DAILY LIFE ON

The Old Colonial Frontier

The Greenwood Press "Daily Life Through History" Series

The Age of Sail
Dorothy Denneen Volo and James M. Volo

The Ancient Egyptians
Bob Brier and Hoyt Hobbs

The Ancient Greeks
Robert Garland

Ancient Mesopotamia
Karen Rhea Nemet-Nejat

The Ancient Romans
David Matz

The Aztecs: People of the Sun and Earth
David Carrasco with Scott Sessions

Chaucer's England
Jeffrey L. Singman and Will McLean

Civil War America
Dorothy Denneen Volo and James M. Volo

Colonial New England
Claudia Durst Johnson

Daily Life during World War I
Neil M. Heyman

Early Modern Japan
Louis G. Perez

18th-Century England
Kirstin Olsen

Elizabethan England
Jeffrey L. Singman

The Holocaust
Eve Nussbaum Soumerai and Carol D. Schulz

The Inca Empire
Michael A. Malpass

Maya Civilization
Robert J. Sharer

Medieval Europe
Jeffrey L. Singman

The Nineteenth Century American Frontier
Mary Ellen Jones

Renaissance Italy
Elizabeth S. Cohen and Thomas V. Cohen

The Spanish Inquisition
James M. Anderson

Traditional China: The Tang Dynasty
Charles Benn

The United States, 1920–1939: Decades of Promise and Pain
David E. Kyvig

The United States, 1940–1959: Shifting Worlds
Eugenia Kaledin

The United States, 1960–1990: Decades of Discord
Myron A. Marty

Victorian England
Sally Mitchell

DAILY LIFE ON

The Old Colonial Frontier

JAMES M. VOLO AND DOROTHY DENNEEN VOLO

The Greenwood Press "Daily Life Through History" Series

GREENWOOD PRESS
Westport, Connecticut • London

Library of Congress Cataloging-in-Publication Data

Volo, James M., 1947–
    Daily life on the old colonial frontier / James M. Volo and Dorothy Denneen Volo.
      p. cm.—(The Greenwood Press "Daily life through history" series, ISSN 1080–4749)
    Includes bibliographical references and index.
    ISBN 0–313–31103–X (alk. paper)
    1. Frontier and pioneer life—North America. 2. North America—History—Colonial period, ca. 1600–1775. 3. Europe—Territorial expansion—Social aspects. 4. North America—Ethnic relations. 5. Indians of North America—Government relations—To 1789. 6. Indians of North America—First contact with Europeans 7. Fur trade—Social aspects—North America—History. 8. France—Relations—Great Britain. 9. Great Britain—Relations—France. I. Volo, Dorothy Denneen, 1949– II. Title.
    E46.V65   2002
    970.02—dc21   2002016104

British Library Cataloguing in Publication Data is available.

Library of Congress Catalog Card Number: 2002016104
ISBN: 0–313–31103–X
ISSN: 1080–4749

First published in 2002

Greenwood Press, 88 Post Road West, Westport, CT 06881
An imprint of Greenwood Publishing Group, Inc.
www.greenwood.com

Printed in the United States of America

The paper used in this book complies with the Permanent Paper Standard issued by the National Information Standards Organization (Z39.48–1984).

10 9 8 7 6 5 4 3 2 1

All photos were taken by the authors. Maps © Arcadia Editions Limited.

Contents

Chronology

1558	Elizabeth I ascends the throne of England.
1558–1603	Reign of Elizabeth I of England.
1560–1589	Reign of Henry III of France.
1560–1648	Catholic Counter Reformation actively pursued.
1565	Spanish destroy a French Huguenot settlement on the St. John's River in Florida.
	Spanish settlement at St. Augustine founded.
1568	Spain establishes missions in Florida.
1570	Spain establishes a mission in Virginia that is destroyed by Indians.
1572	In France, Catholics massacre more than 20,000 French Calvinists known as Huguenots, on St. Bartholomew's Day.
1573	Royal Orders for New Discoveries establishes strict rules for the formation of Spanish settlements.
1577	Spain establishes a mission in Georgia.
1580	Spain absorbs Portugal and its colonies.
1587	Queen Mary of Scotland executed.
1587–1588	Anglo-Hispanic Wars.
1588	English defeat the Spanish Armada.
1593	Dutch expel the Spanish army from the Dutch Republic.
1597	Yamasee and Timucuan Indians destroy five Spanish missions in Georgia and north Florida.
1601	First French trading post, at Tadoussac, established.
1603	James Stuart (James VI of Scotland) becomes King James I of England.
1603–1625	Reign of James I.
1604	French trading post at St. Croix in the Bay of Fundy established.
1607	English establish a colony at Jamestown, Virginia.
	Micmac-Abenaki trade war in Maine and Nova Scotia.
1608	French establish a post at Quebec.

1609	Samuel de Champlain involved in a Native American battle on the shores of Lake Champlain.
	First Anglo-Powhatan War.
	Henry Hudson explores the Hudson River.
1613	Catholic mission founded on Desert Mountain Island, Maine.
1614	Fort Orange, a trading post of the New Netherlands Company (Dutch West India Company), established at Albany, New York.
1618–1648	Thirty Years' War in Europe.
1620	Plymouth plantation established.
1622	Powhatan Indians massacre 400 Virginians.
1625	Charles I ascends the English throne.
	Mohawk-Mahican conflict begins the Beaver Wars.
1625–1649	Reign of Charles I.
1626	Dutch enter the Mohawk-Mahican War as Mahican allies. The Dutch are defeated.
1628	The Mahicans are defeated, leaving the Iroquois a trade monoply with the Dutch in Albany.
	Recollet fathers withdrawn from New France.
1629	Sir David Kirke, an English privateer, seizes Quebec.
1629–1632	First English occupation of Quebec.
1630	Massachusetts Bay colony established.
1631	Militia service formalized in Massachusetts and Virginia.
1633	Maryland colony established.
	La Compagnie des Cent Associés, the Company of One Hundred Associates, is given a large grant of land in New France.
	First Roman Catholic church built in Canada.
	Abenaki mission located at Penobscot.
1636	English open a trading post at Agawam, Massachusetts.
1637	Pequot War.
1638	New Haven colony established.

1639	Connecticut colony established.
1640	Portugal again becomes an independent kingdom.
	French begin supplying firearms to the Huron.
1640–1649	English Civil Wars.
1641	French establish a post at Sault St. Marie.
1642	Sulpician fathers found a mission at Montreal.
	First captivity of Father Isaac Jogues by the Iroquois.
	Dutch destroy two native encampments near Hackensack, New Jersey.
1643	A child-king, Louis XIV, ascends the French throne.
	New England Confederation formed.
1643–1715	Reign of Louis XIV.
1644	Rhode Island colony established.
	Iroquois blockade the Ottawa River.
	French soldiers escort the Huron fur fleet to Montreal.
	Powhatans attack the Virginia colonists.
1645	Brief peace between the Iroquois and the French.
1646	Abenaki mission located at Norridgewock.
	Second captivity and murder of Father Isaac Jogues.
1649	Great Huron Dispersal begins.
	The Hurons and Petuns are dispersed by the Iroquois.
1649–1658	English Republican Period.
1651	The Neutrals are dispersed by the Iroquois.
	Susquehannock-Mohawk War.
1653	Father Joseph Poncet captured and released by the Iroquois.
1654	English open an Indian college at Harvard.
	The Eries are dispersed by the Iroquois.
	First great Ottawa fur fleet arrives in Montreal.
1655	Jesuits establish the mission of Ste. Marie among the Iroquois at Onandaga.

1656	Groseilliers and Radisson bring a great fur fleet to Montreal.
1657	Cathedral of Notre Dame de la Paix opened in Quebec.
1658	Iroquois again blockade the Ottawa River fur fleets.
	Jesuits abandon their mission at Onandaga (Ste. Marie).
1660	English Restoration (Charles II).
	First Roman Catholic bishop sent to Quebec.
	Defense of the Long Sault.
1660–1685	Reign of Charles II.
1661	Jean-Baptiste Colbert appointed French finance minister.
1663	Control of New France transferred from the One Hundred Associates to the Compagnie des Habitants.
	Senaca-Susquehannock War.
1664	Royal governor appointed to New France.
	An intendent of justice, police, and finances appointed to New France to act as business manager for the French king.
	Carignan-Salieres regiment sent to New France.
	English capture New Amsterdam.
1665	French establish a string of forts along the Richelieu River.
1666	Great London Fire.
	French attempt a campaign against the Mohawks. They fail.
1667	French attempt a second campaign against the Mohawks. They burn several Mohawk villages.
	The Iroquois agree to peace with the French.
	English sovereignty over New Netherlands made permanent.
1668	English open a trading post at Pennacock in Maine.
1669	Colbert appointed French marine minister.
1670	The Pueblo Indians stage a significant rebellion against Spanish rule.
	Recollet fathers return to New France.

1671	Jesuits establish a mission at Michilimackinac.
1673	Increased persecution of Quakers under the Test Act of 1673.
	System of Parallels and *First System of Fortification* introduced by the Marquis de Vauban.
1674	Papacy creates the diocese of Quebec.
	Compagnies Franches de la Marine sent to India and West Indies.
1675	Nathaniel Bacon's Rebellion in Virginia.
	King Philip's War begins in New England.
	The Susquehannocks are destroyed by the Iroquois.
1676	French fortify Michilimackinac.
1679	La Salle explores the Detroit region of the Great Lakes.
1682	Pennsylvania colony established by Quakers.
	Iroquois resume hostilities with New France.
1683	Abenaki mission established at St. Francis.
	Compagnies Franches de la Marine sent to Quebec.
	French establish Fort de Baude.
1684	Beaver Wars end.
1685–1688	Reign of James II.
1688	William of Orange overthrows James II as king of England.
	Glorious Revolution begins.
	Jacob Leisler's Rebellion in New York.
1688–1698	King William's War (the War of the League of Augsburg).
1688–1701	Reign of William III (William and Mary).
1689	Abenaki Indians attack Pemaquid, Maine.
	Abenaki Indians attack Fort Penobscot, Maine.
	French Indians attack Dover, New Hampshire.
	French settlements at LaChine raided by the Iroquois.
1690	Indians and French attack Schenectady, New York; Salmon Bay, New Hampshire; and Fort Loyal on Casco Bay in Maine.

	Sir William Phips wins an easy victory at Port Royal, Acadia.
	Frontenac repells a major English expedition against Quebec.
1693	Abenaki Indians attack York, Maine.
	Mohawks make peace with the French after a vigorous attack on their villages.
1694	The Jesuits abandon all their missions in Iroquoia.
1696	English trade board takes control of colonial policy.
	Indians attack the English fort at Pemaquid, Maine.
1697	King William's War ends with the Peace of Ryswick.
	English occupy part of Nova Scotia (Acadia).
1699	Cadillac founds Detroit.
	French extend their colonies in America to Louisiana.
1701	Queen Anne ascends the English throne.
1701–1714	Reign of Queen Anne.
1702	English attack St. Augustine, Florida.
1702–1713	Queen Anne's War (the War of Spanish Succession).
1703	English attack Pensacola, Florida.
1704	Indian raid against Deerfield, Massachusetts.
	Failed attempt to capture Port Royal in French Acadia.
1706	Franco-Spanish expedition attacks Charlestown, South Carolina.
1707	Second failed attempt to capture Port Royal in French Acadia.
	English again attack Pensacola, Florida.
1709	Quebec expedition abandoned by the English Crown.
1710	Four loyal Mohawk chiefs arrive in London.
	The colony of Carolina made into two separate colonies—North and South.
1711	Tuscarora War.
	Quebec expedition again abandoned by the English Crown.
1713	Treaty of Utrecht signed.

1714	George of Hanover becomes King George I of England.
1715	Scottish Rebellion.
	Yamasee War.
	King Louis XIV of France dies. The French throne passes to his five-year-old son, Louis XV.
1717	English establish an Indian mission on the Kennebec River.
1719	Initial work begun on Fortress Louisbourg on Cape Breton Island.
1724	English attack the mission at Norridgewock, Maine.
1729	*Modern French System* of fortification instituted by military engineers.
1730	Fort Oswego established on Lake Ontario by the English.
1730–1742	English begin War of Jenkins' Ear against Spain.
1732	Founding of the buffer colony of Georgia.
1735	Extent of the Walking Purchase determined.
1740	Cartegena expedition ends in disaster.
1740–1748	King George's War (the War of Austrian Succession).
1745	English colonials take Fortress Louisbourg.
1745–1746	Final Scottish Rebellion ends with the Battle of Culloden.
1746	Regular army units, Troups de Terre, arrive in Quebec from France.
1748	Treaty of Aix-la-Chapelle ends King George's War.
	English are firmly established in Annapolis Royal, Nova Scotia.
	Fortress Louisbourg returned to France and strengthened.
1749	Fort St. Frederick, at Crown Point, built by the French.
1751	English open a trading post at the forks of the Ohio River.
1753	Governor Robert Dinwiddie orders the French from the Ohio country.
	Forts Duquesne, Machault, LeBoeuf, Presque Isle, and Niagara built by the French.

1754   A skirmish at Fort Necessity in the wilderness of western
            Pennsylvania between French colonial troops and Virginia
            provincial troops commanded by George Washington begins
            a world war.

            Fort Cumberland, at Wills Creek, built by the English.

            Roger's Rangers recognized as a formal establishment.

            Virginia votes funds to build several military posts and to
            fortify with stockades several garrison houses.

            Benjamin Franklin and his supporters are able to get funding
            for a series of forts along the Delaware and Susquehanna
            Rivers.

1754–1763   French and Indian War in America.

1755   Additional regular French army units arrive in Quebec.

            Baron Dieskau appointed French military commander in
            New France.

            Regular British army units arrive at Alexandria, Virginia.

            General Edward Braddock arrives in North America.

            Alexandria Conference.

            Fort Carillon, at Ticonderoga, built by the French.

            Braddock's defeat at the Monongahela.

            Fort Edward, in New York, built by the English.

            Battle of Lake George. Baron Dieskau killed.

            Fort William Henry, on Lake George, built by the English.

            Pennsylvania votes to build four major forts in Northampton
            County.

            Governor Charles Lawrence of Nova Scotia captures Fort
            Beausejour and disperses the French residents in all of Aca-
            dia.

1756   Seven Years' War begins in Europe.

            Marquis de Montcalm appointed French military com-
            mander in New France.

            William Johnson made a baronet and superintendent of In-
            dian affairs by King George II.

1757   Fort Oswego destroyed.

English detachment ambushed at Sabbath Day Point on Lake George.

Fort William Henry taken by the French. A massacre of the English by the Indians follows.

A botched attempt is made to retake Fortress Louisbourg.

William Pitt becomes prime minister of England.

1758   Roger's Rangers fights the Battle on Snowshoes.

Fort Bedford and Fort Ligonier built.

Major James Grant's detachment destroyed by Indians.

Forbes Campaign takes Fort Duquesne from the French.

Lord Augustus Howe killed near Ticonderoga.

General Ambercrombe fails to take Fort Carillon at Ticonderoga.

Fortress Louisbourg falls to the English.

1759   Roger's Rangers attacks and burns the Abenaki village at St. Francis.

General Amherst takes Fort Carillon at Ticonderoga and Fort St. Frederick at Crown Point.

An English colonial army attacks and destroys Fort Frontenac.

Fort Niagara falls to William Johnson.

French retreat to Detroit, burning many of their western posts and forts.

Fort Stanwix begun by the English.

Fort Pitt begun by the Englsh.

Amherst threatens Montreal.

General James Wolfe defeats the French under the Marquis de Montcalm at Quebec. Both commanders are killed.

1763   Peace of Paris. France loses almost all its possessions in North America except a few islands in the Caribbean.

1764   Pontiac's Rebellion.

Battle of Bushy Run.

1769	Eleazer Wheelock opens an Indian school at Dartmouth.
	Spain takes possession of Louisiana.
1770–1775	Anglo-American relations deteriorate.
1775	Battles of Lexington and Concord begin the American Revolution.

Introduction

It is hardly possible to imagine a more picturesque field for the nov-
elist as well as the historian, than the wilderness farms of the heroic
settlers [and] families who planted their crude homes in the new
country.

—Emanuel Spenser, historian

Unaware of the potential wealth of the Americas, Spain was initially
disappointed by the discovery of a continental landmass that blocked
the ocean passage to the fabulous spices and riches of the East Indies. It
was the Spaniards who first called America a wilderness, a world where
civilized man was an alien presence; a world that lacked the control and
order common in the Old World from which they had come; and most
importantly, a world without the stamp of more than a thousand years
of Christianity. One remarkable characteristic of this New World wilderness was the constant presence of the native population. Yet opinion
varied among European intellectuals as to whether the natives of North
America were children of the devil who might be exterminated and
whose land might be appropriated without remorse, or simple heathens
whose spiritual salvation was the responsibility of all good Christians.
This type of thinking affected native-European relations to a marked
extent.[1]

Beyond the geopolitical boundaries of European claims and counter-
claims, of sovereignty and possession, was a frontier of culture, spiritu-

ality, and economic exchange. In their frontier outposts, the Dutch, Spanish, French, and English came to take what riches the continent offered. They also came to settle, to build, and to develop the land, but with the less noble desire to own the land and to impose on the New World wilderness their own view of civilization. Many times the native inhabitants were treated with appalling disregard and cruelty. Under the pressure of expanding settlement into their traditional surroundings, the Indian population often relinquished any disputed territory, simply giving way to white encroachment by relocating to an adjoining region. At other times they fought to hold or regain what was theirs.

The frontier region, which is the focus of this book, was the interface between the older American wilderness and European-style civilization. To the Europeans, it teemed with undomesticated and unfamiliar beasts, and even its indigenous peoples seemed perplexing, uninhibited, and violent. The frontier was both a place and a process. It was not a clear line along which contending cultures collided, but rather a disrupted region in which explorers, traders, missionaries, colonists, and native peoples came into contact and interacted. The frontier population altered the wilderness of North America and planted the seeds of religious, economic, and political change that would sprout over the next two centuries into a young American Republic.[2]

Among these seeds were the weeds of persistent hostility found among Europeans—rooted in deep and genuine religious and political antagonisms formed during the Protestant Reformation. These dominated much of the thinking and politics of many generations of settlers on the colonial frontier. Many early colonists attempted to transplant the emotionalism of the religious and theological controversies raised by the Protestant Reformation in Europe to the colonies in America. The Catholic kingdoms of Europe, which had little success in stopping the Protestant movement that swept their domains in the sixteenth century, were not going to allow "heretics" to infect their holding in the New World. Protestants held similar antipathetic feelings toward Catholics of all nationalities, distrusted them, and believed that they represented the anti-Christ.

The Spanish found America rich in gold. Yet the search for the fur trade, rather than the search for gold, proved the driving force behind much of the exploration and settlement of North America, and it dramatically altered native American culture, material possessions, economic activity, and society. It was the abundance of furs in the northeast quadrant of the continent and the almost inexhaustible market for them in Europe that produced some of the most far reaching changes in North America. In the northeast quarter of the continent the English, Dutch, and French established trading posts in the interior ever nearer to the source of the furs, and here the final struggle for control of the North American continent took place.

While the frontier population viewed Indians as obstacles to progress, potential adversaries, or mere nuisances, they perceived other Europeans (even those of their own nationalities) as competitors—vying for the same trade agreements, arable land, and geographically strategic positions. European politics and warfare continually spilled over into the American wilderness, making those who populated the frontier regions dread enemies for no reasons other than those of their rulers many thousands of miles away. Consequently, many colonial governments tried to establish military and economic alliances with the native population. This inadvertently introduced great suffering and unspeakable terror to the frontier experience.

The most enduring and harmonious relationships with the native American population were formed by the French, who attempted with some success to peacefully coexist with the Indians, living with them, marrying into their families, and converting them to Christianity. However, the native possessors of the land sometimes proved resistant or even aggressive in the defense of their rights. Many attempted to stand their ground and repel the European invaders. This was especially true when native peoples encountered the Spanish, who enslaved them and used them as laborers and beasts of burden everywhere they went. Finally there were the English, who sought to remove the Indians from the land by treaty, contract, bargain, or force. It can be said with some justification that the French embraced the Indians, the Spanish crushed them, and the English displaced them.[3]

The colonial history of North America has had much written about it by historians, but the view of the period imparted by them has often been one of a simple prelude to the revolutionary climax that was to come in the English colonies. The equally important French colonies are often treated as a simple background to Anglo-American development. Much of the serious research in this area has rightly dealt with colonial governments, battles, commanders, and military personalities. However, the lives of the civilians who populated the frontier have been largely left to the more dramatic, if less authentic, pens of the romantics who write adventure stories and screenplays.

The works of Francis Parkman, including seven volumes written between 1865 and 1892, left an indelible stamp on all subsequent writing about the period of the French and English colonial wars. His research was prodigious and very few errors or omissions have been detected by subsequent researchers. However, it is clear that Parkman harbored anti-Catholic, anti-native American, and pro-British prejudices in his writings that have gone uncorrected in many twentieth-century textbooks. His opinions have also been reflected in popular literature and the cinema.

Nonetheless, Parkman's reports of factual events were detailed and exhaustive, and his work remains a foundation for all future study in this area.

The frontier novels of James Fenimore Cooper have helped to establish a picture of colonial settlement and Anglo-Indian relationships for most students of the period. Yet Cooper emphasized manners and scenes in his novels characteristic of Americans and an America that did not exist when the frontier was actually being settled. The frontier wastelands traveled by Hawkeye, the frontier hero in *The Last of the Mohicans*, took on the romantic imagery of scenery in Cooper's work, which was understood by his contemporaries but largely lost on later generations of readers, television viewers, and movie fans. Moreover, Cooper fashioned an oversimplified structure of intertribal relations and alliances for his readers. Yet he has had a profound effect on how the colonial frontier period was viewed for more than a century because he appealed to the emotions of his readers, and aroused their imaginations and patriotism. His work was highly regarded by the Victorians of the Civil War period because it derived from the principles of the American Revolution and the young American Republic, but it failed utterly to provide an accurate picture of the multinational and multitribal complexities that existed on the colonial frontier.

This book is designed to dovetail the wealth of sources contemporary with the colonial frontier period with these popular histories, novels, and screenplays in order to provide a more complete and accurate picture of life on the frontier. Among these sources are diaries, journals, letters, colonial and military documents, maps, tracts, narratives, and personal reminiscences. The reports of missionaries and the anecdotal narratives of captives serve to record much about the native American lifestyles and cultures that would otherwise be lost. The hazards of frontier life are reported as the participants would have experienced them in their own microcosm rather than in a grand overview of colonial history. In this regard, the reports of average citizens, traders, and militiamen, available in period newspapers, letters, and reports, have been incorporated wherever possible into the discussion of military and political events.

The main theme that runs through this work is the great struggle between France and England for control of the North American trading empire from 1608 to 1763. The desire to establish a fur trade monopoly, shared by both the Europeans and the native Americans, and the consequences of fur trade on the culture and society of each, are closely scrutinized from the days of early European–native American contact to the end of the French and Indian War. The authors have attempted to study the impact of European contact on America in the areas of society, culture, economics, and religion during the period. Nonetheless, the details of the military struggle remain of great weight and importance, and it is hoped that this work will integrate into the body of military and political knowledge the details of the lifestyles of the frontier population and of the principal native American communities with whom they were to interact.

Statistical information about the period and its people has been presented wherever it has been found to be reliable. Many significant historical sites have been visited by the authors to provide photographs and illustrations that are intended to add authenticity to the text. Dedicated reenactors of seventeenth and eighteenth century life have provided information, artifacts, and authentically reconstructed clothing and accoutrements. The authors—educators, historians, and historical reenactors—hope that this work will reflect as accurately as possible a picture of colonial frontier life.

NOTES

1. The authors have decided to use a number of terms to describe the native inhabitants of the Americas. These include *native American, native people, and native population*, as well as the term *Indian*, which was most commonly used by those writing at the time of the events. The authors have eschewed the use of derogatory terms in this regard, and have replaced them wherever they appear in contemporary texts.

2. See Colin G. Calloway, *The Western Abenakis of Vermont, 1600–1800: War, Migration, and the Survival of an Indian People* (Norman: University of Oklahoma Press, 1990), 27.

3. Gary B. Nash, *Red, White, and Black: The Peoples of Early America* (Englewood Cliffs, NJ: Prentice-Hall, 1982), 111.

1

Wilderness and the Promised Land

The wood was so thick, that for a mile at a time we could not find
a place of the size of a hand, where the sunshine could penetrate,
even in the clearest day.
                          —Conrad Weiser, colonial Indian agent

Spain was the recipient of far greater wealth than other European powers
because it was the first to sack the largest, richest portions of the Americas. By 1543 the Spanish had explored and claimed a vast portion of
North America, and they had an idea of the broad outlines of the continent. The Spanish conquered all that is Mexico today and raped the
Incan and Aztec empires of their treasures. Moreover, they journeyed
through present-day Georgia, South Carolina, North Carolina, Alabama,
Mississippi, Arkansas, parts of the Tennessee River valley, the Appalachian Mountains, and the great Southwest. Six decades before the English established their first permanent settlement at Jamestown, the
Spanish established a mission in Virginia. Their record of exploration
and conquest was not only incredible, it was unrivaled: "In a single generation the Spaniards seized more new territory than Rome could acquire
in five hundred years."[1]
     Yet the woodlands of the northeast quadrant of North America and
the fertile lands along the Atlantic coast seemingly held little attraction
for the Spanish. Although they had seen forests, rivers, animal life, and
fertile soil to rival all that was in Europe, they did not covet the natural

wealth of the region. This is understandable when one considers the mighty empires, monuments, temples, and treasures the Spaniards had found elsewhere. A Spanish courtier wrote: "[W]hat need have we of what is found everywhere in Europe? It is toward the south, not toward the frozen north, that those who seek their fortune should bend their way; for everything at the equator is rich." Spain seemingly abandoned the northeastern woodlands to its European rivals—chiefly England and France—to do with as they pleased. Yet as the sixteenth century closed neither France nor England had established a colony in the New World, and Spain was still busily exploiting its claims in Latin America, the West Indies, and Florida.[2]

WILDERNESS

Many Europeans described America as a wilderness, but most areas of the world considered wilderness today are remote, inhospitable, or bereft of natural resources. Regions filled with wildlife, timber, fresh water, and fertile soil, as was America in the seventeenth and eighteen centuries, generally do not evoke the necessary quality of desolation associated with a wilderness tract. Yet for most European immigrants the concept of wilderness was heavily freighted with a myriad of personal meanings and symbolic devices.[3]

When Pilgrim leader William Bradford stepped off the *Mayflower* in Plymouth, Massachusetts, in 1620, he described himself as entering "a hideous and desolate wilderness filled with evil and capable of making man revert to savagery."[4] Bradford's wilderness was intimately tied to his religious concepts of good and evil. For many early immigrants like Bradford, the American wilderness was seen from this religious perspective not as a remote and desolate expanse, but rather as "a sanctuary from a sinful and persecuting society . . . [a] wild country . . . in which to find and draw close to God . . . a testing ground where a chosen people were purged, humbled, and made ready for the land of promise."[5] The wilderness drew to itself a self-righteous people like the Pilgrims precisely because it was harsh and forbidding. Like John the Baptist, Moses, and Elijah in the Bible, they sought out the wilderness as a place to pray and be nearer to God.

In Europe the mountain peaks and cliffsides were the only landforms that had not been put into production by the sixteenth century. Possibly for these reasons many Europeans tended to link the concept of wilderness with uncultivated land that was rocky, heavily wooded, and inhabited only by wild beasts—an area of forests, crags, and cliffs. Many of the areas of the Americas were very close to being absolute wilderness. A traveler in the Appalachian Mountains in 1736 recorded: "We were between two high and steep mountains . . . on both sides were frightfully high mountains and rocks. . . . The wood was so thick, that for a mile at a time we could not find a place of the size of a hand, where the sunshine could penetrate, even in the clearest day."[6]

By comparison, native Americans exhibited little antipathy toward the concept of wilderness. Indian religions accepted a relationship between man and the natural regions of the world that bordered on love. They recognized man as one with all living things. Moreover, for them, the wilderness did not have connotations of evil and disorder, but rather those of natural order and the very essence of deity. It should not be surprising, therefore, that European explorers, missionaries, and settlers failed to understand the native American's close relationship with and deep regard for the land.

For the Europeans, the thought that North America was a wilderness was a great advantage to the newcomer who wished to establish a claim on the land. Just how wild a region qualified as a wilderness to the minds of colonial settlers is not certain. Some small amount of civilization seems to have been permitted, while any form of civilization that failed to demonstrate its influence in European terms—fences, buildings, or roadways—seems to have been dismissed. The first settlers in America took such matters quite seriously.

FRONTIER

To the European mind of the seventeenth century the concepts of wilderness and civilization were at opposite ends of a spectrum with a scale in between suggesting a thorough shading or blending of the two at the center, which was called "the frontier." The frontier was possibly best described in European terms as "Ploughed"—a balance between man's needs and God's clockwork nature.[7] "The frontier [was] the outer edge of the wave—the meeting-point between savagery and civilization." The greatest cities of Europe were small and unsophisticated by comparison with those of today, yet London or Paris were certainly well along toward a synthetic condition of life remote from the fields and pastures of the seventeenth-century peasant. On this scale, the modest New World settlements of the seventeenth and eighteenth centuries, even those highly urbanized ones in New Amsterdam and Quebec, were nothing but outposts on a wilderness frontier.[8]

DISPOSSESSING THE INDIAN

It is certain that the native population felt the repercussions of European contact generations before the first settlers actually arrived in their country, but the physical reality of meeting on the frontier placed serious limitations on both the Indians and the settlers. The commonly held idea

The wilderness was much more forbidding than this Victorian print would suggest. Not until the nineteenth century did such impenetrable forests, waterfalls, and rock formations take on the mantle of scenery.

that colonists craved to own property and that Indians did not "distorts European notions of property as much as it does Indian ones."[9] Both groups recognized ownership in terms of what could and could not be done with property in terms of its disposition. Both assigned boundaries to its possession—although those of the Indians were somewhat less definite than those of whites. And finally, both groups were granted their ownership of the land by a sovereign agency. In the case of the colonists this was almost always the Crown; for the Indians it might be their clan, their tribe, or another tribe such as the Iroquois Confederacy.

Nonetheless, from the very beginning of the colonial period it was clear that the native inhabitants were being dispossessed of their land. To a greater or lesser degree, many Europeans wished to wrap their occupation of Indian land in the cloak of legitimacy. The early Dutch and English settlers carefully purchased the land rights of tribes occupying coastal areas and recorded the deeds; the Moravian settlers of Pennsylvania conscientiously paid various Indian claimants for their lands several times. However, lands that appeared to be vacant were simply occupied by European immigrants. As late as the eighteenth century a prominent officeholder in Pennsylvania determined that the colony was "quite destitute of Indians" and the land was thereby open to lawful settlement.[10]

Native Americans rarely abandoned a region in the face of European advance. The New England coastal region occupied by the Pilgrims was destitute of people due to an epidemic that ravaged the native population shortly before the Pilgrims' arrival. The French found the St. Lawrence River valley unoccupied by native settlements due in large part to the effects of recent intertribal warfare in the region. Nonetheless, there was a good deal of Indian movement along and behind the supposed border between settled and unsettled regions. "Even the Anglo-French frontier was not clearly defined as Indians traveled and traded back and forth among the French and the English."[11]

Questions surrounding the property rights of the native Americans were fundamental to the European concept of ownership and the European way of thinking concerning the disposition of property. Most believed that land could be claimed by right of discovery, and traditions dating to before the Crusades allowed Christians everywhere to dispossess non-Christians of their property. A second theory, based in law and called *vacuum domicilium*, allowed that land not occupied and settled was forfeit to those who took up residence and improved it. Thus ownership of the land could be established if it were a wilderness, or if the original inhabitants had failed to build villages or had abandoned their fields. To the European mind a land was unoccupied if it failed to exhibit structures such as buildings, fences, roads, and other characteristic works of civilization common to the European experience. Since the native American culture eschewed such structures and favored moving between several fertile areas for seasonal, social, and subsistence purposes, the Europeans considered much of the land they saw uninhabited or abandoned in good conscience.

Europeans who arrived in the eighteenth century were favored with an unanticipated stroke of good fortune as migrating tribes, driven into the interior by apprehension of the Europeans in coastal settlements, established hunting trails, cleared land, and settled villages near water transportation in the wilderness. When German and Scotch-Irish settlers pushed into these areas they reaped the advantages of this preparatory work in much the same way as the Pilgrims had occupied the abandoned fields of coastal New England.[12]

Many explorers resorted to the expedient of claiming all the land drained by certain waterways by virtue of discovery. While Europeans used rivers as gateways to the continent, beyond the fall line, which separated the coastal plain from the piedmont, the going became hard, and all semblance of ownership was murky. In most cases, the claimants to thousands of square miles of territory had not seen more than twenty paces beyond the banks of the nearest navigable body of water.[13]

Meanwhile the English were content to establish their colonies on the more easily accessible Atlantic coastal plain, seemingly content to be hemmed in by the Appalachian Mountains. Nonetheless, colonial charters issued by English monarchs granted lands from the Atlantic coast inland without reference to any definitive western terminus other than the western ocean. Both Virginia and Pennsylvania claimed lands in the Ohio River valley under such charters. Under its royal charter the Connecticut colony laid claim to lands in Ohio until after the American Revolution even though the colonies of New York and Pennsylvania intervened geographically. Such ad hoc methods established long-lasting competing claims for native American lands among many colonies and served as points of dispute among Europeans of different nationalities as well as among the native population.

THE WALKING PURCHASE

William Penn's "Walking Purchase" resorted to a similar ad hoc method when buying land from the Indians. Negotiated by William Penn in the seventeenth century, it encompassed all the land drained by the Delaware River from a certain point "back into the woods, as far as a man can go in a day and a half" and back to the river again. The length of a day's journey inland was never meant by the Indians to be a precise measurement; nor was it ever thought that the line would be paced off. Such accuracy did not figure in the native American concept of land-ownership. While the Delaware tribe meant to convey the use of a strip of land thirty miles long and a few miles deep along the river, in 1735 Penn's descendants took advantage of the lack of precision in the agreement to vastly expand the grant to the disadvantage of the native population.

The Pennsylvania proprietors hired two agents, Timothy Smith and John Chapman, to clear the way for a monumental effort. A straight-line path was cut through the forest prior to the measurement. Three walkers (Solomon Jennings, James Yates, and Edward Marshall) were engaged to travel this line with horses and riders providing food and water. The day-and-a-half-long walk quickly turned into a 150-mile marathon that encompassed much of the Lehigh River valley and the land on which the cities of Bethlehem and Easton, Pennsylvania, now reside. The line was then squared off to run parallel to the river, which ran at that point in a great bend, so that the region encompassed by the return trip to the river now took four days to walk and ended at Laxawaxen Creek. So extensive was the expansion of the original agreement, that the Delawares were left no land in the province of Pennsylvania at all. The Penns thereby achieved one of the greatest land frauds in American history.[14]

INLAND WATERWAYS

Rather than being a trackless wasteland, the colonial frontier was actually crisscrossed by a network of well-established water routes. Just as surely as the Appalachian Mountains stood as a barrier to easy entry into the interior of North America from the English colonies on the Atlantic coast, the St. Lawrence River served the French of Canada as a convenient water route to the Great Lakes and the whole center of the continent. French control of this vital waterway is often cited by historians as a key to the continent. Although a simple survey of a map would suggest that the French had an advantage, the available water routes to the interior actually used by the French and the English were nonetheless approximately equivalent.

On the St. Lawrence River, medium-sized ships were able to sail a considerable distance inland to the limits of navigation. One of the most important obstacles to navigation was at the narrows between Montreal and Lake Ontario. Here the LaChine rapids prevented the passage of large vessels, while at the other end of the lake the great cataract of Niagara Falls stalled even the passage of canoes. The Hudson-Mohawk river system served the English in somewhat the same manner as the St. Lawrence served the French. The limit of navigation by sailing vessels on the Hudson was at the falls near Albany. Thereafter, goods and passengers were transferred by hand to canoes, or bateaux, capable of being operated by human power on the Mohawk or on the streams and lakes of the Adirondack region.

Both systems led to the Great Lakes, yet the French started the quest for a North American empire with an advantage. Before the end of the seventeenth century Samuel de Champlain journeyed up the Ottawa River to the west, then northward toward Hudson Bay, westward to Lake Ontario and Lake Huron, and along the Richelieu River southward into the lake that bears his name. Only chance kept the French explorers that followed him from descending further into the Hudson River valley and planting a colony on the Atlantic Ocean somewhere near Manhattan Island.[15]

The geography of North America, available to any school child by simply opening a text book or an atlas, was hidden from early explorers and missionaries. Their knowledge of the interior was often sketchy, superficial, and uncertain. For most of the continental interior, there were no maps at all. Even the most successful explorers had no inkling of the details of most of the topography of the continent. A voyage of 500 miles from the mouth of the St. Lawrence took French explorers to the LaChine rapids near Montreal. Another 500 miles by canoe brought them only to Detroit, with 500 more miles of unexplored lakes before them. It would take Europeans hundreds of years to record the actual contours of the continent on maps, while native Americans simply carried the interlocking pattern of streams, rivers, and lakes in their minds.[16]

From the early part of the seventeenth century the French tried to penetrate the interior of the continent and comprehend its geography. French interest in the topography of the continent was not rooted in exploration for its own sake. Indeed, such a concept was "alien to Europeans before the onset of the Romantic movement of the nineteenth century. Pious Europeans explored for souls; the rest explored for riches." Within three decades of the founding of the French post at Quebec City (1608), Etienne Brule traveled to Lake Erie, and the Jesuit missionaries Brebeuf and Chaumont wintered with the Indians west of Lake Ontario. In 1679 Robert de la Salle sailed up the St. Claire River and passed through Lake St. Claire at Detroit. Each of these early explorers reported the richness of the Great Lakes region in terms of furs, and the reports, spreading rapidly across Europe, ensured that the French would not be alone in coveting control of the region.[17]

At a time when the line of mountains was the boundary between the English settlements and the wilderness interior, there were three significant water routes through the mountains into the interior. Besides the Hudson River, the major rivers of the northeastern Atlantic seaboard in this region are the Delaware and the Susquehanna. All three rivers found their headwaters in the mountains east and southeast of the Great Lakes. The tributaries of the Delaware and Susquehanna Rivers are almost completely entangled in this region. The headwaters region was occupied by the Iroquois Confederacy and the riverbanks were the homes of many

The native American bark canoe remained the most frequently used means of transportation other than walking. The canoe in this mid-nineteenth-century print is essentially the same as that used for hundreds of years by native Americans. They were lightweight, strong, and maneuverable. A single canoe was capable of carrying almost 800 pounds.

subtribes of Delaware, Shawnee, and Susquehannock nations, making it one of the most densely populated centers of native American life east of the Mississippi River. Major centers of native American life were located near these watercourses in the present-day states of New York and Pennsylvania.

The Susquehanna River gave the indigenous populations of this region the best water route to the Chesapeake Bay and the south. The Delaware River gave access to southeastern Pennsylvania, western New Jersey, and the lower part of New York. The river continued through the Delaware Water Gap to form the boundary between the colonies of Delaware and New Jersey, and exited into Delaware Bay. For almost their entire length the Hudson, Delaware, and Susquehanna Rivers were navigable by canoes with only short portages between entering and exiting points around small falls and rapids.

CANOES

Without the native watercraft known as the canoe, or the larger bateau, most travel in North America would have been impractical. Jolicoeur

Charles Bonin, a French soldier serving in New France during the French and Indian Wars, has left a detailed description of a canoe of the period:

Canoes are the most frequently used water transport in upper Canada because they are light enough to make the necessary portages around the frequent rapids. They are made of light wooden strips as thick as a strong lath, bent half double, then curved in a half circle. They are placed four or five inches apart with the ends attached to a slender pole bound with wooden straps like barrel hoops. Five crossbars are placed along the inside of the canoe which is from twelve to twenty feet in length or more. These crossbars hold the canoe open . . . across the widest part and narrows toward both ends. The framework is covered on the outside with birch bark sewed together with wooden withes. The seams are then covered with gum or resin to keep them watertight. These boats are very light. Loaded, they are easily managed by two men, one at each end.[18]

Nonetheless, the canoe did not guarantee unimpeded passage during all seasons of the year. Streams swollen by meltwater and heavy rains were just as impassable as those that turned into a long wet puddle of boulders in the dry seasons. Travelers often had to exit their vessels and drag them through shallow water and across bars of gravel and sand. Such circumstances were hard on both the paddlers and the canoes, which were often scraped so badly as to warrant repair on the stream bank. Fortunately, the materials needed to accomplish the repairs were easily available from the forests along the route. It should be remembered that these canoes, unlike the recreational craft used today, were almost always fully loaded either with trade goods or furs.

PORTAGES

The key to the inland waterways of North America proved to be a pattern of short land bridges where goods and boats could be manhandled overland from one water route to another known as portages. The native Americans had discovered these interconnections through centuries of travel. East of the Mississippi River the important portages could be divided into three distinct systems. Those that went east–west along the St. Lawrence River valley and through the Great Lakes region gave access to the furs of the western plains. Others gave a north–south passage from Hudson's Bay through the Great Lakes to the Mississippi River and its tributaries such as the Ohio and Tennessee Rivers. Finally there was a series of portages leading northward from the Hudson River valley through the Lake George–Lake Champlain valley and the Richelieu River to the St. Lawrence River.

For the French, the major stumbling block to easy movement of trade goods to the west was the great falls in the Niagara River as it flowed between Lake Erie and Lake Ontario. The portage around the falls required a tortuous route along the Niagara River gorge of more than a dozen miles. The location of the outlet of the river into Lake Ontario was strategically important, and the French built a fortified trading post there. The passage of Niagara Falls, taken together with the numerous rapids in the St. Lawrence, made French navigation into the interior more difficult than it seemed at first glance.

For the English, the major difficulty in moving west lay in the four- to five-mile distance between the headwaters of the Mohawk River and the westward-flowing Wood Creek near present-day Rome, New York. This almost flat land bridge between watercourses was called the Great Carrying Place. Here the British built a series of forts during the French and Indian Wars. The carry from the Mohawk was not difficult, and the current of Wood Creek swept travelers first to Oneida Lake, then to the Oswego River, and finally into Lake Ontario. Once in Lake Ontario the English faced the same difficulty in moving further west that was posed to the French by Niagara Falls. The outlet of the Oswego River into Lake Ontario was also fortified by the British.

THE HUDSON-RICHELIEU CORRIDOR

The English settlements at New York and the French settlements in Canada were connected by water through the Hudson River–Richelieu River corridor. England and France found that they were being funneled by this circumstance into the same region of the continent, fated by geography to come into conflict in what would become the capital region of New York State. Of course the same water route that promised the English easy access to Canada, afforded the French access to the New York frontier. Both sides raced to control the significant portages along this route, and some historians consider it the most heavily fortified and important strategic route in North American military history. The Hudson-Richelieu route was used many times in the colonial period by both French and English armies.[19]

There was a portage from the upper reaches of the Hudson that gave access to the north into Canada through Lake George. This portage of more than a dozen miles was also called the Great Carrying Place. The water exit from the Hudson was at present-day Fort Edward, New York, and the entrance was at the south bay of the Lake Champlain system. The latter place was called Wood Creek.

Finally, there was a particularly important portage at the falls in the LaChute River through which Lake George emptied into Lake Champlain. Nearby was a peninsula of land known as Ticonderoga, which was to become one of the most sought after strategic positions in all of North America. No fewer than four critical military operations took place

This photograph was taken during the summer in a region near the Mohawk River valley. The trail, about six feet wide, is typical of those used by native Americans and early settlers. It requires constant cutting to keep it open.

there. Ironically, the French left the position unfortified for more than a century and a half. Thereafter, it passed from the French to the British during the French and Indian Wars, from the British to the Americans during the Revolution, back to the British for a brief period, and finally back to American hands.

INDIAN TRAILS

Frontier exploration and settlement was greatly influenced, and somewhat eased, by the existence of a relatively well articulated network of Indian trails and paths. These provided ready access to the major river valleys, stream crossings, portages, and mountain passes of the region. Paths led to many of the best agricultural lands in the interior where the open nature of the woodlands—especially in the major river valleys— made the land rather more favorable for early settlement than the virgin woodlands and forested hillsides.[20]

Before the advent of bulldozers and other mechanized earthmovers, cutting roads through the forests by hand was generally viewed as an onerous and backbreaking task to be avoided if at all possible. Indian trails rendered the heavily forested areas encountered by early explorers and settlers less of a barrier than they might have otherwise posed. Although the native Americans, lacking wheeled vehicles, failed to develop wide roads, settlers found that they could "ride on horseback without inconvenience in the woods, and even with a cart in most places." In 1685 Thomas Budd wrote: "The trees grow but thin in most places, and very little under-wood. In the woods groweth plentifully a coarse sort of grass, which . . . soon makes the cattle and horses fat in Summer."[21]

Many Indian routes were well-beaten paths, two to three feet wide, worn into the ground by centuries of use, and easily located. The regular traffic of the indigenous population—which seems to have been quite widespread and far reaching—kept the major trails from one region of the country to another fairly clear throughout the year. However, the native population tended to walk in single file, and many minor paths were difficult to locate or seemingly disappeared over rocky or wet ground. Moreover, the entrance of whites into certain regions caused many of the less frequented paths to become obscured by brush or obstructed by windfalls as the Indians withdrew and discontinued their use. Some of these trails came to be known to whites as "blind Indian paths," the true course of which were known only to the few Indians who had not left the locality. Nonetheless, Indian paths continued to be used by whites to define the boundaries of purchases and land grants, sometimes creating difficulties in future years when assessing the legitimate limits of ownership between those who had conflicting legal interests.[22]

The region just west of Albany was an important hub of Indian trails that served the entire northeastern colonial frontier. Here, near the confluence of the Mohawk River and Schoharie Creek (Fort Hunter, New York), was one of the principal population centers of the powerful Mohawk nation known as Teantontalogo, or the Lower Mohawk Castle. The Upper Mohawk Castle, at Canajoharie some thirty miles further inland, had a larger population. Onondaga in the Finger Lakes region of western New York was the practical seat of native American government for most of the Northeast. While a trail from Albany along the bank of the Mohawk led to the great council fire of the Iroquois at Onondaga, the most important trail in the region was the Onondaga Trail, which followed the course of the Susquehanna River from south to north. The Susquehanna route (whether taken by foot, horseback, or canoe) was the route most commonly used by native Americans traveling between the Mohawk country of central New York to the tribal lands of the Delaware nation on the coast.[23]

Finally, there was the Warrior's Path, which followed the Shenandoah River valley through the backcountry of the English settlements to the southern colonies. Every year parties of Iroquois from New York descended the Warrior's Path to the south to attack their traditional enemies among the Cherokees. In the eighteenth century colonial preachers from Pennsylvania traveled the Warrior's Path south through Maryland and the valley of the Shenandoah River, making converts as far south as the Carolinas and Georgia. Other than the Braddock and Forbes roads built by British armies in Pennsylvania between 1755 and 1758, no land route was more important than the Warrior's Path in bringing settlers to the frontier.

TRANSPORTATION

The Indian trails and paths were difficult, but they were passable for men and packhorses. Consequently, packhorse trains of ten to twelve horses were initially the main carriers of trade goods. Drovers and their helpers often walked along these trails driving sheep, pigs, or cattle to market with the help of dogs. The Braddock and Forbes roads, however, were built to support wagons, carts, and artillery. In Pennsylvania, large wagons known as Conestogas were developed to take advantage of these roads. Capable of carrying tens of tons of goods, these wagons required six horses to pull them at even a slow pace. The Conestoga cargo wagon was the principal means of transport to the interior Appalachians. Beyond the reach of the military roads, two-wheeled carts pulled by horses or by oxen outnumbered the larger wagons. Elegant carriages, two-wheeled chairs, and chaises were used in the cities but were not seen on the frontier.

During any season of the year frontier travel was uncomfortable and hazardous, but wet and cold weather proved the most adverse. Rivers and streams swelled with the rain or melting snow, and perfectly dry roads could become quagmires in a downpour. The whole process was made more dangerous during Indian hostilities. Ironically, one of the best times to avoid Indians was in winter, when travel was almost impossible. These circumstances made the local tavern-keepers good people to know, as they could best inform the traveler of potential dangers, convenient detours, and other local conditions.

TAVERNS

Unlike the infrequent groups of passing settlers, wagoners, drovers, and packtrain riders created a continuous demand for accommodations along the main trails and the major roads. As a result a series of taverns, inns, public houses, and ordinaries were established along the most popular routes to service their needs. The differences between these establishments is largely lost on modern students of the period, but each performed specialized services providing a combination of room, board, liquor, or entertainment. Stabling facilities and pens for livestock were also important. In the backcountry most taverns and inns were uncouth,

**Davis Tavern in Marbletown in southern New York State served as a road-
side tavern for many years before and after the American Revolution. It
is now an antique shop. With its dual entrances and wood shuttered
windows, the building is typical of a structure that served as both a home
and a business.**

small, and remarkably similar, but they served as important symbols of
advancing civilization for hundreds of immigrants.

The distances between these establishments was approximately a day's
travel by wagon or afoot depending on the difficulty of the passage, and
many inns and taverns were strategically located at river crossings and
ferries to attract trade even if others were nearby. An average distance
between refreshments and lodging was about ten miles. On the Boston
Post Road in 1697 there were twenty-six taverns along the 274 miles
between Boston and New York, but the road that ran from Hartford to
Springfield 54 miles along the Connecticut River had twelve in 1725.[24]

Before the temperance movement gained popularity in the middle of
the nineteenth century, taverns and alehouses were in many cases considered respectable men's clubs, and served as public centers for political
gatherings, assemblies of merchants and local farmers, and fertile fields
for the recruiting of soldiers. These establishments typically provided
wholesome entertainment in the form of card games, bowling, shuffle-
board, music, and singing for wearing travelers.

Men, and even boys as young as twelve, were allowed to buy whatever alcoholic beverages they wanted. Popular drinks in cold weather

were hot buttered rum and a concoction called "flip." The common variety of flip was a mixture of rum, beer, and brown sugar into which a hot poker was plunged. The heat warmed the mixture without seriously diminishing its alcohol content. Warm-weather drinks included many kinds of beer, ale, porter, cider, wine, and a long list of liquors. If ice was not readily available (and it usually was not), drinks could be chilled by placing the bottle on a rope or in a water bucket and hanging it in the cool water of a well. The temperature of the water in a well is rarely higher than 45 degrees even on the warmest day.[25]

Frontier tavern-keeping was rarely a full-time occupation, and many farmers and merchants simply put aside a room or two of their normal household as a public service, which also provided a second income. Nonetheless, these tavern-keepers generally required licenses for their operations, and their services came under the scrutiny of detailed legislation. The work of serving food and drink often fell to the female members of the family. The widows of tavern-keepers often continued the business long after the deaths of their husbands, and a remarkable number of establishments seemingly had no male proprietor that anyone could remember.

As the traveler approached a city or town, taverns and inns improved and became more specialized. Most had a main area known as a taproom set aside with numerous chairs and tables for eating and drinking before the fireplace. Throughout the colonial period taverns remained the domain of men, but it would not arouse any undue attention to find an elderly female proprietor, serving girls, a minister's wife having dinner with her husband, or a lady on a journey having dinner in a tavern.[26] Nonetheless, women did not travel without their husbands or fathers, nor did they stay alone in taverns or inns for any reason other than absolute necessity. Separate sleeping arrangements, other than loft space, were often totally wanting, and the taproom or other public rooms were turned into sleeping chambers after food and drinks were no longer being served. Large bundles of straw-filled ticking (fabric) were often laid out on the floor in the absence of bedsteads. When women did travel, they planned ahead of their trip to stay in the home of a relative or made other arrangements through a local minister.[27]

NOTES

1. Robert Leckie, *A Few Acres of Snow: The Saga of the French and Indian Wars* (New York: John Wiley & Sons, 1999), 33.

2. Peter Martyr as quoted in David J. Weber, *The Spanish Frontier in North America* (New Haven: Yale University Press, 1992), 38. See also p. 56.

3. Roderick Nash, *Wilderness and the American Mind* (New Haven: Yale University Press, 1971), 1.

4. Louis B. Wright, *The Atlantic Frontier: Colonial American Civilization, 1607–1763* (New York: Alfred A. Knopf, 1951), 124.

5. Roderick Nash, 16.

6. Paul A. W. Wallace, *Conrad Weiser: Friend of Colonist and Mohawk, 1696–1760* (Lewisburg, PA: Wennawoods, 1996), 80–82. A number of sites with similar characteristics came to be known as "The Shades of Death." See Louis M. Waddell and Bruce D. Bromberger, *The French and Indian War in Pennsylvania, 1753–1763: Fortification and Struggle During the War for Empire* (Harrisburg; Pennsylvania Historical and Museum Commission, 1996), 46.

7. Roderick Nash, 6.

8. Frederick Jackson Turner, *The Significance of the Frontier in American History* (New York: Henry Holt, 1920), 2.

9. William Cronon, *Changes in the Land, Indians, Colonists, and the Ecology of New England* (New York: Hill and Wang, 1983), 69.

10. Quoted in Gary B. Nash, *Red, White, and Black: The Peoples of Early America* (Englewood Cliffs, NJ: Prentice-Hall, 1982), 98.

11. Colin G. Calloway, *The Western Abenakis of Vermont, 1600–1800: War, Migration, and the Survival of an Indian People* (Norman: University of Oklahoma Press, 1990), 17–19, 27.

12. Gary B. Nash, 99.

13. Francis Jennings, *The Ambiguous Iroquois Empire: The Covenant Chain Confederation of Indian Tribes with English Colonies from its Beginnings to the Lancaster Treaty of 1744* (New York: W. W. Norton 1984), 27.

14. Wallace, 97–99. Edward Marshall thereafter lived on an island in the Delaware River near present-day Marshall's Creek, Pennsylvania, where the Indians later took their revenge, killing his wife and son and wounding his daughter. Marshall escaped the raid without injury.

15. John Keegan, *Fields of Battle: The Wars for North America* (New York: Alfred A. Knopf, 1996), 92.

16. Ibid., 76, 89–90.

17. Ibid., 96–97.

18. See Andrew Gallup, ed., *Memoir of a French and Indian War Soldier: Jolicoeur Charles Bonin* (Bowie, MD: Heritage Books, 1993), 38–39n.

19. Keegan, 93. This same route was used by both American rebels and British troops during the American Revolution.

20. Peter O. Wacker, *The Musconetcong Valley of New Jersey: A Historical Geography* (New Brunswick, NJ: Rutgers University Press, 1968), 30–37.

21. Edward Armstrong, ed., *Good Order Established in Pennsylvania and New Jersey in America by Thomas Budd* (New York: Williams Gowans, 1865), 44.

22. Wacker, 27.

23. Wallace, 25–26, 35, 78.

24. Bruce C. Daniels, *Puritans at Play, Leisure, and Recreation in Colonial New England* (New York: St. Martin's Griffin, 1995) 141–145.

25. Recent American tastes in beer and other beverages call for large quantities of ice, but European tastes, even today, call for wines and beers to be properly cooled only to the temperature of well water.

26. Daniels, 154. See also Sarah Kemble Knight, *The Journal of Madame Knight:*

A Woman's Treacherous Journey by Horseback from Boston to New York in the Year 1704. (Boston: Small, Maynard, 1920).

27. Parke Rouse Jr., *The Great Wagon Road from Philadelphia to the South* (New York: McGraw-Hill, 1973), 97–101.

2

The Eastern Woodland Culture

The men threw their blanket loosely over one shoulder "holding the upper side of it by two corners, with a knife in one hand, and a tobacco-pouch, pipe &c. in the other. Thus accoutered they walked about their villages or camps."

—Jonathan Carver

THE NORTHEASTERN WOODLAND INDIANS

No single set of material characteristics has been found to unite the diverse nations that made up the native Americans into a single people. Ethnologists have therefore settled on a commonality of language as a gauge to determine lineal relationships among the tribes. There were two great linguistic stocks of native peoples in the northeastern quadrant of North America. One of these was Algonquian and the other Iroquoian. As these native Americans left no written records of their own, much of what is known about them was reported by Jesuit missionaries and white captives, neither of whom can be considered unbiased and objective. It is important, therefore, for students of the colonial period to recognize the conjectural nature of much of what is written about the life and appearance of native peoples.[1]

Algonquians

The Algonquian-speaking peoples, represented by such tribes as the Abenakis, Micmacs, and Montagnais in the north and the Ottawas, Ojib-

A typical scene found in an early period native American camp. Note the
bark shelter at the rear of the encampment, the skins drying at the right, and
the firepit in the foreground. A wide variety of baskets and naturally available food are present. The tall crockery pot was used for boiling food. There
are no metal tools in this camp, which has been re-created at a New Jersey
historic site.

was, and Potawatomis in the lakes region, were active and transient in
the precontact period roaming and hunting in the great wilderness forests of present-day Canada and the Great Lakes. They hunted and for-
aged in small bands who came together annually for fishing, summer
encampments, or religious ceremonies. Unfortunately the Algonquian
peoples of the Atlantic coastal region were destroyed or dispersed by
war and disease in the seventeenth century. Almost nothing of their material culture has survived that was not drastically changed by early
European contact, and the surviving reports of their lifestyle made by
ethnocentric and biased European observers remain highly suspect.

Iroquoians

The Iroquoian-speaking peoples, generally represented by the Iroquois
and their relations known to the French as Hurons, were more settled
in their lifestyle than the Algonquians. Their culture was organized
around an annual agricultural cycle, established political institutions,
and permanent, fortified villages. Although they may have traveled an-

nually to hunt in the grasslands or fish in waters far removed from their homes, they were considerably more sedentary than the Algonquians. Much is known of the Iroquois Confederacy of the Five Nations (later Six) because of their close alliance with the English in the final struggle for empire with the French. Less is known of the Hurons and their associated cantons (tribal groups) because of their great dispersal at the hands of the Iroquois in 1649.[2]

Invaders. The Iroquoian-speaking nations seem to have pressed back the Algonquians to the north and northeast from the Ohio River Valley some time before the period of European contact, but certainly not too far removed from the end of the fifteenth century. The Hurons apparently formed the northern wing of this migration, and their four tribal groups passed north of Lake Erie and Lake Ontario. The Hurons ultimately settled in the Georgian Bay–Lake Simcoe area of the present-day province of Ontario. Meanwhile the five related cantons of Iroquois (Seneca, Cayuga, Onondaga, Oneida, and Mohawk) passed to the south of the lakes to occupy present-day central New York State. The Cherokee and Tuscarora nations, also of Iroquoian lineage, found homes flanking the southeastern Atlantic seaboard. The Mohawks seem to have made the northernmost incursions into present-day Canada, having displaced an unidentified people known as the Adirondacks.

The five Iroquois nations were noted for their chronic hostility toward several tribes who lived great distances from them. Among these were the Catawba nation of the southeast and the Ojibwa and Illinois nations of the west. This long-standing hostility was explained in Iroquois tradition as having roots in their original displacement of the precontact nations. However, they also maintained an internecine feud with their relations in the south, the Cherokees, which seems to have begun in the historical period. Iroquois warriors traveled more than thirty days on the Warrior's Path to raid in Cherokee territory.

Simply because certain tribes spoke the same language did not mean that they were allied in a political or economic sense. In the precontact period a wide-ranging alliance of the Algonquian peoples with the Hurons was established. The Hurons seem to have outnumbered the Iroquois at this time and to have broken with them politically. Nonetheless, after fifty years of warfare the retreating Algonquians seemingly consolidated their resistance to the Iroquois invasion.

The Laurentian Iroquois. Most historical accounts regard the St. Lawrence River and Lake Champlain as the northern and eastern boundaries of region known as Iroquoia, leaving most of the present-day province of Quebec and all of New England in Algonquian possession. However, when Jacques Cartier visited the St. Lawrence River valley in 1535 and again in 1541, he found there at least eleven established villages of Iroquoian-speaking natives. The village of Hochelaga, which he visited on the site of present-day Montreal, was certainly Iroquoian. These villages had all disappeared seven decades later when Samuel de Champlain explored the area, to be replaced by roving bands of Algonquian-speaking hunters like the Montagnais and Nipissings. For lack of a better name, historians have called these missing native peoples the Laurentian Iroquois.

Both Huron and Mohawk traditions claim the Laurentian Iroquois as their own, but neither convincingly explains their disappearance. An aged Indian who claimed to have been a resident of the island of Montreal in the period before the French regime, was reported to have told a Jesuit: "The Huron, who were then our enemies, drove our forefathers from this country. Some went toward the country of the Abenakis, others toward the the country of the Iroquois, some to the Huron themselves, and joined them." Champlain benefited from the peaceful access afforded him by a surprisingly vacant but immensely rich region when he established his small wooden stockade at Quebec on the former site of the Laurentian Iroquois village of Stadacona in 1608.[3]

LIFE IN THE SOUTHEASTERN WOODLANDS

Historians have very little information about the southeastern woodland Indians largely because their traditional cultures were wildly misrepresented and purposely destroyed by the Spanish. Nonetheless, there were a few descriptions left by early European observers and captives. It would be impossible to describe in detail the many nations that peopled this vast region. Suffice it to say that they resembled their neighbors to the north, for whom there were many descriptions by contemporary observers, and that they shared many of their religious and cultural characteristics.

As many as five different languages were spoken among the native peoples of the southeastern woodlands. Besides Algonquian, the most common language was the Muskhogean tongue, which was spoken by the Creek, Choctaw, Chickasaw, Timuca, Natchez, and Seminole nations among others. The Siounan language, most commonly spoken by the Winnebago and Sioux on the western plains, was also the language of the Tutelo, Catawba, and Yuchi in the southeast. Caddo was spoken by the peoples of Arkansas, Louisiana, and parts of east Texas, while the Cherokee and Tuscarora of Tennessee, northern Georgia, and the Carolinas spoke an Iroquoian tongue that marked them as recent invaders.

THE APPEARANCE OF THE WOODLAND INDIANS

The eastern tribes who occupied North America were not all that different in appearance from that of other woodland Indians, making it unnecessary and redundant to describe each nation separately. Many of the items of clothing worn by these nations were generic and designed around the same set of available materials, which were chosen largely for their practicality. Individual and tribal differences were largely in the decoration of these items. It seems certain that there were more similarities in dress than there were differences. There is a particularly incomplete picture of the appearance of the Atlantic coastal tribes, and many of the contemporary European accounts and illustrations that are available have proven to be untrustworthy.

Nonetheless, early descriptions tell of painted deerskin robes, brass ornaments, and copper pipes. The surviving clothing artifacts that serve as examples of these nations have remarkable refinements in cut and exhibit such sophistication in assembly that it is uncertain whether they were affected by European contact. Although the basic garments were of native construction, the native style may have been looser and less tailored than a rudimentary inspection might suppose. The long period of contact between the eastern woodland nations and whites resulted in "a gradual Europeanization of their art and technology," and the multitribal reorganizations that followed the native dispersions of the Beaver Wars of the seventeenth century may explain the hybridized appearance of many native objects now in museums.[4]

Louis Antoine de Bougainville, who spent many years among the various native tribes, noted: "I see no difference in the dress, ornaments, dances and songs of these different nations. They are naked save for a breechclout, and painted in black, red, and blue, etc. Their heads are shaved and feathers ornament them. In their lengthened ear lobes are rings of brass wire. They have beaver skins for covering, and carry lances, arrows, and quivers made of buffalo skin."[5]

C. Keith Wilbur, an expert in historical dress, notes: "As elsewhere in the woodlands the usual dress of the day was a breechclout and moccasins. Any travel through the brush and brambles called for protective leggings and shirts. Cooler weather could be met with the insulation provided by a feather or fur cloak. The air pocketed fur was worn against the skin. Women might also wear skirts of soft deerskin or woven grass or the pliable inner bark of trees."[6]

It would probably be an error, however, to assume that native American costume made of deer or other animal skins was uniformly of their natural color. Spanish explorer Hernando de Soto reported that the skins used in native American clothing in the sixteenth century were well dyed: "The color being given to them that is wished and in such perfection that when of vermilion they look like very fine red broadcloth and when black . . . they are of the purest."[7]

The Effect of European Contact

Once the tribes came in contact with the Europeans, selling them furs for trade items, they gladly adopted cloth shirts made of linen, and blankets, loincloths, and leggings made of coarse wool. "The men of every nation differ in their dress very little from each other, except those who trade with the Europeans."[8] A great number of the male Indians began to dress in jackets and vests mixed with loincloths, Indian leggings, and footwear. The women were not so quick to give up their traditional clothing styles, but they readily replaced skins and woven grass with colored broadcloth nonetheless.[9] Lieutenant Henry Timberlake, who was familiar with the Cherokee, noted: "[T]hey have now learnt to sew, and the men as well as women, excepting shirts, make all their own cloaths . . . [in] their favorite colors of blue and red."[10]

Hair

The women generally wore their straight, black hair long with beads, wampum, or feathers for decoration—"so long that it generally reaches to the middle of their legs and sometimes to the ground." They sometimes wore a small cap or coronet of brass or copper on their heads.[11] With regard to their hair, Jolicoeur Charles Bonin, a French soldier, noted of Indian women:

They keep it long, full and shiny; taking care to rub it frequently with bear grease which thickens it, and covering it with powder made of rotten wood. They make it as large as one's fist, then wrap it with eel or snake skin. This pigtail is flattened on the back, and rounds a little higher up. As their hair very often grows long, they turn it up halfway down, making the pigtail thicker, and as large at the bottom as it is at the top.[12]

A center hair roach was most common on the head of male Indians, but some tribes allowed the hair to grow to great length. William Bartram, who traveled among the Muskhogeans, reported that the men shaved their heads leaving only a narrow crest or comb beginning at the crown of the head, where it is about two inches broad and about the same height. The hair was "frizzed upright," but as the crest moved farther to the back of the head, it gradually widened to cover the "hinder part of the head and back of the neck" in a lank of hair terminating in a tail or tassel, the length of which was ornamented in various ways. Male Indians had no patience for facial hair and plucked it out by the root with clamshell twisters.[13]

The term *Huron* was a colloquialism for these people that referred to the curious scalplock dressed in a ridge or roach down the middle of the head. Although the Iroquois also wore their hair in this manner, the term was almost uniquely applied by the French to these people with whom they were most familiar. The term *Iroquois* was adapted by the French from the Algonquian name for these people, *Iroqu*, which meant "rattlesnake." The scalplock was the objective of the widely misrepresented process of scalping. The taking of a scalp or hairlock as a trophy or proof of having killed an enemy in warfare was an ancient native American custom. The Europeans—who traditionally took whole heads for this purpose—did not introduce scalping to the Indians. They did formulate and foster the payment of bounties based on the presentation of scalps. The frontier population of Europeans seems to have been particularly terrorized by reports of scalpings.

Hats and Headdresses

Among the Muskhogean-speaking peoples, Bartram found a "very curious diadem or band, about four inches broad . . . encircling their temples." This was decorated with stones, beads, wampum, porcupine quills, and a large plume or feather "of crane or heron" set in the front peak.[14] Similar caps were worn by Iroquoian peoples. On the other hand, Peter Kalm, who traveled among the Huron, found that they wore no hats or caps whatever, and when among the Abenaki, he reported women who had "funnel-shaped caps."[15] Colonel James Smith, who spent some time in western Pennsylvania with the Caughnawagas, noted the use of red handkerchiefs in place of hats.[16] Finally, John Knox, who traveled among the Micmac tribe of northeastern Canada, noted the use of a turbanlike headgear by both males and females.[17]

James Adair, who studied the southeastern tribes from 1735 to 1744, described the men as fastening several sorts of beautiful feathers to a lock of hair on the crown of their heads, "frequently in tufts; or the wing of a red bird, or the skin of a small hawk. And every Indian nation when at war trim [decorate] their hair after a different manner through contempt of each other. Thus we can distinguish an enemy in the woods so far off as we can see him."[18]

Outer Clothes

Both genders wrapped a piece of cloth about six feet square around themselves by way of outerwear. This was sometimes described by Europeans in terms of the Roman toga.[19] The Hurons were described as using "a shaggy piece of cloth, which is either blue or white, with a blue or red stripe below. This they always carry over their shoulders, or let it hang down, in which case they wrap it around their middle."[20] In inclement weather the Indians "fasten their blanket below with their

A contemporary likeness of the Mohawk sachem and war leader Tiyanoga, known to the English as King Hendrick. Note his clothing, especially the ruffled shirt, which represents the finest in native regalia. The pipe toma-hawk in his hand and the gorget around his neck were symbols of his im-portance. Tiyanoga was a loyal friend and ally of the English. He was killed during the Battle of Lake George on September 8, 1755.

belts, and make them pass over the head like a monk's hood, arranging them so well that they expose only their nose and hands."[21] Otherwise the men threw their blanket loosely over one shoulder, and even in the hottest weather they might be seen strutting about their villages.[22]

It was noted that the blankets supplied by the French were "made in Normandy of very fine wool, and better supplied by the English which are coarser."[23] The Hudson's Bay Company established a "point" system that valued blankets as to their quality or size. The higher points were of greater value. Men and women reportedly used blankets of two or three points for outer garments, while the children were provided with slightly smaller blankets down to one point. It should be noted that the point system was not universally used by all traders, and it was often imitated by unscrupulous persons to cheat the Indians.[24]

Basic Men's Garments

Most Indian men could not be persuaded to use trousers, "for they thought these were a great hindrance in walking."[25] Jean-Bernard Bossu reported that the male war leaders of the southern nations went "naked, like the other warriors, and the scars on their bodies distinguished them from their men and take the place of military commissions."[26] This report seems extreme, but the men certainly had a great aversion to the wearing of breeches, "for to that custom, they affix the idea of helplessness and effeminacy."[27] They wore instead a slip of cloth or dressed skin known as a breechclout, which was about half a meter wide, and a meter and a half long.[28] This they put between their legs and tied around their waists with a conveniently broad belt or cord. A French soldier noted, "The two ends of the loincloth are folded over in front and in back, with the end in front longer than the one in the back."[29] Another observer noted it was "like a short apron or skirt."[30]

Both men and women seem to have favored the European style of shirts, but they were reported to have left the collars and cuffs open, as fastening them "would be a most insufferable confinement to them."[31] "Young people are dandies, and the women are fond of wearing ruffles bordered with lace. They never take them off, except to sleep, until they are used up for time, and finally they become black from use."[32] Peter Williamson, a captive in Pennsylvania in 1754, noted, "The better sort have shirts of the finest linen they can get . . . but these they never put on till they have painted them of various colours . . . and they never pull them off to wash, but wear them till they fall apart."[33]

The consumption of shirts among Indians was very great. A plain men's shirt could be bought for a large beaver pelt or deerskin. With ruffles the price doubled, and for children a smaller pelt or skin was

These native American reenactors are dressed for cooler weather. They wear furs for warmth and carry French-style weapons.

charged. Shirts were sometimes decorated with vermilion mixed with grease.[34]

The Ottawas were reported to have developed, instead of shirts, "a kind of waistcoat of blue or red cloth, cut in pieces, so that with four or six cords they can cover half the body and the arms."[35] Richard Smith, who toured the great river valleys of the Hudson, Mohawk, Susquehanna, and Delaware near the end of the French and Indian Wars, noted of the natives that he saw even at that late date: "Cloathing they use but little, sometimes a shirt or shift with a blanket or coat, and sometimes the latter only, without linen."[36]

Basic Women's Garments

There is no evidence that women wore loincloths. Instead they wore a skirt of deerskin or cloth. They took a square piece of cloth similar to that used as an outer wrap, which they placed around their waists as a "sort of loose petticoat" reaching only to the middle of the leg. Elizabeth Hicks, a captive in Ohio, made such a petticoat or skirt for herself, describing it as "formed by doubling the cloth so far as to have one fold a quarter of a yard below the other; this is wrapped round the waist, and reaches a little below the knee." The skirts were reportedly covered with "brass runners and buckles" by way of ornamentation, and the edge was sometimes bordered with red or other colored strips of material.[37]

An observer noted of women's fashion in body garments: "Those who trade with the Europeans wear a linen garment [shirt] the same as that used by the men; the flaps of which hang over the petticoat. Such as dress after their ancient manner, make a kind of shift with leather, which covers the body but not the arms."[38] The leather used to make the basic native shift was reportedly deerskin, wild ox, or elk. "The arms, to the shoulders, are left naked, or are provided with sleeves which are sometimes put on, and sometimes suffered to hang vacant from the shoulders." The design of the shift among Canadian nations fell from the shoulders to below the knee in one piece.[39]

The garment covered the shoulders and the bosom and was fastened by a strap passing over the shoulders and gathered about the waist by a belt. Waist belts seem to have been made of leather, twisted bark fiber, a wide strip of broadcloth, or woven yarn. They were used with either shirts or shifts to bring in the garment about the waist. One observer also noted that "the Indian females continually wear a beaded string round their legs [hips], made of buffalo-hair . . . [which] they reckon a great ornament as well as a preservative against miscarriages, hard labor, and other evils."[40] In general, each woman had one basic body garment that was worn as long as it would last and was then thrown away "without any attempt at cleanliness" being made in the interim.[41]

Children's Garments

Until they were four or five children went entirely naked in good weather, and they were provided with a little blanket in which to wrap themselves in bad. Thereafter children seem to have worn the same styles and designs as their parents with the exception of size. Girls were noted to wear shifts much shorter than the matrons. The Reverend Reuben Weiser recounted the details of native children's clothing worn by a young German captive girl named Regina after her rescue from the Abenaki in 1744:

They had a kind of sack, made of deer-skin, just large enough to go over the body, and extending from the hip-bones almost down to the knees. This curious bag-shaped garment was either kept up by being tied around the waist with a bark string, or supported by suspenders over the shoulders, also made of bark. The arms, legs, and all the upper part of the body were naked and exposed to the cold; still, in very cold weather, Regina had also a small, dirty, thin blanket and moccasins and leggings.[42]

Leggings

Both males and females wore leg coverings. Called leggings, leather stockings, mitasses, or Indian gaiters, all were essentially the same item of clothing. They were worn for protection against thorns or brush, and may have helped in avoiding snakebites. "The legs are preserved from many fatal accidents that may happen by briars, stumps of trees, or under-wood, &c. in marching through close, woody country."[43] Nicholas Cresswell, who traveled widely through the backcountry, considered leggings an essential item: "These are pieces of coarse woolen cloth wrapped round the leg and tied below the knee with a string to prevent the snakes biting you."[44]

Leggings were usually made of leather or coarse cloth—scarlet wool was reported to have been a favorite among the Great Lakes tribes. Pierre Pouchot, commandant of Fort Niagara, described women's leggings as stockings "made of flannel cloth fringed with red, white, or blue. This gaiter is sewed up following the shape of the leg, with four finger breadth of stuff outside the seam. This strip is bordered with ribbons of different colors, mingled with designs of glass beads, which forms a very pleasing effect. . . . Besides this they wear garters of beads, or porcupine quills, bordered four fingers wide, which are tied on the legs."[45] Another observer reported that the leather stockings "hung full of the hoofs of the roe deer in the form of bells, in so much as to make a sound exactly like castagnettes."[46]

John Knox, a contemporary journalist, gave a very full account of the construction and use of leggings and described the adoption of these useful and necessary items by whites:

They should be at least three quarters of a yard in length . . . [and] three quarters wide, then double it, and sew it together from end to end, within four, five, or six inches of the outside selveges, fitting this long narrow bag to the shape of the leg; the flaps on the outside, which serve to wrap over the skin, or fore-part of the leg, tied round under the knee, and above the ankle, with garters of the same color. The army have made an ingenious addition to them, by a tongue, or sloped piece before . . . and a strap fixed to it under the heart of the foot. . . . For my part, I think them clumsy, and not at all military; yet I confess they are highly necessary in North America.[47]

Woolen and leather leggings of the native American style were adopted by most frontiersmen and rangers. Many French and English troops serving on the frontiers would appear in uniform coat, waistcoat, and shirt only to be clothed from the waist down in moccasins and breeches topped with Indian leggings.

Note the snowshoes and leggings in this period illustration of an
Indian warrior. Even though this is a winter scene, he is clad only
in a breechclout. Beside his musket, he carries both a traditional
warclub and an iron tomahawk. The beads in his hand may be a
Catholic rosary.

Footwear

Almost every schoolchild knows that Indians wore leather moccasins on their feet. Several styles of moccasin construction have been identified as being that of Algonquian, Iroquoian, or other tribal type. A one-piece construction, "an ancient form," seems to have been favored by the tribes of the southeast.[48] One observer noted that the skin was "gathered at the toe and are sewn above and behind with a raised flap on either side. This is turned down over the cord below the ankle which ties on the shoe." The front seam and side flaps were often covered with an appliqué of woven porcupine quills or decorated woolen cloth.[49] In the eastern areas of Canada a separate top, or vamp, covered the instep and was sewn to the body of the shoe with a thick puckered seam. In the Great Lakes region both styles seem to have been used. A more complicated design, requiring three pieces and often attributed to the Iroquoian peoples, had a separate sole of tough leather to which the sides of the moccasin were stitched with deer sinew. There was a seam along the top of the foot and at the heel. This style also had flaps that turned down over the ankle.[50] The folded edges as well as the fronts and backs could be decorated with ribbons, dyed porcupine quills, glass beads, and tiny copper bells.[51]

The women made the footwear for the men as well as for themselves using deer sinew or a thread from the bark of a linden tree that the French called "bois blanc." The bark was taken from the inside nearest the wood, boiled in water for a time, and pounded with a wooden club until it became soft and fibrous. The women then sat twisting the fibers into a thread by rolling it on their thighs. The bark thread so manufactured was the equal of "a fine hemp cord."[52]

The leather skins were sometimes dressed in the European manner and at other times left with the fur on them.[53] "They make their shoes for common use out of skins of the bear and elk, well dressed and smoked, to prevent hardening; and those for ornament out of deer-skin, done in the like manner; but they chiefly go bare-footed."[54] It was also noted that the natives frequently went without moccasins but found that they usually wore their leggings even when barefoot.

The Indians also had shoes for winter wear "formed like laced boots."[55] Reported to be quite efficient, these boots were very warm and relatively dry. "They wrap their feet with pieces of blanket, and the sides of the shoe form a half boot which prevents the snow from getting in, while their feet would freeze in European shoes as many have unhappily proved."[56]

Body Paint

Peter Kalm noted the use of body paint among the Hurons of Lorette in French Canada:

Many of them have the face painted all over with cinnabar [red vermilion]; others have only strokes of it on the forehead and near the ears; and some paint their hair with the same material. Red is the color they chiefly use in painting themselves, but I have also seen some who had daubed their face with black [denoting death or war]. . . . They formerly made use of a reddish earth, which is to be found in the country, but as the Europeans brought them vermilion, they thought nothing was comparable to it in color. . . . Verdigris [was used] to paint their faces green. For the black color they make use of the soot off the bottom of their kettles, and daub the whole face with it.[57]

A French soldier serving in the middle of the eighteenth century noted that the natives painted themselves by dipping their fingers in the color with which they wanted to paint their faces and dragging them across and down the face forming stripes:

Many . . . tribes . . . are satisfied with painting the face and body in different colours, first rubbing themselves with bear grease, and then daubing on black, red, blue, and green. This is an ordinary decoration for them. Often, when they are at war, they use it, they say, to frighten or intimidate their enemies. . . . They also paint prisoners black when they intend to kill them, as well as painting themselves black when they return from war after losing some of their men.[58]

Tattoos

The Indians tattooed various designs on their bodies that remained as long as they lived. On their faces they impressed figures of snakes, scrolls, lines of tears, and other symbols of importance to them. John M'Cullough, a captive among the Delaware, believed these "hieroglyphics . . . always denote[d] valor."[59] Jean-Bernard Bossu, a contemporary observer, noted, "If anyone should take it into his head to have himself tattooed without having distinguished himself in battle, he . . . might have the design torn off him, skin and all."[60]

The color most used in tattooing was black. Peter Kalm did not recall ever seeing any other. However, he noted, "The men who accompanied me told me that they also use red paint and that black and red are the only colors used."[61] Other contemporary observers described tattoos in red, black, blue, and green—"all bright colors." The blue and green could be made from verdigris, a copper acetate compound, which varies from blue, to blue green, to green depending on its various chemical structures. Verdigris was a particularly poisonous compound if taken internally, but seems to have had no ill effect when applied to the skin. The red dye came from cinnabar, which the French and English traders called "vermilion." The black was made by taking a piece of alder wood, burning it completely, and allowing the charcoal to cool. Gunpowder, being black, was also used on occasion to color tattoos.[62]

The chosen pigment was pulverized, usually by rubbing it between the hands. This powder was put into a vessel of water and allowed to stand until it was well saturated. When the natives wished to paint some figures on the body, they first drew the design on the skin with a piece of charcoal. When a man wanted to have his entire body tattooed, he stretched out on a board, and the tattooer marked out as much of the desired design as could be inscribed in one sitting. The persons being tattooed, both men and women, would rather die than flinch during the process. The women bore the pain "with the same courage as the men in order to please them and to appear more beautiful to them." Nonetheless, the operation was bloody and dangerous, as infection could easily set in and cause the subjects to lose their life.[63]

A contemporary journalist noted that to make the image, a tattooer used a needle, "made somewhat like a fleam"—employed by physicians to let blood—or an instrument said to have had several needles fastened together between two pieces of wood:

[They] dip it into the prepared dye and with it prick or puncture the skin along the lines of the design previously made with the charcoal. They dip the needle into the dye between every puncture; thus the color is left between the skin and the flesh. When the wound has healed, the color remains and can never be obliterated. The men told me that in the beginning when the skin is pricked and punctured, it is rather painful, but the smart gradually diminishes and at the expiration of a day the smart and pain has almost ceased.[64]

No form of antiseptic seems to have been used, and a brief infection seems to have been an expected part of the process. Another observer noted that "the blood must flow from the part thus cut by the tattooer's stroke, a swelling follows, forming a scab which falls off after a few days. Then the wound is healed and the tattooing or pattern stands out clearly. The healing takes a shorter or longer time depending on the amount of tattooing done. It is very curious to see a man tattooed in this way, especially when the entire body is tattooed in colors."[65] One observer noted that in the later part of the colonial period the custom of tattooing was dying out among the Indians.[66]

Jewelry and Ornaments

Native Americans were fond of wearing finger rings and earrings even before their contact with Europeans. Naturally occurring copper and gold were in use by the Indians for generations. Both men and women used naturally occurring coarse diamonds, garnets, amethyst crystals,

These modern-day native Americans have chosen to serve as Indian reenactors during public portrayals of the French and Indian War and American Revolution. They attempt to portray an accurate picture of the lifestyle of their ancestors. Note the metal arm band, earrings, and nose ring as well as the mix of European and native clothing.

and other smooth or polished stones in their jewelry. Soapstone, a soft mineral of gray to green color, was often fashioned into pendants, ornaments, and other geometric shapes by rubbing it with damp deerskin or sawgrass dipped in fine sand. Of course, any stone or bit of metal with an interesting shape could be worked into a piece of decoration. Holes could be bored with relative ease in soapstone with a pointed stick dipped in sand.

After European contact natives quickly acquired brass and silver rings and crosses; medals representative of Catholic saints; large and small bells; pendants cast in the shapes of turtles, bears, and birds; and brass and silver wire. A warrior of the Delaware nation was noted to have had "a large triangular piece of silver hanging below his nose that covered almost the whole of his upper lip."[67] The European traders also supplied items of brass, silver, and tin such as arm plates, wrist plates, ear bobs, and gorgets. The gorget was a metal plate suspended below the throat from a cord worn around the neck. It had a lima bean shape and could be from four to eight inches long. "Both sexes . . . commonly load the parts [of the body] with each sort in proportion to their ability of purchasing them." They were especially fond of these items if they were received as gifts and "would never part with them for the sake of the giver."[68]

Ear Loops. The native women bored small holes in their ear lobes through which they passed earrings and pendants much as women do today. However, the women generally avoided the custom of some young men who distinguished themselves by creating giant loops in their earlobes. Women never followed this practice. The young men could not extend their ears in this manner unless they had been tested as warriors. The ear loops were reported to have reached a diameter of four inches.[69] "The young heroes cut a hole round almost the extremity of both their ears, which till healed, they stretch out with a large tuft of buffalo wool mixt with bear's oil. They then twist as much small wire round as will keep them extended in that hideous form."[70]

The following description of the Indians at a native wedding feast survives from the 1740s. It is useful in giving an overall picture of the Indians in what could be considered their finest dress:

I observed the dresses of the wedding guests. The squaws were covered with a blanket and round their wrists, arms, necks, and ankles were several strings of wampum. Some of them had on their heads a cap of coarse cloth as wool, others a sort of a coronet of party colored feathers. The men and boys were likewise covered with a blanket without any embellishments except some of them had a hole in the thick or lower part of their ear big enough for me to put my finger through, and in this hole was put sundry strips of fine cloth of several colours which cloth hung down their shoulders like a fore horse's top knot. Some of them had their pipe run through their ear and hung by the bole. One Indian I observed had a hole bored through the bridge of his nose and through it was put a ring of brass from which hung a pendant stone of a pearl colour and about the shape and size of a Thrush's egg.[71]

VILLAGE LIFE

The Iroquoian-speaking peoples lived in permanent fortified villages having substantial populations. Iroquoian villages were usually built near a lake or riverside but were set back to prevent surprise attack by canoe-borne raiders. Villages were always located near a source of fresh spring water. They were surrounded by as many as four concentric rows of palisades (fences of stakes) topped with a scaffold from which the walls could be defended. At the beginning of the seventeenth century Champlain found some stockades that were thirty-five feet high, and it seems that the Hurons built much more imposing structures than the Iroquois. That this was due to fear of the Iroquois, as suggested by some contemporary observers, is probably not true.[72]

The Laurentian Iroquois village of Hochelaga (Montreal) was described as surrounded by cultivated lands and fields of maize, beans, and squash:

The town [was] round in shape and enclosed with three rows of timbers in the shape of a pyramid crossed on top, having the middle stakes perpendicular, and the others at an angle on each other, well joined and fastened in their fashion. It is the height of two lances [25 feet] and there is only one entrance through a gate which can be barred. There were in the town about fifty houses, each fifty steps [100 feet] or more in length and twelve or fifteen [25 to 30 feet] wide, all made of wood covered with bark and strips of wood as large as a table, sewn well together artificially in their way. Within there were several rooms [sleeping alcoves]. In the center of the house there was a large space used as a fireplace, where they eat in common, each man retiring afterwards to his rooms with his wife and children. Likewise they have lofts or granaries in their houses, where they store their corn, out of which they make their bread.[73]

The Algonquian peoples were still roaming in extended family groups of about twenty persons in the historical period. They were most active in winter and came together as a tribe when the warmer planting season approached to make maple sugar and to plant their fields. Because of their seasonal cycle of living, these tribes generally did not establish permanent cities or large-scale villages with extensive stockades. Nonetheless, fifty to one hundred dwellings, or wigwams, could be scattered about a semipermanent town with rudimentary fortifications. These structures were made of bark supported on a framework of saplings and small tree trunks sunk into the ground and bent over into a dome with a door opening and a smoke hole. The bark coverings could be stripped and carried to the next seasonal campground. As with most Indians of the eastern woodlands, the towns were moved about every ten years because the fields became too depleted for further cultivation.[74]

Jolicoeur Charles Bonin has left a detailed description of an Algonquian village in his memoir of the French and Indian War:

[An Algonquian] village has no plan. It is a group of cabins of various shapes and sizes. Some are as long as a shed. They are all built and covered with tree bark, with the exception of a strip in the roof about two feet long, to let out the smoke from a fire of the same size. On each side of a cabin, there are beds made of bark spread on sticks and raised seven or eight inches above the ground. The exterior of these cabins is sometimes covered with a mixture of earth and brush to keep out the wind. The doors are likewise of bark hung from the top like blinds, or fastened on one side with wooden withes, making a swinging door.

In general, [the natives] fortify better than they house themselves. Villages may be seen stockaded like redoubts, making provision for water and stones. The piles and the stones used to build them have battlements able to withstand a siege. But they must live near their enemies and fear being surprised, if they entrench themselves in this manner.[75]

This photograph was taken in a Iroquoian longhouse that stood for many years outside the visitor
center on the site of Fort William Henry at Lake
George in New York. Note the sleep alcoves, storage
shelves, and birchbark canoe. The structure has
since been removed.

The coastal Algonquian-speaking peoples had smaller villages of ten
to twenty dwellings. The northeastern coastal nations had semipermanent dwellings much like those of the north-central peoples, but the mid-
coastal tribes and the nations of the southeastern woodlands seem to
have favored a more permanent scaled-down longhouse between
twenty-five and fifty feet in length with straight sides and a dome-
capped roof. The longhouses were arranged in orderly rows on a central
plaza with extensive gardens all around. If the village was stockaded,
the longhouses were more tightly bunched together.

In southern New England there were also longhouses of a different
profile. These structures were the basis for the Quonset huts used in
World War II by U.S. forces. "Instead of vertical sides and a rounded
roof, the saplings forming the sides were bent in a continuous arc." These
"half-cylinders" were shingled with bark or reed mats, and they held six
to eight families. For smaller groups or single families a wigwam with
a circular or oval floorplan was erected. The northern Algonquians built
permanent Iroquois-style longhouses and more temporary cone-shaped
dwellings (tepees) covered with birchbark shingles that could be carried
from place to place.[76]

Clans

The clan was a female-oriented institution. It offered a structure to aboriginal society that was organized around common female ancestors. When a man married, he moved in with his wife and her relatives. These matrilineal relatives would join to build a large clan-oriented longhouse, to clear and tend the outlying fields, and to care for and educate the young. The clans took names from among a number of animals, birds, plants, and even mythical beings; but wolves, bears, foxes, elk, deer, hawks, and eagles predominated. Some Algonquian peoples separated their clan-based tribal government along "sky" and "earth" divisions known as moieties. The sky clans were named for birds and were dedicated to the pursuits of peace, the adjudication of blood feuds, and the promotion of harmony, while the earth clans were devoted to preparations for war, defense, and policing the tribe. The political leaders of the tribe were chosen from sky clans, and the war chiefs were chosen from the earth clans. This dual division of power among the clans was found in diverse forms in many Algonquian communities.[77]

All the material wealth of the clan belonged to the women, including the fields, dwellings, and the village itself. The daily life of most woodland Indians centered on the extensive fields of their three main crops—maize, beans, and squash—that surrounded the village. An observer noted "a considerable Indian town inhabited by the Senecas. . . . The low lands on which it is built, like all the others, are excellent, and I saw with pleasure a great deal of industry in the cultivation of their little fields. Corn, beans, potatoes, pumpkins, squashes appeared extremely flourishing."[78]

The fields were cultivated by the women of the clan. For this reason many historians believed that the more settled tribes gave greater political and social power to females. Certainly among the Iroquois, the clan or lineage was accounted through the female line. Such a situation is known as matrilineal, but it is far removed from a matriarchy in which the women actually rule the tribe. Jolicoeur Charles Bonin noted of the French Indians, "Perhaps no nation in the world scorns women more than these savages usually do." Yet under the matrilineal principle the women of the Iroquois nations, at least, enjoined a good deal of power. It was the senior clan matrons who chose the next leader from among the available males of the same matrilineal line as their predecessor.[79]

"As a rule of thumb the number of longhouses in a village indicated the emphasis placed on the clans." Those tribes with more permanent villages tended to be matrilineal, calculating clan lineage through the mother. "On the other hand, the more mobile tribal villages with small family-sized and less permanent wigwams tended toward patrilineal clans." This association between the two concepts may be seen as an

It would be an error to believe that native American women failed to voice their opinions. These native American reenactors have set up an encampment at a living history weekend. Note the woman's loose outer garment and long hair as well as the face paint on the man at the right.

oversimplification that masks deeper social relationships. Nonetheless, the clan structure played an important role in the socialization of native American youth, and it was the basis for village and tribal politics.[80]

Blood Revenge

The system of clans also provided a basis for the concept of blood revenge. Much of the intertribal raiding and counter-raiding among the native Americans was fueled by revenge. Small groups of related warriors would slip off into the wilderness to seek out and kill the members of other tribes with whom they had a grudge, usually based on the death or mistreatment of one of their own clan members. In this regard Bonin noted, "When . . . injured, he is capable of going [600 miles] or more to surprise his enemy and satisfy his revenge with blood." Blood revenge caused hostilities to drag on for long periods.[81]

The clan structure allowed for the ease with which male captives might be adopted as clan members. This feature of clan-based Indian society figured prominently among the coureurs de bois, woodsmen, captives, and fur traders who married native women and had children with them.

All of their progeny were considered full clan members because questions of legitimacy flowed through the females. Men like Charles Michel de Langlade, who was French-Ottawa, and the French-Seneca Joncaire brothers, Daniel and Chabert, maintained their status as clan members as they moved among the native Americans speaking at their councils and leading their war parties, while among many Europeans they were looked down upon as mere "half-breeds" who were useful in dealing with the Indians but unsuited for "proper" society.[82]

Child Rearing

Jolicoeur Charles Bonin has left a description of the raising of children among the French Indians. Because of its remarkable detail, his depiction is important even though the observations were sometimes ethnocentric, chauvinistic, and otherwise indifferent to the feminine or native point of view:[83]

The women bear children, usually unattended and without pain but always away from their dwellings,[84] in a little shelter built for this purpose forty or fifty days previous in the woods, or sometimes in their fields. . . . These mothers nurse their own children. . . . care for them, and carry them on their backs with a small board twenty-five or thirty inches long, bent at the upper end. . . . [T]his is fastened with straps, and carried with the child's head upright under the plank's curved end. . . . [T]he child is changed when necessary.

When it leaves the cradle, the child is not interfered with in any way. He is given complete liberty to roll about on his feet and hands, in the woods, in the snow, and even in the water, when he is strong enough. He learns to swim like a fish. All this helps a great deal in making these children strong, supple, and agile. Ordinarily, when they are three or four years old, their mother leaves them to themselves; not through harshness and indifference, but because they believe nature must be let alone and unhampered.

Bows and arrows are put in the hands of children at an early age, and they become expert in their use in a short time. They are made to fight each other, and, sometimes, one would be killed if care were not taken to separate them. The losers are so ashamed, that they do not rest until they have revenge. For this reason they seem born with a desire for glory.

The only education children receive is by hearing their mother and father tell the brave deeds of their ancestors and their tribe. They become enthusiastic over these stories, and grow up and imitate what they have been taught to admire. Kindness is used in correcting them, never threats. . . .

The giving of a name ends the period of early infancy. The ceremony is carried out with a feast attended only by persons of the same sex as the child that is to be named. He is held on his mother's knee, and given the name of a dead warrior in his family. Children are usually thought of as belonging more to the mother than to the father. Since they are brought up with this notion, they respect their father only as the master of the dwelling.[85]

Each child belonged to the clan of his mother and lived in a clan house with his mother's relations. While this did not disqualify the father from taking a critical role in the life of his children, the most important males in a boy's life were undoubtedly his mother's brothers, or his maternal uncles. These would be the ones who instructed him in the skills that he would need as an adult.

Besides practice with the bow and arrow or throwing tomahawks and knives, Indian children played at a number of games. In good weather, running, jumping, and climbing contests abounded as they would among any group of children. A remarkable development was the vigorous and unrestrained game known to the Jesuits as lacrosse. Played with a long-handled net and a leather ball, lacrosse pitted two teams in a contest to score the ball through a goal. The game could cover many acres of ground and involve many hundreds of players. Winter games included a form of ice hockey without skates and a game known as Indian snakes in which a long stick was propelled along an icy trench for distance. Many of these games involved both adults and children playing together.

The Vision Quest

Puberty was an important time in the life of a child as it marked, more distinctly than it does for teens today, the passage from childhood to the status of an adult. The search for a protecting or guiding spirit through the experience of a metaphysical vision was an important part of this transition. The vision quest was common to most native American peoples, but unlike the nations of southwestern North America, the tribes of the northeastern quarter seem to have eschewed the use of mind-altering drugs in the process. However, tobacco may have been burned as a ceremonial offering to ensure success.

Young men generally embarked upon their vision quest when their maternal uncles thought that they were fit in terms of physical and behavioral maturity. Then in the isolation of a wooded spot, cliffside, or mountaintop of some mystical importance, a young man would fast alone for up to ten days. The physical stress created by the denial of food and water usually brought on a hallucination or vision. In this state he would search for a guardian spirit, usually represented by an animal totem that he would follow for his entire life. During his quest the young man might put together a small bag of totems or special items of meaning to himself.

The timing of the vision quest was somewhat less problematic for young women. At the onset of her first menstrual period, a young woman would seclude herself in the same type of shelter as that used by the women of the tribe for giving birth. Here she would fast, denying herself food and drink, until her unseen guardian would make a dream visitation and give her directions for her duties as an adult.

A young person who was favored by a vision might have an experience with a clear meaning, or might have to consult with a shaman, or wiseman, as to an unclear experience. By this means the relations of the young could effectively direct the efforts of their adolescents. Nonetheless, young persons favored by many spirit helpers in their vision quests were considered fortunate. Young men, or in some tribes young women, so favored might themselves become shamans. After a successful vision the young persons might paint their heads red as a sign of having reached adult status.

Marriages

Although many marriages were arranged by parents, the parties concerned do not appear to have been forced to marry without their consent. Promiscuity among teenagers was common,[86] and among some tribes the girls were not urged to marry at an early age, "for they are permitted as many trial marriages as they wish."[87] Nonetheless, there was a formal courtship procedure that was dictated by tribal traditions. These customs seem to have changed from people to people, but they usually involved the giving of presents. Among the Algonquians, a prospective husband presented a trumpline halter, a kettle, and a firelog to his intended. These gifts were based in practical considerations and represented very little in the way of romance.

The woman's acceptance of these gifts signified her acceptance of her role as a wife. The trumpline, worn across the forehead and used to help support loads carried on the back, showed that she would carry; the kettle, that she would cook; and the firelog, that she would not only provide the firewood, but would do everything else required to establish a household. She was also expected to cultivate the fields, help to carry game, transport the bark sheets used to mark wigwams, and to make and repair moccasins.[88]

The woman gave her intended husband only a bag of Indian tobacco and sweet sumac leaves. As Indian men almost always had a pipe in their mouths or hands, the tobacco may have signified their position as husband. An observer noted that "the men glory in their idleness." Certainly the prospective husband's duties were limited, "save for hunting, fishing, and war." Among the Algonquians, the husband was also required to build and repair the family dwelling, while among the Iroquoian nations he moved into an established dwelling with his wife's relations, and it is unclear whether or not he was required to help them in maintaining it.[89]

Polygamy was common among many tribes, with the Algonquians

sometimes marrying all the sisters in a family, "a custom based on the notion that sisters get along better with each other than with strangers." Nonetheless, the Algonquians also recognized two types of wives, one of whom was subservient to the other. It was into this class that many white women captives were placed if they married a native warrior. In some tribes blood relationship was scrupulously regarded. One did not marry a relative or a member of one's own clan. However, a widower might marry his dead wife's sister or some other female relation. This person might be chosen for him by the clan matrons, and the process ensured that the children of the previous marriage would be brought up in the clan tradition. A widow might be required to do the same thing with regard to her dead husband's brothers. Yet if she had no children and was still young, she might be allowed to seek a husband elsewhere.[90]

It would be a mistake to think that these concepts concerning matrimony were hard and fast rules. Even within a single clan there were many variations. Among the Iroquois, for instance, both polygamy and polyandry (many husbands for one woman) were practiced. Among some nations men had wives at every place where they hunted, yet there were some clans who recognized marriages only among themselves. Divorce was recognized in different ways. Couples might agree to stay together only as long as they were happy; others agreed to separate only for good cause. A man who abandoned his wife might have to face retaliation by her relations, and a woman who left her husband for another man without his consent and the approbation of the clan matrons, could "have a bad time of it." In this regard the clan matrons served in place of a divorce court, deciding if the cause warranted the separation.[91]

Adultery among some nations, as opposed to promiscuity, merited extreme punishment. Jealousy not only disturbed the peace of the family but also sent shudders of unrest throughout the clan. A disgraced husband might cut off the nose of his straying wife, while two husbands might exchange wives "to increase their happiness." The women of the Iroquois, Mahican, and Shawnee nations were reported to be excessively jealous. "When a woman discovers that her husband loves another, her rival had better beware; especially as the faithless husband dare not defend her in any way without dishonor."[92]

Traditional Religions

An exhaustive study of the many religions, diverse rituals, and complicated ceremonies of the woodland nations is beyond the scope of this work, but certain characteristic elements can be highlighted. The religions of the Iroquoian, Algonquian, and many other woodland Indians was dualistic. Good and evil existed in the world, and the objective of humans was to please friendly spirits and to mollify unfriendly ones. The Iroquois believed in a creator, Orenda, who embodied the health and creativity of nature. The ceremonial spirits of maize, beans, and squash—the "Three Sisters"—were examples of how the Iroquois assigned spiritual personality, or manitou, to all the materials things around them.

The Indians treated their environment with a respect that matched their technology, but not with adoration. In the deeply religious world of woodland Indians there were supernatural beings, the spirits of animals, plants, sun, sky, and earth from whom the natives sought guidance.[93] This aspect of their religion led some of the Jesuit fathers to misinterpret their religion as the worship of animals, rocks, and trees— a concept at odds with the native Americans' daily life of hunting, chopping, and burning. Moreover, the Indians generally took from the environment around them until it was exhausted. They hunted and fished until the game would no longer support them. They burned the forest underbrush to open the woods for the hunting of game. They girdled trees to kill them and farmed the land until it refused to yield. Then they moved on without attempting to revitalize the area.

Cannibalism was one of the most striking aspects of their religious life. The traditional name for the Mohawks among other nations meant "man-eaters." The ritual eating of an enemy was an attempt to assimilate the power of the victim no less than the consumption of a deer or bear was thought to provide fleetness of foot or great strength. The practice of cannibalism does not seem to have died out until the late eighteenth century.[94]

The Ceremony of the Dead, or the condolence ritual, was widespread among the tribes. Condolence rituals cleansed those who were in despair of their grief and helped to refocus the attention of the living on the needs of the survivors. The replacement of dead family members with captives, or those adopted for the purpose, was not only an attempt to maintain the size of the tribe but was also a means of raising up a successor to fill an important position in clan life. Moreover, a great reverence was given to the bones of the dead, and when a village was moved the bones of those who had died in the interim were taken to the new village site with great ceremony.

Mask societies were another notable element of woodland religion. The False Faces were a "medicine" society, not in terms of "magic" but rather in terms of healthcare. A carved wooden mask, usually of grotesque portions and details, when worn represented a mythological being invoked by the wearer to aid mankind in the elimination of disease. Society members might blow tobacco smoke through the mouth of a mask upon the sick to heal them. Another mask society was the Corn Husk Faces, whose members wore masks during the midwinter rituals connected with farming. Almost all of the woodland nations gathered annually for the Green Corn, midwinter, and harvest rituals, where the activities of the mask societies were prominent.

Among the Shawnee, Creek, Choctaw, Chickasaw, and other tribes of southeastern North America, the Green Corn celebration was of immense importance. It lasted from four to eight days, and was an occasion for amnesty, forgiveness, and absolution from guilt. The ceremony involved purging oneself to cleanse the body and the lighting of new fires in the hearth to cleanse every home. The Shawnee were unique among native American nations in that they believed the creator to be a female. However, their world view, or cosmology, was similar to that of most other peoples. The world was an island on the back of a great turtle who swam slowly through the oceans supported at its corners by four enormous animal spirits such as snakes.[95]

Shamans played a significant role in all these festivals and other religious matters. However, they were not priests or ministers in the European sense. Hunters and warriors would consult shamans because they had many spirit helpers and had shown wisdom in the past. Among the Ojibwa and Chippewa of the western Great Lakes there was an actual priesthood known as the Midewiwin, or Great Medicine Society. These priests, both male and female, possessed various degrees of competency that required training and initiation. The formation of such an organized body may have been in response to a great fear of sorcery among these people, for they had a pantheon of evil spirits who were in conflict with the supreme spirit known as Manito, or Midemanido.[96]

The Life of an Iroquois Wife

In the midst of the French and Indian War (1758) fifteen-year-old Mary Jemison was captured by the Shawnee near Gettysburg, Pennsylvania. Shortly thereafter she was turned over to a Seneca family and adopted into their clan. In the first year of her adoption she was married to a Delaware warrior who was living with the Seneca. One year later her first son died almost immediately after birth. In the fourth year of her captivity she had a second child, Thomas. Although free to return to her white community at the end of the war, she chose to spend the rest of her life as an Indian wife living in an Iroquois village. Her description of the daily labors of the women in this village is detailed and interesting. It is even more important in that the Iroquois women, themselves, left no written records of their daily lives:

I . . . had become so far accustomed to their mode of living, habits and dispositions, that my anxiety to get away, to be set at liberty and leave them, had almost subsided. With them was my home; my family was there, and there I had many friends to whom I was warmly attached. . . .

Our labor was not severe; and that of one year was exactly similar, in almost every respect to that of the others without that endless variety that is to be observed in the common labor of white people. Notwithstanding that Indian women have all the fuel and bread to procure, and the cooking to perform, their task is probably not harder than that of white women, who have those articles provided for them; and their cares certainly are not half as numerous nor as great. In the summer season, we planted, tended and harvested our corn, and generally had all our children with us; but had no master to oversee or drive us, so that we could work as leisurely as we pleased. We had no ploughs . . . but performed the whole process of planting and hoeing with a small tool that resembled, in some respects, a hoe with a short handle.

Our cooking consisted in pounding our corn into samp or hommany, boiling the hommany, making now and then a cake and baking it in the ashes, and boiling or roasting our venison. As our cooking and eating utensils consisted of a hommany block and pestle, a small kettle, a knife or two, and a few vessels of bark or wood, it required but little time to keep them in order for use. . . . In the season of hunting, it was our business, in addition to our cooking, to bring home the game that was taken by the Indians, dress it, and carefully preserve the edible meat, and prepare or dress the skins. . . .

One thing only marred my happiness . . . and that was the recollection that I had once had tender parents, and a home that I loved. Aside from that consideration . . . I should have been contented in my situation.[97]

NOTES

1. Archeology and historical ethnology suggest that both linguistic groups built their cultures on a precontact Mississippian or "temple mound" civilization of which the earliest Europeans to enter the interior may have seen the dying remnants.

2. See George T. Hunt, *The Wars of the Iroquois: A Study in Intertribal Trade Relations* (Madison: University of Wisconsin Press, 1972), 39.

3. Ian K. Steele, *Warpaths: Invasions of North America* (New York: Oxford University Press, 1994), 63; Francis Jennings, *The Ambiguous Iroquois Empire: The Covenant Chain Confederation of Indian Tribes with English Colonies from Its Beginnings to the Lancaster Treaty of 1744* (New York: W. W. Norton, 1984), 28–29 n. 8.

4. Michael G. Johnson, *American Woodland Indians*, Men-at-Arms, vol. 228 (London: Osprey 2000), 41.

5. Louis Antoine de Bougainville, *Adventures in the Wilderness: The American Journals of Louis Antoine de Bougainville* (Norman: University of Oklahoma Press, 1964), 118.

6. C. Keith Wilbur, *The Woodland Indians: An Illustrated Account of the Lifestyles of America's First Inhabitants* (Guilford, CT: Globe Pequot Press, 1995), 54.

7. Wilbur, 54.

8. James F. O'Neil, ed., *Their Bearing Is Noble and Proud: A Collection of Narratives Regarding the Appearance of Native Americans from 1740–1815* (Dayton, OH:

J.T.G.S., 1995), 38. See also Jonathan Carver, *Travels Through the Interior Parts of North America in the Years 1766, 1767, and 1768* (Minneapolis: Ross & Hanes, 1956), 222–231.

    9. Peter Kalm, *Peter Kalm's Travels in North America* (New York: Dover 1964), 560.

    10. Henry Timberlake, *Lieutenant Henry Timberlakes's Memoirs* (Marietta, GA: Continental, 1948), 86, 150.

    11. Timberlake, 75–77.

    12. O'Neil, 29. Quoting a French Soldier, Jolicoeur Charles Bonin, *Travels in New France*, from the 1941 edition published by the Pennsylvania Historical Commission, Harrisburg, PA. See also Andrew Gallup, ed., *Memoir of a French and Indian War Soldier: Jolicoeur Charles Bonin* (Bowie, MD: Heritage Books, 1993), 215.

    13. Ibid., 77–78. Quoting William Bartram, *A Journey from Pennsylvania to Onondaga in 1743*, from the 1751 edition; and *Travels Through North and South Carolina, Georgia, East and West Florida*, from the 1791 edition.

    14. Ibid.

    15. Kalm, 563.

    16. O'Neil, 16. Quoting Col. James Smith in 1755.

    17. Ibid., 19. Quoting John Knox from the 1769 London edition of *An Historical Journal of the Campaigns in North America for the Years 1757, 1758, 1759, and 1760.*

    18. Ibid., 2. Quoting James Adair from the 1775 London edition of *The History of the American Indians, Particularly Those Nations Adjoining to the Mississippi, East and West Florida, Georgia, South and North Carolina, and Virginia.*

    19. Ibid., 2–3. Quoting James Adair.

    20. Kalm, 471–472.

    21. Pierre Pouchot, *Memoir upon the Late War in North America Between the French and English, 1775–1760*, vol. 2 (Roxbury, MA: E. Elliot Woodward, 1866), 215.

    22. Carver, 222–231.

    23. Pouchot, 190.

    24. Ibid., 215.

    25. Kalm, 560.

    26. O'Neil, 31. Quoting Jean-Bernard Bossu, who traveled among the nations of Louisiana and Alabama from 1751 to 1762.

    27. Ibid., 2–3. Quoting James Adair.

    28. Having the hair or fur removed by scraping after soaking in a vat of oak bark, the leather was tanned by rubbing in the brains of deer mixed with rotten wood made into a powder.

    29. O'Neil, 29. Quoting Jolicoeur Charles Bonin.

    30. Kalm, 556.

    31. Carver, 224.

    32. Pouchot, 187.

    33. O'Neil, 14. Quoting Peter Williamson in his own publication of 1757 titled *French and Indian Cruelty.*

    34. Ibid., 33. Quoting Alexander Henry.

    35. Pouchot, 190.

    36. Richard Smith, *A Tour of Four Great Rivers: The Hudson, Mohawk, Susquehanna, and Delaware in 1769* (New York: Charles Scribner's Sons, 1906), 83–84.

37. O'Neil, 45. Quoting Elizabeth Hicks.

38. Carver, 225.

39. O'Neil, 2–3. Quoting James Adair.

40. Ibid.

41. Ibid., 44–45. Quoting Alexander Henry, esquire. The issue of "cleanliness" was reported by Elizabeth Hicks.

42. Reuben Weiser, *Regina, the German Captive* (Baltimore: T. N. Kurtz, 1860), 132–133.

43. O'Neil, 19. Quoting John Knox.

44. Nicholas Cresswell, *The Journal of Nicholas Cresswell, 1774–1777* (New York: Dial Press, 1928), 61.

45. Pouchot, 188.

46. O'Neil, 43. Quoting Bernard Romans, *A Concise Natural History of East and West Florida* (Gainesville: University of Florida Press, 1962), who first published his work in 1775.

47. Ibid., 19. Quoting John Knox.

48. Johnson, 42.

49. O'Neil, 29. Quoting Jolicoeur Charles Bonin.

50. The one-piece, knee-high "Apache" boot, which combined a moccasin with leggings, was not used in the eastern woodlands.

51. O'Neil, 29. Quoting Jolicoeur Charles Bonin.

52. Kalm, 564.

53. Carver, 222–231.

54. O'Neil, 2. Quoting James Adair.

55. Pouchot, 187–193.

56. Ibid., 215.

57. Kalm, 471–472

58. O'Neil, 28. Quoting Jolicoeur Charles Bonin.

59. Archibald Loudon, *A Selection of Some of the Most Interesting Narratives of Outrages Committed by the Indians in Their Wars with the White People* (London: S. Hooper and A. Morley, 1808), 292.

60. O'Neil, 30–31. Quoting Jean-Bernard Bossu.

61. Kalm, 577.

62. O'Neil, 28. Quoting Jolicoeur Charles Bonin.

63. Ibid., 31. Quoting Jean-Bernard Bossu.

64. Kalm, 577–578.

65. O'Neil, 28. Quoting Jolicoeur Charles Bonin.

66. Loudon, 292.

67. Ibid., 258.

68. O'Neil, 4–5. Quoting James Adair.

69. Ibid., 16. As reported by Col. James Smith.

70. Ibid., 4. Quoting James Adair.

71. Isabel M. Calder, *Colonial Captives, March, and Journeys* (Port Washington, NY: Kennikat Press, 1935), 16.

72. Hunt, 39.

73. Elizabeth Metz, *Sainte Marie Among the Iroquois* (Syracuse, NY: Midgley, 1995), 22.

74. Wilbur, 55.

75. See Gallup, 223.

76. Wilbur, 77–78.

77. Ibid., 55–56.

78. Albert E. Stone, ed., 377.

79. See Gallup, *Letters from an American Farmer and Sketches of Eighteenth-Century America by J. Hector St. John de Crevecoeur* (New York: Penguin Classics, 1986), 216.

80. Wilbur, 78.

81. See Gallup, 216.

82. Allan W. Eckert, *Wilderness Empire* (Toronto: Bantam Books, 1980), 123.

83. For instance, the authors doubt that Bonin had firsthand knowledge of the painless births experienced by Indian women. He also fails to specifically detail the correction, or lack thereof, of male children, leaving the reader to assume that male children went without correction of any sort.

84. Since Bonin's memoir was translated from French to English, the authors have changed the term *cabin* to *dwelling* in an effort to maintain an authentic image of village life.

85. See Gallup, 221–222.

86. Wilbur, 65.

87. See Gallup, 220.

88. Ibid., 221–222.

89. Ibid., 222.

90. Ibid., 219.

91. Ibid., 219.

92. Ibid., 220.

93. Johnson, 37.

94. Ibid., 33

95. Ibid., 37.

96. Ibid., 36.

97. See James E. Seaver, *A Narrative of the Life of Mrs. Mary Jemison* (Syracuse, NY: Syracuse University Press, 1990), 30–34. Mary Jemison's narrative was given to Dr. Seaver in 1823 and first published by him in 1824.

3

The Tomahawk and the Cross

In England the acceptance of either the Roman Church or the Church of England quickly became inexorably linked with the political survival of the nation. Adherence to the church of Rome "came more and more to be identified in popular thinking with hostile and alien powers."

—Louis B. Wright, historian

The part played by religion in the development of the colonial frontier cannot be overstated. The questions of religious affiliation and the establishment of state-sponsored churches loomed large in the colonial period as legitimate causes for rebellion, social strife, the confiscation of property, imprisonment, and execution. No fewer than seven of the colonies founded by the English in the seventeenth century were established specifically for religious motives. Five of these colonies were established by English Puritans in New England: Plymouth (1620), Massachusetts Bay (1630), New Haven (1638), Connecticut (1639), and Rhode Island (1644). The two others were the Catholic colony of Maryland (1633) and the Quaker colony of Pennsylvania (1682). Of these, the Pennsylvania colony was considered by contemporary observers as the most successful.

French, Portuguese, and Spanish colonies, though not free of religious turmoil, closely coordinated the economic and social objectives of their governments with the purposes and goals of the Roman Catholic Church, even if they did not directly coordinate in their efforts with the papacy. The French came to the New World to convert the Indians and pack out furs. While they aligned the purposes of their explorations with their religion, the financial benefits of the fur trade generally escaped the church fathers in France. Nonetheless, a great deal of wealth in terms of land and political power was bestowed upon the French missionary orders, particularly the blackrobed Jesuits.

Spanish explorers and colonial administrators were conspicuously attended by the Franciscan fathers of the Roman Catholic faith. A mendicant (begging) order, the friars eschewed all temporal wealth, but sought power in the spiritual sense nonetheless. Like the Spanish, the Portuguese ultimately sought to acquire vast riches and to create a great national wealth not through "the healthy excitement of exploration and adventure, but [through] gold and silver." The absorption of Portugal and its colonies by Spain in 1580 ended the period of Portuguese colonization and made Spain a more important colonial power, but much of the treasure brought back to Europe by Spanish treasure galleons found its way into the coffers of the Roman Catholic Church or the pockets of the Protestant merchants of northern Europe.[1]

RELIGION IN EARLY AMERICA

Europe was swept by great religious wars and moral awakenings during the colonial period that resulted in waves of religious zealots and exiles crossing the Atlantic. Spanish and French Catholics accepted their mission to convert the Indians and rid the New World of heresy. Protestant Walloons and Huguenots, Dutch Calvinists, English Puritans, Quakers, Scotch-Irish Presbyterians, German Lutherans, Baptists, and Dunkers, and Moravians were all moved by much the same spirit. Many factors caused life on the frontier to be difficult. Religious bigotry was only one of these. Influential clergymen, both Catholic and Protestant, encouraged the raising of armed forces and instructed the faithful that to bear arms one against the other was to do God's work.[2]

The frontier digested a wide variety of immigrants, but most of them were within the same religious compass of essential Protestantism. An estimate of the number of religious congregations in the English colonies at the close of the colonial period has been made and gives a total of more than 3,100 almost equally distributed among the three regions of New England, the Middle Colonies, and the Carolinas. The Congregationalists had 658 mostly in New England. The Presbyterians were strongest in the Middle Colonies with 543. Scattered among the colonies were Baptists with 498, Anglicans with 480, Quakers with 295, German and Dutch Reformed with 251, and Lutherans with 151. The Methodists with 37 were largely found in Maryland and Virginia. The Catholic churches were mostly confined to Maryland and numbered about 50;

while a very small undetermined number of Jewish synagogues—composed of Shepardic Jews whose ancestry lay in the Iberian Peninsula—were found mostly in New York City.[3]

Nine of the colonies had established churches. The Anglican Church was established in all the colonies south of Pennsylvania and in New York City. The Congregationalists were established in New England. Only Rhode Island and Pennsylvania lacked a state-sponsored church, but in the latter the Quakers tightly controlled the legislature and dictated their pacifist ideals to the entire colony. Much of New York, which included the hills of Vermont, was free to follow whatever religion it chose.[4]

New Spain

The Spanish established a temporary mission to the Indians in Virginia as early as 1526, eighty years before the founding of the first permanent English settlements in nearby Jamestown. The Spaniards threatened immediate attack and certain destruction on any Protestant settlements in the New World just as surely as they had moved forward to conquer the spiritual beliefs of the native Americans in Mexico. "Cast them out by the best means possible," wrote Philip II to his governor general in Mexico. Pedro Menendez de Aviles, appointed adelantado (military chieftain) of Florida, wrote to the king in 1565 that Protestants and American Indians held similar beliefs, rooted in Satanism: "It seemed to me that to chastise them . . . would serve God Our Lord, as well as your Majesty, and that we should thus be left free from this wicked sect."[5]

The Spanish clergy viewed the native American population as lost in a wilderness of paganism. Unfortunately the worst precepts of an intolerant religious inquisition in Europe crossed the Atlantic with the priests. A Spanish missionary wrote: "Once idolatry is known, one must not rest until it is altogether eliminated. . . . Conversion must be total: no individual, no fraction of the individual, no practice, however trivial it may seem, must escape." Armed with such a powerful bias, the Spanish justified their treatment of the Indians and the total elimination of their culture. If the Indians resisted they could be killed or enslaved and their lands and possessions forfeited.[6]

Franciscans led the religious crusades in New Spain. The Franciscans more than any other order accompanied the early Spanish explorers in North America. This order of friars, or brothers, lived only on alms, wore simple robes and sandals, and walked everywhere with their donkeys and mules in tow renouncing the horse as a symbol of aristocracy. Although they wore no armor and carried no weapons, the friars were almost always accompanied by at least a small escort of soldiers. They went about their missionary work with a special urgency, brought on by rivalries with the Jesuits, to firmly establish themselves among the natives.[7]

In 1565 they established the settlement of St. Augustine on Florida's east coast, and within three years there were missions on the south and west coasts of Florida and in Georgia and South Carolina.[8] The missions generally preserved the Indians from physical destruction, but the friars made no attempt to preserve the culture of the native peoples they encountered. Quite the reverse, the Franciscans had as their goal the weakening of the indigenous religions and culture and the establishment of their own values among the Indians. The Pueblo Indians staged a significant rebellion against this form of acculturation in 1670 by destroying almost every church and mission in Spanish New Mexico, and many of the Indians of Florida remained recalcitrant into the nineteenth century.[9]

Spain ruled vast areas of the Americas for 200 years before the struggle for the North American empire began in earnest. Yet Spain never really figured as a possible competitor in the struggle. Several factors combined to eliminate the Spanish from the contest. With their strength dangerously overextended, the Spanish found it increasingly difficult to stop intrusions into their vast American empire. As a consequence of the English victory over the Armada in 1588, Spain never again rose to the position of a great naval power. The defeat of the Armada also gave the Dutch a brief respite from Spanish aggression in Europe, and they continued to harass the Spanish until 1593, when the last Spanish soldier left Dutch soil. In 1640 Portugal threw off the yoke of Spanish rule, further weakening Spain's position in Europe and complicating its administration of the American colonies.

With Spain's power seriously reduced and with the impending elimination of Dutch competition in 1688, when William of Orange became king of England, only France or England had a feasible chance of wresting control of North America. The French army was in ascendancy on the continent of Europe, and the English fleet controlled the sea-lanes. The struggle for political and military supremacy that spilled over into the American wilderness in the eighteenth century pitted English Protestants against French Catholics, and involved the native Americans of the region in a war on the frontiers marked largely by religious devotion, secular bigotry, and appalling inhumanity.

The Atlantic Frontier

At the end of the seventeenth century the English colonies were confined to the Atlantic coast and coastal plain from the Penobscot River in Maine to the Ogeechee River in Georgia by the Appalachian Mountains. On the south they were astride the Spanish settlements in Florida and in the north they faced an uncertain and changing border with the French that ran through the forest wilderness. The frontier remained an ambiguous boundary shifting through the forest with every European treaty.

With the exception of a few Catholics who settled in Maryland, the English who came to America were almost all Protestants, but they represented a large number of discrete, if not mutually antagonistic, religious sects. The flood of emigration from each Protestant sect can be closely tied in time to periods of increasing persecution and harassment in Europe. Adherents of the Church of England, or Anglican Church, who flooded to the southern colonies during the protectorate of Oliver Cromwell, dominated the colonies of Virginia, Delaware, and even Maryland. New England was founded by Puritans who fled either the intimidation of James I in the 1620s or the persecution of his nephew, Charles II, in the 1660s. Consequently, New England was most hospitable to followers of the Congregational Church. The Scotch-Irish who came to America, beset by conflicts with both the Anglicans and Catholics in Ireland, were nearly all Presbyterians. Quakers, drawn by William Penn's assurance of religious toleration, initially settled in Pennsylvania, which was clearly the best-known and the most tolerant of all the English colonies. The Germanic settlers were divided into many related Protestant pietist sects including Moravians, Mennonites, and Dunkers. Methodists and Baptists were found in small numbers throughout the colonies. Finally, the Dutch, and their religious brethren, the Flemish Walloons and French Huguenots, considered religious dissenters and nonconformists by most of Europe, maintained their presence only in those regions of the English colonies originally settled by Holland.[10]

The outstanding exception among the settlers of the English colonies were the Catholics of Maryland. These were served by Jesuits under Father Andrew White until 1645. The work of the Jesuits was hampered by Puritans and other malcontents who were allowed access to the colony, and also by the hostility of the Susquehanna Indians, who lived at the head of the Chesapeake Bay. Many Catholics remained in the colony of Maryland after Protestantism had been established there by law during the English Civil Wars (1640–1649). However, their churches and missions were plundered, and the priests who did not escape into the interior were sent to England for trial. The Piscataway Indians of Maryland, almost completely Christianized by the Jesuit fathers, sought refuge from the new Protestant government with the Delawares and the Iroquois to the north. Here they lost all distinction as a unique people.

Nathaniel Ward, a Puritan writer from New England, proclaimed in 1647 the limits of religious toleration that this diversity of settlers could expect in the New England colonies: "I dare take upon me to be the herald of New England so far as to proclaim to the world, in the name of our colony, that all Familists, Antinomians, Anabaptists, and other [religious] enthusiasts, shall have free liberty to keep away from us, and

such as will come, to be gone as fast as they can, the sooner the better."
Rather than championing religious freedom, at least during their first
generation, many of the English colonies were possessed of a level of
religious orthodoxy and self-inflicted conformity unmatched in Europe.
These devout people found the role of religion in their daily lives mag-
nified by the relative seclusion of their frontier communities, where loneliness and awe of the surrounding forest added to the pressure to bond
more closely with their fellow religionists.[11]

New France

In 1633 a group of entrepreneurs known as La Compagnie des Cent
Associés, the Company of One Hundred Associates, was given a large
grant of land in New France. In return for the right to trade for furs and
appoint a governor in New France, the Hundred Associates promised to
settle 4,000 colonists within ten years, protect them, and support the
Catholic missions to the native population. Initially the sole spiritual
ministers of the colony were to be Jesuits. Crown policy ensured that the
settlers were wholly Roman Catholics. No one whose devotion to the
church was suspect was allowed to emigrate to New France. If there was
any doubt concerning their devotion to the faith, French emigrants were
required to renew their baptismal and confirmation vows before the
church fathers in Quebec. Two forces governed the lives of these settlers.
"One was the specter of death haunting them from the fringe of the
wood in the Satanic form of the Iroquois. The other was the church and
their religion."[12]

Francis Parkman described how he believed the Catholic faith mani-
fested itself in New France:

Over every cluster of small white houses glittered the sacred emblem of the cross.
The church, the convent, and the roadside shrine were seen at every turn; and
in the towns and villages, one met each moment the black robe of the Jesuit, the
gray grab of the Recollet, the formal habit of the Ursuline nun. The names of
saints, St. Joseph, St. Ignatius, St. Francis, were perpetuated in the capes, rivers,
and islands, the forts and villages of the land; and with every day, crowds of
simple worshipers knelt in adoration before the countless altars of the Roman
faith.

Yet Parkman's descriptions were based on his visit to Quebec in the last
half of the nineteenth century, and while historians laud his exhaustive
research and the meticulous preparation of his manuscripts, the facts
present a slightly different picture of religious life in New France in the
seventeenth century from those that he gleaned 200 years later.[13]

It is quite certain that both the French colonists and the native Amer-

A street in the Ancienne Ville, or Old City, of Quebec at the bottom of the great cliffs that overlook the St. Lawrence River. Here General Montcalm and Governor Frontenac may have walked. Little has changed here since the days of the French regime except that the streets are now lined with museums, shops, and restaurants that appeal to the modern tourist. Nonetheless, a visitor to the Old City will immediately note the flavor of the seventeenth and eighteenth centuries.

ican converts to Catholicism were wholly dependent for their religious survival on just a few priests. Franciscan Recollet friars were among some of the earliest explorers of French North America. The Recollets accompanied Champlain in his explorations but were withdrawn from Canada in 1628 and did not return until 1670. With a scarcity of secular priests, the colonists were compelled to rely on the missionary orders, particularly the Jesuits. A small community of Sulpician fathers was founded in Montreal in 1642, yet they numbered only four priests a decade and a half later.

A census of the clergy in Quebec in 1686 shows that they made up a much smaller number than their ultimate influence on events in New France would suggest. There were 44 secular priests, 43 Jesuits, 12 Recollets, 12 seminary students, 28 Ursuline nuns, 13 sisters of Notre Dame, 26 Hospital nuns of the Mercy of Jesus, and 16 Hospital nuns of St. John. The Jesuits controlled all the missions to the Indians in New France, including one in Illinois (established in 1690), while the Recollets served Cape Breton, Acadia, the Seminary of Quebec, and a mission at Tamarois (1690) on the west bank of the Mississippi River.

The first church in New France was built in Quebec in 1633, but it was destroyed by fire seven years later and its replacement was not undertaken for a decade thereafter. The new building, Notre Dame de la Paix, was opened in 1657. Although only one hundred feet long by thirty feet wide, it was described as "a cathedral made of stone . . . large and splendid." To the tiny French community of Quebec it was a tremendous achievement. With its gold and silver ornaments, its statues, and its stained glass, Notre Dame stood in sharp contrast to the churches of the other districts of New France, which may have been crudely built wooden structures without adornment. Rather than the "countless altars" described by Parkman, it was more common to have no church at all, as it was not believed proper to consecrate a building that was not solidly built and durable. By 1680 only seven Catholic communities in New France had church buildings with walls of stone.[14]

For most Catholic settlements there was no resident priest. The number of Frenchmen in New France was so small, possibly no more than 3,000, that it was impossible to assign a priest to each of the scattered settlements and farmsteads. Consequently the available clergy were assigned to parishes comprising many hundreds of square miles of wilderness territory. A parish might reach for fifty miles along a river and a day's walk into the interior, for it was largely by canoe that the priest made his spiritual visits to his flock. Practically every house and important native village in New France stood in sight of some body of water navigable by this functional native craft. With a servant to help paddle a canoe in the rivers and streams, or pull a sledge along their frozen surfaces in winter, the solitary priest commonly carried a portable altar, a communion set, a bottle of holy oil and a few supplies into the forests. Under these conditions he managed to minister to his entire flock three or four times a year.

Jesuits. The Jesuit fathers stand out in the history of New France. It is quite clear that much of the early history of New France revolves around the struggles of the Jesuit missionaries to hold their own against the aggressive Iroquois. Parkman devoted one of the seven volumes that composed his monumental study of this period solely to the Jesuit order in New France. As a religious order, the Jesuits were widely feared and hated in Europe even by other Roman Catholic orders because of the control they were able to exert over political and economic events. The order was founded by Ignatius Loyola in 1540. They had no distinctive habit, but were noted for the simple black cassocks that they wore. The blackrobed Jesuits also harbored a quiet distaste for cooperation with other religious orders and ultimately dominated all the other groups of clergy in New France. Moreover, they openly challenged the ministers of the civil government with remarkable success.

To some extent the grandiose designs of the Jesuits had been encouraged by the fact that Cardinal Mazarin, prime minister of the French government since 1642, had failed to appoint a bishop over New France. Until 1656 the church in Canada was presided over by the father superior of the Jesuits in Quebec. In 1657 steps were taken to remedy the situation by creating a bishop for Quebec. "If anyone had a right to nominate a bishop for Quebec, the [Jesuits] claimed the right was theirs."[15]

The Jesuits in France chose Francois Xavier Montmorency de Laval. The church, however, proposed a compromise. Laval would be appointed the pope's apostolic vicar in Canada and given a vacant bishopric in Arabia to lend him ecclesiastical stature. This arrangement was acceptable to the Jesuits, who believed that through Laval they would rule Canada.

The Bishop of Quebec. The immediate result of Bishop Laval's arrival in Canada in 1660 was a hostile encounter between the new apostolic vicar and the governor-general of New France, Pierre de Voyer, Comte d'Argenson. D'Argenson was the fifth man to hold the post of governor under the original system of civil government, and he had shown his willingness to defend Canada against the incursions of the Iroquois, personally leading a group of volunteers into the forest in pursuit of an Onondaga raiding party. However, he was no match for the Jesuit bishop who systematically took every opportunity to belittle his position and authority.[16]

Since the time of Champlain the governors of Canada had ruled the civil government under the auspices of the Hundred Associates and in cooperation with the Council of Quebec. The council was a group made up of representatives from three municipal districts (Quebec, Trois-Rivières, and Montreal), the administrator of Montreal, and the father superior of the Jesuits. The representative members were nominated by the powerful fur trade interests who made up the Hundred Associates. The nominees were approved by the king and appointed by the governor-general of all Canada. The functions of the council were legislative and administrative, but in practice they affected the life of the colony very little.

It was upon the governor's authority that Laval launched his most telling attacks. At first he demanded as apostolic vicar to concur in the approval of the appointments to the council. Winning this point, Laval then insisted that he had the power to excommunicate transgressors for civil as well as religious offenses. He then railed against the use of alcohol as an item of exchange in the fur trade. There was also a series of small battles over precedence in processionals, the order of speaking at public events, and other protocols. In almost every encounter with d'Argenson, Laval chipped away some of his power as governor. D'Argenson found himself perplexed and increasingly frustrated. At length, in 1661, he asked to be replaced.

In fairness to d'Argenson, his replacement was no more successful than he had been in stemming Laval's quest for power, and the system for governing New France was overhauled by the Crown in 1664. Although the bishop retained much of the power that had been won, the governor was no longer appointed by the Hundred Associates. Thereafter, the governor was nominated by the Ministry of Marine in France and appointed directly by the king. The council was made larger, ultimately expanding to twelve persons. Finally an intendant of justice, police, and finances was appointed to act as a business manger for the King. The intendant had powers that could be exercised without consulting the council, and he was positioned as a barrier between the civil government and the bishop so that the church could no longer interfere in purely civil matters. The first intendant was Jean de Talon, who made great strides in reinvigorating economic growth in Canada from 1665 to 1672.

Many colonial officials in French America discreetly questioned the motives of the Roman Catholic clergy, suggesting that the Jesuits in particular considered New France their own private domain established ostensibly for the conversion of Indian souls, but lucrative in a layman's economic sense nonetheless. This attitude was openly expressed in a report to the colonial ministry in Quebec by Antoine de la Mothe, Sieur de Cadillac, founder of the French trading post at Detroit:

[T]he missionaries should act in good faith, and . . . though these Reverend Fathers come here only for the glory of God . . . nobody can deny that the priests own three-quarters of Canada. From St. Paul's Bay to Quebec . . . the greater part belongs to the Jesuits or other ecclesiastics. The upper town of Quebec is composed of six or seven superb palaces belonging to Hospital Nuns, Ursulines, Jesuits, Recollets, Seminary priests, and the bishop. There may be some forty private houses, and even these pay rent to the ecclesiastics.[17]

Like many of the government officials in New France, Cadillac was "not an especially religious man," and he was an undoubted critic of the French fathers. If France was to develop economically, he understood that a government entrenched in religion might gnaw away at the achievements of enterprising men like himself. His attitude openly antagonized some of the resident priests, especially Father Superior Carheil of the mission at Michilimakinac, with whom he almost came to blows. "I do what I can to make them my friends," he wrote, "but, impiety apart, one had better sin against God than against them . . . for the offense is never forgiven in this world, and perhaps never would be in the other."[18]

Although there was friction between the Jesuits and the civil authorities, the order seems to have had a genuine desire to convert the native population to Catholicism and to establish firm foundations for the continued growth of the church among the native Americans. The Catholic religion, with its rituals, mysteries, and tales of miracles ascribed to a legion of saints, proved very appealing to the Indian concept of spirituality. In the end the Jesuits were able to confound their detractors by the "single-hearted devotion of their missionary work among the Indians." The reports that the blackrobed fathers sent home to France were combined into seventy massive volumes known as *The Jesuit Relations*. Their devotion and self-sacrifice, the hardships they endured, and their triumphs or martyrdoms were all set down in meticulous detail. These volumes serve as a major source of information about early French America, but there is little recorded about the parish priests who came to serve the scattered flock of inhabitants.[19]

From the historic record it seems certain that Bishop Laval's actions were not aimed at personal aggrandizement. The church, his order, and the conversion of the Indians to Christianity seem to have been the absorbing forces in his life. "Winning the savage souls that roamed [Canada] to the Cross stirred his blood. . . . He shared the Jesuit dream of some day converting all the wilderness area into a kind of Peaceable Kingdom."[20] Laval established a seminary in Quebec in 1663, recalled to New France the Recollet fathers in 1670, and fought the alcohol trade to the Indians. Appointed bishop of Quebec (instead of Arabia) in 1674, Laval served until 1688, when he resigned and returned to France. During this period he fought to maintain the prerogatives of the clergy over the civil government that he had created.

Having handpicked his own religious successor in 1688, Laval returned to Quebec when the man was recalled in 1694. He served as Quebec's religious leader again until 1705, having battled with six governors and seven civil administrations. The last three years of his life were spent in quiet retirement.

THE INDIAN MISSIONS

Bishop Laval led the most successful effort at Christianization in the history of the Jesuit order. He did not hesitate to send his blackrobed fathers upon missions into the wilderness if he thought there was the slightest chance of winning souls. These undertakings, often made by lone priests, entailed incredible hardships. "A missionary destined for this great work must make up his mind to lead a very strange kind of life, and endure unimaginable destitution of all things; to suffer every inclemency of weather, without mitigation; to bear a thousand impertinence, a thousand taunts, and often, indeed, blows from the Infidel Savages, who are at times instigated by demons—and all this without human consolation."[21]

Nonetheless, Jesuits brought energy and dedication to the task of converting the native Americans. Father Jacques Bigot considered himself an essential bridge for the Indians between their traditional ways and the lifestyle thrust upon them by European contact. Father Sabastien Rasles (sometimes spelled Rale') spent more of his life living among the Abenaki than he did in European society. He learned their language and wrote an Abenaki-English dictionary, which is preserved at Harvard University. He was trusted by the Indians and was allowed to speak at their most solemn councils. Father Isaac Jogues returned two times to his missionary duties even though he had been horribly tortured and mutilated by the Iroquois. He was finally killed on his third attempt to bring Catholicism to the natives by Iroquois warriors.

Excavations of archeological sites known to have been Jesuit missions in New York and New England have turned up brass rings and silver or brass crucifixes that were handed out by the missionaries among the Indians. Father Jean Enjalran requested additional crosses, rings, and rosaries, reporting that he had stripped himself of almost everything in giving such gifts as rewards for reciting the catechism or being baptized. Although the Jesuits felt that these items helped them win converts, it is quite certain that many native Americans wore these tokens as mere decorations, not knowing their religious meaning and regarding them as any other amulet or charm. Similarly the Indians often believed that the priests, by "throwing water upon [their] heads," subjected them to the will of the governor of Canada and exercised a special spiritual power over them.[22]

New Englanders dismissed the French missionary activity as mere subversion of native allegiance and displayed little understanding of the dedication of the Jesuits to the conversion of souls. It was widely believed by the English settlers—and not without supporting evidence—that the Jesuits of New France actively incited the Indians against the English frontier settlements because of their Protestantism. The missionaries were accused of bringing presents of powder, ball, and guns to the tribes and of announcing the support of the French government for their raids. The French civil authorities viewed the missions as the equivalent of outposts guarding the main avenues to New France. In fact, most were situated just far enough from the border of English settlement to make it difficult for the English to attack them by surprise.

There were a number of the villages composed of native American converts to Catholicism well located to serve this purpose. The earliest Catholic mission in what was to become New England was founded in 1613 on Desert Mountain Island, Maine. This was almost immediately destroyed by Englishmen, and the priests were carried off to Virginia. Two important Abenaki missions were located at Penobscot (1633) on the Maine coast and Norridgewock (1646) on the Kennebec River. Both villages supported missions kept by the Jesuit fathers. Penobscot was one of the farthest outposts of the French influence at the end of the seventeenth century. Abenaki villages were also located at Trois Rivières, and on the St. Francis River. St. Francis was a particularly active launch point for war parties planning attacks on the English settlements, as the river opened a practical route by canoe to the New England border.[23]

Many of the Abenaki of Maine removed themselves to the St. Francis mission of Father Jacques Bigot as early as 1683, making it one of the most successful strongholds of Catholic Indians in New France. The mission housed, besides the Abenaki, a large number of related Algonquin Indians who were refugees from King Philip's War (1675) in New England, and a smaller population of Caughnawaga Indians of Iroquoian lineage. A great deal of intermarriage had taken place among the Algonquian refugees and the Abenaki. The inhabitants of St. Francis soon acquired among the English a reputation as devout Catholics and unshakable allies of the French. This flourishing mission was attacked in 1759 by a force of rangers under the command of Colonel Robert Rogers and completely destroyed. Its church with all its records were burned and an estimated 200 warriors were killed.

The Caughnawagas, originally from Ossernenon near Auriesville, New York and considered cousins of the Mohawks, had separated from their Iroquois relatives in the historical period mainly due to their adoption of Catholicism, but they maintained a kinship bond with the more English leaning Mohawks. Compelling evidence seems to indicate that the French colonial ministry actually gave explicit instructions to Abbe' Francois Piquet, a Sulpician priest of Montreal, to establish a separate mission 100 miles up the St. Lawrence River from Montreal (called La Praire) for the purpose of winning over to the French the Caughnawaga Iroquois of that region, the present-day site of Ogdensburg, New York.

The use of Christianized Indians for the purpose of carrying war to the English frontier settlements was a matter of French crown policy. It was understood among the officials at Versailles that "in most cases the movements of war-parties upon the frontiers were generally first ordered or sanctioned or suggested by Louis [XIV] himself." A French official wrote, "If Abbe' Piquet succeeds in his mission, we can easily persuade these savages to destroy Oswego." Another official suggested that, as the French and English were ostensibly at peace, "The only means that can be used for such an operation in times of peace are those of the [Caughnawaga] Iroquois." The French were hard pressed, however, to convince the Caughnawagas to attack the Mohawks, and the English could not convince the Mohawks of the faithlessness of their brethren.[24]

The war party that attacked Pemaquid, Maine, in 1689 was known to have been composed of warriors from the missions at Penobscot and Norridgewock who set out in their canoes and gained the advantage of

speed by traveling to the point of their attack on the Kennebec River.
These same missions, predominantly populated by the Abenaki, were
thought to have served as a rallying point for the attack on the English
at York, Maine, in 1693. The Indians were supposed to have been incited
to make war by their priests, particularly fathers Jacques Bigot, Sabastien
Rasles, and Louis Thury, all of whom seem to have had great influence
among the Abenaki.[25] These observations were based on the reports, narratives, and journals of English captives taken by the raiders, and they
must be viewed with some skepticism.[26]

   The hatred toward Catholics, and toward Jesuits in particular, was
deep-seated and engendered among the English from an early age. John
Giles, a young English boy captured by Indians in a 1689 raid on Fort
Penobscot, Maine, and carried off to Canada, noted:

[A] Jesuit of the place had a mind to buy [ransom] me. . . . He gave me a biscuit,
which I put in my pocket, and not daring to eat it, I buried it under a log, fearing
he had put something in it to make me love him. When my mother [who had
also been captured] heard talk of my being sold to a Jesuit, she said to me, "Oh,
my dear child, if it were God's will, I had rather follow you to your grave, or
nevermore see you in this world, than you should be sold to a Jesuit; for a Jesuit
will ruin you body and soul."

The theme of anti-Catholicism and anti-Protestantism should not be underestimated when studying the events that took place on the frontiers
in this era.[27]

   The almost continuous warfare between the French and English colonies after 1690 exposed the Indian missions to attack and made the
missionaries marked men. In *The Jesuit Relations* it was observed that
Father Rasles, in particular, had become "odious to the English," as they
were convinced that his endeavors to confirm the Abenaki in the Catholic
faith constituted the greatest obstacle to their plan of settling the interior
of New England. "[T]hey put a price on his head; and more than once
they had attempted to abduct him, or take his life." Finally a large force
of Englishmen and allied Indians was raised in 1724 to attack the mission
at Norridgewock. The attack completely surprised the inhabitants, who,
having few warriors among them, fled to the other side of the river from
the English:

Father Rasles, warned by the clamor and the tumult . . . promptly left his house
and fearlessly appeared before the enemy. He expected by his presence either to
stop their first efforts, or at least to draw their attention to himself alone. . . . As
soon as they perceived the missionary, a general shout was raised which was
followed by a storm of musket-shots that was poured upon him. He dropped
dead at the foot of a large cross that he had erected in the midst of the village.[28]

Huron Conversion

The Huron were initially the power base of the French–native American alliance. Jesuits who came to Huronia in the first part of the seventeenth century were very successful in converting them to Catholicism. Increasing Jesuit linguistic competence, expanding trade, and French diplomacy tied the Hurons to the French. After 1640 Catholic Hurons were supplied with guns, and more than half their population was considered Christianized. Unfortunately, the Huron and the Iroquois were openly hostile to one another. Minor blood feuds, raids of outlying villages, and attacks on hunting parties characterized the relations between these powerful nations. In 1642 the raids escalated into war as the Mohawks cut off the Ottawa River fur trade route and the Seneca completely destroyed a frontier Huron village. The Mohawk and Seneca virtually exterminated the Hurons during 1649. From thirty villages, more than 7,000 refugee Hurons fled to all points of the compass. The resident Jesuit priests were killed, or they made their way in terror to Quebec. The dispersal of the Hurons "was a cultural catastrophe with widespread consequences."[29]

Iroquois Conversion

A large part of New York and Pennsylvania served as the home of the Iroquois Confederation. Through an unfortunate circumstance Champlain had gained for the French an enmity with the Iroquois by siding with their Montagnais, Algonquin, and Huron enemies in the early days of French colonization (1609). Though the Iroquois were involved with the Dutch at the beginning of the historical period, they were largely self-serving in their dealings with the English in the seventeenth century. However, they remained bitterly anti-French for more than a century. For these reasons no permanent Catholic mission to the Iroquois was ever established within the limits of their confederacy.

Isaac Jogues. It was hoped that the Iroquois could be attracted to the French if they shared their religion. Many attempts to draw off the Iroquois from English influence by this means were attempted. The best known among these were the journeys of Father Isaac Jogues through the Mohawk River valley. In 1642, Jogues, possibly the best-known Jesuit missionary in colonial history, was captured by a party of Iroquois and taken to a Mohawk village near Auriesville, New York. Jogues and his companions (among whom were several Hurons) were cruelly treated. The Hurons were burned at the stake. Joques had his nails torn from his fingers, two fingers crushed, and a thumb sawed off. Of the two lay brothers who accompanied him, one was killed and the other was adopted into the tribe. Jogues was ransomed by the Dutch fifteen months after his capture and returned to France. In 1646 he set out again to establish a mission among the Iroquois. He was again captured in the company of a Huron, brought to the village at Auriesville, and tortured. This time he was killed, and his head was placed on the palisades that surrounded the village. The site of his martyrdom is now a Jesuit memorial.

Ste. Marie Among the Iroquois. In 1653 Father Joseph Poncet was captured by Mohawks near Montreal. He was also tortured but was released to carry overtures of peace to Quebec. As a consequence, although the peace feelers were thought to be insincere, the Jesuit mission of Ste. Marie was established near the capital of Iroquoia at Onondaga in 1655. A party of fifty French colonists and half a dozen Jesuit priests built a palisaded enclosure and wooden chapel on the shores of Lake Onondaga. Mission stations were established with each of the five Iroquois nations, with the Onondaga, Cayuga, and Oneida seemingly most open to the Jesuit influence, and the Mohawk and Seneca less so.

However, many Iroquois accepted the tenets of Christianity selectively without total acceptance or rejection of the new beliefs. "The Indians seem more often to have sought to add to [their] spiritual arsenals than to fill spiritual vacuums . . . to have taken on Christianity as another weapon for assuring their well-being, without abandoning traditional ways of life." As the missionaries attempted to extract a total acceptance of Catholicism and an abandonment of traditional practices, the more skeptical among the Iroquois became increasingly influential. For this reason the Jesuits had favored bringing their converts into mission settlements where they could be supervised. Nonetheless, a little more than a year after Ste. Marie had been built, hostilities broke out near Montreal, and by 1658 it was thought prudent to close the mission. During the next three decades only sporadic attempts were made to Christianize the Iroquois nations.[30]

In 1666 the French decided to chastise the Mohawks. The first attempt misfired, but in 1667 under the Marquis de Tracy a force of 1,100 men descended into the Mohawk River valley burning one village after another. As the attack came late in the season the Mohawks lost much of their crops for the winter and faced starvation. They therefore joined with those tribes of the Iroquois Confederacy more inclined toward the French, and sued for peace. The peace treaty entered into in 1667 left New France in relative peace for twenty years. However, as renewed war in Europe approached in the last decade of the seventeenth century, the Catholics among the Iroquois increasingly withdrew from the Mohawk River valley toward the Catholic missions in Canada. By 1694 all of the Catholic missions in Iroquoia had been abandoned, and a schism had taken place between the traditional and Christianized Iroquois.

This photograph is of the interior of the compound of the Ste. Marie Among the Iroquois historic site near Syracuse, New York. The re-created Jesuit mission is less than a mile from the actual location of the mission. On the day the photograph was taken the historical interpreters were finishing a large cross to be erected before the wooden chapel on the right. The building on the left was the residence of the missionaries and their helpers.

English Missions to the Indians

The zeal and influence of the French Jesuits has rightly given them a disproportionate place in the history of colonial America. However, their missions were not the only efforts put forth to Christianize the natives. The largely abortive efforts of the English to bring Protestantism to the native peoples of New England came too late and were prosecuted with too little vigor to tie the Indians to them through the instrument of religion. Moreover, the Protestant faiths seem to have lacked much of the mysticism and ceremony that drew the natives to Catholicism.

Thomas Mayhew Jr. began preaching the Protestant faith to the Wampanoag Indians on the island of Martha's Vineyard in 1640, and after the epidemics of 1643 and 1645 a large number of the survivors made the Christian religion their own by blending the new faith with their own traditions. This form of conversion was unacceptable to most of the Puritan ministers. In 1641, John Elliot translated the Bible into the native dialects of Massachusetts and set about teaching the native Americans to read it. Elliot established fourteen "praying towns" in which the natives were expected to assume European manners and dress. An Indian college was opened at Harvard in 1654, and when Elliot died in 1667 he left a number of native-born preachers among his flock. However, during King Phillip's War in 1675 the colonists rounded up all the "praying Indians" and imprisoned them. After the crisis the praying towns were reestablished, but they were now viewed as Indian "reservations" in the worst sense of the word.[31]

In 1717, in an effort to attract the Abenaki, the Reverend Joseph Baxter attempted to establish a mission on the Kennebec River of Maine. The Reverend Cotton Mather unrealistically hoped that this mission would attract a "considerable number of our eastern savages . . . from the pop- ish to the Protestant religion." In 1735 the Massachusetts government appropriated money to place a minister among the natives at Fort Drum- mer on the Connecticut River. Neither mission was considered wholly successful.[32]

After the French and Indian War, in 1769, Reverend Eleazer Wheelock opened a school in Hanover, New Hampshire, to natives recruited from St. Francis and elsewhere. This is considered the founding of Dartmouth College. Nonetheless, the Iroquois clearly rejected Wheelock's request to educate their youth. Mary Jemison, who lived among the Iroquois for sixty years, noted, "I have seen . . . the effects of education upon some of our Indians, who were taken when young from their families, and placed at school before they had had an opportunity to contract many Indian habits, and there kept till they arrive to manhood; but I have never seen one of those but what was an Indian in every respect after he returned."[33]

Failure of Protestantism Among the Indians

Puritan missionaries, innately rigid in their concepts of propriety and good form, tried to force the Indians into "praying towns" where their customary wardrobe, ornaments, and language were looked upon with scorn and with an insistence that they be eradicated. In 1645, Emmanuel Downing, an English Puritan, wrote in a letter, "I doubt whether it be a sin in us, having power in our hands, to suffer them [the Indians] to maintain their worship of the devil."[34] Even among the English-leaning Iroquois, the French were viewed as more accepting of Indian ways.[35] "Brother," said an Onondaga diplomat to the English, "you must learn of the French [priests] if you would understand, and know how to treat Indians. They don't speak roughly; nor do they for every little mistake take up a club and flog them."[36]

Only the English Quakers and German Moravians seem to have made any inroads among the natives in terms of the Protestant religion. None- theless, a visitor to a Moravian mission in Seneca country in western Pennsylvania reported: "Their wandering life is not fit to receive the benefits of our religion which requires a sedentary life; they forget in the woods the precepts they have learnt, and often return as ignorant as ever. Their women who are most constantly at home appeared on the contrary tractable, docile; they attended prayers in their chapel with great modesty and attention."[37]

Many of the Indians who converted to the Protestant faith seem to have taken every opportunity to revert to their traditional religion in much greater numbers than did those who undertook to become Catholics. This may be due to the fact that the Catholic missionaries went to the native villages to build their churches and chapels, lived among them, and decorated them with all the religious paraphernalia that had been abandoned by Protestantism. The Jesuits, in particular, became totally immersed in the Indian culture and way of life.[38]

Yet it would be an oversimplification to credit such concepts as the sole cause of the failure of Protestantism among the native Americans. Growing interests in trade and mercantilism, and the increasing acceptance among the colonists of many Protestant sects, finally seem to have blunted the nascent English programs of native conversion more than the use of corporal punishment or the absence of religious trinkets. The ranks of English Protestantism, disordered by sectarian wrangling and doctrinal bickering in Europe, utterly failed to pry the Catholic Indians from the French because of the protestant missionaries' lack of organization and common purpose. In this way the more dogmatic and focused Catholic missionaries among the French had a distinct advantage. Ultimately, however, economic inducements and geopolitical factors appear to have been more persuasive than the influence of religion in the battle for control of the North American continent.

NOTES

1. G. J. Marcus, *The Formative Centuries: A Naval History of England* (Boston: Little, Brown, 1961), 86; Alfred Thayer Mahan, *The Influence of Sea Power Upon History, 1660–1783* (New York: Dover, 1987), 50–53.

2. Paul A. W. Wallace, *Conrad Weiser, Friend of Colonist and Mohawk: 1696–1760* (Lewisburg, PA: Wennawoods, 1996), 51.

3. See North Callahan, *Royal Raiders: The Tories of the American Revolution* (New York: Bobbs-Merrill, 1963), 125–126.

4. Ibid., 126.

5. David J. Weber, *The Spanish Frontier in North America* (New Haven: Yale University Press, 1992), 69.

6. Tzvetan Todorov, *The Conquest of America* (New York: Harper Perennial, 1987), 204; Wallace, 57.

7. Quoted in Weber, 92.

8. Ibid., 94–96. In 1769, with much of the continent lost to the English, the

driving force behind continued Franciscan mission building would be in the person of Father Junipero Serra of California.

9. Ibid., 120–121.

10. Ralph Bennett, ed., *Settlements in the Americas: Cross-Cultural Perspectives* (Newark: University of Delaware Press, 1993), 147. Pietism placed its emphasis upon inner spiritual life and denied the need for formal ecclesiastism. Although Puritanism was essentially a pietist form of religion, it was largely distinct from the Germanic sects.

11. Daniel J. Boorstin, *The Americans: The Colonial Experience* (New York: Vintage Books, 1958), 7.

12. Walter D. Edmonds, *The Musket and the Cross: The Struggle of France and England for North America* (Boston: Little, Brown, 1968), 79.

13. As quoted in John H. McCallum, ed., *Francis Parkman, The Seven Years War: A Narrative Taken from Montcalm and Wolfe, The Conspiracy of Pontiac, and A Half-Century of Conflict* (New York: Harper Torchbooks, 1968), 17.

14. Edmonds, 79–82.

15. Ibid., 43–44.

16. The Hundred Associates appointed governors for three decades (1633–1663). There were six in all: Champlain (1633–1636) was the first. Montmagny (1636–1648) was second and served the longest of the six. The third and fourth were d'Ailleboust (1648–1651) and de Lauson (1651–1658). The fifth was d'Argenson (1658–1661) and the last was d'Avaugour (1661–1663). Thereafter the governor was chosen by government ministers in France and appointed by the king. Louis de Buade, Comte de Frontenac et Pelluau, known simply as Frontenac, was twice appointed royal governor.

17. See Allan W. Eckert, *Wilderness Empire* (Toronto: Bantam Books, 1980), 5–6.

18. Ibid., 4.

19. Wallace, 117; Edmonds, 82. Full translations of *The Jesuit Relations* can be found in most college libraries and on the Internet. They make fascinating reading.

20. Edmonds, 93–94.

21. Ibid., 97–98.

22. Colin G. Calloway, *The Western Abenakis of Vermont, 1660–1800: War, Migration, and the Survival of an Indian People* (Norman: University of Oklahoma Press, 1990), 46–49.

23. Samuel Adams Drake, *The Border Wars of New England, Commonly Called King William's and Queen Anne's Wars* (Williamstown, MA: Corner House, 1973), 150 n.

24. Drake, 11, 146; Eckert, 126–127.

25. Colin G. Calloway, ed., *Dawnland Encounters: Indians and Europeans in Northern New England* (Hanover, NH: University Press of New England, 1991), 86.

26. See Drake, 76, 154.

27. Ibid., 33.

28. Calloway, ed., *Dawnland Encounters*, 81–82.

29. Ian K. Steele, *Warpaths: Invasions of North America* (New York: Oxford University Press, 1994), 70–71.

30. Calloway, *The Western Abenakis*, 51.

31. Colin G. Calloway, *New Worlds for All: Indians, Europeans, and the Remaking of Early America* (Baltimore: Johns Hopkins University Press, 1997), 74–75, 83.

32. Ibid., 171.

33. James E. Seaver, *A Narrative of the Life of Mrs. Mary Jemison* (Syracuse, NY: Syracuse University Press, 1990), 32. Mary Jemison's narrative was given to Dr. Seaver in 1823 and first published by him in 1824.

34. Louis B. Wright, *The Atlantic Frontier: Colonial American Civilization, 1607–1763* (New York: Alfred A. Knopf, 1951), 124.

35. Calloway ed., *Dawnland Encounters*, 59–60.

36. Calloway, *New Worlds*, 171.

37. Albert E. Stone, ed., *Letters from an American Farmer and Sketches of Eighteenth-Century America by J. Hector St. John de Crevecoeur* (New York: Penguin Classics, 1986), 377–378.

38. Calloway, *Dawnland Encounters*, 60.

4

Intertribal Trade and Warfare

The great dispersal of Indian nations by the Iroquois "was a cultural
catastrophe with widespread consequences."
—Ian K. Steele, historian

MAHICANS

The Algonquian-speaking Mahicans, called Loups by the French, lived
south of Lake Champlain at the headwaters of the Hudson River near
present-day Saratoga, New York.[1] According to tradition, their land
rights stretched from the Housatonic River in Connecticut and Massachusetts to a point west of the Hudson River. However, contemporary
maps show that they had a large number of villages on the north shore
of the Hudson River near Albany and at least one village on an island
in the mouth of the Mohawk River. The Mahicans were among the first
natives to trade with the Dutch in this region and appear to have acted
as middlemen in the diffusion of fur trade goods as far north as the St.
Lawrence River valley during the first quarter of the seventeenth century. Indians traded for social and political reasons as well as economic
ones, and it is very likely that many Mahicans from New England were
attracted to the Hudson River valley solely in order to be in proximity
to the Dutch trade at Fort Orange near Albany.[2]

The Mahicans jealously guarded their middleman status with the
Dutch much to the consternation of the neighboring Mohawks, who had

also made contact with the Dutch. The Mohawks were just west of Albany with many of their important villages in the Mohawk River valley. By reason of their proximity the Mohawks sought to exercise what they considered to be their natural prerogatives with regard to access to the Dutch. The Mahicans resented the presence of Mohawks in and around the trading post, and were buoyed by the annoyance which was freely expressed by the Dutch traders who were chafing under Mohawk interference with the trade coming from the "French Indians" living in the St. Lawrence River valley. Isaac de Rasiers, secretary to the Dutch governor, wrote to the directors of the New Netherlands Company, "I beg your Honors to authorize me to go with 50 or 60 men on an expedition to drive them [the Mohawks] off."[3]

For almost two decades the Mohawks connived to gain some precedence in the existing trade system by peaceful means. They were particularly incensed by the tribute levied against them by the Mahicans when they came to trade with the Dutch in what was arguably their own backyard. Finally in a concerted effort to disrupt the Mahican trading advantage and replace it with their own, the Mohawks opened a trade war with them in 1624. Although the initial clashes were unrecorded, it seems certain that the Mohawks were the aggressors in the ensuing conflict known as the Mohawk-Mahican War.

THE MOHAWK-MAHICAN WAR

In 1625, with the encouragement of the Dutch, the Mahicans attacked the easternmost village of the Mohawks, probably Schaunactada, which was situated near Schenectady, New York. As both sides were still using traditional weapons, the attack was little more than a skirmish. But as territorial integrity and prestige ranked high in the process of native American warfare, the Mahicans gained the upper hand by boldly invading what was unquestionably Mohawk territory. For some time thereafter the war swung back and forth with the Mahicans suffering almost as badly as the Mohawks. A contemporary Dutch observer noted of the conflict, "There have been cruel murders on both sides."[4]

Daniel van Krieckebeeck, commander of Fort Orange, probably thinking that his guns would help the Mahicans to overpower the Mohawks, accompanied a group of Mahicans with four or five soldiers on a subsequent raid in 1626. A few miles from the fort the party was set upon by the Mohawks, who seem to have caught them in a storm of arrows. The commander and at least three of his soldiers were killed along with upwards of two dozen Mahicans. One Dutchman escaped to report the details of the battle by jumping into a nearby body of water. The Dutch were horrified to learn that the Mohawks had burned their captives and had eaten part of one Dutchman. Having had his former aggressive attitudes somewhat altered by the outcome, Isaac de Rasiers rather disingenuously characterized the result as a "disaster caused by the reckless adventure of Krieckebeeck."[5]

The Mahicans now appealed for support to the Indians living near the French, but these natives demurred largely due to the continued intercession of the French governor, Samuel de Champlain, who wished to prevent the war from becoming a regional affair that would negatively impact the volume of trade coming to Quebec. Nonetheless, some of the Alqonquians in New England became involved. These nations had been enemies of the Mohawks on other occasions, but the extent of their involvement seems to have been limited to the detachment of small raiding parties into the southern Berkshires and the Lake George region.

Little more can be known about the extent of the Mohawk-Mahican War because the native American nations involved kept no written records and because there was no further involvement by Europeans. According to a detailed native tradition, the last major battle of the war was a decisive one. The Mohawk and Mahican forces were arrayed against one another on an island in the Hudson River. The island has not been identified, but such set-piece gladiatorial encounters were not unusual in native American warfare. Champlain had blundered into a similar affair between the Mohawks and a force of Montagnais at Crown Point in 1609.[6] According to the account, the Mahicans were winning the contest until a group of Mohawks sprang from ambush, launching a furious attack and killing many Mahican warriors. The Mahicans then sued for peace.[7]

The natural ferocity and military discipline of the Mohawks had finally beaten the Mahicans and had effectively eliminated them as competitors for the Dutch trade. The surviving Mahicans were driven into New England or took refuge at Schagticoke on the Hoosic River in New York. Jonas Michaeleus, minister of the Dutch Reformed Church in New Amsterdam, wrote in 1628, "The Mahicans have fled and their lands are unoccupied." Nonetheless, the Mohawks continued to harass the Mahican refugees in their villages in southwestern Vermont and western Massachusetts for many years. Thereafter, the Mahican position became more difficult due to their conflicting allegiances with their Algonquianspeaking relations in New England and New France and with the Dutch, whom they valued as friends and trading partners, but who were soon allied with their former enemy, the Mohawks.[8]

MOHAWK MONOPOLY

The immediate effect of the end of the Mohawk-Mahican War on the frontier was a rapid destabilization of the balance of power that had existed among the native tribes of the region. The war spoiled the trade

in furs for the English traders far to the east in New England. For their part, the French were disappointed at the increased power of the Mohawks, who were their implacable enemy. The businesslike Dutch immediately moved to acquire the vacant lands of the Mahicans and seem to have avoided any long-lasting enmity among the Mohawks for having taken arms against them. In fact, a fur-trading coalition was created between the victorious Mohawks and the Dutch that proved beneficial to both.

The Mohawks now held and strove to maintain a trading monopoly with the Dutch. They imposed onerous conditions upon the tribes who wished to trade with them, extending even to the nations of their own confederation. In an attempt to underscore their new position, Mohawk war parties passed down Lake Champlain to raid the French settlements in the St. Lawrence River valley and disrupt the northern fur trade. They attacked and destroyed the Montagnais village at Trois-Rivières, and during the next two decades Mohawk war-parties constantly filtered back and forth across the Lake Champlain and Connecticut River valleys from Agawam to Quebec. As a result, many of the Algonquian-speaking peoples of frontier New England were driven north to the French missions, and the natives who remained in the region went out of their way to avoid offending the Mohawks.

Although they were much weakened by the losses that they sustained in these efforts, the Mohawks emerged from this period of upheaval as a dominant power in the northeast. Prior to the Mohawk-Mahican war the Dutch had traded a little over 5,000 pelts with both Iroquoian- and

Algonquian-speaking peoples. After the war, the Dutch trade with their Mohawk middlemen alone increased in volume to over 7,000 pelts in its first year. In two years almost 10,000 skins of all kinds were being traded, and five years later the trade had increased to 30,000 skins. Although the Mohawks kept no formal record of the sources of their furs, it is almost certain from their subsequent actions that they were exhausting the beaver and other valuable fur-bearing species in all of Iroquoia. It was from this period that the position of the Iroquois in the conduct of the fur trade assumed its unprecedented importance.[9]

Herein appears to lie both the genesis and the continued motivation behind the policies, alliances, and aggressive actions of the Iroquois in the mid-seventeenth century. Propelled by circumstances set in motion by the Mohawks of their confederacy, the remaining Iroquois followed a desperate course, striving to achieve total control of the fur trade by diverting the fur coming from the interior into their own hands. The almost ceaseless intertribal conflicts fought by the Iroquois have been characterized as the "Beaver Wars."[10]

THE HURON TRADING EMPIRE

Southwest of Quebec, in a great triangular area now part of the province of Ontario, was the land of the Huron. This was a populous and rich region east of Lake Huron and bounded on the southwest by Lake Erie and Lake Ontario and capped on the north by the Ottawa River. Historians' knowledge of Huronia relies almost completely on the reports of the French Jesuit fathers who served there. It seems certain that in the historical period the Huron had become almost exclusively a trading nation. Father Jean de Brebeuf reported that the Huronia in summer was "stripped of men." Using their neighbors as sources of foodstuffs and other trading materials, the Hurons seemingly "spent the entire year in the act of trading or in preparing for it."[11]

The Hurons were great friends of the French. They used their friendship to control all the trade in the north country and the Great Lakes in much the same way as the Iroquois controlled the trade with the Dutch. Yet in their self-appointed role as master traders the Hurons seemingly lived at peace and at ease with their neighbors. The economy of Huronia was almost purely agricultural, with maize and fish being the principal articles of food. The Hurons established firm alliances with their neighbors, on whom they relied for those things that they could not or would not produce for themselves. The easy conditions of life in Huronia, with its many lakes, rivers, and fertile meadows, made this arrangement relatively easy to maintain. So effective were the Hurons at bringing out furs that no French traders penetrated Huronia before the middle of the seventeenth century.

The immediate neighbors of the Hurons were related to them and included the Petuns, the Neutrals, and the Eries. While the Eries seem to have acted in total independence of the Hurons, the Petuns, who lived just to the west of the Hurons, were totally subjugated to them providing tobacco, beans, squash, and maize to Huron villages. The Attiwanda-ronk, or Neutral tribes, raised a great deal of tobacco, hemp, and meal in the area around the falls of the Niagara River. They were the source of much of the flint that was bartered among the tribes, but they did not trade very far from home. The Hurons treated the production of the Petuns and Neutrals as their own, using their corn, meal, and other materials as items of exchange in the fur trade with other Indians. In return they carefully guarded their relations against possible competitors.[12]

The Hurons' penchant for trade allowed them to establish a brisk commerce with the neighboring Nipissings, who were themselves great fur traders in the far north and west, accumulating a large stock of beaver skins and buffalo robes. They also speared almost numberless whitefish in Lake Nipissing, which they dried and freely traded. Their pelts, robes, and dried fish were exchanged with the Hurons in return for corn, meal, and beans. The Allumettes and Iroquets, who controlled the portages around the rapids in the Ottawa River, the Ottawas of the upper Great Lakes, and many other Algonquian tribes wintered near the Hurons and had very friendly, if businesslike, relations with them. The Montagnais of the Saguenay River region near Tadoussac produced great quantities of deer and moose skins and allowed no other tribe than the Hurons to trade with them.[13]

Using means similar to those agreed upon with the Nipissings, the Hurons annually gathered up and delivered to the French traders at Quebec the entire accumulation of furs gathered by the native peoples of an immense territory. "Such an economy would function very well so long as the complex and intimate tribal relationships upon which it depended were undisturbed." Not only the Hurons, but all the participating tribes, seem to have found an economic niche in this system of intertribal relations, with each trying to maintain the middleman status with their immediate neighbors. Yet only the Hurons seem to have been able to take on the role of master traders, acquiring furs from all the nations of the north country and funneling them into French warehouses in Montreal, Trois-Rivières, and Quebec by way of the Ottawa River.[14]

Beaver, otter, buffalo, deer, moose, and even seal skins from Hudson Bay were loaded in great bales by the Hurons onto a great fleet of canoes. Throughout the late summer and early fall, twenty, forty, and sixty canoes came down the Ottawa River at a time. At Allumette Island, the Ottawa River was obstructed by dangerous rapids, and the passage involved a considerable portage of canoes. It was the custom of the local Allumette and Iroquet nations to charge a considerable toll upon the value of the passing trade. Although they numbered only 400 warriors, they were respected by the more numerous Hurons and feared by the French.

INTERTRIBAL NEGOTIATIONS

It seems certain that as early as 1633 the Iroquois were seeking a trade alliance with the Hurons and the French in order to establish themselves as key players in the fur trade of Canada. How this circumstance arose is somewhat obscure. However, it may have had something to do with the fact that Quebec was seized by Sir David Kirke, an English privateer, in 1629. Neither the Hurons nor the Iroquois kept written records of their negotiations, and there were no substantial records of intertribal activities and proposals kept during the brief English occupation (1629–1632). Some historians have accused the Iroquois of insincerity in making these overtures, but the Iroquois were certainly trying to find an accommodation with the recently returned French traders. The Mohawks, the least inclined toward the French of the Iroquois, had swallowed injury and insult to remain on good trading terms with the Dutch in 1629, and they would do so again when the English conquered the Dutch in 1664.[15]

The Jesuit Relations, written contemporaneously with the events, reflects that the Mohawks managed to effect a friendly understanding with the Montagnais in 1635, and were trying to deal peacefully with the Hurons as late as 1640. It should be remembered that the Iroquois achieved their greatest successes by a judicious blend of aggression and diplomacy. There is, however, every reason to consider the French untrustworthy in these circumstances. The French were greatly concerned that growing friendly relations between these disparate native groups might result in the Iroquois diverting Huron furs to the Dutch. Both the colonial officials and the priests became willing instruments in an effort to stop any diversion of trade.[16]

Despite the occasional revenge raids on the Huron made by small bands of Seneca, there was little in the way of open warfare on the frontier between Huronia and Iroquoia. In response to the pleadings of their priests, the Hurons broke the general peace in 1639 by capturing a number of Seneca who were quietly fishing on Lake Ontario. Twelve of these were brought to Huron villages as captives and were burned to death. Shortly thereafter a large body of Senecas who were rallying to the defense were defeated by Huron raiders, and many were taken to Huronia to be tortured and burned. The whole Iroquois Confederacy was reported by Jesuit sources to have been in great fear of the Hurons launching an attack on their villages at this time.

The Iroquois again attempted trade negotiations in 1640, but their proposals were largely disregarded. The Hurons were openly "fearless and even contemptuous of them."[17] Throughout the year the situation remained the same. The mass of the Iroquois generally stayed on watch in Iroquoia while an occasional Huron was killed by frontier war parties. But the Iroquois were in a difficult position economically. With their own sources of fur exhausted by more than a decade of over-trapping, their position of importance with the Dutch traders at Fort Orange was in jeopardy. In an attempt to strengthen their position an Iroquois delegation made a petition of peace to the French at Trois-Rivières. These overtures resulted in French assurances of friendship and cooperation "so vague as to give the Iroquois no privileges at all."[18]

THE BEAVER WARS

Having been rebuffed by the French, the Iroquois quite consciously undertook a series of trade wars with the French Indian allies. They began by raiding the fur brigades on the Ottawa River, and they attacked a small outlying Huron village in 1642. Although the blockade of the Ottawa was effective, the Hurons mounted a counteroffensive, putting a force of 500 Iroquois warriors to flight. The Iroquois then extended the war to the Iroquets, dispossessing them of their position of control on the lower Ottawa River. The Iroquets fled to winter under the protective eyes of the Hurons. In the following year the Iroquois completely closed the Ottawa River to the transportation of furs. By the summer of 1644 only one fur fleet in four reached Quebec. The Hurons attempted to bypass the Ottawa River route by detouring overland to the north, but any Huron parties who passed near Iroquoia were annihilated.

The French response to these circumstances was to give military aid to the Hurons in the form of twenty soldiers, who traveled into the interior and wintered in the Huron villages. The soldiers returned with the fur fleet in the summer with almost 40,000 livres worth of fur. The Iroquois, "learning of the presence of French soldiers," abandoned any raids that had been planned on this fleet and let it be known that they would entertain any messages of peace sent by the French. Both the Hurons and the French were deeply worried by the effectiveness of the Mohawk blockade and were in the proper frame of mind to resume negotiations.[19]

The result of these peace feelers was a great conference with the Iroquois that included the French governor, Charles de Montmagny, Hurons, Montagnais, Allumettes, and other tribes. The French position with regard to an overall peace prior to this conference was that it must include all of their Algonquian-speaking allies. The Iroquois had shown a marked lack of enthusiasm for this particular proposal in the past, and their attitude was hardly diminished in the current circumstances. Nonetheless, the French were particularly eager to conclude a peace that would end the interruption of their trade. Consequently, they included in the treaty terms that abandoned the Algonquian nations to the whims of Iroquois aggression. The Allumettes on the Ottawa River remained particularly apprehensive of Mohawk aggression and doubtful of their sincerity.

This flawed peace held inviolate for some time, even for the Allumettes. In 1646 the greatest fur brigade in the history of the trade arrived at Montreal from Huronia. More than eighty canoes fully packed with prime furs had traversed the Ottawa River without the slightest challenge from the Iroquois. So many bales of fur had been withheld during the Iroquois reign of terror that the traders exhausted their supply of available trade goods.

The Iroquois had entered into a commercial treaty with the hope of improving their own position, but they benefited not at all from the renewal of trade. Their main reason for entertaining a treaty had been to increase trade and economic interaction for themselves, and it seemed that the terms of the agreement had not effectively improved their position. As long as the Hurons held the Georgian Bay–Lake Simcoe region, they controlled almost the entire fur trade of the Northeast. There seemed to be no possibility of the Iroquois trading with other nations without violating the treaty. If the fur trade was to continue as it had in the past, with the Iroquois standing on the outside looking in, then they would repudiate the treaty.

The Hurons had not been united in accepting the peace. Their policy toward the Iroquois had long been one of economic encirclement and isolation. When the Mohawks heard that the Hurons were negotiating an alliance against them with the Susquehannocks of Pennsylvania to their south and had tried to divide the Iroquois Confederacy by enticing the Onondaga into a separate agreement, they began to look upon the treaty with complete distrust.

In 1648 the treaty was broken. Having the support of the Senecas, who had continued a separate series of revenge raids on the Hurons in the interim, the Mohawks waylaid and killed the Huron ambassadors to the Onondaga. Meanwhile the Senecas assumed a strategic position on the Huron frontier and cut off all communications between Huronia and the Susquehannocks. The Mohawks then attacked a Huron trading fleet within sight of Montreal, but they were repulsed. This fleet of fifty to sixty canoes manned by 250 warriors was worth a quarter of a million livres. This defeat was somewhat offset by a successful Seneca attack on a frontier Huron village.

THE GREAT DISPERSAL

The original strategy of Mohawk attacks in the St. Lawrence and of Seneca raids on the frontier of Huronia was not producing the desired results. Therefore, in March 1649 the Mohawks and Senecas launched

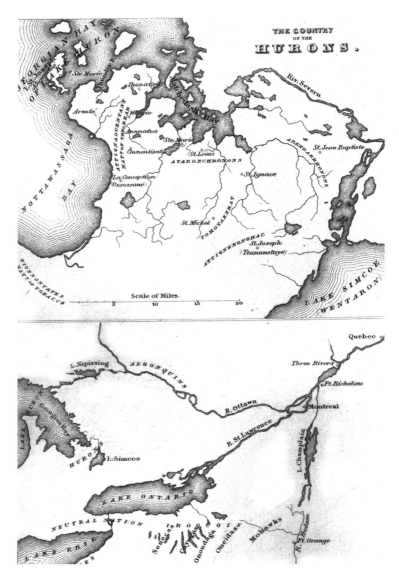

Francis Parkman's map of Huronia and Iroquoia from his book
The Jesuits in North America in the Seventeenth Century **(1867).**

the equivalent of an aboriginal blitzkrieg. Rather than being unsophisticated, frenzied, and disorganized, the plan of war that they formed was shrewd, sober, and minutely organized. It was based on a series of sudden, unremitting, and massive assaults for which the Iroquois were to become notorious.

A thousand Seneca and Mohawk warriors quietly left Iroquoia in small groups in the autumn of 1648 and hunted in Ontario throughout the winter. In late winter they assembled in the forests of Huronia and fell upon the Huron town at the French mission of St. Ignace. Attacking at dawn through the last of the melting snow, these warriors caught the Hurons totally unaware, taking many captives and killing all but three Huron warriors. The attackers then immediately made a forced march to the village at St. Louis three miles away and completed another successful attack before nightfall. By dawn of the next day they were outside the main Huron stronghold. Before they could mount a third attack in little more than twenty-four hours, the Hurons, having been warned by the retreating survivors of St. Ignace, counterattacked. Hampered by more than 100 captives and already carrying heavy spoil, the Iroquois retreated with moderate losses. All the way back to Iroqouia they were hounded by 700 Petun allies of the Hurons.[20]

The Hurons had been totally unprepared for an attack of this magnitude and scope. The Iroquois had attacked the very center of Huronia with a singleness of purpose and organization that was daunting. No army of native warriors of such a size had ever before been seen in North America. So well guarded had been their plan that they had entered Huronia, concentrated their force, and swiftly moved to the attack without the least warning being raised by the Hurons or their allies. Nonetheless, the Hurons had driven them off with the loss of perhaps 200 warriors compared to about 300 Hurons lost in defending the villages. The Petuns responding to the needs of their ally suffered no losses.

With these facts in mind there seems to be no convincing explanation for the abject terror that now seized the entire Huron nation. Fear seems to have divested them of both common sense and strategic judgment in this crisis as "they incontinently fled in all directions." By May 1649, fifteen Huron villages had been abandoned, and between 6,000 and 8,000 refugees had crowded onto St. Joseph Island, where the Jesuits had a mission. Nothing seems to have been able to move them from their chosen refuge, not even hunger and death. Even before the next winter set in, the Hurons were starving. Thousands died. The surviving remnants of the tribe, about 500 persons, retreated to Quebec the next spring to take up residence at Lorette. Other refugees ran to the territories of the Petuns, the Neutrals, or the Eries, where they quickly lost their individual tribal identity.[21]

The Petuns, Neutrals, and Eries were completely astonished at the consequences of the Iroquois attacks but did not immediately become apprehensive about their own safety. Then in December 1649, they received news from friends and allies that the Mohawks and Senecas were again in the field. The Petuns bravely went in search of the invaders, but could not find them. Two days later the Petun village at St. Jean was attacked in the absence of their warriors. Little was reported of the details of this attack, as the Europeans at the village were killed. Good sense and prudence born of experience now overtook Petun courage. The tribe dispersed with the same speed, but without the wild disorder of the Hurons. Some of the Petuns went to St. Joseph, but most sought the protection of the Ottawa Nation, which proved a wiser course. Both the Petuns and the Ottawas then fled before the Iroquois menace to Green Bay in Wisconsin.

After the Huron dispersal, the Neutrals abandoned their neutral stance in favor of the Iroquois and took the Huron refugees as slaves and captives. Unfortunately, the Neutrals had played host to the negotiations that the Mohawks and Senecas had considered a Susquehannock-Huron conspiracy. This made them a perceived threat to the ultimate Iroquois objective of total control of the fur trade. The Mohawks and Senecas decided that it was better to defeat the Neutrals immediately before they could engage in another such conspiracy.

In 1651, almost 600 Iroquois stormed a Neutral town, killing the old and the young and dispersing almost 1,600 persons. The Neutrals then attempted a counterattack, taking a Seneca town on the frontier of Iroquoia and scalping 200 Seneca warriors as a warning to the Iroquois. Notwithstanding this bravado, for the third time in as many years, the willingness of an Indian nation to continue a confrontation with the Iroquois evaporated as the Neutrals scattered. Many fled to the neighboring Eries. Others went to the Ottawas near Green Bay. Ironically, most of the Neutral territory, noted for its fertility and easy living, remained virtually uninhabited for many years thereafter and served as a hunting ground for the Iroquois.[22]

The Eries were the least known of the Iroquoian-speaking peoples who inhabited Huronia. Until the time of the dispersal, no white man was known to have visited them. They were thought to have occupied the northwest shore of Lake Erie, but at the time of the dispersal were actually living south and west of the lake with the Senecas on their eastern border. Just why they moved is unknown. The warriors of the Erie were reported to number about 2,000 and they were noted as brave and disciplined fighters. They were aggressive in their dealings with the Iroquois confederacy, and the addition of refugees from the Hurons, Petuns, and Neutrals seems to have stirred up their willingness to go to war against their Seneca neighbors.

By the summer of 1654 it was becoming obvious to the Eries that they would be the next target of the Iroquois war machine. Reports reached them that the greatest native army ever raised in Iroquoia was about to descend upon them. More than 1,800 Iroquois warriors, now including warriors from all members of their confederacy, were assembling. Part of this force, about 700 warriors, attacked the principal Erie town that summer. The Eries defended their palisades with great courage. In a scene better imagined to take place before a medieval European castle, the Iroquois built counter-palisades and used scaling ladders to mount the defenses of the Eries. When the stockade was breached the Iroquois fell upon the Eries, and those who were not killed or captured fled the region.

Though small groups of the Eries continued to fight over the next few years, their tribal identity was just as surely destroyed by the Iroquois as had been that of the Hurons, Petuns, and Neutrals. Whereas the Hurons who fled south toward the Ohio River Valley became known as Wyandots, the Minguas (Mingos) who terrorized western Pennsylvania in the eighteenth century were undoubtedly the remnants of the Eries. Some of the Neutrals finally penetrated to the far south, and may have become part of the Catawba nation of the Carolinas. The Petun refugees kept a far greater part of the tribe together than all the other dispersed nations by fleeing to the Ottawas and removing to Green Bay. Thereafter they reentered the history of the intertribal fur trade with the founding of Detroit almost half a century later.

By the end of the dispersal period, the Iroquois, and the Mohawks in particular, appeared to have attained all of their war aims. The Mohawks and the Seneca nations had shown how a series of single devastating blows, if struck against one target at a time, could defeat a wide array of potential enemies. As with the Mahican war, their unremitting focus and willingness to swallow their pride for the moment in order to achieve a greater goal seemed to have served the Iroquois well.

THE FIRST SUSQUEHANNOCK WAR

In 1651 and 1652 the Mohawks also tried to make a lightning conquest of the Susquehannocks, but were not able to force either their surrender or their dispersal. Little is known of the First Susquehannock War, as there were no Europeans involved and the Jesuits were not among the Susquehannock nation. It is quite certain that the Susquehannocks were receiving firearms from the Swedish colonists in the Delaware Bay. They were reported to have fitted their villages with several small cannons from this source. Nonetheless, when the Dutch conquered New Sweden in 1655, the Susquehannocks became their customers, and active aggression between this nation and the Mohawks seems to have subsided.[23]

THE ONE LONGHOUSE

In the mist of all this turmoil, the governor of New France, Jean de Lauson, held a great peace council in 1653 with the Iroquois nations, and the Jesuits agreed to establish a mission among the Onondaga, who had initiated the peace talks. In a short time representatives of the Mohawks appeared at Quebec to protest the settlement of a mission among the Onondaga and asked that it be among the Mohawks instead. According to the Jesuits in attendance, the Mohawk diplomats described the Iroquois confederacy in terms of the traditional longhouse in which they lived:

We, the five Iroquois nations, compose but one longhouse: we maintain but one fire; and we have, from time immemorial, dwelt under one and the same roof. Well then, will you not enter the longhouse by the door, which is at the ground floor of the house? It is with us Mohawks, that you should begin: whereas you, by beginning with the Onondagas try to enter by the roof and through the chimney. Have you no fear that the smoke may blind you, our fire not being extinguished, and that you may fall from the top to the bottom, having nothing solid on which to plant your feet?[24]

It was from this speech that the imagery of a single longhouse came to represent the Five Nations of the Iroquois for Europeans. The Mohawks were the keepers of the eastern door, the Senecas the keepers of the western door. The Onondagas were the keepers of the great central fire, and the Cayuga and Oneida were the younger brothers who lived among them. A general peace ultimately resulted from this conference that covered all of the northeastern fur country with all five Iroquois nations freely roaming the St. Lawrence River valley and dealing with the French.

ENTER THE OTTAWA

In 1654 a great fleet of canoes filled with furs appeared on the Grand River bound for Montreal. This was manned largely by the ubiquitous Ottawas. It was from this period that the Grand River became known as the Ottawa River. The Mohawks were particularly taken aback by this event, but they were again buoyed in 1655 when there was no fur fleet at all. Nonetheless, in 1656 two French fur traders, Medard Chouart Des Groseilliers and Pierre-Esprit Radisson, who had gone out into the northwest to collect the furs themselves, appeared on the Ottawa River with fifty canoes loaded with furs and manned once again by Ottawa paddlers. This was to prove a fateful accomplishment.

In 1658 the French policy toward the Iroquois suddenly shifted under the new governor, d'Argenson. Immediately before his arrival three Frenchmen were killed and their farms pillaged. Iroquois war parties were suspected, and d'Argenson immediately led a fruitless pursuit into the forests. It is clear that the governor overreacted to the situation thereafter. The Jesuit mission to the Onondaga at Ste. Marie was hurriedly withdrawn, and d'Argenson ordered "the arrest, throughout the French settlements of all the Iroquois that should present themselves, from whatever quarter they might come." Several Mohawks were seized at Trois Riviers and sent as prisoners to Quebec.[25]

The Mohawks felt that the imprisonment of their men was unjust and were prepared to go to war. Yet the Seneca, who had been their main support in the wars of dispersion, had recently expressed that they were war weary. Understanding that an attack without Seneca aid was impractical, and fortified by a new treaty with the Dutch, the Mohawks again began blockading the Ottawa River. So effectively did they do this that the commerce of New France almost came to a halt. It was reported by a contemporary observer that of 360 canoes that attempted the run only 7 got through.[26]

Montreal was in a constant state of alarm as long as the Mohawks blockaded the Ottawa River. Small bands, breaking off from their watch of the river, would terrorize the French habitants by destroying their livestock and menacing solitary farmers. In all the north country not only was the fur trade interrupted, but settlement was threatened. In the winter of 1659–1660 a large number of Mohawk bands wintered on the Ottawa River, and the French, knowing the recent method of Iroquois strategy, apprehended an assault on their settlements in the spring.

THE DEFENSE OF THE LONG SAULT

In an attempt to avert the coming blow, Dollard des Ormeaux raised a band of young men and French Indians and ascended the Ottawa River to ambush the Iroquois. At the section of the river containing rapids known as the Long Sault, Dollard and his men built a crude fortification—little more than an entrenchment strengthened by a few logs. Here they awaited the Iroquois. As the Indians shot down the rapids in their canoes, Dollard opened fire upon them from the bank. The Iroquois were initially taken aback, but their increasing numbers forced Dollard and his men into the shelter of their fort. For eight days he and his small band of volunteers fought savagely. In the end, however, they were overpowered.

Those Frenchmen who were not killed in the battle were tortured and burned at stakes overlooking the river. Contemporary accounts record seventeen monuments to this torture decorating the bank. Nonetheless, Dollard's attempt had been heroic, and it had inflicted so severe a loss upon the Iroquois that they withdrew into their own territory and left Montreal unmolested for a time. Moreover, the local Algonquian-speaking peoples were buoyed by this defense, and the French policy of toleration for the aggressive trade wars of the Iroquois was largely suspended. It is generally supposed that the French would have countered the Iroquois victory with a large-scale military stratagem of their own except for the impending change in governors in 1661 from the aggressive d'Argenson to the generally ineffective Baron Dubois d'Avaugour (1661–1663).

THE IROQUOIS ARE HUMBLED

In 1663 the colony of New France was placed under royal control, and a new form of government was initiated under the first royal governor, Chevalier de Mezy (1663–1665). Although de Mezy's administration was short-lived, the arrival of the Carignan-Salieres regiment, which had gained great renown in the Turkish Wars, was specifically designed to put an end to Iroquois aggression. The second royal governor, Daniel de Remy, Sieur de Courcelle (1665–1672), gave precedence to the military viceroy, the Marquis de Tracy, during the viceroy's stay in the colony, but de Courcelle chaffed when de Tracy did not immediately move to eliminate the Iroquois threat.

In 1666, de Courcelle led a raid of his own devising into Mohawk territory that badly misfired, but de Tracy led a better-organized campaign in 1667 with a force of 1,100 men. He burned many Mohawk villages and destroyed their crops, but there was little loss of life, as the occupants had prudently withdrawn. Nonetheless, the attack had its desired effect. Dismayed by the specter of further disaster or impending starvation, the Mohawks joined with the other members of their confederacy in humbly seeking peace. Notwithstanding doubts and suspicions on both sides, with great ceremony and exchange of presents a solemn treaty was made at a great conference in Montreal in 1667.

THE GREAT PEACE

For more than two decades the Iroquois remained at peace with the French. More importantly, the whole north country was at peace, and the fur trade was free to move forward unimpeded. Even the Mahicans, who had fought the Mohawks for more than four decades, succumbed to Iroquois diplomacy. Meanwhile the English had quietly displaced the Dutch in New Netherlands in 1664, and they applauded the peace. The removal of Dutch sovereignty, made permanent by treaty in 1667, did not immediately eliminate the traders of that nation. However, with time it did substitute potentially more powerful English competitors in the same role who had not yet demonstrated the expansionism that would characterize England's policies in the eighteenth century.

It would be an error to believe that the Iroquois had been forced into a one-sided peace agreement by French determination. Throughout the period, European observers seem to have failed to recognize the intricacies of intertribal diplomatic and economic manipulations. Iroquois policies were rarely so straightforward as to include a simple unilateral surrender. One person who understood was Jolicoeur Charles Bonin, a French soldier serving in North America who wrote, "The character of these people is a mixture of simplicity and trickery, nobility and meanness, vanity and politeness, good nature and treachery, valor and cowardice, humanity and barbarity."[27]

It is certain that the Iroquois were responding to many circumstances when they made peace in 1667. Among these the Jesuits reported a recent epidemic that had ravaged the villages of Iroquoia and had killed many hundreds of warriors. Additionally, a coalition of northern tribes had shown remarkable resistance to the Iroquois by "utterly destroying" a large party of Mohawk warriors in New England. These two circumstances may have left the Iroquois, who probably could field no more than 2,500 warriors in good times, in a weakened military condition. On the other hand, the Iroquois may simply have been repositioning themselves with respect to the English occupation of Dutch territory. Notwithstanding the ambiguity of these circumstances, it seems certain that the Iroquois were using their newfound accord with the French to help prosecute a renewed war with their neighbors to the south, the Susquehannocks.[28]

THE SECOND SUSQUEHANNOCK WAR

The Susquehannocks were noted as a redoubtable enemy of the Senecas, who had previously fought against them but had failed to achieve a decisive result. Although thought to inhabit a large region of present-day Pennsylvania, the Susquehannocks were a far ranging people who sent hunting and war parties west into the Ohio River valley and well north of Lake Ontario. The Senecas and the Susquehannocks continually annoyed one another with small excursions in an attempt to patrol the borders of their respective territories and to stave off the likelihood of a clandestine buildup of invasion forces.

The reasons for the outbreak of a major conflict between these two related peoples at this point are obscured by the same lack of direct evidence that affects the study of all the intertribal wars of the seventeenth century. However, it seems clear that the causes of the conflict were rooted in the interdiction of the fur trade in 1663. The importance of this war was that the English colonies of Maryland and Delaware took an active part in an intertribal trade conflict for the first time and significantly affected its outcome.

The Senecas were increasingly harassed by Susquehannocks as they tried to move furs across the region that is now the New York–Pennsylvania border. The Seneca carried their beaver skins to Albany "with great inconvenience and by long and perilous routes," with the Susquehannocks laying ambushes for them all along the way in a manner similar to that of the Mohawks along the Ottawa River. In order to defend their caravans the Senecas were reported by Jesuits to have devoted half their force in warriors as escorts.[29]

In the ensuing war the Susquehannocks were again supported by the firearms and small cannons formerly supplied to them by the Swedes. The cannons were not used tactically, but they were of great value strategically as a defense for the main Susquehannock village. Maryland initially sent gunpowder and fifty armed men to help defend the main Susquehannock village. Allied to the Susquehannocks were the remnants of the Eries, hereafter known as the Minguas, and the Shawnee, who made their first appearance as an aggressive force in intertribal warfare in this conflict.

The Seneca were not alone in their adversity. The Cayuga, "younger brothers" of the Seneca, seem to have suffered a great disaster at the hands of the Susquehannocks. Many of the Cayuga were driven north from their tribal lands into the now vacant region north of Lake Ontario. The Onondaga who occupied the territory immediately adjacent to that of the Cayuga felt constrained to take some part in the war. Ironically, the Mohawks seem to have ignored the difficulties of their confederate nations, and the Oneida initially refused to aid the Senecas.[30]

Nonetheless, the Senecas and their allies were reported to have raised a force of between 800 and 1,600 men to invade Susquehannock territory in 1663. The Seneca assault of the main Susquehannock village was unsuccessful because of its seemingly impregnable stockade and cannons. In an attempt to win concessions by diplomacy rather than might, the Seneca sent twenty-five representatives to the village to treat with the defenders. These were seized and burned at stakes raised upon the stockade in full view of the besieging Seneca army. The Senecas retreated in frustration.

For several years the Seneca continued the fight by promoting a continuous series of small raids. The Oneida finally joined them in 1664 and attacked the Delaware allies of the Susquehannock living on the Chesapeake Bay, to the outrage of the officials in Maryland. Finally, Cayuga territory was again invaded, and a relief force of Senecas was cut to pieces. Thereafter, it became evident that the Senecas simply could not deal with the Susquehannocks. The Seneca repeatedly appealed to the French, but Frontenac, the royal governor at the time, essentially refused to help them.

Suddenly, in 1675, the Susquehannocks were reported to have been destroyed. The exact reasons for their demise are not clear but seem to have included the involvement of the English. One scenario suggests that a force of Iroquois defeated the Susquehannocks in battle and that the survivors fled south along the frontiers of Virginia and Maryland, where they were exterminated or sold as slaves by whites. It is altogether possible that a decisive battle between the Iroquois and Susquehannocks in the wilderness might go unrecorded. The ubiquitous Jesuits seemingly knew nothing of the details of the Susquehannock dispersion beyond the fact that they were gone, leaving their sudden disappearance a mystery. A few were still reported to be living in eastern Pennsylvania as late as 1763.

THE END OF THE BEAVER WARS

With the exception of some minor expeditions against the tribes to the west, by 1684 the Iroquois attempt to achieve a fur trade monopoly was over. They had been wedded to the idea of trading furs at Albany throughout their struggles. When the English took possession of New Netherlands from the Dutch, the Iroquois skillfully switched their focus from one group of traders to the other. They also quickly saw that English goods were superior to those of the French and many times cheaper. However, the Indian nations of the Great Lakes could no longer be made to recognize the Iroquois as middlemen. The Five Nations of the Iroquois and the Mohawks in particular, had expended the lives of their young men in making war and, ironically, had exhausted their ability to use war as a tool of economic success.

More importantly, by the last decades of the seventeenth century Frenchmen had ascended the rivers and lakes into the interior to trade for furs directly with the native trappers. Medard Groseilliers and Pierre Radisson, Louis Joliet and Jacques Marquette, and particularly Robert Cavelier de la Salle had demonstrated the advantages to the Indians of dealing directly with the French. The active interposition of Frenchmen, or any Europeans, into the fur trade upset the underpinnings of a century of intertribal trade wars and complicated the shape of the world for the Iroquois beyond their ability to refashion it more to their liking.

Yet the Iroquois were astute politicians, subtle diplomats, and determined strategists who had proven that they would not give up at the slightest setback. They began to ponder a wiser policy. Might not the assumption of a great neutrality between the French and English in the future better serve them than warfare? They had never before attempted to play one competitor against the other, yet this would be their position throughout most of the eighteenth century. This decision marked the end of the Iroquois attempt to gain a trading monopoly by purely military means, and it opened a new phase of carefully crafted diplomacy and brinkmanship.

NOTES

1. Contrary to opinions revolving around James Fenimore Cooper's use of the term *Mohicans* in the title of his most famous novel, both the terms *Mahican* and *Mohican* refer to the same people and are equally correct. The authors have chosen to use the *Mahican* as it is most common term in Dutch documents of the period. Conversely, the name *Mohegan* refers to a tribe more closely tied to the Pequots of eastern Connecticut.

2. Shirley W. Dunn, *The Mohicans and their Land, 1609–1730* (Fleischmanns, NY: Purple Mountain Press, 1994), 233.

3. Ibid., 97.

4. As quoted in ibid., 99. The observer, Domine Jonas Michaeleus, was lamenting the downturn in the volume of fur coming from the interior to New Amsterdam.

5. Ibid., 98.

6. Guy Omeron Coolridge, *The French Occupation of the Champlain Valley from 1609 to 1759* (Fleischmanns, NY: Purple Mountain Press, 1999), 11–12. For the use of the term *gladiatorial*, see Ian K. Steele, *Warpaths: Invasions of North America* (New York: Oxford University Press, 1994), 66.

7. H. P. Biggar, ed., *The Works of Samuel de Champlain*, vol. 6 (Toronto: Champlain Society, 1933), 3.

8. Dunn, 99. The Mahicans of Massachusetts were later known as the Stockbridge Indians. Those who remained in New York were often called the Schagticoke, or River Indians.

9. George T. Hunt, *The Wars of the Iroquois: A Study in Intertribal Trade Relations* (Madison: University of Wisconsin Press, 1972), 32–35, 53.

10. Francis Jennings, *The Ambiguous Iroquois Empire: The Covent Chain Confederation of Indian Tribes with English Colonies from Its Beginnings to the Lancaster Treaty of 1744* (New York: W. W. Norton, 1984), 113. See Dorothy V. Jones, *License for Empire: Colonialism by Treaty in Early America* (Chicago: University of Chicago Press, 1982).

11. Hunt, 55, 63.

12. Ibid., 96. The Neutrals were not inept with regard to canoes, but their territory in Huronia was devoid of the birch and elm trees needed to build them.

13. Ibid., 64.

14. Ibid., 59.

15. Jennings, 43.

16. Hunt, 68.

17. Ibid., 72–73.

18. Ibid., 74.

19. Ibid., 76.

20. Ibid., 92. Hunt is one of the few historians to report the details of this momentous event. Others dismiss the entire episode and its aftermath in a single paragraph.

21. Ibid., 93.

22. Ibid., 98.

23. Jennings, 110.

24. See Elizabeth Metz, *Sainte Marie Among the Iroquois* (Syracuse, NY: Midgley 1995), 53. To complete the metaphor, the Mohawks were the keepers of the eastern door, the Seneca the keepers of the western door, and the Onondaga the keepers of the central fire. These three were the "older brothers" of the confederacy, with the Oneida and Cayuga being the "younger brothers." All important confederacy business was done at councils held at Onondaga.

25. Metz, 105.

26. Hunt, 104.

27. Andrew Gallup, ed., *Memoir of a French and Indian War Soldier: Jolicoeur Charles Bonin* (Bowie, MD: Heritage Books, 1993), 216.

28. Hunt, 134–135.

29. Ibid., 139.

30. Jennings, 130.

5

Anglo-America: The English Colonies

Every homestead was a log cabin. No brick houses then; no frame-houses except in towns. What did they encounter! The deadening of trees, their gradual falling, the logging and burning, the clearing, the rude plowing amidst the stumps and roots—what exciting, toilsome times! Custom made the solitude and independence of their life, happiness.

—John Sherman, Ohio senator, 1890

ANGLO-AMERICA

The earliest English colonists called their New World home Virginia in honor of the unmarried Elizabeth I, the Virgin Queen. The Pilgrims referred to their settlements as New England. The Royalists in the southern colonies called them the Carolinas in honor of King Charles I. The Catholics called their home Maryland. Parts of New Netherlands were renamed New York and New Jersey when the English took them from the Dutch; and Pennsylvania was named for its founder. Finally, Georgia was dedicated to the reigning English monarch at the time of its establishment.

The circumstance of having separate names for different portions of the English colonies, unlike the French who called their entire colony New France, mirrored the entire scope of English colonial settlement in North America. The English colonial structure was almost as confused as the many names that described it. Some colonies were virtually self-governing while others were ruled by governors appointed by the Crown. Still others were under the jurisdiction of proprietors or trustees. No two were alike in their governance, and it should be remembered that no two were settled by a single distinct and homogeneous population of immigrants.

Unlike the French and Spanish colonies, most of the English colonies were virtually independent in their formative years. Indeed the governance of each was not only unique, it evolved with time. The Glorious Revolution of 1688 seems to have been a watershed in this regard. When James II became king, he attempted to cancel many of the royal charters under which the colonies were formed. He succeeded in placing the entire Atlantic coast from Maine to Delaware under the Dominion of New England under a royal governor, Sir Edmund Andros; but William III, who replaced the deposed James II, reissued many of the original charters in a modified form. Nonetheless, Massachusetts was partitioned, and both it and the new colony of New Hampshire became royal colonies. Meanwhile Rhode Island retained its right to elect its own government, and Connecticut retained its original charter by refusing to yield it up and hiding it in an oak tree.[1]

The royal colonies of New York and New Jersey were particularly unfortunate in their court-appointed governors, many of whom proved to be arrogant, dishonest, or incompetent. The proprietary colonies of Pennsylvania and Maryland were somewhat more fortunate in their governance. Pennsylvania was converted into a royal colony for a brief time, but the proprietorship was reinstated by the beginning of the eighteenth century. Maryland underwent a political and military upheaval in 1688 because its founder, George Calvert, the First Lord Baltimore, had been a Catholic. It was thought that the Catholics in Maryland might support the deposed king instead of the stalwartly Protestant William III. It was not surprising, therefore, that William answered a petition of the colony's Protestant settlers by appointing a Protestant royal governor.

The two southern colonies known as the Carolinas began as a single entity, but by 1710 a separate governor was appointed to each. This date marks the separation of North and South Carolina. The tract of land that became Georgia in 1732 was given to a set of eight trustees under a limited charter, but at its expiration the colony reverted to the king, with Lord Granville being the sole remaining trustee with any interest in the colony.

Delaware remains an enigma in the colony period, and it is almost certain that Lord De la Warr never saw the colony named for him. Delaware was originally founded by the Swedes. It was captured by the Dutch and then seized by the English. Delaware was claimed by both Maryland and Pennsylvania in the early colonial period and was considered part of the latter throughout most of the eighteenth century. It was not considered an independent colony until the eve of the American Revolution. Similarly, Maine was part of Massachusetts, and Vermont part of New York, until after the War of Independence.

WAVES OF MIGRATION

At least four large waves of English-speaking colonists migrated to the colonies between 1620 and 1775. Each of these had its own religious affiliations, speech patterns, social rank, and genealogy. It has been found that immigration to the New World from Britain was not a random flood of diverse people, but rather the sequential movement of four separate and distinct sets of Britons, each with unique characteristics. While all four waves shared a common language and adherence to the Protestant faith, they spoke different dialects, built their houses differently, held diverse views on business and farming, and had different conceptions of public order, power, and freedom. These people brought to the English colonies the basis for many of the regional variations that can still be seen in American society today.[2]

The earliest English settlers—Jamestown settlers in Virginia in 1607 and the Pilgrims of Plymouth, Massachusetts, in 1620—were few in number and do not warrant inclusion in a discrete wave of their own. Nonetheless, the first mass migration into the English colonies was made by Puritans very much like the Pilgrims. These came from the east of England to Massachusetts during a period of eleven years from 1629 to 1640. The second wave—very much like the Jamestown settlers—was composed of a small Royalist elite and a larger number of indentured servants from the south of England. They came to Virginia from approximately 1642 to 1725. The third movement was composed of persons from the northern midlands of England and Wales who came to the Delaware River valley from 1675 to 1725. Finally, the fourth wave—composed mostly of Scotch-Irish—was from the borders of northern Britain and northern Ireland. They settled in the Appalachian backcountry of the southern colonies from 1718 to 1775. The distinctive folkways of these four groups created an expansive pluralism in America that remains one of the most important characteristics of the United States today.[3]

REASONS FOR MIGRATING

Although these waves of migration overlapped, there was a definite correlation in time between the identity and number of each migrant group and certain political circumstances taking place in Britain. During the Anglo-Hispanic Wars of 1587–1588 few attempts at English colonization were made, but after the Spanish Armada was defeated in 1588 a number of colonization schemes were revived like the ill-fated plan by Sir Walter Raleigh to found a colony on Roanoke Island. Among Raleigh's goals in supporting the settlement of coastal Virginia was the establishment of bases for the interdiction of Spanish treasure fleets in the Straits of Florida.

The death of Elizabeth I and the accession to the throne of James Stuart (James I) almost immediately resulted in the founding of the Virginia Companies of Plymouth and London. The Jamestown settlement (1607) and the Plymouth colony (1620) were the direct results of James I's policies as king. In the first instance, it was the hope of the Crown to tap the wealth that Spain had shown to exist in the Americas. In the latter, James sought to rid himself of the potential political annoyance represented by the most radical of the Puritan minorities. He freely assented to their request to emigrate.

It was during the repressive reign of Charles I (1625–1649) that the great Puritan migrations to New England took place. The English Civil Wars (1640–1649) actually saw a reverse flow of immigrants as one-third of young Puritan males trekked back to England to fight in the parliamentary armies. With both the monarchy and the House of Lords abolished, Oliver Cromwell came to serve as Lord Protector of England during the Republican Period (1649–1658). In these years Royalists and Catholics (Papists) migrated to the southern colonies in great numbers to avoid the Puritans—a trend that was reversed in 1660 with the Restoration of the monarchy.

The persecution of Quakers under the Test Act of 1673 led William Penn to devise his plan for a Quaker colony in the New World, and the rigid enforcement of the act over the next decades increased Quaker migration to western New Jersey and Pennsylvania. Finally the great Scottish Rebellions of 1715 and 1746, and the persecution and repression that followed their failure, caused large numbers of Scots and Scotch-Irish to enter the colonies during those periods. The violent repression of the Scotch highlanders after the Battle of Culloden drove many more immigrants to the colonies than might otherwise have come.[4]

SOCIAL CLASS

The earliest English immigration to America was made by people with many professions, trades, and skills. Highly skilled craftsmen (5 percent) and merchants (5 percent) made up a small proportion of immigrants, while those with ordinary skills (38 percent) were more widely represented. Most immigrants were farmers or agricultural workers (40 percent) of some kind, and the remainder (12 percent) were identified as laborers. These statistics can be somewhat misleading, however, as very young persons may have been identified as laborers or farmers for lack of a more definite occupation. Remarkably the gentry and upper classes were so few in number as to be statistically insignificant. With the exception of the Royalists among them, who migrated during the English Republican Period to escape Puritan persecution, there was no need or purpose for any of the upper classes to immigrate to America.[5]

AGE DISTRIBUTION

Most immigrants to the English colonies came in family groups. It has been estimated that the ages of the immigrants were fairly random in their distribution. Records from the late colonial period, after the French and Indian War, indicate that only the elderly, those over sixty (less than 1 percent), seem to have been underrepresented. The largest group (39 percent) was composed of those between twenty-five and fifty-nine; the smallest (25 percent) by children under fourteen. The remaining group (35 percent) was remarkable in that it was composed of older teens and young adults between fifteen and twenty-four. "[A]mong those . . . still young and healthy enough to endure a long sea voyage, the tales they heard of freedom and opportunity in the New World and of the crying need for cheap labor made their hearts leap with that stranger joy of hope."[6]

Women and girls made up approximately half of the earliest immigration to the English colonies. This was in sharp contrast to the almost total lack of female representation in New France. In the later colonial period male migration to the English colonies seems to have dominated that of females by a ratio of 3 to 2. The mix of genders was more equal in the southern colonies than in New England.[7]

It would be an error to accept the unsupported claim that the life expectancy of colonials was much shorter than that of modern Americans. The average age at which people died was driven down by very high rates of infant mortality, death due to disease and accident among the young, and death among young women in childbirth. Those who survived adolescence seem to have had a life expectancy well into their seventies. It should be noted that military service was demanded of men up to the age of sixty in almost all of the colonies. This would suggest that men of this age were still expected to be vigorous and healthy.

LITERACY

It is generally accepted that the Puritans who came to America could read the Bible, as the reading of the Holy Scripture by the individual was a foundation stone of their religious belief. It is also generally assumed that the elite among the Royalists were as educated as those in their social class in Britain. Certainly the large number of diaries, journals, and letters that survive, written by the officers and common soldiers of the provincial armies, show an ability to write. Although their spelling and grammar leave much to be desired, there is every reason to believe that each was literate by eighteenth-century standards.

Many anecdotes from the period have survived about the level of illiteracy among frontier settlers, however. Some of these have been kept alive, even presently, by well-meaning, but otherwise misguided, docents and local antiquarians. Some unwary historians have been led to believe that the literacy of the frontiersmen was uniformly low, and that their speech patterns and written word were of inferior quality. Careful research suggests that this was not the case.[8]

In the seventeenth century, men on the frontier seem to have had a literacy rate of approximately 50 percent. This figure improved to 65 percent by the early eighteenth century. The standard used for defining literacy in these cases was "the ability to sign one's name, a skill that runs parallel though slightly below reading proficiency and likewise runs parallel though slightly above the ability to write." As would be expected, literacy varied greatly with wealth and social class, but it also varied from one ethnic group to another. Based on the examination of wills, deeds, and other public documents, German Protestants and French Huguenots may have been 90 percent literate; while the Scotch-Irish may have been much less so. Nonetheless, fewer than 30 percent of lowland Scots used a "mark" rather than a signature on surviving documents from the mid–eighteenth century, suggesting that as many as 70 percent could write. Ironically, literacy rates in the coastal settlements seem to have been higher in the early colonial period than they were later, and higher among the gentry and craftsmen than among laborers. These patterns in America mirror similar findings for Britain during parallel periods of time.[9]

The availability of books and other reading material can be used as a good indicator of literacy. A few exceptional families owned large collections of books in the backcountry. Forty or fifty volumes was considered a vast library even in the late eighteenth century, but a lack of books in the frontier communities not does not necessarily lead to the conclusion of widespread illiteracy. It was rather a matter of the poor availability of books in general and the priority given to moving tools, provisions, livestock, and firearms through the wilderness on poorly constructed roads. In most frontier estates that reached probate, at least a few books were included in the inventories. These were generally primers, prayer books, practical handbooks on farming, and treatises on medicine. An unusual number of books on mathematics and surveying can be found, denoting not only literacy but mathematical acumen. Nonetheless, the most common book to be found on the frontier was the Bible.

There is evidence that literacy was also associated with gender. Males may have been twice as likely as females to be literate among southern- and middle-Atlantic settlers. In New England the difference was not so pronounced. This evidence needs to be viewed with great care, however. Women were often taught to read because they needed to read the Bible for themselves and to their children. Sometimes female indentures, children when their contracts were signed, were promised reading lessons during their tenure. However, it seems that many of the women who were readers were not taught to write because society saw no need for them to do so. By comparison to the nineteenth century, when women were prolific writers of personal accounts, there were many fewer in the colonial period who left diaries and journals. If writing ability was assumed as the only indicator of literacy, then many more females may have been readers than previously thought.[10]

MEANS OF EMIGRATION

There were three means of coming to America if one did not have the money to do so. Through a system of bounties much like those used to enlist soldiers for the military, agents of the colonial proprietors assembled groups of Britons who contracted themselves to work for a specified number of years for wages. These were represented to be artisans, mechanics, husbandmen, and laborers by the agents, but many—possibly the majority—were from among the economic refuse of the British Isles. In the late colonial period the process of migration became more materialistic, with loads of settlers being crowded into ships whose holds were filled beyond capacity. Many hundreds died at sea due to the spread of disease among the closely confined passages, and some died of starvation when unscrupulous shippers failed to provide enough provisions for the voyage.

Second, through the institution of indenture, tens of thousands came to America as indentured servants with the hope of receiving land or carving out a farmstead of their own at the end of their terms of service. These were given a social status that was little more than that of white slaves, and many of them failed to survive their contracts. Others renewed their indentures at the end of their term and never achieved the status of freemen. Ironically, the indenture provided a stability and predictability to economic life that many unskilled workers sought out because they feared the chronic unemployment that characterized Europe. However, they found that willing workers were a scarce commodity in America, largely because the frontier offered land to anyone willing to work for themselves.

Finally, many persons of black heritage came to America as slaves with no hope of improving their lot. The English, who began the settlement of North America, did not initially envision the use of race-based slave

These historical interpreters of the Pilgrim period, a man and a woman, are aboard the re-created vessel known as *Mayflower II*, which has its home port in Plymouth, Massachusetts, near Plymouth Rock and only a short distance from the Plymouth Plantation historic site. Their clothing is typical of the period of early colonization.

laborers, favoring the use of black and white indentured servants or wage laborers instead. Recent research in this area suggests that the first blacks brought to Virginia were not slaves at all, but black indentures. However, the colonial proprietors and plantation owners found that indentures and wage earners resisted discipline, ran away, attacked their employers, and demanded better treatment more often than black slaves freshly imported from Africa. Consequently, the number of white indentures diminished with time and the number of African slaves increased. The few black indentures quickly became lost in the multitude of black slaves as the distinction between the two blurred with time.

Largely through these three means the thirteen English colonies had, by the time of the French and Indian War (1754), accumulated a population estimated at 1.3 million persons, black and white. This was an overwhelming population advantage over New France, where the population never exceeded 80,000, but the French were massed along a densely populated stretch of the St. Lawrence River that was perhaps eighty miles long. The majority of the English population clung to the coastal settlements and cities, leaving the frontier regions sparsely populated by comparison.

PURITANS AND PILGRIMS

When Elizabeth I ascended the throne of England in 1558, she attempted to ameliorate the religious tensions that racked England by affecting a religious compromise between the Church of England and the Catholic population. Such a compromise was largely unacceptable to those English who remained vehemently anti-Catholic or who viewed the Anglican Church as a corruption of true Protestantism barely distinguishable from the Roman faith. They were disgusted by the remnants of Catholicism found in the continued use of Latin-style vestments and rituals, and they found the Anglican clergy just as overbearing and oppressive as the Roman hierarchy. These Protestants wanted greater purity in the Anglican Church and were known as Puritans.

Puritanism was more than a religious movement. It was also a response to ongoing changes in English society. The center of the Puritan sect could be found in the rural countryside of England, where village life was structured according to a fixed order. While Puritans applauded the right of the each man to worship as an individual in a more direct relationship with God, they retreated from the idea of individuals breaking free from most traditional social and political restraints. In this way the Puritans were social conservatives. Through a regenerated social and political order, Puritans hoped to restore discipline and equilibrium to their society. They stressed a work ethic and were not beyond scrutinizing others for signs of waywardness.[11]

The Puritans formed congregations in which men and women could work together for the mutual salvation of the community. They were not beyond using the machinery of government to coerce those who disagreed with their ideas of Christian purpose. Queen Elizabeth ignored them, but they were persecuted and harassed by her successors, James I and Charles I. Within two decades, Puritan leaders became convinced that their religious and social ideologies could not be carried out in England with a Stuart on the throne.

Having initially sought religious toleration among the Dutch, a group of Puritans (the Pilgrims) were the first religious exiles to reach America. In 1620 about 100 Puritans, together with artisans and laborers of other Protestant sects, settled at Plymouth, Massachusetts. Here they hoped to find "rest from the world . . . in the peace of primitive places" where there existed "the conditions requisite for the absorption of man's soul in God's."[12]

Their settlement was a totalitarian political and social commune. Although the Mayflower Compact was the first document to formalize a government based on the consent of the governed, its signers proved to be authoritarian, restrictive, and narrow-minded. Yet the Pilgrims freely agreed to give up their diversity in order to accomplish the great goals of their community. They generally accepted the idea that the rights of each settler would be sacrificed to the security of the community and that their government would control, direct, or compel most of their daily activities.

The Plymouth plantation grew slowly for a decade, but a great Puritan migration from England began in 1630 when 700 colonists arrived. By 1640 more than 12,000 people had come to the shores of New England. Surrounded by available and generally vacant land,[13] many Puritans began to move away from the centers of authority. They spread out along the Massachusetts coast or formed settlements along the rivers of Connecticut.

The strict central authority envisioned by the Pilgrim fathers quickly created dissension and conflict among the individual towns that sprang up on the edge of the frontier. Notable among the dissenters was Roger Williams, who arrived in New England in 1633. Williams deplored the Puritans' continued attachment to the Church of England and had no intention of changing his own religious views to conform with those of earlier settlers. As a result of his outspoken belligerence he was banished from the Massachusetts colony and escaped his oppressors by forming a colony of his own among the native people of Rhode Island. Another notable was Anne Hutchinson, who quickly became the center of a movement that stressed the mystical elements of Puritanism. The orthodox Puritan clergy of Boston arranged to have her arrested and banished for preaching erroneous theology in 1636, but Anne escaped their reach and followed Roger Williams to Rhode Island.

Individualism like that expressed by Williams and Hutchinson proved to be the greatest threat to the Puritan theocracy in New England. Regardless of the number of people banished, the colony could not have remained a monolith of absolute Puritanism. An increasing tide of immigration, the expansion of frontier settlements, trade with neighboring colonies, and interaction with the native peoples all worked against the concept of maintaining a closed community established on a single, immutable set of religious foundations.

FRONTIER RELIGION

Succeeding generations of New Englanders worked their way inland by 1710, and within only a few years had established churches, ministries, and in many cases altogether new religious sects. Among the earliest settlers of the New Jersey frontier were those who described themselves as Presbyterians, Episcopalians, or Baptists from the New England colonies. Many individual preachers came to dominate these flocks, and local churches became "citadels of pietism in the wilderness" where frontier populations "sang, prayed, exhorted, admonished, and searched their own souls and one another's."[14]

Nonetheless, many frontier families settled so far from the precincts of any established church that their children were raised with no formal religious instruction. As late as 1768, William Frazer, a missionary serving in western New Jersey, wrote that "a great many families . . . call themselves Church of England people from no other principle as I can find than because it was the religion of their fathers [and many had] arrived to the age of 40 who never in their lives had been to hear a church minister."[15]

THE SCOTCH-IRISH

Beginning in the first decade of the eighteenth century, the Scotch-Irish (also called Ulster Scots) began to arrive at the port of Philadelphia. They were predominantly Presbyterians taking their basic beliefs from the scriptural interpretations of John Knox. Having chaffed under the yoke of English rule in Scotland and northern Ireland, the Scotch-Irish were accustomed to act independent of the mainstream churches. Having pushed the Irish Catholic population out of Ulster, these Scots formed a hatred for the English during the attempt to force Anglicanism upon them. They detested the members of the Church of England for their intolerance and despised the tolerant Quakers for their pacifism. Although the beliefs of the Scotch-Irish Presbyterians and the New England churches were similar, the two groups chose separate paths in America.

On the frontier, the tough-minded Scotch-Irish held to their contrary views. Large numbers of them were either actively anti-English or unwilling to work cooperatively with English authorities. Unlike the Quakers, who scrupulously paid for Indian land, the Scotch-Irish unabashedly believed that they were foreordained by Scripture to take their land from the Indians, by force if necessary. "On the frontier, the Scotch-Irish were hewing their way through the woods, killing Indians when it suited them, and developing a righteous indignation against the restraining orders which came from the government."[16] Even contemporary members of the Presbyterian movement became critical of the Scotch-Irish attitudes, claiming that they were "productive of confusion . . . and the most wicked and destructive of doctrines and practices."[17]

Tracing the movements of the Scotch-Irish immigrants has proved difficult for historians and genealogists because a large number of British colonists, who were also Presbyterians with Scottish or Irish surnames but not part of this immigrant group, may have moved to the frontier from New England. The bloody repression of the Scottish Rebellion of 1745–1746 also greatly increased the number of Scottish immigrants who had no Irish connection. These were inexorably intermingled in the surviving genealogical evidence with the true Ulster Scots.[18] It seems certain that the Scotch-Irish who began to arrive in 1728 turned largely toward the Maryland, Virginia, and Carolina frontiers. There is also evidence of a movement of Scotch-Irish families from Philadelphia northward into northern New Jersey. The peak periods of Scotch-Irish emigration thereafter were in 1741, 1755, and 1767, and they continued to trickle onto the frontiers in lesser numbers by passing through the settlements to live on the very edge of civilization until the American Revolution.[19]

The French and Indian War had an important effect on the frontier outposts, and many hundreds of Scotch-Irish fell victim to the depredations of the Indians. Nearly all of the inhabitants of certain regions of the frontier were driven back into the more settled areas by the threat of Indian attack. Thereafter, many Scotch-Irish settlers elected to remain away from the frontiers, thereby permanently erasing the evidence of their early pioneering efforts from the available records.[20]

THE DUTCH

The Calvinist Dutch, and their religious brethren, the Flemish Walloons and French Huguenots, had a significant influence on frontier life. Their greatest concentration was to be found on the island of Manhattan in the settlement of New Amsterdam and at Fort Orange on the Hudson River at Albany. Coming largely from these older settlements established in the seventeenth century, the Dutch penetrated the frontier by expanding their settlements along Indian trails, rivers, and their tributaries.

Given an early start in the exploration and settlement of the New Netherlands colony, the directors of the Dutch West India Company in Holland nonetheless had great difficulty in finding settlers of an appropriate type from among the native Dutch. The directors of the company therefore enlisted a number of foreign religious refugees among their settlers to America. The company's own orders required all settlers to be members of the Dutch Reformed Church (a Calvinist faith), and this may account for the large proportion of Walloons and Huguenots who answered the call. Walloons were French-speaking Calvinists from the southernmost provinces of the Spanish Netherlands. The Huguenots were Protestant refugees from within France. Both the Walloons and Huguenots were targets of the relentless persecution of the Catholic regimes of Spain and France, respectively. A great wave of Huguenot emigration began in 1685 when the Edict of Nantes was revoked and French Protestants were once again made subject to religious persecution.

The early activities of the Dutch West India Company are not clear in the historical record mainly because its business records were systematically destroyed in the nineteenth century. Yet from surviving letters and other miscellaneous documents much can be known of the early history of the Dutch colony. The Dutch Reformed minister Jonas Michaelius was a prolific letter writer. When Michaelius arrived in New Amsterdam in 1628 to oversee the organization of the Dutch Reformed religion in the colony, he found that there was no formal establishment of religion. The erection of churches for religious denominations other than the Reformed sect was forbidden, but a substantial number of Spaniards, Portuguese, and Italians—all nominally members of some Protestant sect—were permitted their private religious worship. Michaelius quickly exerted himself in an effort toward religious conformity among the settlers, but found that he sometimes had to give his sermons in French for the Walloons and Huguenots at the service who understood Dutch only poorly.[21]

By 1653 there were several Dutch Reformed ministers less tolerant than Michaelius serving the colony. Of the religious sects in their midst, only a growing number of English Presbyterians seem to have followed an "acceptable" form of worship. Ostensibly fearing the spread of heresy in the colony, these ministers railed against any deviation from the prescribed forms of worship and praised the Dutch governor, Peter Stuyvesant, when he jailed a group of Lutherans for worshiping contrary to the law. The directors of the Dutch West India Company in Holland, valuing profit over orthodoxy, ordered Stuyvesant to release those who had been jailed and to tolerate variations in worship as long as they were held privately. Even a small conclave of Sephardic Jews, those whose ancestry lay in the Iberian peninsula, was tolerated. It is clear from other surviving papers, however, that the Dutch in New Netherlands held a particular hatred for the French Jesuits of Canada that went beyond mere theological differences to include "all things Catholic."[22]

The flood of Dutch emigration to New Netherlands survived the change to English governance under the managers appointed by the Duke of York in 1664, and it was bolstered by accession to the English throne of William of Orange in 1688. His acceptance of the English throne, and the decade of war with France that followed, created an alliance of Dutch and English interests that helped to reinforce anti-Catholic sentiment in the English colonies. Dutch emigration to America remained significant until about 1735. Hundreds of families came by boat to the present site of New Brunswick, New Jersey, to ascend the rivers advancing north and west into New Jersey and Pennsylvania.

They also came south from the older Dutch settlements on the Hudson River. A number of Dutch settlements were scattered along the route known as the Old Mine Road (U.S. Rt. 209) from Ulster County, New York, south into and beyond the Delaware Water Gap of Pennsylvania. The Dutch quickly dominated the local area. In 1737 there were no fewer than four Dutch Reformed churches serving both sides of the Delaware River from present-day Port Jervis, New York, to the water gap—a distance of only forty miles. The influence of the Dutch was so strong that several families with English roots were attending Dutch churches and speaking the Dutch language as their own within two decades of their arrival.[23]

QUAKERS

Quakers, or Friends, made extraordinary efforts to develop the Delaware River valley and southeastern Pennsylvania, and their influence contributed strongly to the formulation of a uniquely characteristic colonial frontiersman and settler. William Penn personally directed the development of his royal grant of land in America during the seventeenth century, and by the beginning of the eighteenth century his efforts had created the most successful of all the English colonies as measured by contemporary standards. In 1739 Andrew Hamilton, a Pennsylvania lawyer, ascribed the success of the colony to the form of government dictated by Penn in 1682 in his *Frame of Government for Pennsylvania*.

In dictating the form of government for his colony, Penn strayed from his Quaker belief in decentralized authority. Yet some historians have suggested that the success of the colony can actually be found in the inability of Quakers to run an efficient government under Penn's rules while strictly following their religious tenets. "Even in the earliest years, they were able to govern only by compromising one principle after another." They thereby avoided some of the creeping paralysis that affected the rigidly orthodox governments of New England.[24]

Penn recruited his Quaker population disproportionately from among the Cheshire and Welsh farmsteads of England. He could not have found a better group to settle the frontier than these Quaker farmers. For generations they had successfully carved a living in a difficult environment, and they combined their religion and farming experience into a spiritual framework that well served the economically challenging conditions of the frontier. The subsequent settlement pattern, agricultural policy, and behavior largely reflected their religion and led to their economic dominance in the eighteenth century.

Quakerism was begun in seventeenth century England by George Fox and Margaret Fell. The first adherents to the new sect—many of whom were of Welsh ancestry—were drawn largely from farmers who lived on the fringe of the cultural, economic, and social mainstream. Quakerism was a radical religion that attracted these generally independent people by preaching the virtues of the family as the basic disciplining and spiritualizing authority in society as opposed to that of magistrates and church prelates. Thanks in part to their devotion to the decentralization of authority, many Quakers were more comfortable in the vast spaces of the American forests than were the New Englanders who had come from more densely populated villages in the southeast of England.[25]

Quakers devoted themselves to their religious duties by creating nearly autonomous moral households. Everything in the Quaker household—wives, children, and business—was subjected to a familial order based in morality. The burden of producing, sustaining, and incorporating morality, and civic and economic virtues, into the household was taken on by the entire family and supported by the community. Outside authorities such as an intolerant established priesthood, an authoritarian upper class, or even a pedantic university system were considered "not only unnecessary but even pernicious."[26]

The Quaker community gave unprecedented moral authority within the household and within the congregation to the women of their sect. They thereby radically changed the traditional English household, especially in the areas of authority over child rearing, courtship, and marriage. Women were encouraged to discuss and legislate on "women's matters" in specially designed women's meetings set up for the primary purpose of controlling courtship and marriage within the community. No fewer than twelve female "ministers" have been identified as being active between 1690 and 1765 in the region of initial Quaker settlement.[27]

Quaker fathers devoted a great deal of their energy to the accumulation of land that would be devolved onto their sons, or would otherwise benefit their daughters. The availability of large tracts of undeveloped land was one factor that caused the overwhelming majority of Quaker children in America to marry other Quakers locally and stay within the Quaker meeting discipline. The Quakers on the frontier quickly found themselves related to one another not only by religion but also by shared genetics. This web of kinship was partly responsible for the strong community ties exhibited by a community of people who were otherwise defiantly anti-institutional.[28]

In applying their principles Quakers relied heavily upon a religious and spiritual form of human relations. They radically reorganized their church from one that required the performance of a series of external disciplines and the reception of a well-prepared sermon, as among the Puritans, into one in which the silent meeting and a personal conversion took precedence.[29]

The first town named by Penn in 1682 was Chester, which was situated on the Delaware River. Here the land-claim boundaries of Pennsylvania, Delaware, and New Jersey almost came together. The basic unit of Quaker settlement was the family farm of about 250 to 300 acres—an initial size to which much was added with time. The holdings were widely dispersed, and Quaker farmers were accustomed to moving about on horseback over an undulating and often flat countryside. All roads tended with time to lead to the meeting house. By 1720 every township in Penn's original grant to the Quakers had a meeting house. Pennsylvania roads, unlike those in other sections of the colonial countryside, tended to form as the spokes of a wheel with the meeting house at the hub. Remnants of this characteristic road pattern can be observed even today in this region of the state. The city of Gettysburg, Pennsylvania (noted for the American Civil War battle fought there in 1863), exhibits this pattern of development.

THE GERMANS

The German settlers in America were generally Lutherans, but they are often confused with several other related Protestant sects belonging to the Pietist tradition. The settlement of German Lutherans on the frontier is generally thought to have come later than that of the Pietist groups, and many historians consider them to have come nearly destitute to the frontiers. However, like the Pilgrims of New England, the German Protestants on the frontier were noted for their somber clothing and sparse households, which may have been more illustrative of their dedication to a conservative simplicity rather than to their poverty.

Many scattered German-speaking settlements were establish on the frontier early in the eighteenth century. A large number of Palatine Germans, who had originally settled the Mohawk River valley and the Schoharie lands in New York, emigrated to the Delaware River valley and Berks County in Pennsylvania. Many of these were disgruntled remnants of the Palatine emigration to the Hudson River plantations of Robert Livingston in New York that had begun in 1710. In 1717 another group of Palatines whose ship was blown off course for New York landed in Philadelphia. Striking overland for New York on the Old York Road, many of them, having become enamored with the region, chose to settle along the way in Pennsylvania and New Jersey. The Palatines (incorrectly called Pennsylvania Dutch) maintained close relations among themselves.[30]

Beginning about 1740, a separate flood of German Lutherans began to enter the colonies, and the pace of this immigration did not falter until the advent of the American Revolution. By 1750 they had penetrated into the far northwestern portion of New Jersey and west into the region of Reading and Harrisburg, Pennsylvania. They tended to separate themselves from other groups, a process aided by their lack of the English language. Joshua Gilpin, traveling through this region, noted, "I never knew before the total want of a language for in this respect we might as well have been in the middle of Germany." Isolated in this manner the Germans achieved a far greater social solidarity than any other group on the frontier.[31]

The German Baptists were leaders among those who first experienced a great religious awakening in America. On the whole they were sober and collected, and their religion valued simplicity, justice, and mercy.

This detail from a print in the authors' collection is of a street scene in Philadelphia in the early part of the eighteenth century. Note the slave with the basket in the foreground, and the cart and wagons in the background. Substantial buildings like these could be found in the city because Pennsylvania, as one of the most successful of all the English colonies, attracted wealthy and prominent persons as well as immigrant pioneers.

They tried to revive plainness of dress and manner in their everyday lives. They attempted to reinstitute many of the customs of the early Christian Church such as the washing of feet and complete immersion for baptism from which they became known as "Dunkers." Dunkers eschewed religious and denominational controversies as unchristian, preferring pleasing, contemplative, and reaffirming sermons to those that espoused dogmatic confrontation and brutal orthodoxy within the congregation.[32]

MORAVIANS

The Moravians were among the least fanatical of the Protestant sects who came to America. With roots in the teachings of John Huss and John Wycliffe, the Moravians (Fratres Unitas) had become one of the most important Protestants groups in central Europe at the beginning of the seventeenth century. Nonetheless, they suffered decades of persecution in the Thirty Years' War (1618–1648) being hounded from their homes until only a few faithful families were left in the sect by the end of the century. In 1722 almost the entire surviving Moravian congregation could be found on the estate of their protector, Count Nikolaus von Zinzerdorf of Saxony. From there they began to spread their faith to the West Indies, Africa, Asia, and North and South America. From their London center they influenced John Wesley, a leader in the evangelical movement in the Anglican Church and the founder of Methodism. By 1735, many Moravians had turned to the New World for religious freedom.

Although the Moravians professed a common unity among all Christians, this goal proved too high-minded for most persons dedicated to a more narrow field of church dogma. Moravians refused to take an oath or to bear arms in times of war. Consequently, they were viewed with a good deal of suspicion by the majority of other German Protestant sects on the American frontier.[33]

In 1735 the first Moravians entered North America through Philadelphia. The headquarters of the Moravian mission in America was located for a long time in the town of Bethlehem on the banks of the Lehigh River. From here they established additional settlements, particularly at Nazareth, to which they built a substantial wagon road. The Moravians conscientiously paid the Indians for the land that they settled. In fact, by 1755 they had paid for it several times distributing funds to various groups of Indians over the years as new claims were made against them.[34]

During 1743 two Moravian preachers, Leonhard Schnell, a German, and Robert Hussey, an English convert from Anglicanism, traveled the Warrior's Path south through Maryland and the valley of the Shenandoah River making converts as far south as the Carolinas and Georgia. Schnell found the frontier people spiritually hungry because they had had no minister for many years. He was particularly successful in converting emigrant Germans in these frontier communities who had not heard a sermon in the German language for several years.[35]

After a missionary tour of more than 500 miles on foot, the two preachers returned to Pennsylvania by sea. Soon their missionary work bore fruit as other Moravians began settlements at Bethabara, Bethania, and Salem in North Carolina. From Salem the Moravian preachers set out to preach on the frontier, "miraculously [preserving] some of the Christian virtues of medieval monasticism: altruism, self-denial, meditation, industry, frugality, and selfless submission to discipline."[36]

AFRICANS

There was a significant African presence on the frontier. Almost all the Africans who came to America came as slaves. Ethnologists have determined that most African Americans can be traced by lineage to one of only thirteen tribes who inhabited the western part of the African continent. These tribal societies were largely agricultural ones. The blacks who came to America as slaves, therefore, were already experts in farming methodologies and animal husbandry.

Some blacks of African heritage came to America as freemen, wage earners, sailors, artisans, and craftspersons. Many of these moved out onto the frontier to escape white prejudice in the coastal communities. While this was particularly true of the southern colonies, it should be remembered that race-based slavery was not isolated there. It was a legally recognized institution throughout the English colonies, and many New England communities had large numbers of black slaves counted among their populations.[37]

The black frontier experience was otherwise little different than that of white settlers. Native Americans were no more tolerant of blacks invading their lands than they were of whites. Black families were just as likely to be attacked and slain as were white families, and blacks were given no special consideration when it came to adoption or torture. A significant exception to this was the case of the Florida wilderness, where Indians and escaped black slaves seem to have formed an alliance to resist both the Spanish and the English. This alliance lasted well into the nineteenth century.

In the earliest years of black slavery, the new arrivals from Africa depended heavily on their own tribal religions and cultural practices. With time many African religious practices came to be fused with Christianity. Yet white English society deemed the simplest vestiges of African culture as pagan, innately evil, and inconsistent with Christianity. In New England, among the Puritans, even the most remote hint of aboriginal religious practice brought charges of witchcraft, incarceration, torture, or worse. White ministers, therefore, absolutely forbade the simplest forms of African culture to be retained by blacks and strove to completely eliminate any cultural memories from among blacks living in the New World.[38]

NEW- AND OLD-STYLE CALENDARS

On May 22, 1752, King George II approved a bill that reformed the calendar then in use and eliminated eleven days from the year. The bill, passed by Parliament, proposed that all of Great Britain and its colonies switch from the Julian calendar, which had been used for centuries in one form or another, to the Gregorian system, which had been implemented in much of the Catholic world in 1582. The act stipulated that the day following Wednesday, September 2, 1752, would be Thursday, September 14, 1752. Moreover, New Year's Day in England would move from March 25 to January 1.

The problem that instigated the change was that the old calendar was imprecise as to the actual length of the year. The Julian cycle was more than eleven minutes short, causing the beginning of the astronomical "New Year" to drift through the calendar as the missing minutes, hours, and days accumulated over the centuries. Hipparchus of Alexandria had noticed the difference in the second century A.D. by taking careful astronomical observations of Earth's relative position with the stars, and in the centuries that followed Arab astronomers and others had proven that the old calendar was simply wrong.

Parliament took great pains to minimize the problems that would be associated with the changeover that would skip all the dates between September 2 and September 14, 1752. These included matters of banking, the celebration of holidays, the payments of debts and rents, and the duration of indentures and contracts of every kind. Wages and interest were to be paid without counting the missing eleven days, but the dates of birth before the reform and the computation of age for legal matters continued to be based on the old style. Although it was impossible to ignore the new dates in matters of commerce and public business, many Protestants refused to acknowledge the reform privately.

Beginning in 1753, the marking of many of the inscriptions on tombs and graves as *O.S.* (Old Style) or *N.S.* (New Style) became common. It was said that Catholic and Protestant graves from this period could be sorted out by these markings. The change also led to a number of riots in England. In Bristol several people were killed when they rioted to maintain Christmas Day on January 5 (*Old Style*) rather than December 25 (*New Style*). A popular rhyme of the anti-reform protesters was:

> In seventeen hundred and fifty-three
> The style was changed to Popery.[39]

In Anglo-America much less notice was taken of the reform. Benjamin Franklin noted in *Poor Richard's Almanac*:

Be not astonished, nor look with scorn, dear reader, at such a deduction of days, nor regret as for the loss of so much time, but take this for your consolation, that your expenses will appear lighter and your mind be more at ease. And what an indulgence is here, for those who love their pillow to lie down in peace on the second of the month and not perhaps awake till the morning of the fourteenth.[40]

FARMING

Growing tobacco saved the southern colonies from extinction once the quest for gold and precious metals had been quelled by failure. Tobacco was used in lieu of cash payments and as collateral for loans. Tobacco bonds, which encumbered the profits of future crops, were even accepted in lieu of taxes. But intensive tobacco farming was hard on the soil, stripping it of valuable nutrients that could not easily be replaced in an era before synthetic fertilizers.

Settlers in the backcountry added new acreage to their farmsteads each year by clearing the land. Those considered the most able farmers cleared the land by cutting down all the trees in early summer, hauling off the valuable logs and leaving the least valuable wood and branches on the ground until the following spring. This was scavenged for firewood during the winter, and the leavings were burned in the early spring to complete the clearing. The burning left a layer of fine ash to fertilize and soften the ground between the remaining stumps. The stumps were usually allowed to rot of their own accord, but they could be pulled after a few years with the help of team of oxen. Once the stumps were removed, the rocks and boulders could be dragged to the edges of the field on a sledge and dumped. In the winter these stones could be made up into walls for the enclosure of sheep or cattle, but only on the oldest farms were stone walls laid up in this manner.

Indian corn was usually planted in a new field, which was commonly prepared by the use of a hoe alone. This and the axe were the most widely used farm implements on the frontier. The average farmer devoted most of his fields to hay, which could be planted among the stumps because it was gathered with the use of a hand sickle. The plow could be driven through the open ground between the stumps or in meadows, but it was not generally used until the majority of the stumps, roots, and rocks were removed. The French required that habitants clear about two acres of new ground each year, and English farmers were capable of doing about the same. The average farmer tended about eighteen acres of crops on a hundred-acre farm. The acreage not put directly into crop production was used as pasture and woodlots, or was left as fallow ground to recuperate from several seasons of overfarming. Small kitchen-garden plots, which included a variety of herbs and greens, surrounded the family home.

The native American farmer was not unlike the colonial one. Both followed the annual cycles of preparing the ground, planting, tending, and harvesting dictated by the seasonal changes in the weather. Colonial agriculture was different in that both men and women tended the crops. Colonists tended to segregate their crops into single-species plots having furrows, while the Indians mixed their corn, bean, and squash plants in hillocks scattered about their fields. The Indian method was less efficient in terms of space, but their fields were easier to weed and required less detailed preparation of the soil. Both colonials and native Americans grew corn, beans, squash, pumpkins, cucumbers, some tubers such as potatoes or yams, and the ubiquitous tobacco plant. Only the Europeans produced wheat, rye, barley, flax, and hay. Colonials grew medicinal plants in small plots near their homes, while Indians generally gathered such plants from the wild.

Both colonials and Indians used seaweed, clam and oyster shells, fish, ashes, and bonemeal to improve their soil. Neither the colonials nor the Indians spent a great deal of time using animal fertilizers, however. This may have been because virgin land was plentiful, but also because fertilization was a new idea to the colonists. It was not until several decades had passed that the earliest settlers noticed a change in the soil that they were farming. At first it had been dark, almost black, but with time its color became lighter, and crop yields fell. Scientific agriculturalists in England, like Jethro Tull, believed that active cultivation of the soil was the secret of its fertility. Deep plowing was his answer to diminished crop yields, as this helped to dry out wet land and allowed the soil to better utilize rainfall.

Jared Elliot, a minister and doctor from Connecticut, correctly believed that the fertility of the soil was associated with the organic matter that it contained. He showed that the addition of swamp mud to the soil increased the yield and improved the crops, and he was one of the first to note that certain crops rebuilt the soil. Ultimately, he was able to show that animal manures, cover crops of red clover and timothy, and a year's rest between plantings could significantly improve agricultural production. Later experiments showed that root crops such as turnips and carrots helped the soil. Moreover, turnips could be used as winter feed for livestock.[41]

Husbandry

The greatest difference between native American and European agricultural practices was that of animal husbandry. Natives had no conception of the breeding or ownership of animals. The deer, beaver, bear, and moose of the frontier were not owned until they were killed during the hunt. Colonials claimed year-round ownership during the life of their livestock. Moreover, the pigs, cattle, sheep, and horses of Europeans were far different than the wild prey usually consumed by Indians.

It can be said that the greatest visible differences between Indian agriculture and colonial farming were hogs and hay. Hogs were of great value to the colonials because they reproduced themselves in large numbers and fed themselves in the brushwood. Unlike sheep and goats, they were able to hold their own against the depredations of wolves and other carnivores. They required almost no care until the fall slaughter, and provided meat that preserved well when salted, smoked, or pickled. Besides, pork was much more tasty than preserved beef or mutton that had grazed in the open woodlands. A long-legged variety of hog, somewhat leaner than modern types, was favored by colonials. The hogs needed to be good walkers because they were often driven in herds to market.[42]

MAKING HAY

The Indians had no need for hayfields because they kept no livestock, but their abandoned fields quickly became overgrown with grasses and brush. Early settlers often loosed their livestock to graze in these fields, but the native grasses proved less nutrious than European varieties. The animals imported from Europe often brought with them as part of their manure common European grass seeds from their shipboard fodder. These grasses, spreading naturally in the older settlements, were obviously superior to native grasses. This led colonial farmers to import English grass seeds such as bluegrass and white clover to the frontier.

Making hay was a difficult and time-consuming task. The hayfield was cut by hand, dried in the sun, turned to dry the reverse side, and then gathered for storage. Hay could be stored in a barn or loft for winter feeding, or it could be gathered up into a stack or mound. The shape and structure of these haystacks differed from one community to another and seems to have been dictated by the country of origin of the local settlers. Hay could usually be made from the same field twice a year. It required one cleared acre to produce the hay needed to winter a cow or an ox, and a little more, plus some grain, to winter a horse.[43]

WOLF HUNTS

The cry of a wolf surely must have chilled the blood of the early settlers. To the frontier farmers the call represented a threat that was economic as well as personal. Wolves preyed on the livestock, which provided a substantial part of the comfort, sustenance, and wealth of the settlers. As early as 1645 the Massachusetts General Court complained of "the great loss and damage" suffered because the wolves killed "so great numbers of our cattle." As farmers brought increasing numbers of domesticated animals into the frontier region, the wolf population grew, and the number of attacks increased.[44]

In an effort to stem the ravages of these predators, town meetings throughout the colonies voted bounties for each wolf killed. These ranged from cash payments from as little as twopence to as much as ten shillings, in cash or bushels of grain. Indians who hunted wolves were sometimes paid with gunpowder and shot. All owners of livestock in the town were required to contribute to pay the bounties awarded. Such payments created a market for wolves that appealed to many, especially Indians. Nonetheless the bounties created problems of their own. Bounties were sometimes claimed for wolves that were caught at great distances from a town. In fact, they might even have been preying on the livestock of another town entirely. Some hunters tried to collect twice on the same wolf's head. To prevent this, towns resorted to cutting off the ears of a redeemed wolf and burying them separately from the rest of the head.[45]

Full-scale wolf hunts were sometimes organized. A contemporary notice informed residents: "It was voted and agreed that the next Thursday should be the day to go upon this work of killing wolves. . . . All persons to be ready by seven of the clock in the morning and meet upon the hill at the meeting house by the beat of the drum."[46] Another strategy used against wolves called for clearing swamps, thickets, rubbish yards, waste grounds, and "harboring stuff" that provided shelter for wolves.[47]

Wolf heads were nailed to posts and doors to publicize their capture. Particularly bothersome wolves could be a nuisance and their capture brought momentary prominence and an additional reward to the lucky hunter. Israel Putnam, famous for his daring escape from the British in Connecticut during the American Revolution, was already noted for his bravery after he single-handedly captured and killed a wolf that had been terrorizing his town.

NOTES

1. This act made no practical difference, but the traditions of Connecticut make much of it nonetheless.
2. David Hackett Fischer, *Albion's Seed: Four British Folkways in America* (New York: Oxford University Press, 1989), 6. This work is essential reading for those doing research in the area of cultural and social history during the colonial period. Fischer called these categories of characteristics "folkways."
3. Ibid., 6–11.
4. See the chart offered in ibid., 804.
5. Robert Leckie, *A Few Acres of Snow: The Saga of the French and Indian Wars* (New York: John Wiley & Sons, 1999), 258.
6. Ibid., 259.
7. Fischer, 610, 610 n.
8. Ibid., 716.
9. Selma R. Williams, *Demeter's Daughters: The Women Who Founded America, 1587–1789* (New York: Atheneum, 1976), 109.
10. See Dorothy Denneen Volo and James M. Volo, *Daily Life in Civil War America* (Westport, CT: Greenwood Press, 1998); and James M. Volo and Dorothy Denneen Volo, *Encyclopedia of the Antebellum South* (Westport: Greenwood Press, 2000).
11. Gary B. Nash, *Red, White, and Black: The Peoples of Early America* Englewood Cliffs, NJ: (Prentice-Hall, 1982), 68–69.
12. Paul A. W. Wallace, *Conrad Weiser: Friend of Colonist and Mohawk, 1696–1760* (Lewisburg, PA: Wennawoods, 1996), 51–53.
13. Much of the native population of coastal New England had succumbed to

disease brought from Europe by fishermen and traders leaving cleared fields and untended orchards behind for the English to occupy.

14. Wallace, 53.

15. Henry Race, "Rev. William Frazer's Three Parishes: St. Thomas's, St. Andrew's, and Musconetcong, New Jersey, 1768–1770," *The Pennsylvania Magazine of History and Biography*, 12 (1888), 214.

16. Louis B. Wright, *The Atlantic Frontier: Colonial American Civilization, 1607–1763* (New York: Alfred A. Knopf, 1951), 224.

17. Parke Rouse Jr., *The Great Wagon Road from Philadelphia to the South* (New York: McGraw-Hill, 1973), 59.

18. Rouse, 54.

19. Fischer, 606.

20. Peter O. Wacker, *The Musconetcong Valley of New Jersey: A Historical Geography* (New Brunswick, NJ: Rutgers University Press, 1968), 40–42.

21. Wright, 164–168.

22. Ibid., 10.

23. Wacker, 42; George W. Cummins, *History of Warren County* (New York: Lewis Historical, 1922), 73.

24. Daniel J. Boorstin, *The Americans: The Colonial Experience* (New York: Vintage Books, 1958), 43.

25. Ralph Bennett, ed., *Settlements in the Americas: Cross-Cultural Perspectives* (Newark: University of Delaware Press, 1993), 146.

26. Ibid., 149.

27. Ibid., 169.

28. Ibid., 152–153.

29. Ibid., 152, 157.

30. Wacker, 35–36.

31. Ibid., 50–51; Joshua Glipin, "Journey to Bethlehem," *The Pennsylvania Magazine of History and Biography* 46 (1922), 25.

32. Wallace, 54.

33. Ibid., 56.

34. Ibid., 72.

35. Rouse, 37–42.

36. Ibid., 78.

37. The state of Connecticut had 3,000 slaves among its population as late as 1848.

38. See James M. Volo and Dorothy Denneen Volo, *Encyclopedia of the Antebellum South*.

39. David Ewing Duncan, *Calendar: Humanity's Struggle to Determine a True and Accurate Year* (New York: Avon Books, 1998), 287. Many countries where the Greek Orthodox religion was common refused to change over to the new calender until the twentieth century.

40. Ibid., 288. The grave monuments of George Washington and Thomas Jefferson bear *O.S.* and *N.S.* marks, respectively.

41. For a short history of these concepts, see U.S. Department of Agriculture, *Early American Soil Conservationists* (Washington, DC: Soil Conservation Service, 1990).

42. William Cronon, *Changes in the Land, Indians, Colonists, and the Ecology of New England* (New York: Hill and Wang, 1983), 129.

43. Ibid., 142.

44. Ibid., 132.

45. Ibid., 132–133.

46. Elizabeth George Spears, *Life in Colonial America* (New York: Random House, 1963), 83.

47. Cronon, 133.

6

Family and Household

If ever two were one, then surely we . . .
—Anne Bradstreet, "To My Dear and Loving Husband"

Men and women on the colonial frontier spent most of their time living
and working side by side. A wife was expected to manage the household
and to care for the children, but she was also expected to help in the
economic affairs of her husband, acting as his representative or even his
surrogate, if the situation warranted. A husband was expected to provide
for his family and to guide and educate his children. The daily routines
and tasks of a husband and a wife might have been very distinct, but
they worked toward a common goal, the well-being of the family. A
husband and wife, and in fact all family members, were interdependent.
Each and every member was expected to contribute to the welfare of the
family unit as their gender, age, and ability permitted.

Marriage was presumed for all adult men and women. There simply
was no acceptable place for sexual expression outside of marriage. This
was particularly true in New England, where legal as well as religious
authority prohibited any extramarital sexual activity. Communities
feared that unmarried mothers would not be able to provide for themselves and would ultimately be a drain on the community. If pregnancy
occured outside of marriage, the couple was expected to wed or face the
wrath of the community. Consequently, contemporary records show a

remarkable number of "early term births" six or seven months after their parents were married.

Generally, the selection of a career was a prerequisite for a man to assert his freedom from childhood and establish himself as an adult. Only after a man had chosen a career and was financially solvent was he able to contemplate marriage and children. If he came from a family of wealth, a man had numerous employment options within certain expectations. In seventeenth-century New England he was expected to choose an occupation useful to God, his community, and his family. As the eighteenth century progressed, however, considerations became more secular. Decisions as to who would farm, who would be apprenticed, or who would be sent for advanced schooling were made to benefit the family as a whole. These determinations were not always equitable from the individual's point of view, but this was a secondary consideration to a greater good—the welfare of the family. Those young men who had few family connections or wealth were subject to serving out their lives as laborers. Of course in America, one could strike out into the forests to carve out a farm. But as settlements grew, farming opportunities became more limited, and more young men were forced farther into the wilderness in order to find sufficient land to set up a farmstead of their own.

Women did not have even the limited choices provided to men. The few occupations open to them produced little income. Women who remained unmarried often lived with other relatives. If they were not the female head of the household, they were awkwardly placed in the family scheme. Many of these women made their contribution by spinning flax and wool. They would spin for their own household and could also bring in additional income by spinning for other families. It is from this practice that the term *spinster* has come to refer to an older unmarried woman.

When it came to the selection of a wife, a man searched for a woman with a good temper and a virtuous demeanor. Certainly, a woman who was fair of face was desirable, but with the demographics of the time good looks probably were a secondary consideration. Men outnumbered women in seventeenth-century settlements, a situation that persisted into the eighteenth century and remained true even longer on the frontier. Upon the death of his wife in 1732, Thomas Clap, a minister in Windham, Connecticut, recorded these thoughts about his selection of a spouse: "I thought I wanted one near Friend & Acquaintance, that should be another Self & Help-Meet for me. Among all the Qualifications of an Agreeable Consort. I seemed more especially to have in my View these Two viz. A steady Serene & Pleasant Natural Temper, and True Piety: For these Two Qualifications seemed most directly to Conduce my real

Comfort, Contentment & Happiness both in this World and that which is to come."[1]

Naturally, some men sought a woman who came with a dowry or an annual allowance. Such a quest might even be inspired by a young man's family hoping to improve its own situation with a judicious union. Generally, once a woman married all of her property and money came under the control of her husband.

COURTSHIP

When a man became interested in a woman he had to move carefully, or he risked gossip and possibly legal action. Custom dictated that he speak to both the young woman's parents and his own in advance of any active courtship. The effect of a disapproval by the young man's parents caused the typical personal tensions such a polarization would naturally spawn. Usually, however, their only control over his actions was based in economics. Failure to select a young woman acceptable to his parents might cause them to withhold a marriage gift or even limit a future inheritance.

Samuel Sewall noted in his diary: "Col. Wm. Dudley calls, and after other discourse, ask'd me (leave) to wait on my daughter, Judith . . . I answered it was reported he had applied to her and he said nothing to me . . . His waiting on her might cause some Umbrage: I would speak with her first."[2] Samuel Sewall was not pleased with the prospect of having Col. Dudley as a son-in-law, and Dudley's failure to observe convention did not advance his situation. Less than two months later Sewall wrote, "Mr. Cooper asks my consent for Judith's Company; which I freely grant him."[3]

The advice of friends and relatives, who often acted as intermediaries between the couple, was also sought. After Sewall's rebuff, Col. Dudley sought an intermediary to assist him in his petition. Two weeks later Sewall noted: "Gov. Dudley visits me . . . speaks to me on behalf of Col. Wm. Dudley, that I would give him leave that he might visit my daughter Judith. I said 'twas a weighty matter. I would consider of it."[4] If Sewall gave Dudley any consideration because of the intercession of the governor, it did not change his opinion of Col. Dudley. Judith and William Cooper were married about five months later.

Nonetheless, such allies could ascertain the true feelings of each of the parties and parents prior to the commencement of formal courtship. This saved both the man and the woman potential embarrassment if one was not interested in the other. In small communities, everyone would be aware if a young man was making frequent visits to a young woman. If such visits suddenly stopped, the rejected party would be subjected to certain humiliation and gossip.

If the consent of a willing young woman's parents was not attained beforehand, the young man risked being brought into court for stealing the affections of their daughter. New England records have numerous instances of young men being fined for such offenses. If a young woman was of age, however, she could not legally be prevented from marrying her suitor. As with the young man, her parent's major weapon was financial.

Once married, a man was required to provide for his wife and children. A husband and wife may have labored together for the benefit of the entire family, but when financial hardship loomed, both the courts and the community looked to the husband to supply a remedy. In his 1712 sermon, "The Well-Ordered Family," Benjamin Wadsworth reminded husbands of their divine mandate to "contrive prudently and work diligently that his Family, and his Wife particularly, may be well provided for."[5]

This obligation continued through divorce, illegitimacy, and even after his death. Children born outside of wedlock were usually left unrecognized until their father's death, at which time they might be remembered in a will. However, many illegitimate children found themselves at odds with their legitimate siblings even when a favorable will was outstanding. The courts tended to uphold the rights, and desires, of the eldest legitimate son in most cases where there was friction between siblings over an estate.

A WOMAN'S PLACE IN THE HOME

Colonial law permitted women more freedom than the common law of England. Benjamin Franklin wrote to his wife as he set sail for England, "I leave Home and undertake this long Voyage more cheerful, as I can rely on your Prudence in the Management of my affairs; and education of my dear child."[6] Women in the colonies were permitted to act as agents for their absent or busy husbands, and many did. In fact, colonial wives were expected to assist their husbands in any way that they could. Many husbands came to rely on their wives' skills. Sewall reported in his diary: "gave my Wife the rest of my cash £4.3 &8 and tell her she shall now keep the Cash; if I want I will borrow of her. She has a better faculty than I at managing Affairs: I will assist her."[7] Some married women were even empowered to make contracts, an action that women in England were not allowed even with the permission of their husbands. One of the most striking differences between the colonies and England in such matters concerned the transfer of real estate. In the colonies both the husband and the wife executed the deed by which title passed. Deeds had to be acknowledged by both spouses. Moreover, in certain cases, a wife would be asked to verify her signature and attest that it had been given voluntarily and without undue duress by her husband.

CHILDBEARING

In marriage a woman entered a cycle of pregnancy, birth, and nursing that set the bounds of her life for the remainder of her childbearing years. For many women, twenty- to thirty-month intervals stretched from the birth of one child to that of the next. During pregnancy a woman was expected to have amassed a set of "childbed linen." A portion of this assemblage may have been handed down from her mother. The remainder was the product of the woman's own needle. As much ceremonial as pragmatic, the linens and infant wear were of the finest linen the family could afford and would be adorned with embroidery and lace.

Labor and delivery were not only momentous occasions for the family, they were community events as well. At the first stage of labor, the husband would send for the midwife, who would be on hand for the birth and remain with the family for a brief interval afterward. Other female friends and relatives would also attend to assist in the birth. Samuel Sewall recorded the following events in his diary at the time of the birth of his fourteenth child: "My Wife had some thoughts the Time of her Travail might come, before she went to bed; But it went over. Between 4 and 5 a.m. I go to prayer, Rise make a Fire, call Mrs. Ellis, Hawkins. Mary Hawkins calls Midwife Greenlef." Later in the day he made a second entry: "My Wife is brought to Bed of a Daughter about two p.m." Two days later, his wife, Hannah, fell ill: "Sabbath-day night my wife is very ill and something delirious. Pulse swift and high." Four days later he noted: "Nurse Hill watch'd last night. Wife had a comfortable night."[8]

All children were breast-fed until they were weaned as toddlers. A mother who was incapable of producing enough milk for her child needed to find a "wet nurse" as a substitute. Nonetheless, the newborn infant was often given to another woman to nurse for the first few days. The nurse was also available to help with complications following childbirth. It was not uncommon for a nurse to remain with the mother and child for an extended interval.

This population explosion in the house as labor progressed required that a large number of people be fed. One of the responsibilities of the expectant mother was to provide refreshment for those in attendance during the childbirth. "Groaning cakes," "groaning beer," and other items that would not spoil were made in advance of the expected event.

Sewall made note of a dinner that was given two weeks after the birth in appreciation to the women who attended his wife during the delivery: "My Wife Treats her Midwife and Women: Had a good Dinner, B'oiled Pork, Beef, Fowls; very good Roast-beef, Turkey-Pye, Tarts, Madam

Usher carv'd, Mrs. Hannah Greenlef; Ellis, Cowell, Wheeler, Johnson, and her daughter Cole, Mrs. Hill our Nurses Mother, Nurse Johnson, Hill, Hawkins, Mrs. Goose, Deming, Green, Smith, Hatch, Blin. Comfortable, moderate weather; and with a good fire in the stove warm'd the room."[9]

Sometimes plans were disrupted. At the birth of their ninth child Sewall wrote: "My wife was so ill could hardly get home . . . at last my Wife bad me call Mrs. Ellis, then Mother Hull, then the Midwife, and through the Goodness of God was brought to Bed of a Daughter . . . Mrs. Elizabeth Weeden, Midwife. Had not Women nor other preparations as usually, being wholly supris'd, my wife expecting to have gone a Month longer."[10]

Death due to childbirth was a genuine fear, for it was the leading cause of mortality for women. Before the birth of one of her children, Anne Bradstreet composed a poem to her husband acknowledging the risk that loomed: "How soon, my Dear, death may my steps attend." She voiced her concern for the children she would leave behind and bid her husband, "These, O protect from step Dames injury."[11] Husbands too worried. Benjamin Bang was concerned about his pregnant wife. In his diary he noted, "My dearest friend is much concerned being in and near a time of difficulty." He tried to bolster her and dissuade her frightful dreams. Of one such nightmare he wrote, "I put it off slightly for fear of disheartening her but directly upon it dreamed much the same myself of being bereft of her and seeing my little motherless children about me which when I awoke was cutting to think of."[12]

INFANT MORTALITY

Loss of a child was a frequent occurrence. One in ten infants did not survive the first year of life, and four out of ten children died before age six. Common diseases that stole away these infants included measles, diphtheria, whooping cough, mumps, and chicken pox. Hannah and Samuel Sewall had fourteen children and one child stillborn. Seven of the children died within twenty-five months of birth. Anne Lake Cotton gave birth to nine children in twenty years. She lost her first child two months before the birth of her second child. The next four survived infancy but the last three died at or shortly after delivery.[13] Mary Holyoke gave birth to twelve children in twenty-two years. Only four survived infancy.[14]

Accidents claimed children too. Frontier households were bustling, cluttered places that were not always child-safe. Open fires, kettles of hot water, privy holes, unfenced ponds, and open wells were daily dangers to a toddler or a small child. Busy adults and older children could easily lose sight of one of the smaller children in a crowded household.

Alice Walton returned from visiting her husband in the field to find her toddler missing. She questioned an older child, who responded, "It was here just now presently." The child was found drowned in an unfenced water hole. Nicholas Gilman's cousin "narrowly escaped drowning being fallen into a kettle of Suds." Fortunately, the mishap was seen, and the child was "pulled out by his heels" in time. Hannah Palmer's daughter was not so fortunate. While Hannah was still recovering from giving birth and grieving the loss of twin daughters who died five days prior, her daughter fell into a kettle of scalding water and died the following day.[15]

Some parents dealt with the tenuous presence of children with a certain emotional detachment. They avoided focusing intense care upon any single child. Whatever defenses they employed, the pain of loss, no matter how frequent, surely caused intense grief. Anne Bradstreet wrote several poems in memory of grandchildren lost in infancy. Grandson Simon Bradstreet lived but a month and a day: "No sooner come, but gone, and fal'n asleep, Acquaintance short, yet parting caus'd us weep."[16] It was common for children to be compared to items of a frail and fleeting nature. Portraits of children often depicted them with a single blossom as a reminder of how transient their time on earth might be. Grandchild and namesake Anne Bradstreet expired at age three years and seven months. On this occasion Anne wrote:

> I knew she was but as a withering flour,
> That's here to day, perhaps gone in an hour;
> Like as a bubble, or the brittle grass,
> Or like a shadow turning as it was.
> More fool then I to look on that was lent,
> As if mine own, when thus impermanent.[17]

CHILD REARING

A woman's responsibilities were greatly added to by the burden of rearing a family. Fathers were responsible for the education of their children, and they were the ultimate authority in matters of discipline. Issac Norris wrote of his two daughters, "They are a constant care as well as great amusement and diversion to me to direct their education aright and enjoy them truly in the virtuous improvement of their tender minds."[18] Contemporary historian William Alexander noted, "A father only is empowered to exercise a rightful authority over his children, and no power is conferred on the mother."[19] Mothers, however, attended to the everyday care of the children. This, of course, was in addition to their myriad other duties. After the birth of her second child, Esther Burr wrote in her 1756 journal, "When I had but one child my hands were tied, but now I am tied hand and foot . . . how shall I get along when I have got ½ dozen or 10 children I can't devise."[20]

Frontier children were expected to become productive contributors to the family as soon as they were able. Only in infancy were they treated simply as children with no responsibilities. As early as three years old, children were given simple chores. Not only did this help to instill a sense of responsibility, but it kept them occupied as well. Young children gathered goose feathers, picked berries, and helped process food. Older children plaited straw, weeded the garden, and knitted stockings.

Playthings were few and simple. Boys played with marbles, balls, whistles, small boats, toy soldiers, wooden animals, and whatever else a loving father might carve from a piece of wood by a winter's fire. Girls mimicked their mother's activities playing with whatever bowls and spoons were not in use. They played with moppets or dolls made from scraps of fabric or pieces of wood. Many dolls were more like a log with a face than a baby's image. Outside, children used their imaginations and nature's playthings to fashion garlands of flowers, small boats of leaves and pods, and whistles from blades of grass. As children grew older, chores increased with ability and made greater demands on their playtime. A large, healthy family was a tremendous resource to a colonial farmer.

THE EDUCATION OF CHILDREN

Almost all education was provided informally on the fringes of the frontier. Parents had the responsibility to educate their children in the manners and morals of their community. Where settlements were more established, an organized effort was made to provide more formal instruction. Some children were sent to dame schools as early as three years old, where they were introduced to the Three R's. These schools were extremely basic and held in the house of the school mistress in order to enable her to attend to her household chores as well as to her students. Once the children reached an age where they were needed at home or in the fields, their education usually ceased. Reading received the greatest emphasis. Believing that the inability to read was an attempt by Satan to keep people from the Scriptures, the Puritans of Massachusetts passed a law in 1642 that all children be taught to read.

Female literacy in the rural areas remained stagnant at about 33 percent for the entire period.[21] The education of young women was viewed as less essential when compared to that of young men. A period newspaper quoted an anonymous father advising his wife on how to educate their daughter:

Teach her what's useful, how to shun deluding;
To roast, to toast, to boil and mix a pudding;
To knit, to spin, to sew, to make or mend;
To scrub, to rub, to earn & not to spend.[22]

While parents surely loved their children, their demonstrations of affection in some ways differed from those of today. Puritans believed that children were born empty of knowledge and goodness and full of will. "The Four Ages of Man" by Anne Bradstreet well illustrates this attitude:

When Infancy was passed, my Childishness,
Did act all folly, that it could express . . .
From birth stained, with Adam's sinful fact;
From thence I 'gan to sin as soon as act.
A perverse will, a love to what's forbid:
A serpents sting in pleasing face lay hid.
A lying tongue as soon as it could speak,
And fifth Commandment do daily break.[23]

Puritan parents had the responsibility of breaking the spirit of independence in a child if they would hope to bring that child to God. This was achieved through harsh and restrictive supervision. Children were corrected not only to teach them socially acceptable behavior but also because they bore the mark of Original Sin. Sewall, recording an incident of a badly behaving four-year-old son, concluded with a biblical reference to Adam: "Joseph threw a knob of brass and hit his sister, Betty on the forehead so as to make it bleed and swell; upon which, and for his playing at Prayer-time, and eating when [saying Grace], I whip'd him pretty smartly. When I first went in . . . he sought shadow and hid himself from me behind the head of the Cradle which gave me sorrowful remembrance of Adam's carriage."[24]

Children were lectured about the sudden deaths of other children and were required to read intimidating verses from the Bible. They were taught never to be confident of their salvation. Sewall recorded his daughter's breakdown while reading from scripture: "Betty can hardly read her chapter for weeping; tells me that she is afraid she is gone back, does not taste that sweetness in reading the Word which she once did; fear that was once upon her is worn off. I said what I could to her, and in the evening pray'd with her alone."[25]

The Quaker attitude toward children was quite different. Households were child-centered. It was believed that young children should be protected from the world and nurtured within a controlled environment. Parents preferred rewards to punishments and as children grew older, they appealed to their reason. William Penn advised parents to love their children "with wisdom, correct them with affection: never strike in passion, and suit the correction to their age as well as fault. Convince them of their error before you chastise them."[26]

Children of Dutch settlers enjoyed a carefree youth of simple pleasures. Parents were open in their displays of affection for their youngsters. Anne Grant, traveling in colonial New York, reported: "You never entered a house without meeting children. Maidens, bachelors, and childless married people all adopted orphans and all treated them as if they were there own."[27] She described picnics, parties, and other fun activities for children that took place regularly. Contrary to New England practice, she noted: "Indeed, it was on the females that the task of religious instruction generally devolved. . . . [T]he training of children . . . was the female province."[28]

GIVEN NAMES

Parents sometimes selected names for their children that were of deeply religious significance. After naming his daughter, Sarah, Sewall wrote: "I was struggling whether to call her Mehetable or Sarah. But when I saw Sarah's standing in the Scripture, Peter, Galatians, Hebrews, Romans, I resolv'd on that side."[29] Other times they chose attributes that they hoped would flourish in their child's life. This was a carryover from England, where during the late sixteenth and seventeenth centuries such a practice was in vogue among Puritans. Comfort, Deliverance, Temperance, Peace, Hope, Patience, Charity, Submit, and Silence were common names. Roger Clap named his children Experience, Waitstill, Preserves, Hopestill, Wait, Thanks, Desire, Unite, and Supply. Sometimes events provided the inspiration for a name. Susanna Johnson named the child born during her Indian captivity, Captive. Widow Dinely lost her husband husband in a snowstorm. When their baby was born, she named the child Fathergone.[30]

Children were also named for deceased siblings. Necronyms—names of the dead—were given 80 percent of the time when a child of the same sex was later born. Ephraim and Elizabeth Hartwell of Concord, Massachusetts, lost their five children, Ephraim, Samuel, John, Elizabeth, and Isaac, to "throat Distemper" in a single month in 1740. The parents survived and had nine more children, named Elizabeth, Samuel, Abigail, Ephraim, John, Mary, Sarah, Isaac, and Jonas.[31]

In Pennsylvania and Delaware, Quaker babies underwent a ritual known as nomination. The infant's name was selected by the parents, certified by friends, witnessed by neighbors, and finally entered into the register of the meeting. Quakers tended to name their firstborn children after grandparents. They were careful to acknowledge both sides of the family, going so far in some cases as to name the firstborn female to commemorate the paternal line and the firstborn male to honor the maternal line. This tradition was particularly popular in the Delaware River valley. Other favored names came from the Bible. John, Joseph, and Samuel were popular for sons; while Mary, Elizabeth, and Sarah were often chosen for daughters. From time to time, families chose attribute names for daughters. Among these were Patience, Grace, Mercy, and Chastity.

WIDOWHOOD

Some families experienced the trauma of losing a father. Legally, the death of the male head of the household meant the dissolution of the family. The archaic term, *relict*, used in reference to his survivor, paints a very accurate picture of the widow in colonial times. The widow was simply a remnant, a leftover from a relationship that no longer existed. Following the husband's death, household inventories were taken in preparation for the redistribution of resources that would take place. By law, a widow commonly inherited one-third of the household goods. She was also entitled to use or receive income from a third of the real estate for the rest of her life or until she remarried.

Some husbands made explicit pleas in behalf of their wives in their wills. Tristram Coffin directed son Nathaniel to "take special care [of his mother and] provide for her in all respects." His brothers all contributed a fixed sum annually to help support their mother.[32] If a woman had minor children, as a widow she might be permitted to retain control of the entire estate until her sons came of age. The courts routinely granted the widow administration of the husband's estate in such circumstances. A study of ninety-three New Hampshire widows between 1650 and 1730 found that 75 to 80 percent of the women were given joint administration even in the event of grown sons. On some occasions, however, not only was the estate managed by a man, but a male guardian would be appointed for her children.[33]

Some widows were hesitant to remarry. For the first time in their lives they found themselves in control of their finances. William Alexander explained that men "exercised nearly a perpetual guardianship over them (women) both in their virgin and married state, and she who, having laid a husband in the grave, enjoys an independent fortune, is almost the only woman who among us can be called free."[34]

If a widow had been left in a comfortable financial situation, remarriage had its risks. A widow who remarried gave up all her unprotected property to her husband. She would once again have to defer to the generosity of her husband for her personal needs and those of the household. Widower Samuel Sewall pursued the widow Dorothy Denison asking her what financial allowance she felt he should bestow on her annually. Despite a generous offer on his part, she refused him, leaving him to note in his diary, "She answer'd she had better keep as she was, than give a certainty for an uncertainty."[35] In addition to her own security and comfort, a widow had to worry about the security of her children's inheritance. If she chose imprudently, her new mate could squander the wealth meant for the children of her prior marriage.

Naturally, many women missed the companionship and emotional support of a spouse, but it was socially acceptable for them to find fulfillment with their children. It was not unusual for a widow to live with the family of one of her adult children. Even though she would have to acquiesce to her daughter or daughter-in-law as female head of the household, she held a socially acceptable place in the household.

Widowhood for men was different. Dependency on grown children was not as acceptable for a man as for a woman. Many men from all economic stations promptly remarried. Loss of a wife affected the entire household negatively. A wife provided essential services to the family and without her it functioned poorly. Besides the emotional loss of a loving spouse and companion, a widower experienced a void in his household. On their deathbeds many young women urged their husbands to remarry. This concern for their surviving spouse was less out of regard for his happiness as for the welfare of their children. A mother knew that the vacancy she left would put tremendous strain on the family. Mary Clap told her husband to "get another Wife as soon as you can . . . one that will be a good Mother to the Children."[36] Cotton Mather reflected on his widowed state, "My family suffers by it in several instances."[37]

Remarriage was also more attractive for a man. In addition to regaining essential services for his household, it allowed him to regain social respectability. Marriage was the only venue that permitted sexual expression. Unmarried men were viewed to some extent as a sexual threat to the community. Financially, a man stood to gain from remarriage. Whatever a woman brought to a marriage became her husband's property. The only monetary risk he assumed was the possibility of having to provide for additional children.

Samuel Sewall's courtship of his third wife, the widow Mary Gibbs, was composed more of legal negotiations than of romantic flirtation. In both letters and personal conversations, the sixty-nine-year-old Sewall discussed the monetary effects of the potential union. In his diary he made note of a conversation: "her sons to be bound to save me harmless as to her Administration; and to pay me £100 provided their Mother died before me: I to pay her £50 per annum during her life, if I left her a Widow." Sewall was concerned because if a man married a woman before her late husband's estate was settled he risked becoming liable for his debts. Mary, naturally, was concerned about burdening her sons financially. Finally, after several letters and meetings between Sewall and Mary's sons, a prenuptial agreement was reached. Sewall agreed to forgo the £100 provided that her sons indemnified him against the debts of their father's estate. However, he did reduce Mary's annual stipend to £40. The couple was married shortly thereafter.[38]

HOUSEHOLD SERVANTS

In the earliest of settlements households often included servants. Between the 1640s and 1670s many settlers emigrated to the American colonies as indentured servants. Most were drawn from English agricultural workers. Agents scoured the English countryside making grand promises about the opportunities that awaited them in the colonies. A ballad relating the miseries of one poor maiden who was deceived by unscrupulous assurances became popular in seventeenth-century England. It opened with:

> This girl was cunningly trappan'd,
> sent to Virginny from England
> Where she doth hardship undergo,
> there is no cure it must be so
> But if she lives to cross the main,
> she vows she'll ne'er go there again.[39]

These servants entered into a contract that paid for their transport to the colonies. In return they agreed to labor for a set number of years. The number of years varied greatly, but averaged a little more than four years. Contracts could be made directly with the future employer or with other merchants who would sell the contract upon arrival in the colonies.

A small percentage of servants were drawn from the English prisons. Former convicts were released from incarceration on the condition that they would migrate to America as servants. Usually, their contracts were for double the term of service. While some colonists saw this as good value for their investment, others avoided such labor, uncomfortable at the thought that there might be behavioral difficulties with such a person.

Servants were forbidden to engage in anything that had the potential to interfere with their work. A mistress could physically discipline her servants, and whippings were not uncommon. Servants were not permitted to drink and certainly not to marry. Pennsylvania servants James Hall and Margaret Ryan ran away and married. After thirteen days, they were returned at a cost to their master of nine pounds. As their punishment, the court decided that each would have to serve an additional thirty days for running away, five months for the nine-pound expense, and a year for marrying. A female servant who became pregnant was liable to her mistress for the additional costs incurred for a midwife, a nurse, and any subsequent child rearing. Since few servants were in a position to pay for such expenses, their time of servitude was commonly extended eighteen to twenty-four months. The ratio of women to men in the colonies was such that many female servants easily found husbands upon the completion of their service.

INDENTURES

Many laws governed the manner in which the indentured person could be treated. Indentured servants were entitled to care during illness, and the time of service lost could not be held against them. They could not be sold out of the colony of emigration nor could they be cheated out of their freedom dues—those items due them at the conclusion of the indenture. Overall, indentured servants were given a legal status similar to that of children. The Pennsylvania colonial assembly passed legislation that gave indentured servants two suits of clothing, a new axe, a grubbing hoe, and a weeding hoe as freedom dues.[40]

Disputes between indentured servants and masters occasionally made their way into the courts. The most common complaint by servants was that the master or mistress was not attending to the welfare of the servant. There were also specific claims that the master failed to provide proper clothing or food. The majority of charges against servants were for running away or stealing. Other common complaints included unruly behavior, fornication, profanity, and sexual misbehavior. Mary Dudley of Massachusetts wrote to her mother complaining of her indentured servant: "If I bid her do a thing she will bid me do it myself . . . If I should write you all the reviling speeches and filthy language she hath used towards me I should but grieve you."[41] Penalties for offenses varied from one colony to another and evolved as time progressed. In cases of a servant's unlawful absence from duty, Maryland extended the contract by twice the number of days absent. In 1666 the penalty was increased to ten days for every one absent. In 1683, Pennsylvania added lashing to the imposition of five additional days for each day of unlawful absence. Anyone found to be assisting a runaway was required to pay the master twenty pounds and an additional five pounds to the court.[42]

By the 1680s and 1690s the free-flowing supply of emigrating indentured servants began to subside, and their numbers fell steadily through the remainder of the colonial period. In the Chesapeake region an average of only two women per year emigrated as indentured servants from 1718 onward. This was due in part to the improving economy in England, which left fewer individuals willing to leave their home in order to sell themselves into bondage.[43]

SLAVES

The shortfall of indentured workers was easily filled by the increasing number of slaves being brought from Africa. Slave markets provided an abundant source of labor that was found to be less restrictive than indentured servitude. Once purchased, slaves were the master's property until death or sale. Indentures were limited by time. At the end of the contract, the bond servant was free to leave. Additionally, indentured servants were more likely to bring grievances against their master to the attention of authorities and to seek legal action.

Slavery was accepted in the North, but it was not as widespread as in the South, where the plantation economy demanded an abundant source of low-cost labor. The early Dutch settlers of New Netherlands, however, made extensive use of slave labor. Their manors along the Hudson River, like their southern counterparts, required more laborers than the sparse settlements could provide. The Dutch employed slaves both in the household and on the farms. Some large farms in Narragansett region of Rhode Island and in eastern Connecticut also utilized slaves in larger numbers.[44]

The small farmers of New England did not need workers in such abundance. Large families and dependent relatives usually supplied what was needed, but sometimes they did require more hands than their family could provide. Early diaries of northern colonists and Indian captivity records mention slaves by name. The situation of these slaves would have been vastly different from the lot of the plantation slave. Slaves in New England had to be more skilled than the average southern plantation worker. They had to be able to work in the cornfield and cabbage patch, tend the stock and the dairy, and repair a fence or a cradle. Contemporary newspapers offered an abundance of advertisements describing slaves who were "brought up in husbandry," "fit for town or country," or "understanding the farming business exceedingly well."[45]

A frontier slave lived side by side with the family sharing the same labors, food, and residence. Madame Knight, on her journey through the primitive settlements between Boston and New York, complained that settlers were "Too Indulgent (especially the farmers) to their slaves: suffering too great familiarity from them, permitting them to sit at table and eat with them."[46] They were treated in much the same way as whites bound to service. Madame Knight also noted a dispute between a master and his slave "concerning something the master had promised him and did not punctually perform; which caused some harsh words between them; But at length they brought themselves to Arbitration." The master was ordered to pay the slave forty shillings "and acknowledge his fault."[47] Slaves experienced constant contact with white society. It is

The team of oxen in this print from the authors' collection represents the prime motive power that colonists could expect to have to do their heavy work. Oxen pulled wagons, carts, and plows. The African American drover in the background was probably a slave. The colonial frontier farmer generally worked alongside his slaves, sharing the sweat and toil, but not the profits of their joint labors.

likely that both male and female slaves in the North acculturated relatively rapidly, as they did not receive the reinforcement of African heritage that their southern counterparts did.

The vast majority of frontier farmers worked the land themselves, and few owned any slaves. However, many white farmers may have harbored the desire to accumulate enough money to buy one or two slaves, as this raised them to a new social status in the eyes of their neighbors. Nonetheless, most frontier farmers who owed slaves in the period before plantation slavery became an institution worked in the fields beside them, ate the same foods, lived in the same style of dwelling, and wore essentially the same functional clothing.

APPRENTICESHIPS

Another source of labor during this period came through the apprentice system. Children who were orphaned or whose families were unable to support them could be apprenticed to learn a skill. Samuel and Elizabeth Edeth bound their seven-year-old son, Zachary, until he was twenty-one to John Brown to be instructed "in his employment of husbandry." They explained their action saying that they had "many children and by reason of many wants lying upon them, so as they were not able to bring them up as they desire[d]."[48] In addition to the obvious trades of joyner, blacksmith, or printer, children were also apprenticed to learn farming, reading, and ciphering. A widower with no inclination to remarry might apprentice his daughter and ask that she be taught to read. It is likely that she would be bound to a family who wanted a young girl to help with the household chores. The daughter would learn the skills in which her mother would have instructed her and be taught how to read as well. Financial burdens and single parenthood were not the only reasons for "sending out" children. This custom was particularly popular among Puritans, who sent their pubescent children to other respectable homes to learn a skill or apprenticed them to a trade. Samuel Sewall sent out his three daughters—Hannah to learn housewifery, Elizabeth to learn needlework, and Mary to learn to read and write. His son, Samuel, was bound as an apprentice. While the parents' intentions may have been in their child's best interest, apprenticeship was sometimes a painful experience. Sewall made the following entry upon Hannah's departure: "[M]uch ado to pacify my dear daughter, she weeping and pleading to go [home] with me."[49]

The contracts that legalized the apprenticeship were considered indentures. They specified what duties and behaviors were expected of the servant and what the master or mistress was required to provide in return. It was not unusual for prohibitions to certain social activities to be specified in the indenture. A servant might be required "not [to] play at Unlawful Games nor Contract Matrimony."[50] They might be forbidden to "haunt taverns."[51] The term of service could last for a specific time or until the child reached a certain age. At the satisfactory conclusion of the term the apprentice would be given certain essentials that would allow them to go out on their own. Generally this involved a provision of clothing and a set of essential tools for the former apprentice to ply their newly learned trade.

After her father died, Rebekah Goslee was apprenticed by her guardians. The 1756 indenture stated that she would "well and faithfully serve [Timothy Hale and his wife Rebecca]. . . . Keep his or their commandments lawfull and honest. . . . Not do hurt nor damage to her . . . master nor his mistress nor consent to be done of others. . . . Not waste the goods of her . . . master nor lend them to any person without his consent . . . not either by day or by night absent herself from her . . . master's or mistress' service, but in all things as a good and faithful servant demene herself."[52]

In return, the Hales were expected to "take reasonable pains to instruct her and also to teach her to read the English tongue." They were also required to supply Rebekah with "sufficient wholesum and complete meat, drinking, washing and clothing and lodging." Rebekah was indentured until she was eighteen years old. At the end of her time of service the Hales had to supply Rebekah with "double apparel," which meant that she would have clothing "to have and to ware as well as on the Lord's Day as on working days." She was to have clothing of both "linen and wool, shoes, stockings and all other." Additionally, Rebekah was to be given "one good cow and one English Bible."[53]

Slave, bondswoman, or apprentice, the frontier female servant spent her days engaged in the activities of her mistress. She cooked, cleaned, sewed, and washed. She tended the fire, worked in the garden, and looked after the children. If the mistress saw fit, the servant could be hired out to work for another family who might need temporary help to assist with a labor-intensive activity or to provide nursing. If the mistress was generous, the servant might be permitted to keep all or part of any fees earned while on assignment. It was likely for the servant to sleep in a garret or in the kitchen. For many their bed was nothing more than a ticking (fabric) filled with straw.

The supervision of male servants and apprentices fell to the husband. Like their female counterparts, male servants on the frontier often worked side by side with their masters, plowing, harvesting, and tending animals. Placing unsupported children as indentured servants relieved the community of the need to maintain the unfortunate youths and provided them with skills to enter society as productive adults. Many of these children were apprenticed to learn farming, husbandry, or the skills of a stockman. In 1770 eight-year-old Benjamin Jeffords was indentured by the selectmen and "overseers of the poor" in Preston, Connecticut, to learn the skill of husbandry. At age twenty-one Benjamin's service was to be completed. At that time, in addition to two suits of workman's clothing, Benjamin was to receive "a Bible and ten good store of sheep" with which he might begin his own career.[54]

NOTES

1. Lisa Wilson, *Ye Heart of a Man: The Domestic Life of Men in Colonial New England* (New Haven, CT: Yale University Press, 1999), 47–48.

2. M. Halsey Thomas, ed., *The Diary of Samuel Sewall, 1674–1729*, vol. 2 (New York: Farrar, Straus and Giroux, 1973), 927.

3. Ibid., 935.

4. Ibid., 931.

5. Wilson, 103.

6. Carl Holliday, *Woman's Life in Colonial Days* (Boston: Cornhill, 1922), 132.

7. Thomas, 496.

8. Ibid., 459.

9. Ibid., 460–461.

10. Ibid., 264.

11. Joseph R. McElrath Jr. and Allan P. Robb, eds., *The Complete Works of Anne Bradstreet* (Boston: Twayne, 1981), 179–180.

12. Clifford K. Shipton, *Sibley's Harvard Graduates* vol. 17 (Boston: Historical Society, 1975), 480.

13. Laurel Thatcher Ulrich, *Good Wives: Image and Reality in the Lives of Women in Northern New England, 1550–1750* (New York: Vintage Books, 1991) 129.

14. George Francis Dow, ed., *The Holyoke Diaries*, (Salem, MA: Essex Institute, 1911), 73.

15. Ulrich, 157.

16. McElrath and Robb, 188.

17. See Ibid., 187.

18. David Hackett Fischer, *Albion's Seed: Four British Folkways in America* (New York: Oxford University Press, 1989), 508.

19. William Alexander, *The History of Women from the Earliest Antiquary to Present Time: Giving an Account of Almost Every Interesting Particular Concerning That Sex Among All Nations, Ancient and Modern*, vol. 2 (Philadelphia: J. H. Dobelbower, 1796), 343.

20. Susan Burrows Swan, *Plain and Fancy: American Women and Their Needlework, 1650–1850* (Austin, TX: Curious Works Press, 1995), 36.

21. Reliable literacy figures are difficult to attain for this period, as the definition of literacy varies from source to source.

22. See Selma R. Williams, *Demeter's Daughters: The Women Who Founded America, 1587–1787*, (New York: Atheneum, 1976), 111.

23. See McElrath and Robb, 37–38.

24. Thomas, 300.

25. Ibid., 349.

26. Fischer, 509.

27. Anne Grant, *Memoirs of an American Lady: With Sketches of Manners and Scenery in America As They Existed Previous to the Revolution* (New York: Samuel Campbell, 1805), 62.

28. Grant, 29.

29. Thomas, 324.

30. Alice Morse Earle, *Child Life in Colonial Days* (New York: Macmillan, 1940), 15.

31. Fischer, 96.

32. Ulrich, 148.

33. Ibid., 249.

34. Alexander, 338.

35. Thomas, 908.

36. Wilson, 161.

37. Worthington Chauncey Ford, ed., *Diary of Cotton Mather*, vol. 1 (New York: Frederick Ungar, 1911), 476.

38. Thomas, 908.

39. See Williams, 55.

40. Elaine Forman Crane, ed., *The Diary of Elizabeth Drinker* (Boston: Northeastern University Press, 1994), 63.

41. Williams, 60.

42. Cheesman A. Herrick, *White Servitude in Pennsylvania: Indentured and Redemption Labor in Colony and Commonwealth* (Philadelphia: John Joseph McVey, 1926), 166.

43. Carol Berkin, *First Generations: Women in Colonial America* (New York: Hill and Wang, 1996), 108, 152.

44. The social climate on the northern Dutch farms was often different from that on southern plantations. Northern owners commonly absented themselves from the property for long periods of time, especially during the winter. The slaves left on these farms were virtually on their own to manage the property during the owner's absence.

45. Lorenzo Johnston Greene, *The Negro in Colonial New England, 1620–1776* (New York: Columbia University Press, 1942), 103.

46. Sarah Kemble Knight, *The Journal of Madame Knight: A Woman's Treacherous Journey by Horseback from Boston to New York in the Year 1704* (Boston: Small, Maynard 1920), 38.

47. Ibid.

48. Nathaniel Shurtleff and David Pulsifer, *Records of the Colony of New Plymouth in New England*, vol. 2 (New York: AMS Press, 1968), 112.

49. Thomas, 314.

50. Connecticut Historical Society, *Children at Work* (Hartford: Connecticut Historical Society, 1993), 6–7.

51. Ibid., 11.

52. Ibid., 14–15.

53. Ibid.

54. Ibid., 12–13.

7

Hearth and Home

[Mother] was now in the wilderness, surrounded by wild beasts, in a cabin with about half a floor, no door, no ceiling overhead, not even a tolerable sign of a firepace, the light of day and the chilling winds of night passing between every two logs in the building.
                                                —John Sherman, Ohio senator, 1890

Homes on the colonial frontier varied with the means and needs of the families who built them. Often initial construction was limited and additions to enlarge the structure were attached as time and situation permitted. In New England, houses commonly followed one of three plans.

The one-room plan was the most basic pattern and the earliest type of house constructed in the colonies. It continued to be common for small and poorer dwellings and on the frontier into the eighteenth century. The front door of such a structure typically opened into a small vestibule, referred to as a "porch," which contained a steep, narrow staircase that traversed the width of the entry. Sarah Knight, an early eighteenth-century traveler, complained that such a stairway "had such a narrow passage that I had almost stopped by the bulk of my body."[1] To one side of the vestibule was a doorway into the the main room. Generally sixteen feet by eighteen feet, this room was known as the "hall" and it served as a combination kitchen, dining area, living area, and in some cases a bedroom. It had a low ceiling and a double layer of boards on the floor. Some floors had a layer of sand between the boards, probably to act as insulation from the cellar's cold. Wainscoting was used from the early seventeenth century. Broad pine boards were beveled to cover the studs, but posts were exposed. As the century closed, molded pieces were attached to form the earliest paneled walls. The most prominent feature in the room was the large fireplace. The depth of the fireplace extended into the area behind the staircase. The upstairs consisted of a large sleeping area which had a sloping roof in a one-and-a-half-story house and a roof of full height in a two-story house.

The two-room house followed the plan of the one-room house with the addition of a second room to the other side of the chimney and porch. This was called the "parlor." Upstairs were two rooms known as the "hall chamber" and the "parlor chamber." On occasion there was a room projecting over the porch referred to as the "porch chamber." Prior to the nineteenth century, rooms were basically multipurpose. Furniture in first floor rooms was often placed against the walls when not in use and moved into position as needed.

The lean-to plan was the two-room plan with the addition of a room at the rear of the house. This served as a separate kitchen and workspace for other domestic chores but might also accommodate a sleeping area. Above the lean-to was a loft that, as necessity dictated, may have been used for additional sleeping. The roof rafters leaned from one-story eaves at the back against the top of the wall of the main house. A cooking fireplace was also added at the back of the central chimney mass. A common lean-to house had as many as five fireplaces built into a single chimney stack.

During the cold northern winters, ewes, young calves, piglets, and hens were sometimes brought into the kitchen to save them from freezing. Lean-tos and single-boarded sheds provided little protection from bitter winds and heavy snow. In 1640 this practice saved the lives of a Massachusetts family when the reflection of a fire awakened a neighbor's hens: "Mr. Pelham's house . . . took fire in the dead of night by the chimney (and was) ready to lay hold upon the stairs. A neighbor's wife, hearing some noise among her hens, persuaded her husband to arise . . . he did and so espied the fire, and came running in his shirt, and had much to do to awake anybody, but he got them up at last, and saved all."[2]

Windows in seventeenth-century New England homes were few. Many of these homes probably had oiled paper or sliding board shutters rather than glazed windows. Letters to England urged emigrants to bring glass for windows. Windows of this period were in diamond-shaped panes of glass arranged in a lattice pattern typical of those in medieval England. By 1650 glazed windows were commonplace in prosperous homes. Although the windows were relatively small, they were often grouped two, three, or four together to make a wide, horizontal window bank. First-floor windows were often of a casement style or a mixture of casement and stationary. Second-floor windows were frequently fixed units that did not open. In order to overcome the limited availability of light, much of the food preparation and other household chores were performed outdoors when weather permitted.

Entrance to the home was made through a heavy door made of two layers of boards, the outer of which ran vertically and the inside horizontally. It was studded with hand-forged nails driven through both and clenched on the inside. The door was supported on long wrought iron strap hinges. The earliest hinges were made of wood. They had a leather thong that passed through a hole that lifted the latch on the inside. Later hinges were made from wrought iron. At night doors were further secured with a heavy wooden bar placed across the inside.

Sarah Knight described a primitive home she encountered on her journey: "This little Hut was one of the wretchedest I ever saw as a habitation for human creatures. It was supported with shores enclosed with Clapboards laid on lengthways, and so much asunder, that the Light came through' everywhere; the door tied on with a cord in the place of hinges; The floor the bare earth; no windows but such as the thin covering afforded."[3]

In the middle and southern colonies frontier homes were often built of squared or rounded logs. While the Swedish are often given credit for introducing this construction to the colonies, it was embraced by German and Scotch-Irish settlers, who did much to popularize it. Early log cabins were frequently only one room with both front and rear doors. Next to the large interior chimney was a ladder or steep stair that led to a loft. It was not unusual for the structure to later be enlarged to what was called a "saddle-bag" plan with a second room on the other side of the fireplace. The rooms seldom exceeded twenty-four feet in length, as it was difficult to find suitable timber of greater size and this was still reasonable to handle. Another plan, called the "dog-trot," created two rooms that were separate, each with a chimney on opposite ends. The space between was then covered, producing a long breezeway. This area was an ideal living space in warm weather, providing protection from the sun yet permitting the opportunity to capture what breezes there were. In winter it was a practical place to store curing pelts or unused traps.

The Dutch were some of the most skilled bricklayers in Europe. Naturally, they preferred to continue to use brick in the construction of their homes in America. The brick was laid in a variety of patterns, some of which were quite striking. Sarah Knight's description of a Dutch home in New York is typical of those of the period: "The Bricks in some of the Houses are of diverse Colors and are laid in Checkers, being glazed [they] look very agreeable."[4] A brick kiln was built just below Albany

This illustration of a street in Albany, New York, was made in 1805. The buildings clearly show evidence of Dutch influence in their architecture. Note the hay wagon at the end of the street and the shops at the right.

as early as 1630. Albany had many step-gabled brick houses so characteristic of New Amsterdam, but the straight-lined gables prevailed in the more rural counties of New York. When brick was unavailable the Dutch used whatever materials were at hand. Many houses along the lower Hudson River and in New Jersey were built of stone. Stones were gathered from fields or broken from ledges and bound together with mortar made from straw or hair and, when available, lime. Walls were very thick and ranged from one and a half to three feet thick. In the seventeenth-century houses in the Hudson River valley, with the exception of Albany, were one and a half stories high. Two-story houses were an eighteenth-century innovation.

The interiors of Dutch houses were cheerful. Walls were whitewashed or wainscoted. Yellow or blue curtains added color at the windows and other decorations brightened the walls. A traveler remarked: "They affect pictures much [and] set out their cabinets and buffets much with china. . . . They hang earthen or Delft plates and dishes all around the walls."[5] Furniture tended to be simple with the exception, perhaps, of a large chest that would have been brought with the settlers when they emigrated. Smaller objects were stored neatly in cupboards. Beds were commonly built flush into the wall and closed off by curtains or shutters. Of the beds the same traveler noted, "They have their beds generally in

alcoves so that you go thro' all the rooms . . . and never see a bed."[6] Sarah
Knight, who was so critical of most of the accommodations she encountered on her 1704 journey, made this observation of the Dutch homes:
"The inside of them are neat to admiration." She was also struck by the
fireplaces, which she noted "have no Jambs. . . . But the Backs run flush
with the walls, and the Hearth is of Tiles and is as far out in the Room
at the Ends as before the fire."[7]

Inside the frontier home the fireplace was the center of activity. A fire
would burn every day of the year. The central fire warmed the house
and provided a means for cooking. A greenwood lung pole bisected the
chimney flue six to eight feet above the hearth. From it could be hung
chains from which pots could be suspended for cooking. Coals were
raked to the side of the hearth apron to create additional cooking stations
that were more controlled and away from the open flame. A house with
a single fireplace burned between fifteen and twenty cords of wood a
year.[8] While sustaining life with light, heat and means of cooking, the
fireplace also presented a potential danger, as an out-of-control fire
could quickly burn an entire house to the ground. Anne Bradstreet's
home was completely lost in such a fire. She recounted her loss in a
poem:

> My pleasant things in ashes lie.
> And them behold no more shall I.
> Under they roof no guest shall sit,
> Nor at they table eat a bit.[9]

Many homes of this period had "catted" chimneys that consisted of
logs plastered with clay inside and out. Early homes also often had
thatched roofs, which easily caught fire from a stray spark. Toward the
close of the seventeenth century many localities began to pass laws forbidding wooden chimneys and thatched roofs. In 1631 Governor Thomas
Dudley of Massachusetts recorded, "We have ordered that no man shall
build his chimney with wood nor cover his house with thatch [because]
diverse houses have been burned since our arrival."[10] Brick replaced
wood as chimney material as it became available.

Modern images of a colonial fireplace often depict a hearth cluttered
with myriad iron pots, griddles, and skillets. Many of the artifacts that
have survived from the early settlers were from the more prosperous
families and are not typical of the average household. Few frontier settlers had the benefit of such equipment. Probate inventories, taken after
the death of a settler, depict a much sparser scene. Elias Wear of York,
Maine, was killed by Indians in 1707 while traveling between his home
and the village. He left a wife, six children, and an estate of which the
household goods included some pewter, a pot, two bedsteads, bedding,
one chest, and a box.[11]

This historical reenactor is an expert on colonial cooking and the use of herbs. The cap he is wearing is a typical linen laborer's cap of the period. The fireplace at which he is working is in the kitchen of Governor Thomas Fitch's house in Norwalk, Connecticut, which dates from 1740. The kitchen display has many more items than would have been found around a frontier hearth, including a pot crane, a running trammel, a long-handled frying pan, a Dutch oven, and a large cast iron plate known as a fireback. The fireback kept the heat from destroying the stone and mortar at the back of the fireplace, and it helped to radiate heat into the room.

William Googe died in Lynn, Massachusetts, in 1646. The one-room house that he left his wife and three children contained a chest, a chair, an "old chair," a stool, a trunk, and some bedding. Additionally, there were three wood trays, three wood bowls, three wood dishes, some pails and tubs, one runlet,[12] an earthen pot, a skillet, a posnet,[13] a frying pan, a gridiron, and six spoons.[14] These sparsely furnished homes may have included additional items such as hand-carved wooden bowls or trenchers, gourd ladles, scoops, horn cups, or spoons that were considered of so little value that they were not included in probate inventories. The fact that the Googe inventory included several wooden serving pieces indicates that it is likely they were professionally made and of good quality. Similarly, shelves that were nailed or mortised into posts were excluded from these inventories.

Generally, frontier furniture was simple, solid, and painted. It would be an error to believe that frontier homes were decorated with tree stumps and crude tables made of saplings. Much of the furniture consisted rather of backless benches and stools. Chairs, especially those with arms, were a luxury and their use were reserved for the head of the household. Meals were served from a board table made from two or three long planks that rested on a pair of trestles.[15]

Boxes of all sizes were plentiful. There were long boxes for clay pipes, wall boxes for salt and candles, and slant-top table boxes for the family Bible. Larger boxes of chest size that sat upon the floor contained clothing and other possessions. In her will, Jane Humphreys identified each of her boxes individually: "my little chest, my great old chest, my great new chest, my lesser small box, my biggest small box."[16]

The most valued piece of furniture was usually the bedstead. The term *bed* originally referred to the mattress only, which was simply thrown on the floor for sleeping and rolled up out of the way during the day. Mattresses were stuffed with corn husks, straw, bits of felt or wool, or any other soft material that could be spared.

Francis Plumber of Newberry, Massachusetts, was a linen weaver with a sixteen-acre farm. Following his death in 1672, the inventory showed a kitchen that contained pots, kettles, dripping pans, trays, buckets and earthenware, and a bed. The parlor held the bedstead with its bolster, pillows, blanket, and coverlet. A great chest, a table, and a backless bench furnished the hall. Plumber's house contained two upstairs chambers, which were used for storage of foodstuffs and out-of-season equipment.[17]

John Dillingham of Ipswich, Massachusetts owned extensive acreage, livestock and a two-room house when he died in 1635. The inventory of furniture contained in the house listed two bedsteads, one cupboard, two chairs, a desk, and a round table. The house also contained feather mattresses, bolsters, pillows, and coverlets, as well as flaxen sheets and coarse sheets. The coarse sheets were likely for use by the two indentured servants, Thomas Downs and Anne Towle. It is also likely that the mattresses upon which the servants slept were simply thrown on the floor.[18]

LIGHTING DEVICES

Lighting was poor in these homes. Small windows let in limited amounts of light, and once the sun set the fireplace was the greatest source of illumination. The simplest lighting supplement was the pine knot, or what settlers called candlewood. Rev. Higginson described them as "the wood of the pine tree, cloven in two little slices, something thin, which are so full of moysture of turpentine and pitch that they burne cleere as a torch." They were often held in an iron holder, which had a pincer like end that held the wood securely. Because they "droppeth a pitchy kind of substance," a flat stone was often placed beneath them to catch the tar that they secreted.[19] Grease or fat lamps were also used. These lamps were small, shallow containers, commonly iron, in which tallow, grease or oil was placed. The wick was held in a projecting spout. These lamps commonly had a hook and chain link that permitted them to be hung from a nail in the wall or from the back of a chair. For use on a table, they were placed on a chunky wooden stand. Some grease lamps sported a second container, immediately below the first, in order to catch the fat that dropped from the wick.[20] The simplest candles were rushlights. They were made by stripping away the outer layer of common rushes, leaving the pith. This would then be soaked in tallow or grease and allowed to harden. Rushlights were placed in holders similar to those that held the candlewood.

Making traditional candles was labor-intensive, autumn activity. Candles could be made in molds or dipped by hand. On the frontier, dipping was probably the most common form. Tallow was melted in huge kettles. Wicks were attached to candle rods, which were laid across pairs of poles suspended from chairs or stools. In turn each candle rod was dipped in the tallow and placed across the poles to harden. Skill was required to know how to dip slowly enough so that the wax did not dry too quickly and produce brittle candles that would crack. A skilled candle dipper could make 200 candles a day. The quality of a candle depended upon the quality of the fat that was used. On the frontier, every bit of fat from butchered meat, including deer and bear, was utilized. The better the quality of the fat, the firmer and less offensive was the candle.[21] New England settlers were fortunate to discover that the waxy berries from the bayberry bush made very pleasant candles. Swedish naturalist Peter Kalm wrote about them in 1748 after a trip to America: "There is a plant here from which they make a kind of wax. . . . Candles of this do not easily bend, nor melt in summer as common candles do; they burn better and slower, nor do they cause any smoke, but yield rather an agreeable smell when they are extinguished."[22]

CHORES

There are few records to personally illuminate the routine chores of the frontier woman. They were so boring and repetitive, so basic to the family's survival, that they were seldom recorded in diaries and journals. What details have survived of the housewife's day were usually recorded by women of considerable wealth and leisure. Generally, women on the frontier maintained the fire, cooked and preserved food, sewed and repaired clothing, cultivated the vegetable garden, cleaned and laundered, and assisted their spouse in any way they could. Cooking and food preservation probably consumed the largest amount of a housewife's time. Frontier farmer J. Hector St. John de Crevecoeur proclaimed, "If we are blessed with a good wife, we may boast of living better than any people of the same rank on the globe."[23]

FOOD

The earliest colonists ate the same food in much the same manner as the Indians who taught them. These settlers learned how to bake beans in earthen dishes buried among the ashes, to make sugar from maple tree sap, and to pound corn into meal to make a simple cake. The average diet consisted of boiled, stewed, or steamed meats and fish, peas, corn-meal cakes and puddings, and wild berries.[24] Field peas were among the first crops introduced to New England in 1629, and they flourished. Peas were boiled or baked, eaten hot or cold, and could be expected at any meal including breakfast. Settlers learned to cultivate native crops, especially pumpkins, squash, and melons. They eventually planted fruit trees and cultivated vegetable gardens of a wider variety. The gardens were close to the house and commonly planted in raised beds.

As time went on, the settlers learned to adapt the natural foods of the area to their traditional ways of cooking. A Pennsylvania settler wrote: "There was not a bushel of grain or potatoes, nor a pound of meat except wild to be had. But there were leeks and nettles in abundancy, which, with venison and bears meat, seasoned with hard work and a keen appetite, made a most delicious dish."[25] Settlers learned to appreciate the bounty that was theirs for the gathering. Watercress, wild leeks, milkweed shoots, and dandelions were boiled with wild game, as were chestnuts, hickories, butternuts, walnuts, and acorns. Sugar maples yielded sap, which was made into sugar, candy, and syrup. The bounteous amounts of grapes, gooseberries, cranberries, currants, blueberries, strawberries, raspberries, and blackberries were enjoyed fresh in season and made into tarts. Quaker John Kipps wrote back to England that there was "plenty of fish and fowl, and good venison very plentiful, and much better than ours in England, for it eats not so dry, but is full of gravy, like fat young beef."[26] Mahlon Stacy reported a "great store of wild fruits, as strawberries, cranberries, hurtleberries. . . . The cranberries [are] much like cherries for color and bigness . . . an excellent sauce is made of them for venison, turkeys and other great fowl, and they are better to make tarts than either gooseberries or cherries."[27]

Breakfast usually consisted of leftovers or previously prepared foods, as women were usually involved with early morning milking. A typical breakfast might have been toasted bread, cheese, and any leftover meat or vegetables from the previous day. In summer, it may have been accompanied by milk. Dinner (lunch) was the main meal of the day and it would have made the most of the season's offerings. A heavy pudding stuffed into a cloth bag would steam over vegetables and meat, or meat with fresh or dried vegetables would be boiled in water. Supper, too, was a simple meal. It was was often merely a repeat of breakfast or leftovers from dinner. Eating leftovers was not simply a matter of thrift. Prior to refrigeration, there was no safe way to save extra portions for a later date. Eating what remained from a previous meal just made good sense. Summer suppers might have had the added variety of fresh eggs, milk, or a fruit or berry tart. Like breakfast, bread and cheese were often served, or the broth from the boiled dinner was made into a pottage with the addition of oatmeal or barley.

Most meals were served with beer or cider. "Strong" beer was brewed annually in October and in most cases was made by those with expertise in the craft. "Small" beer was a milder beverage that could be made by any housewife. It was brewed every week or so and used shortly thereafter. Crevecoeur reported: "Some families excel in the method of brewing beer with a strange variety of ingredients. Here we commonly make it with pine chips, pine buds, hemlock, fir leaves, roasted corn, dried apple-skins, sassafras roots, and bran."[28] Cider was an excellent way to preserve the apple harvest. The liquid from the pressed fruit was allowed to ferment naturally in the cellar until it was mildly alcoholic. Cider that was served in taverns had a sightly higher alcoholic content due to the fact that sugar was added during the fermentation process.

Menus were reflective of the season's bounty. Spring dinner might have been an eel pie flavored with winter savory. While spring brought reassurance of nature's renewal and promised the bounty of the harvest, it was the least generous of all the seasons. Spring provided little in the way of fresh produce, and stores put away in the fall were greatly depleted by this time. A housewife would have welcomed wild onions, dandelions, and even skunk cabbage to supplement a dwindling supply of root crops such as turnips, parsnips, and carrots. In summer she might have served a leek soup and garden greens. A fall dinner might have included recently slaughtered pork or goose with apples. In winter boiled meats made more appealing with a variety of sauces and produce preserved from the harvest would have been standard fare.

FOOD PRESERVATION

What was available to a family in the winter and spring depended upon a wife's careful preservation of their excess harvest. A woman's expertise in this area was the difference between comfort and starvation through the winter and well into the spring. Food preservation was an ongoing process in response to the seasons. Milk was processed in summer to yield cheeses for the winter. A family who did not have time to plant a garden faced a winter of intense hardship. John Reynolds and his family survived such an adversity on the Pennsylvania frontier. He

Women spent much of their time in food preparation and preservation. Much of their work was done out of doors in seasonable weather.

wrote: "Our bread was flour and water without salt or leaven, baked in the ashes in thin cakes. . . . Bacon was our standing dish of meat. Chocolate with sassafras or wintergreen tea was our drink at meals. Vegetables we had none."[29]

The garden's harvest was stockpiled in a variety of ways. Vegetables such as beets, cabbage, carrots, onions, parsnips, potatoes, radishes, turnips, and winter squash were stored in root cellars, where the climate allowed. In other areas, they were packed in straw and stored in barrels. The straw acted as a barrier to prevent the spread of spoilage to the entire barrel. Carrots were often buried in sawdust or sandboxes. Other vegetables such as corn, beans, and peas were dried and used in cooking. Green corn was preserved by turning back the husk, leaving only the last, very thin layer, and then hanging it in the sun or a warm room to dry. When it was needed for cooking, it was parboiled and cut from the cob. Sweet corn was parboiled, cut from the cob, dried in the sun, and stored in a bag kept in a cool, dry place. Sweet corn was also dried in the husk and then buried in salt. String beans, squash, apples, and pumpkin were strung on thread and hung to dry.

Crevecoeur remarked: "Besides apple we dry pumpkins, which are excellent in winter. They are cut into thin slices, peeled, and threaded. Their skins serve also for beer, and admirable pumpkin-pies are made with them." String beans were strung whole while other produce was sliced thinly and dried in strips. Cabbage was made into sauerkraut. Vegetables and fruits could also be preserved by making them into pureed sauces. Crevecoeur noted, "We often make apple-butter, and this is in the winter a most excellent food, particularly where there are many children."[30]

Fall was the time for slaughtering. While the men may have dispatched the larger animals, a housewife may have slaughtered smaller pigs herself. Pork was a mainstay of the colonial diet. Pigs were easier to keep than other livestock, as they could be fed on most anything, including leavings from food preparation. Pigs did not have to be put to pasture and consumed less feed than cattle, for their weight. Pork could be easily preserved in a number of ways, such as pickling, salting, and smoking. Much of the pork would have been jarred in a solution of brine and stored in the dairy, where the temperature was generally cooler. Some of the pork was also preserved as bacon. The slabs would be salted in tubs for several weeks in early winter before being hung in the chimney for smoking. Crevecoeur remarked: "Our beef by smoking becomes so compact that we commonly shave it with a plane. The thin, transparent peelings, when curled up on a dish, look not only neat and elegant but very tempting."[31]

Baking became an important skill and was traditionally done one day a week. Some homes had exterior, freestanding bake ovens that were protected by a small wooden roof and open-sided structure. Other homes had ovens built into the fireplace. If a house had no oven, baking was done in iron kettles. In New England, brown bread became a staple. The first settlers made this essential from a mixture of wheat and corn. Following a wheat rust in the 1660s rye replaced the wheat. Wheat flour was saved for special occasions and ornamental uses such as the top crust of a pie. Primitive mortars used to grind the corn into meal were a fixture in the frontier home.

THE HERB GARDEN

In addition to vegetables, a housewife planted a variety of herbs in her garden. Herbs were the among the first things planted. Parsley, skirret, and sorrel were harvested for "sallets." Cooked and served hot or cold, with an oil and vinegar dressing, they accompanied many dishes. Herbs also had tremendous value as seasonings for meats that had been heavily salted. Early records and seed lists provide insight into what colonists considered to be essential herbs. In 1631 John Winthrop Jr. ordered seeds for angelica, basil, burnett, dill, fennel, hyssop, marjoram, parsley, rosemary, savory, thyme, and tansey.[32]

On the frontier, herbs served as both spice rack and medicine chest.

The log cabin in this photograph has been reconstructed in the Cape May, New Jersey, area. The building has a single large room, a log-crib fireplace, and a wood-shingle roof. The gardens in the foreground and to the left were used to provide vegetables and herbs for the use of the frontier family.

The tradition of using plants as "physicks" for healing as well as seasoning came along with the settlers from Europe. Garden herbs were likely to be the only medicines available. Hyssop was mixed with honey to make a cough syrup, yarrow was placed on wounds to stop bleeding, and savory was used to treat colic. Many herbs, such as marjoram, had a variety of uses for an assortment of complaints. Tea from marjoram leaves was given to relieve spasms, colic, and indigestion. When chewed, it eased toothaches. Mixed with honey, the leaves lessened bruising. Colonists expanded their knowledge with information gained from the Indians on the use of native plants. The settlers were introduced to bee balm, which was brewed into "Oswego tea" for relief from colic, fever, or colds. Some herbs were used as pesticides to deter flies, fleas, and moths. Herbs also provided dyes. Tansey shoots produced a green grey, yarrow blossoms gave yellow, and the stems and leaves of sweet cicily yielded an olive color.

TEXTILES

A family's attire also depended greatly on the skill and industry of the housewife. Men were involved in the early gathering and processing of wool and flax, but it was a woman's job to spin it, weave it, and fashion it into clothing and linens. In 1656 the Massachusetts General Court passed a compulsory spinning law that detailed weekly spinning quotas and fines for failing to meet assessments. Children helped with textile production as they could. Young girls were set to work sorting, carding, and spinning wool at an early age. Once spun, wool could easily be knitted into caps, stockings, mittens, and dishcloths.

Weaving remained a predominately male occupation and virtually every community of size had its weaver. Households would bring their spun linen and wool to the weaver to be woven into yard goods. The weaver also would have yard goods of his own production available. Households often had small hand or table looms known as tape looms. These were used to weave narrow strips for use as garters, shoestrings, belts, hat bands, stay laces, braces, and tapes. Tapes were essential to secure petticoats, shifts, and aprons. Simply a heddle frame, these primitively shaped boards were cut so that the center of the board had a row of narrow slats pierced by a small hole through which the warp threads passed. The board could be held at the bottom by the weaver's knees and steadied at the top by being tied to the back of a chair. The lightness of these looms allowed them to be carried to a neighbor's house for an afternoon of work and socializing.

Sewing was also an important activity. Clothing on the frontier was utilitarian, but it still required mending, and growing children always needed something larger. A housewife also had to supply her family with all the bed linens and towels they needed. Mastery of the needle was an essential skill for all women at this time. Young girls were taught needle skills at an early age and were expected to master them. While wealthy women may have spent a good deal of time doing fancywork that demonstrated their needle skills in decorative projects, most frontier women engaged in plain sewing.

Textiles were a large part of a family's wealth. Inventories taken for probate commonly listed textiles immediately after landholdings, money, and silver. Clothing was repaired, remodeled, and recycled. Such conservation was not done solely out of frugality; it was less time consuming than making a new garment. When a garment was no longer able to be used, it would be cut down and remade for a smaller family member.

CLOTHING

While fashions changed from the seventeenth to the eighteenth century, the basic clothing of the frontier woman consisted of the same essential items. The basic undergarment was known as a shift. Over this a woman wore her stays and usually several petticoats. The outermost layer consisted of a waistcoat or shortgown and skirt. An apron was generally worn to protect the skirt. Adult women wore a coif or cap to contain their hair. Most frontier families had only one set of "Best" clothes, which were saved for Sundays and special occasions. Cloaks were worn by both men and women for inclement weather.

Men wore long, loose-fitting shirts with wide sleeves. Their breeches, made of wool or linen, came just below the knee and were held closed about the leg with either buttons or buckles. The lower leg was encased in a woolen thread stocking. In the seventeenth century the outer garment worn by men on special occasions was a close-fitting item known as a doublet, but the average laborer or farmer wore a simple pullover garment much like a woolen shirt or jacket. In the eighteenth century waistcoats and long-tailed coats became fashionable, but the day-to-day work clothes remained essentially the same. In the mid–eighteenth century long-legged trousers became more common for work than breeches. Few adjustments in the weight of fabric were made for seasonal variations in temperature.

Children were dressed as small adults. Infants and toddlers were dressed in gender-neutral gowns until the age of five or sometimes seven. These simple garments, which laced down the back, were easy to make and eliminated the need to engage in detailed sewing of garments that children would soon outgrow. Small children also wore a cap, called a biggin, which tied under the chin, and an apron to protect the gown.

Although sewing was a regular part of a woman's routine chores, needlework may have been a welcome opportunity for her to sit down and relax while still being productive. The simplicity of the task even allowed it to be done by the limited light of the fire at night. Sewing could be brought along while visiting or employed while socializing. Such elementary sewing as mending and hemming required little attention and permitted a woman to converse or to listen to someone reading.

From time to time clothing needed laundering. Woolen jackets and petticoats probably never got more than a good beating and an airing but linen shifts, caps, fichus, aprons, and shirts required washing. Households that almost always had a child in diapers mush have engaged in the activity with some regularity.

SOAP

Before the laundry could be done soap had to be made. Soap was a mixture of animal fat and lye that was boiled together in a kettle for many hours. Lye was obtained by pouring water into a leach barrel filled with hardwood ashes. The water would drain through the layers of ash and the lye trickled out a small opening at the bottom and was captured in a small bucket or tub. An olden recipe explains: "The great Difficulty in making Soap come is the want of Judgment of the Strength of the

Lye. If your Lye will bear up an Egg or a Potato so you can see a piece of the Surface as big as a Ninepence it is just strong enough."[33] Six bushels of ashes and twenty-four pounds of grease rendered enough lye to make a barrel of a soft textured soap. This soap was very harsh and seldom used for personal hygiene. A hard soap made from the waxy bayberry was more desirable for toilet use.

NOTES

1. Sarah Kemble Knight, *The Journal of Madame Knight: A Woman's Treacherous Journey by Horseback from Boston to New York in the Year 1704* (Boston: Small, Maynard, 1920), 47.

2. Frances Phipps, *Colonial Kitchens, Their Furnishings, and Their Gardens* (New York: Hawthorn Books, 1972), 27.

3. Knight, 23–23.

4. Ibid., 52.

5. Dr. Alexander Hamilton's *Itinerarium*, quoted in Hugh Morrison, *Early American Architecture: From the First Colonial Settlements to the National Period* (New York: Dover, 1987), 114.

6. Ibid.

7. Knight, 52–53.

8. David Freeman Hawke, *Everyday Life in Early America* (New York: Harper & Row, 1988), 55.

9. Joseph R. McElrath Jr. and Allan P. Robb, eds., *The Complete Works of Anne Bradstreet* (Boston: Twayne, 1981), 237.

10. Phipps, 23.

11. Laurel Thatcher Ulrich, *Good Wives: Image and Reality in the Lives of Women in Northern New England, 1550–1750* (New York: Vintage Books, 1991), 30–31.

12. A runlet was a wooden container of approximately eighteen gallons.

13. A posnet was a small saucepan that rested upon a tripod frame.

14. Phipps, 52.

15. The board table has given us the phrase "chairman of the board," from the custom that the head of the household sat in the chair at the board table, as well as the phrase "room and board," meaning that a hired hand could expect a place to sleep and a place "at the board."

16. Alice Morse Earle, *Customs and Fashions in Old New England* (Williamson, MA: Corner House, 1969), 117.

17. Ulrich, 18–19.

18. Selma R. Williams, *Demeter's Daughters: the Women Who Founded America, 1587–1787* (New York: Atheneum, 1976), 40.

19. Alice Morse Earle, *Home Life in Colonial Days* (Stockbridge, MA: Berkshire House, 1993), 33.

20. These fat lamps are commonly referred to today as "Betty lamps." It is thought by some that the name is a corruption of the phrase "better lamp," which described improved lamps that had a second container to catch the dripping grease.

21. Every bit of grease residue from cooking or fat from meat was utilized for

candlemaking. Beef fat produced candles that were firmer and less unpleasant smelling than those made from pork fat. Frontier families used whatever fat was available, including fat obtained from predators or pests.

22. Earle, *Home Life*, 39–40.

23. J. Hector St. John de Crevecoeur, *Letters from an American Farmer and Sketches of Eighteenth Century America* (New York: Penguin, 1981), 232.

24. New England's coastal waters abounded with mussels, oysters, lobsters, and clams, yet the Puritans consumed these only as a last resort. They preferred the beef and mutton common to the English diet.

25. Marian I. Doyle, "A Plentiful Good Table," *Early American Life* (December 2001), 47.

26. David Hackett Fischer, *Albion's Seeds: Four British Folkways in America* (New York: Oxford University Press, 1989), 541.

27. Ibid.

28. De Crevecoeur, 298.

29. Doyle, 46.

30. De Crevecoeur, 283.

31. Ibid., 299.

32. Richard M. Bacon, *The Forgotten Art of Growing, Gardening, and Cooking with Herbs* (Dublin, NH: Yankee, 1972), 8.

33. Earle, *Home Life*, 254.

8

The French Regime in Canada

I shall be forced to take measures which will insure to our Canadiens and Indians treatment such as their zeal and services merit.
—Pierre de Vaudreuil, governor of New France

The history of Canada during the French regime can be broken down into distinct phases. In 1633 the Company of One Hundred Associates took possession of New France from Florida to the Arctic Circle, and from Newfoundland to the source of the St. Lawrence River and its tributaries. It was understood that they would have a fur trade monopoly and the right to govern the colony as they saw fit as long as they brought 4,000 colonists to settle there within ten years. The dispersal of the Hurons in 1649 changed the nature of the fur trade, however, and in 1663 the colony came under royal control, with the governor and intendent appointed and controlled by the Crown through the Ministry of Marine. The monopoly was broken and transferred to what was called the Compagnie des Habitants. Thereafter, the fur trade was opened to any settler who wished to pursue it.

Two hundred colonists came with Champlain in 1633, but the Hundred Associates conveniently ignored any further obligation to populate the colony. The Hundred Associates was also required to support and defend the Catholic clergy and missions to the Indians. This it did begrudgingly and not without a great deal of friction between the company officials and the ecclesiastics, even though Cardinal Richelieu was one of the major investors.

Most of the French who came to Canada in the earliest group came from northern and western France. A study of their names and backgrounds suggests that they came mainly from Poitou, Charente, Normandy, Pershe, Aunis, and Île de France. Soldiers, priests, workmen, and servants—mostly male—made up the initial groups of settlers.

SEIGNEURS

The Hundred Associates was formed of many men of rank, merchants, and bourgeois in France with Cardinal Richelieu at its head. The king heaped many favors on its members, and twelve of the associates, although born commoners, were ennobled. A series of land grants, some of them including many thousands of acres, were made to these friends of the Crown. These grants were called *seigneuries*, and by 1663 more than sixty had been made. In exchange for the estates and privileges granted by the fur company, it was hoped that the seigneurs would become enthusiastic recruiters of colonists, not only providing the able-bodied settlers but also organizing their ocean crossings and their disposition on the land.

CLERGY

During the period of the monopoly granted to the Hundred Associates the influence of the clergy outweighed their small number, which was probably fewer than 100. Composed almost entirely of Jesuit priests before 1640, they tended to the spiritual wants of the colony and were the sole spiritual ministers for its population. The Jesuit Order was also specifically entrusted with the mission of converting the native population to Catholicism. The father superior of the Jesuits in Canada was thereby made a very influential person. The order seems to have had a genuine desire to establish firm foundations for the continued growth of the Catholic Church among the native Americans.

TRADERS

The fur traders worked for the company and were not considered "colonists" in the normal sense of the term. There were several categories of fur traders who worked under licenses from the company. The *marchand-equipeur*, or merchant outfitter, lived in the colony and purchased the necessary equipment for traveling into the interior. He imported the trade goods and hired the trading personnel. The merchant outfitters came to Canada only to make money. After remaining one or more trading seasons they usually returned to France. The *marchand-voyageur*, or traveling merchant, was a licensed trader who did the actual buying and negotiating with the native trappers. He was sometimes served by an interpreter or a *commis* (clerk). From the beginning of the fur trade monopoly a number of woodsmen and guides were also kept on the company's payroll.

HIRED MEN

Last in line in the fur trade heirarchy were the *engages*, who worked as paddlers, porters, and general laborers. They received room, board, and clothing besides a small stipend in lieu of wages. The engages were young men, some in their teens, who signed a contract to remain employed in the colony for three years, but many remained in New France after their contracts ran out. Many engages bolted from their contracts to take up life in the wilderness as unlicensed fur traders. Recent forensic studies of the remains of several engages show that they lived very harsh lives and probably were required to carry tremendous loads on their backs for long distances. Their remains—mostly bones—suggest widespread malnutrition, a high level of arthritis, and an early death. These symptoms correlate well with a life of exposure to the cold and wet environments found in portaging and paddling canoes into and out of the wilderness.

ARTISANS

Also among the hired men were craftsmen and certain other persons with specific skills unrelated to the fur trade who worked for an annual wage. With an average salary of sixty livres per year there were soldiers, ploughers, diggers, and sawyers. While in France these men would have been fixed in their employment for all their lives, in the colony they had some chance of improving their condition. Craftsmen such as masons, carpenters, smiths, and coopers earned about ninety livres and had the advantage of becoming masters of their own shops more quickly and with less competition than they would have found in Europe. These men generally occupied the towns and within a few decades had apprentices of their own.

In the towns and settlements all of the population was required to observe an evening curfew. They were forbidden to attend public meetings or form private organizations. Reading materials, when available, were generally restricted to religious texts. As with persons of their station in France, the artisans enjoyed no political or religious freedom.

HABITANTS

The real colonists of French North America were the *habitants* (inhab-itants), yet for many decades after the founding of the colony they were few in number. Habitants were considered the permanent residents of New France. They may have been recruited by agents of the seigneur, of the fur company, or of the king. Living on farmsteads cut out of the forests along the rivers and streams of Canada, they found little difficulty in making a living in the rich virgin soil. Providing that they obtained the proper licenses and followed the regulations of the Compagnie des Habitants, individual settlers could find the fur trade quite lucrative, but only young and adventurous men could choose the harsh life of the frontier trader. Most tried fur trading for only a few years, making one or two journeys into the interior before settling down and marrying.

It would be an error to think that the habitants enjoyed any freedom of action in their lives, however. Young men were required to follow strict regulations forcing them to marry, to settle on the land, and to develop farmsteads. Abandoning their land to traffic in furs without a license could bring stiff penalties, deportation, or even death. Because of their small number and wide dispersion along the Canadian frontier, the habitants were openly terrorized by the Iroquois, yet they were generally forbidden to move into town.[1]

Very little is known of the reasons for which habitants emigrated. As all French colonists were required to be Catholic, there does not seem to have been any movement to the New World for religious freedom or toleration. No great social crisis in France seems to have played a role in their departure. These were major considerations for emigration to the English colonies. Aside from three specific groups of settlers who were given cash bonuses to emigrate, the ordinary habitant seems to have come to New France for a wide variety of personal reasons.

LAND

The desire for land may have been a motivating factor. Habitants and hired workers who had worked through their contracts could settle down on an uninhabited parcel of land called a *censive*. These were usu-ally between seventy-five and eighty acres, with a waterfront dimension of about 200 yards and a depth of almost a mile. The French unit of land measure at the time was the *arpent*. The common censive was three ar-pents wide by thirty arpents deep. Most of the settlements were on the St. Lawrence River or other navigable waterways. As the canoe was the main means of tranportation, long, narrow land grants with a minimal water frontage allowed many habitants to share the waterways as an asset much like a system of highways today. The long and narrow cen-

Rivers and streams were the original highways into the wilderness, open to
the traffic of canoes, bateaux, and barges. Only with the passage of time
would roadways be developed along their banks. Few farmsteads were located beyond the view of a body of navigable water.

sive of the French in Canada varied greatly with the more equilateral
and rectangular farmsteads favored by English and Dutch settlers.

The habitant had to respect certain conditions or the censive would be
forfeited. He had to build a home and hearth within one year. He had
to actually live in this structure and clear the land at a rate of two square
arpents (about two acres) per year. Once the habitant became a *censitaire*,
or landholder, he was responsible for paying in cash a rent as well as
fishing and milling fees to the seigneur who actually owned his land.
When parishes were set up nearby by the clergy, the habitant was also
required to pay a tithe to help support the priest and to help erect and
maintain a church building. In the seventeenth century the tithe was set
at one-thirteenth of his crop, but by the beginning of the eighteenth century it had been reduced to one-twenty-sixth.

POPULATION GROWTH

Regardless of their reasons for coming to the New World, the flow of
immigration to New France was very slow indeed, and the development
of the land relied largely on population growth due to births within the
colony. This factor somewhat alleviated the pressure on the local native

population to vacate their lands and may have dampened the hostility toward settlers that was so common in New England. Young men who married before age twenty and girls who married before sixteen were awarded twenty livres each on their wedding day. Fathers with unwed daughters of marriageable age were fined, and young men who remained single too far into their twenties could be denied trading licenses and promotions. A yearly pension of 300 livres was awarded to families having ten living children and 400 livres to families having a dozen or more. In some frontier communities in New France, special privileges were given to the fathers of large families, such as the local command of the militia or the position of town official. Having a large family was not a simple task for settlers carving out a living in the harsh environment of the frontier. The high rates of infant mortality alone would require a woman to be pregnant at almost every possible time during her childbearing years to qualify for these pensions.

THE KING'S DAUGHTERS

Along with a change of control from the Hundred Associates to the Compagnie des Habitants in 1663, the king ordered a census to be taken of the colony of New France. This census showed an amazing lack of French women and girls among the population, which may explain why so many Frenchmen took native American wives. The Crown earnestly attempted to resolve this inequity by finding peasant girls of good character in France to serve as wives for the colonists. These young women were called the King's Daughters, or *Filles du Roi*. The Crown provided each of these girls with a dowry of one hundred livres—ten for personal moving expenses, thirty for clothing, and sixty for passage. A hope chest was also included, filled with necessary household items. The colony gave each newly married couple an ox, a cow, two pigs, a pair of chickens, two barrels of salt pork, and eleven French crowns in cash on their wedding day. In a single decade (1663–1673), 852 young women entered the colony under this program.

Although supposed to be at least sixteen, some of the King's Daughters were actually as young as twelve—a very few others were as old as forty-five. The men's preference was for mature peasant girls who were healthy, robust, and industrious rather than nubile adolescents. The young women who exhibited these qualities had some choice among prospective husbands, while the old and the very young had very little in the way of selection. A plump and buxom figure was considered an asset, as it was considered a sign of fertility.

The King's Daughters were married off with shocking speed once they reached Quebec, as there were six men for every girl over twelve years of age in the colony. The priests and necessary public officials were pres-

With men outnumbering women by six to one, the King's Daughters found a warm welcome in New France.

ent when the girls reached Quebec, in order to expedite the marriages. The girls were expected to make their choice of a husband on arrival, and very little ceremony took place with regard to extensive questioning or courtship between couples. Under the circumstances the men could be expected to be on their best behavior, but at least some of the girls had been sent out by their families against their own wishes. Nonetheless, if the girls behaved badly or were overly uncooperative, they were made to understand that they could be deported. Prostitutes from the streets and alleys of French cities were specifically forbidden from emigrating, and any girl who arrived in the colony pregnant was to be sent home. Given the shortage of women, however, few of the girls were actually returned.

GOVERNANCE

The governors of New France were very important to its development as a colony. While Acadia and Montreal each had a chief executive known as a governor, it was the governor of Quebec who was viewed as the governor-general of the colony. Under the Hundred Associates there were six governors of Quebec. Samuel de Champlain (1633–1636) was the first. Charles Huault de Montmagny (1636–1648) was second and served the longest of the six. It was he that the Indians first called Onontio, or great mountain, from the translation of his name *(mons magnus)*. Thereafter, *Onontio* was the native term used for "governor." The third and fourth governors were Charles Joseph d'Ailleboust (1648–1651), a resolute soldier, and Jean de Lauson (1651–1658). The fifth was Pierre de Voyer, Comte d'Argenson (1658–1661), who was the first to challenge the growing power of the Jesuits, and the last was Baron Dubois d'Avaugour (1661–1663), who had little more success than his predecessor. Thereafter the governor was chosen by the Ministry of Marine in France and appointed by the king. The first royal governor was Augustin de Soffray, Chevalier de Mezy (1663–1665).

FRONTENAC

The development of New France was particularly advanced by Louis de Buade, Comte de Frontenac et Pelluau, who served as royal governor twice: from 1672 to 1682 and again from 1688 to 1698. Possibly the most effective governor of New France in the colonial era, Frontenac came to New France with a brilliant military reputation earned on the battlefields of Holland, Italy, and Germany. He held the rank of Marshall of the Camps under King Louis XIV, and had once commanded a contingent of the French army against the Turks. He was described as intelligent and magnanimous, brave and unflinching; but he was also characterized as proud, imperious, haughty, and vengeful by his contemporaries.

In his first administration (1672–1682) he argued with the bishop of Quebec (Francois Laval), the governor of Montreal (Francois Perrot), and the king's intendant (Jacques Duchesneau). He attempted to awe the Iroquois by attacking their villages and by building a fort named for himself at the mouth of Lake Ontario at Cataraqui, and he sent La Salle to explore the interior of the continent. His continued quarrelling with colonial officials over relatively trival questions of colonial government finally caused the king to recall him in 1682. He was subsequently replaced by two weak and unfit administrators: Le Febvre de la Barre and the Marquis de Denonville.

In 1688 the Iroquois again threatened the existence of the French colony, and Frontenac was recalled to office. After the LaChine raids by the Iroquois had terrorized the colony in 1689, he took up the task of securing New France with energy and ability. Frontenac sent three war parties from Montreal and Quebec to attack the English border settlements in New York and New England. The raid against Schenectady was the first of its type, and it was completely successful in creating panic among the English and winning the native tribes to the French. The attacks on Salmon Falls, New Hampshire, and Fort Loyal, Maine, were equally effective. Encouraged by these offensives he vigorously attacked the Iroquois in their own territory, burning several of their major villages in 1693.

The Mohawks, realizing that he was not a man to be taken lightly, made peace.

The French allied Indians called him the "Great Onontio," a term of high respect. Francis Parkman notes, "Frontenac . . . showed from the first a special facility of managing [the Indians]; for his keen, incisive spirit was exactly to their liking, and they worked for him as they would work for no man else." By Frontenac's orders the Abenakis and other Indians raided all up and down the New England frontier during King William's War. In 1690, Frontenac boldly repelled a major English expedition sent to seize the city of Quebec.[2]

Frontenac's greatest failure was his inability to cooperate with the powerful Jesuits, yet he was a friend and supporter of the Recollet fathers and was buried in their church. His public character was a mixture of good and bad qualities, but his poor qualities were much less evident in his second administration than in his first. He found New France weak and under attack from all sides in 1688, and he left it enlarged, respected, and feared by its enemies ten years later. Frontenac died in office in 1698 after having disciplined the Iroquois in New York. All of New France went into mourning. Under Frontenac's administration New France ceased to be a giant mission and became a colony.

SIEUR DE CADILLAC

In 1694 Frontenac sent a thirty-six-year-old career army officer to command the vital post at Michilimackinac and the mission of St. Ignace. The officer, Antoine de la Mothe, Sieur de Cadillac, was of a good family and had served for almost ten years in Acadia on the Atlantic coast of New France. Cadillac retained the position at Michilimackinac for three years and then retured to Quebec City as a rich man having amassed a great profit by trading alcohol to the Indians for their furs.

During his time in Quebec, Cadillac brought forward a well-considered plan for the establishment of a fortified post along the short route from Lake Huron to Lake Erie along the St. Claire River. This route had been shown by natives to Louis Jolliet in 1668. Nonetheless, the Crown ignored Jolliet's findings for three decades, but it acted on Cadillac's advice almost immediately. In 1699 Cadillac was given a royal mandate to build a fortified post (Fort Ponchartrain) and settlement at Detroit (the strait between Lake St. Clair and Lake Erie), and to ensure that all the western Indian tribes traded furs with the French rather than the Iroquois. Finally, he was to acculturate the Indians to European Catholicism and assimilate them into the French nation. In 1701, Cadillac left Montreal for Detroit with fifty soldiers, fifty colonists, and two priests. Three years later, he caused the closing of the mission at St. Ignace by moving the Michilimackinac garrision to Detroit.

Cadillac also obtained personal title to Fort Ponchartrain and requested a marquisate from the Crown. His request was denied mainly because he failed to consolidated the fur trade between the western tribes and the French. Most of the furs continued into New York and passed through Iroquois middlemen to English and Dutch merchants at Albany. Cadillac was made governor of Louisiana from 1710 to 1717, where he and his son caused a good deal of discontent among the settlers.

PHILIPPE DE VAUDREUIL

Philippe de Rigaud, Marquis de Vaudreuil, came to New France in 1687 as the commander of a detachment of marines. He gained his military experience during seventeen years of service in the king's musketeers in Europe, where he rose to the rank of colonel. Vaudreuil was one of the first to react to the Iroquois attack on LaChine in 1689, and he prepared a brilliant defense of Montreal against further attacks by the Indians. He helped Frontenac defend Quebec during the English siege of 1690 and was made governor of Montreal when Louis Hector de Callieres was promoted to governor-general of Canada.

Vaudreuil succeeded Callieres as governor-general in 1703. His prudence and experience well suited him for the position during the trying years of Queen Anne's War. Unlike Frontenac, Vaudreuil was able to deal with the position of governor without coming into open conflict with the church and colonial officials. He was respected and feared by the Indians of New France, and he constantly strove to strengthen the French alliance with them. He was instrumental in ransoming English captives from the natives during the war years, even adopting one of them, Esther Wheelwright, into his family. Wheelwright ultimately entered the Ursuline covent in Quebec and was appointed mother superior after the English conquest of the city.

Vaudreuil encouraged agriculture, commerce, and education throughout the colony. During his administration the fortifications of the city of Quebec were expanded and strengthened, and a wall was built around Montreal. Fort Niagara was built under his orders at the western end of Lake Ontario. The colony was divided into eighty-two administrative parishes, and a census was taken at the end of his tenure giving a population of 25,000 persons.

MONTCALM

Louis Joseph, Marquis de Montcalm-Gozon de Saint-Veran, was born in 1712. At fifteen he joined the French army as an ensign in the regiment Hainaut. At seventeen he was a captain, and had been under fire in Europe during one of the many battles of the War of Spanish Succession

(Queen Anne's War). Although the title he inherited from his father at age twenty-three was a prestigious one, the estate was poor and in debt. However, the younger Montcalm made a good marriage that brought him money, influence, and ten children. In 1741 during the War of Austrian Succession (King George's War), Montcalm was made colonel of the regiment Auxerrois, and in 1746 he was severely wounded in a heroic stand below the walls of Piacenza. After recovering he was again promoted, this time to brigadier-general, and again wounded.

In autumn 1755 word reached Paris that Baron Ludwig Dieskau had been killed during a battle with the English at Lake George in New York. Dieskau had been the commander of all the regular French regiments in Canada, while the governor regulated the Compagnies Franches de la Marine and the militia. The Marquis de Montcalm was approached by the French minister of war, Marc Pierre de Voyer, concerning the position of commander in chief of all the military forces in Canada. Montcalm was not excited by the prospect of commanding the forces of France in the wilderness of North America when a major war was looming on the continent of Europe, but the war minister prevailed by offering Montcalm's eldest son command of a regiment in France.

Montcalm was made a major-general, and the Duc Francois-Gaston de Levis, afterward a Marshal of France, was named as his second in command. He was to take two battalions of regulars with him to Canada. One belonged to the regiment La Sarre and the other to Royal Roussillon. These would be added to the battalions brought from France by Dieskau. The almost 7,000 regulars under his command were known in Canada as Troupes de Terre.

Montcalm reported directly to the minister of war, but his position would require him to work closely with the French governor of Canada, Pierre Francois Rigaud, Marquis de Vaudreuil. Canadien by birth, Pierre de Vaudreuil was the fifth son of Philippe de Vaudreuil, the former governor during Queen Anne's War, and became governor of New France during the period of the Seven Years' War. It seems certain that Montcalm was apprehensive about his relations with the governor, and for his part, de Vaudreuil found it difficult to see why a general officer from France was now needed. Francis Parkman declared that Pierre de Vaudreuil "distrusted Old France and all that came out of it," including Montcalm. This distrust was enhanced by the fact that the governor had heretofore been considered the commander of the militia and Compagnies Franches de la Marine. Until 1746 these were the only troops needed to defend the colony, but the looming probablity of war in Europe in the 1750s caused a tremendous buildup of regular forces in New France along with a new military commander.[3]

Montcalm was not fully aware of the feelings de Vaudreuil held toward him, and the general may initially have yielded to the governor's experience and knowledge of Canada when formulating strategy. However, Vaudreuil took advantage of Montcalm's attitude of cooperation, claiming unwarranted credit for every successful operation for himself and the Canadiens and denying it to the French troops and their general. Montcalm liked the militia no better than the governor liked the regulars. This had the general result of creating an ill will between the Troups de Terre and the Canadiens. Nonetheless, Vaudreuil wrote to the minister of marine in 1756; "I shall always maintain the most perfect union and understanding with M. le Marquis de Montcalm, but I shall be forced to take measures which will insure to our Canadiens and Indians treatment such as their zeal and services merit." Subsequent events were to make Pierre de Vaudreuil the last governor of New France.[4]

NOTES

1. See W.H.P. Clement, *The History of the Dominion of Canada* (Toronto: William Briggs, 1897), chap. 4.
2. Francis Parkman, *La Salle and the Discovery of the Great West* (New York: Modern Library, 1999), 54.
3. Francis Parkman, *Montcalm and Wolfe* (New York: Atheneum, 1984), 213.
4. Ibid., 269.

9

The Fur Trade

The Indians seemingly "spent the entire year in the act of trading or
in preparing for it."
—Father Jean de Brebeuf

The significance of the fur trade in New England, New Netherlands, and
New France cannot be underestimated. Initially, there were faint rum-
blings of discontent among the native populations as the effects of the
fur trade altered long-standing traditions and intertribal relations, but
the Indians ultimately became more dependent on European trade
goods. As they increased the volume of their hunting to satisfy the demands of the fur trade, many ritual observances that tied the hunters to
the animal world were in danger of being disregarded. The trading posts
in particular were thought to be destabilizing to the rhythm of intertribal
commerce, and they caused the natives to use unfamiliar and dangerous
routes of travel. Nonetheless, as the manufactured goods streamed into
the wilderness there were few natives who could not see their usefulness.[1]

It would be an error to suppose, however, that trinkets, mirrors, and
glass jewelry divested the native peoples of their economic sense, or that
the natives valued their archaic methods of toolmaking and weaponry
as modern observers do from the romantic perspective of centuries. Native Americans were sophisticated in their thinking and vastly pragmatic. Knives and razors of steel, and axes of iron, which replaced those

The knife was a trade item prized by native Americans because of its utility, and by the trader because as a trade item it was lightweight and convenient to transport. This antique knife from the authors' collection has a deer-antler handle and is about eight inches long. The markings on the blade date it as being more than 200 years old.

of stone, were reliable and easy to use and maintain. Not all Indians were equally talented in the manufacture of projectile points, scrapers, and blades, and the raw materials for their manufacture sometimes came from sources many hundreds of miles away. Woolen blankets and linen cloth were more comfortable and more colorful than animal skins, and the tedious process of weaving mats from marsh reeds and capes from grasses was avoided. Vermilion (a bright red pigment) and verdigris (a blue to green pigment), which could be mixed with animal grease to form a body paint, were very popular because they were not readily available from among natural materials known to the natives. A contemporary observer noted, "Many persons told me that they had heard their fathers mention that the first Frenchmen who came over here got a heap of furs from the Indians for three times as much [vermilion] as would lie on the tip of a knife."[2]

Brass and iron kettles allowed them great convenience in preparing their meats, maize, and roots in stews instead of roasting them over the fire or in bark containers. As the dripping fats were no longer lost in the ashes, a great deal of caloric and nutritional value was saved. This was no small matter to a people who hunted and gathered for a living in a subsistence economy.[3] More importantly, European goods gave the natives abilities that they had not before possessed. In this regard steel awls and needles were highly valued. Beads for wampum, cut from oyster shells and polished to size, could now be drilled with ease when compared to the laborious process required when using a bone awl.

Wampum was highly valued as a decoration, a medium of exchange, and a device for recording traditions and agreements. For centuries its manufacture had been limited to coastal tribes who had access to the shells from which it was made. The importation of red, white, and blue porcelain beads, seemingly as highly valued by the natives as the natural product, greatly enhanced the stockpile of this culturally important item. The most dramatic impact of the fur trade, however, may be that it gave the Indians firearms. But this was not an immediate development, and up to 1640 the trade in firearms was small.[4]

NATIVE MIDDLEMEN

The Indians of the Maine coast were trading with Europeans in the sixteenth century, and a surprising abundance of manufactured goods was found among them by settlers in the seventeenth century. One observer noted "very good axes ... and French shirts and coats and razors" among the Indians. In the trading process individual Indian trappers and traders often acted to their own advantage, but those bands who could act as middlemen occupied a "valuable strategic and economic position." Between 1607 and 1615 the Micmacs and eastern Abenakis (both Algonquian-speaking peoples) fought for the position of middlemen in trading furs with the tribes of the interior for manufactured goods available on the coasts of Maine and Nova Scotia. The western Abenaki and their relations among the Algonquians east of the Lake Champlain River valley seem to have controlled the flow of trade goods and furs from the coast and throughout much of New England in the early seventeenth century.[5]

A HIGHLY SPECIALIZED ENTERPRISE

European and native American fur traders differed considerably in the roles that they assumed in the trading process. The Europeans displayed a great division of labor among the traders. Some supplied the capital and political influence to secure a license, others operated the fixed trading posts, and finally some made the face-to-face negotiations with the Indians in the wilderness. The colonies of every European nation represented in North America at the time acquired a corps of negotiators whose prestige among the Indians enhanced their ability to bargain effectively. On the other hand the native Americans who dealt in the fur trade, with the notable exception of the Hurons, usually combined these many roles into a single person. The Indians who hunted were most often the same persons who did the trading. They transported the furs themselves and haggled over the bargain with varying degrees of success. A number of tribes attempted to control this aspect of the fur trade by installing themselves as middlemen. Some tribes welcomed their intervention; others decried it. Decades of bloody intertribal conflict, known as the Beaver Wars, were generated by the resulting commercial competition during the seventeenth century.[6]

TRADING POSTS

European fur traders initially attempted to penetrate the interior of North America by utilizing the same trade routes that the native populations had used for centuries. The Frenchmen who penetrated the interior for the first time had trade as well as exploration on their minds. The two objectives of French enterprise in Canada were the colonization of the country and the development of the fur trade. The fur trade in New France was established in 1601 under a trading monopoly granted to Aymar de Chastes, an aged man who never saw Canada. The post at Tadoussac was near the mouth of the Saguenay River, where it flowed into the St. Lawrence. It was begun by Pierre Chauvin de Tonnetuit, who had been made lieutenant-general of Canada by King Henry IV in 1599. Tadoussac remained a disappointing enterprise, however, because too few furs came into it from the interior. Moreover, the French traders could not enforce their monopoly upon the Basque fishermen who traded in sight of the post with impunity.

In 1603 de Chastes died and his monopoly was secured by Pierre du Guast de Monts. One of the first fur traders to act under de Monts's patent was a Breton sea captain named Francois du Pontgrave, who had come with Chauvin and Samuel de Champlain to New France in 1603. Pontgrave sailed in 1604 with a trading vessel loaded with metal tools, kitchen utensils, and useless trinkets such as bright buttons, caps, ribbons, and cheap jewelry. Their first attempt at creating a trading post was on the island of St. Croix in the Bay of Fundy, but this proved an unhealthy site. A second unproductive year was spent at Port Royal across the bay. The natives who visited these posts told of a bounty of furs from the lakes and rivers of the wilderness interior. The most valuable furs were those of beaver, taken in the winter when the coat was most heavy. If the French wanted these at a reasonable price, they would have to travel inland to get them.

Acting on Champlain's desire to move into the interior, a base was opened at Quebec in 1608. Here was the great natural citadel that had been occupied and abandoned by the explorer Jacques Cartier decades before. Ironically, Quebec, 700 miles inland, had not been Champlain's initial choice for a trading post. Montreal, 500 miles farther into the interior with its forested plains and with its connections to many navigable waterways, was his first choice, but it would have to wait for almost three decades to become the focus of the fur trade in New France. From these beginnings the fur trade became the major commercial activity of the colony, with major trading posts and settlements at Quebec, Trois-Rivières, and Montreal.

One of the most advanced European trading posts in the early fur trade period was that of the Dutch. In 1614 a group of Dutch shipowners had the remarkable foresight to form the New Netherlands Company (Dutch West India Company), a fur-trading monopoly. The small outpost of New Amsterdam was founded at the southern tip of Manhattan Island to support the main trading establishment near the head of navigation of the Hudson River at Fort Orange (Albany, New York). Henry Hudson had traded here with the natives in 1609 and found them cooperative and cordial. The New Netherlands colony soon proved immensely rich in terms of the trade in furs with the native population. There was an easy water route from the fur-rich interior of the continent down the Mohawk River or through the Lake Champlain corridor to Albany, from Albany by way of the Hudson River to Manhattan, and from Manhattan to the sea.

COUREURS DE BOIS

Some of the French who came to Canada found the native American way of life attractive. These coureurs de bois (bushrangers) adapted themselves to Indian life and became skilled woodsmen. Some historians consider them quite picturesque and effective as woods fighters. They have been awarded a great deal of prominence in prosecuting French objectives against the American rangers in the eighteenth-century war for empire. The coureurs de bois, driven largely by a disregard for the fur company's monopoly and by a desire to avoid the church's strict enforcement of religious duties, broke away from the boundaries of the colony to live and trade among the native population. However, in the Canadian fur trade economy of the seventeenth century they were generally considered outside the law. At one point as many as 25 percent of colonists in Canada chose the life of a coureur de bois, and a list of severe penalties was enacted against them as a deterrent to any more colonists joining their ranks.

From time to time, certain persons who were considered coureurs de bois by historians actually found it to their advantage to transfer their allegiance to the fur companies of other European nations. Medard Chouart des Groseilliers and Pierre-Esprit Radisson were two of these.

Groseilliers and Radisson opened the rich Hudson Bay region to the French, but they believed that they were mistreated by the political administration of the colony. They therefore joined the newly formed Hudson's Bay Company of the English, which established trade with the Cree nation of the north. Martin Chartier and Pierre Bisaillon helped to establish the foundations of the fur trade for the English colony of Pennsylvania in much the same way.[7]

THE UPPER COUNTRY

Organizing a fur-trading expedition into the interior was a serious task. References to the *Pays d'en Haut*, or upper country, of New France usually encompassed the Great Lakes region around Michillimakinac and Mackinaw Bay more than 1,500 miles away. Most fur traders were gone from the settlements from May to August, when the rivers were clear of ice, in order to trade in the upper country for furs brought from the west and north by native American trappers. Coureurs de bois often traveled an additional 500 miles to the source of the beaver in the territories of the Miami, Illinois, Sioux, or Assinibione nations.

The basic form of transportation for fur traders was the *canot du nord*, or birchbark canoe. These functional watercraft were sometimes replaced by larger but similarly structured vessels known as bateaux. Canoes and bateaux would be loaded with trade goods for the outward journey and could hopefully hold many large bundles of furs on the return trip. These may have passed through many hands and many have traveled many hundreds of miles from the interior. Only the strongest among the young engages would be recruited for such trips, as they often had to paddle 2 thousand miles upriver to complete their trading. They would then have to return to either Montreal or Quebec before the ice set in.

Packing a canoe for these journeys required a good deal of skill. The fur trader required personal gear and supplies to ensure his own comfort and survival. As many as thirty articles were considered essential. Nonetheless, the fur trader could bargain for food items such as dried corn, peas, beans, and dried meats (jerky), as well as fresh fruits and vegetables. He could hunt for game in the forests and fish in the rivers, but these activities took time from his fundamental objective. Both in value and volume, therefore, trade goods accounted for the greatest part of the load. These could be traded for furs and for other essentials. The major trade goods were broadcloth, woolen blankets, cotton and linen cloth, shirts, metal goods, fishing gear, firearms, ammunition, and gunpowder. Tobacco, liquor, jewelry, trinkets, and other items that the native population might consider luxuries accounted for only a small fraction of the goods traded.

Clothing and cloth may have represented two-thirds of the trade goods brought into the interior. What was meant by the term *broadcloth* is not clear from the surviving records of the fur companies, but it is generally considered by historians to refer to thick, blanket-weight wool in bolts of cloth rather than finished blankets. Blankets may have been white or gray-white with one or more wide red or blue bands woven into them. Traders also were known to carry a lighter-weight red or blue fabric of which the native women were fond for making skirts. Finished clothing items such as twilled coats, woolen capots, bleached and unbleached shirts, and socks were highly regarded but probably came in a one-size-fits-all assortment of colors.

Weapons and ammunition, if they were allowed at all, amounted to about one-eighth of the value of the trade goods. They were heavy but took up little room. Guns, shot, bar lead, bullet molds, and gunpowder were very important trade items, and many traders included them in their loads even if they were strictly forbidden by law. Powder and lead were highly prized by most natives, and as much as 600 pounds of each might be carried in a bateau paddled by twelve men, with proportionately less being carried in the smaller canoes.

Highly prized metal tools and utensils made up about 10 percent of the total cargo of trade goods. Cauldrons and kettles of various dimensions accounted for about half of this category. They were usually made of copper and nested together to save space. Copper kettles were more highly regarded by the natives than iron ones, and were often broken up to provide malleable metal for other purposes. The kettles were referred to as being of two, three, four, or more "fists"—an archaic measure of their volume. The other half of the metal goods was composed of knives, hatchets, scissors, awls, sewing needles, brass and iron wire, chisels, scrapers, and a few metal arrowheads.

LIQUOR

Alcohol was considered a necessary part of the fur trade. Every canoe of trade goods sent into the interior had at least some liquor on board. The Jesuits detested the practice of trading alcohol to the Indians, considering it the most potent weapon of the devil. Its introduction at the missions was thought to lead to the immediate degradation of the Indians. The Indians were at first fascinated by alcohol's hallucinatory effect, but the novelty quickly wore off and was replaced by an almost universal craving. "The introduction of alcohol into [their] hallucinatory world of dreams, demonology, and fractionalized emotions and spiritual beliefs could not have been anything but devastating. With a few drinks of brandy an Indian could release his soul from his body . . . as though they had been looking on from a point of vantage entirely outside themselves."[8]

Although many native peoples made a weak sort of beer from maple syrup or spruce buds, none of the western or northern tribes had discovered the process of fermentation. They therefore had developed no tolerance for strong drink. Moreover, there are theories held by some historians that a physiological cause related to the sugar content of their blood might explain the almost immediate reaction that many Indians had when exposed to strong drink. Regardless of the cause, native Americans exhibited an extraordinary susceptibility to the effects of alcohol consumption, which was utilized and exploited by most fur traders to the detriment of the Indian population.[9]

Whether physiological, spiritual, or cultural, the effect of alcohol on native American behavior was reported by contemporaries as pathological and devasting. "The liquor made them more than quarrelsome; it literally drove them mad." There seemed to be no limit to the senseless violence to which a drunken Indian might resort, and the women were equally affected. "Their habitual modesty evaporated," and they were capable of violent acts that they would not have considered in a sober state. Robert Juet, a sailor on the Dutch vessel *Half Moon*, noted in 1609 that "there is scarcely a savage, small or great, even among the girls and women, who does not enjoy this intoxication, and who does not take these beverages when they can be had, purely and simply for the sake of being drunk." While the Indians quickly learned what alcohol would do to them, they seemed powerless to resist it, and it is certain that many individuals experienced a physical addiction.[10]

The alcohol used in the fur trade was not rum or brandy as such but a watered-down version of strong spirits known to the Canadian habitants as "whiskey blanc." It was made in three strengths. The weakest, one part spirits diluted in thirty-six parts of water, was for tribes new to alcohol; the intermediate strength, for tribes familiar with liquor, was cut by only one-sixth; and the strongest blend was cut by one-fourth. A barrel of brandy or rum, brought into the wilderness with a great expenditure of effort, could be made to provide many times its volume as a trade good. The sometimes lethal effects of even these diluted alcoholic beverages serves to emphasize the utter vulnerability of the native Americans to the unscrupulous methods of many European fur traders.[11]

THE ENGLISH FUR TRADE

The English traders, who, fearing that their native contacts in the New England fur trade would go north to the French or west to the Dutch at Albany, threw themselves into the wilderness in a fur-trading rivalry that would last through the seventeenth and eighteenth centuries. Having established the necessary logistics, the English trading posts "leapfrogged" into the interior following the Merrimack, Connecticut, and

Hudson Rivers. In 1636 John Pychon opened a successful trading post at Agawam well up the Connecticut River near present-day Springfield, Massachusetts, and Captain Richard Waldron established his post at Pennacock on the Merrimack River in 1668. The English had also quietly displaced the Dutch at New Amsterdam in 1664 and taken possession of their trading post at Albany in 1667. They gained the entire colony in 1672. Fort Oswego had been built on Lake Ontario at the mouth of the Oswego River in 1730, and had been reinforced in 1733. Abbe Francois Piquet considered the post at Oswego "a great and evil menace . . . It not only spoils our [French] trade, but puts the English into communication with a vast number of our Indians, far and near."[12]

Following the Treaty of Aix-la-Chapelle, which ended King George's War in North America in 1748, English traders pushed as far west as the Miami River at Pickawillany. The English advances into the border areas west of Virginia and Pennsylvania were largely a product of commercial interests in the colonies outweighing the statecraft that had ended the War of Austrian Succession in Europe. Within a year the trading post at Pickawillany had taken on the look of a fort, and a dozen traders were working there. The goods they brought by packhorse over the mountains were much finer and less expensive than those of the French, and they attracted more than 4,000 Indians from all over the Old Northwest. This even dwarfed the trade of French Detroit.[13]

A contemporary observer noted the list of trade goods made available to native American hunters and trappers by the English by the middle of the eighteenth century:

The goods for Indian trade, are guns for hunting; lead, balls, powder; steel for striking fire, gun-flints, gun-screws; knives, hatchets, kettles, beads, men's shirts; cloths of blue and red for blankets and petticoats; vermilion and verdigris; red, yellow, green, and blue ribbons of English weaving, needles, thread, awls, blue, white red rateen for making moccasins, woolen blankets, of three points and a half, three, two, and one and a half of Leon cloth, mirrors framed in wood, hats trimmed fine, and in imitation, with variegated plumes in red, yellow, blue and green, hoods for men and children of fringed rateen, galloons, real and imitation, brandy, tobacco, razor for the head, glass in beads made after the fashion of wampum, black wines, paints, &c.[14]

In 1751, John Fraser opened a trading post at the confluence of French Creek and the Allegheny River in western Pennsylvania at the village of Venango, close to the Seneca, the Cayuga, and the tribes of the lower Great Lakes. The French response to this post led to dire consequences. The town was completely destroyed and the natives scattered. The main chief, Unemakemi, also known as Old Britain for his allegiance to the English, was killed and eaten by French allied Indians. Although Fraser was fortunately absent at the time of the attack, two of his traders and all his goods were captured by the French. More importantly the French began a program of fort building in the region that is considered by most historians of the period a direct cause of the French and Indian War.

King George's response to these reports was to order Robert Dinwiddie, governor of Virginia to take drastic steps in 1754: "If you shall find that any number of persons shall presume to erect any fort or forts within the limits of the Province of Virginia [which then included the Ohio country], you are first to require of them to peaceably depart; and if they do still endeavor to carry out any such unlawful and unjustifiable designs, we do hereby strictly charge you . . . to drive them off by force." The man chosen to carry out the first part of this command was George Washington.[15]

NOTES

1. Colin G. Calloway, *New Worlds for All: Indians, Europeans, and the Remaking of Early America*, (Baltimore: Johns Hopkins University Press, 1997), 73.

2. James F. O'Neil, ed., *Their Bearing Is Noble and Proud: A Collection of Narratives Regarding the Appearance of Native Americans from 1740–1815* (Dayton, OH: J.T.G.S., 1995), 10–11. Quoting Pierre Pouchot.

3. Native Americans made many body paints and dyes. Ground red ocher was the closest they came to the brilliant red of vermilion and they quickly learned that green could be made from tarnished copper metal. Broken or cracked brass, copper, and iron kettles were also used to make projectile points, blades, and jewelry.

4. Colin G. Calloway, *The Western Abenakis of Vermont, 1660–1800: War, Migration, and the Survival of an Indian People* (Norman: University of Oklahoma Press, 1990), 220.

5. Calloway, *The Western Abenakis*, 43; George T. Hunt, *The Wars of the Iroquois: A Study in Intertribal Trade Relations* (Madison: University of Wisconsin Press, 1972), 167.

6. Francis Jennings, *The Ambiguous Iroquois Empire: The Covenant Chain Confederation of Indian Tribes with English Colonies from Its Beginnings to the Lancaster Treaty of 1744* (New York: W. W. Norton, 1984), 62.

7. Ibid., 64.

8. Walter D. Edmonds, *The Musket and the Cross: The Struggle of France and England for North America* (Boston: Little, Brown 1968), 48, 71.

9. Ibid., 49.

10. Quoted in Ibid., 48.

11. Ibid., 48.

12. Allan W. Eckert, *Wilderness Empire* (Toronto: Bantam Books, 1980), 184.

13. Calloway, *The Western Abenakis*, 40.

14. O'Neil, 20. Quoting Pierre Pouchot.

15. Eckert, 240.

10

The Militia

It is but too well known by the late numerous murders barbarously committed on our borders, that the county . . . is become the only frontier part of the province left unguarded and exposed to the cruel incursions of the Indian enemy. And the inhabitants of these parts have been obliged to perform very hard military duty for these two years past, in ranging the woods and guarding the frontiers.
—Colonel Thomas Ellison, 1757

FRONTIER SECURITY

Lacking large standing armies, colonials relied heavily on provincial forces or local militias for protection against attack or for prosecuting war with others. The colonial militia in particular has usually been seen from the perspective of the English as they came to rely on it in a manner unlike that of the French or Spanish. From the distance of time most milita organizations appear the same, and it has been difficult for historians to separate any differences or discernible peculiarities in the provincial forces that evolved.

The entire frontier, encompassing many hundreds of miles, rarely required massed military force, but there were a number of border areas along which European nations came into conflict with one another. In addition, there were more than half a dozen centers of repeated military interaction between native American peoples and Europeans. Nonetheless, there was one undeniable unifying characteristic of all colonial forces. Whether set against natives or Europeans, the respective colonial governments attempted to enforce unequivocal recognition of their own sovereignty by using the forces that they had at hand. "Border warfare was the only school in which the yeomanry had been trained up, and as soon as the exigency was over they returned to their farms or workshops." Not until the final struggle for control of the continent did armies from Europe join the fray.[1]

The Burgher Militia

The defensive systems of the Dutch at Albany and on Manhattan Island were surprisingly different. After 1630 the Albany colony relied on the good will and intervention of the Five Nations of Iroquois to defend itself. Motivated largely by a desire to maintain a profitable trade in furs, the Albany Dutch found it necessary to maintain an alliance with the powerful Mohawks, who acted as brokers for furs coming from the more remote tribes in the interior. Both the Dutch and the Mohawks had more to lose than would be gained by any mutual hostility. This quickly became the standard for the New York colony, with the Indians serving as hired mercenaries rather than a "burgher militia" providing for defense.[2]

On the other hand, the Dutch around Manhattan Island (New Amsterdam) became more aggressive toward the local natives. Stripped of their economic usefulness by overtrapping the local furs, the indigenous people were required to submit to colonial rule and were treated as an ignorant and brutish people. Dutch-Indian relations consequently deteriorated as the autonomous local tribes continued to resist colonial authority. The settlers finally became incensed when two Dutch farmers were alleged to have been killed by Indians in 1642. A group of eighty armed men, raised into an ad hoc fighting force from among the settlers, fell upon two encampments of natives near Hackensack (New Jersey), indiscriminately killing men, women, and children. This force lacked the order and structure of a true militia. The only body of respectable size raised by the Dutch during the period was sent to sieze the colony of New Sweden in Delaware in 1655. Less than a decade later, when a small English force seized the Dutch possessions in North America, only a tiny garrison of soldiers stood in the way.[3]

Conquistadors and Captains-General

The Spanish feared an uprising if they armed the peasants who populated their colonies. They therefore encouraged private persons to undertake the colonial defense. The *adelantado*, or military chieftain, risked his own capital knowing that the Crown would reward success with titles of nobility, land, and broad governmental powers in the explored regions. Consequently, the Spanish eschewed a militia entirely and provided troops led by Spaniards of noble birth known as *conquistadors*, or captains-general, for the protection of their colonies.[4]

Widely dispersed *presidios*, or garrisons, were established to house these men. From these fortified positions the soldiers sought out and actively engaged those local Indians who demanded their continued independence. By using the advanced technology of their firearms, cannon, and armor to great effect, the Spanish decimated the native populations of Mexico and Central America and smashed their will to withstand colonialism. The surviving Indians were then forcibly removed from the countryside and herded into one of the many missions set up by Jesuit priests or Francisan friars. Herein it was hoped that the Indians would be christianized and made submissive or at least docile.

Until the late eighteenth century, the heart and strength of Spanish American colonialism was in Mexico, with the isthmus of Panama and the islands of the West Indies serving as depots for the transportation of gold to the Old World. But in the swamplands of Florida, in the jungles of South America, and on the borderlands of the Desert Southwest of North America the natives were capable of withstanding the full weight of Spanish aggression. The Spanish presence in these areas was numerically insignificant when compared to the indigenous population and the vast area in which they lived.

The failures of the Spanish military in the New World can be seen in several regions outside of Mexico proper. The tensions in Florida, for instance, resulted in persistent outbreaks of violence directed at the Catholic missions. In South America, although they had raped the riches of Peru, the mighty Spanish armies limited themselves to the coastal regions of the continent rather than undertake a campaign against the native tribes of the interior. And finally in the North American Southwest, the Pueblo Indians staged a significant rebellion against aculturation in 1670 by destroying almost every church and mission in Spanish New Mexico. Although attempts at Christianization had been made for almost a century in this region, the Indians singled out the priests for especially gruesome forms of vengeance. In general, the Spanish military failed to convert and Europeanize the native Americans even though they utilized professional soldiers and mercenaries in an attempt to crush their resistance.[5]

The Carignan-Salieres Regiments

The French in North America embraced a completely different defensive strategy by eschewing any form of military force in their dealings with the Indians. In 1643, a child-king, Louis XIV, ascended to the French throne, and the early decades of his reign kept France embroiled in in-

ternal affairs rather than colonial ones. During this period explorers such
as Champlain, La Salle, and Marquette established many of the French
claims to North America. Unfortunately, the period was also characterized by a great deal of corruption at court sustained in large part by
Nicolas Fouquet, the finance minister.

During this period the king ordered that those who originated any
commercial or religious ventures in New France provide their own garrisons. These scanty garrisons of private mercenaries found it nearly impossible to put up a resistance to the unfriendly Iroquois. Not until 1661,
when Fouquet was finally brought to trial, were the funds available for
the Crown to build a respectable colonial presence. In 1664 the French
government made a commitment of royal troops for the first time in the
form of four companies of infantry (200 men) detached from the regular
army regiments and sent to the West Indies. In Quebec twenty companies (1,000 men) of the Carignan-Salieres regiment were stationed. These
established a string of forts along the Richelieu River in 1665, and raided
into Iroquois country in 1666 forcing the Indians to make a peace. Yet
by 1669 fewer than 100 of these troops remained in Canada. Four hundred of the Carignan-Salieres, their enlistment having run out, elected to
remain as settlers as the regiments were returned to France.

King Louis appointed a new finance minister in 1661. This was Jean-
Baptiste Colbert, who played a significant role in producing the vast
revenue surplus that he used in part to establish the foundations of
French colonialism. Colbert was a mercantilist. Appointed minister of
the marine (navy) in 1669, Colbert quickly incorporated into his administration of the colonies the whole theory of mercantilism that was to
characterize the eighteenth century. He helped to establish both the
French East and West India Companies, and he set about creating a navy,
a merchant marine, and a military force to support and protect them.[6]

Thereafter, the Ministry of Marine controlled the French colonies in
much the same way as the Board of Trade (founded 1696) would control
those of the English. Initially, while the Iroquois maintained their treaty,
the small group of Carignan-Salieres in Canada sufficed to police the
inhabitants of New France, but they failed to have the desired effect
when in 1682 hostilities with the Iroquois resumed.[7]

Compagnies Franches de la Marine. The Ministry of Marine chose to
rely on professional troops to police New France and only raised the
inhabitants of Canada (militia) in the most severe emergencies. During
Colbert's administration, the Compagnies Franches de la Marine were
instituted and sent to the French colonies in India, the West Indies, and
North America. The independent companies (*compagnies franches*) chosen
for colonial duty were formed into a distinct establishment of regular
colonial troops. The men generally volunteered for long term service. As
they were raised, supplied, and administered by the Ministry of the Ma-

rine in France, they were known as the Compagnies Franches de la Marine.[8]

The first compagnies franches were sent to the West Indies in 1674. The first three companies to be stationed in Quebec arrived in 1683 in direct response to the renewed Iroquois threat. Within five years thirty-two companies were serving in New France alone; the last three arrived in 1688 just prior to the opening of King William's War. These units were scattered in forts and outposts over a vast territory stretching from Acadia to the Great Lakes and Louisiana.

Many of the early compagnies franches were hastily recruited, and some historians consider them to have been less effective soldiers than their European counterparts. The French colonial officers posted to frontier outposts were generally unskilled in traditional European tactics and lacked immediate oversight. Yet it has been pointed out by students of French colonialism that the training of the soldiers of La Marine was better than that of the common militia, and their officers had far more freedom of action than their counterparts in the regular army in responding to unrest on the frontier.[9]

Only reasonably good conditions of service and sufficient logistical support were likely to produce good soldiers in New France. Over the years between the initial establishment of the compagnies franches and the end of the Seven Years' War, the number and strength of these troops varied, and it is almost certain that the number of available soldiers in each regiment was usually below that prescribed at their establishment. When they retired, or when the individual regiments were disbanded, many of the soldiers of La Marine took up "the vagabond life of an Indian trader, married the daughter of an Indian chief, and cast [their] fortunes with the denizens of the forrest." This greatly helped to cement the generally good relations established by the French with the Algonquian-speaking peoples of Canada.[10]

The compagnies franches took part in almost every engagement against the enemy in North America from 1684 to 1760. Many of these were small affairs, *petites guerres*, suited to small, mobile units like the compagnies franches. The men of the compagnies franches served as both policemen and soldiers. They were detached in small groups to man many of the outposts of the French fur trade, including Montreal, Niagara, Trois-Rivières, Michilimackinac, St. Frederic (Crown Point, New York), Chambly, and Detroit. Besides the Iroquois, they fought Fox Indians in Wisconsin, and Chickasaw and Natchez Indians in Louisiana. Beginning in 1697 unofficial companies of artillerists were recruited from among the compagnies franches. These were some of the best soldiers in La Marine, and they were trained in the use of cannon and mortars of naval design. Although they suffered setbacks, the compagnies franches "maintained the peace and successfully resisted attempts by the English and their Iroquois allies to expand their influence."[11]

After 1755 the independent companies were augmented by regular army units from France known as Troups de Terre. However, in the unconventional style of frontier warfare, the compagnies franches—often serving with militia and Indian allies—were simply more successful than regular troops. When called on to actively campaign in the Seven Years' War, they gave a good account of themselves. The last of the compagnies franches served in Louisiana until 1769, when they were relieved by Spanish troops.

The private soldier wore the standard military coat of the period used by most European armies. That of the Compagnies Franches de la Marine was a long, collarless, single-breasted coat made of grey-white wool with broad blue cuffs and blue lining, and metal buttons (either brass or pewter). The pocket flaps were set low on the hips and the skirts could be hooked back at the corners. At each corner of the skirts was a reinforcement in the shape of an anchor, a symbol of La Marine.

Long-sleeved waistcoats (vests), and breeches and stockings, known as smallclothes, were also grey-white until 1716, when they were made blue. These were made of wool, but linen was used for summer service. The usual hat was the tricorn with the front raised high and a ribbon cockade on the left side. A cloth forage cap with a long tail was also issued. This was an ingenious affair with a front turn-up and a surrounding wide edge. The forage cap must have been popular as it was retained by the Royal Army into the French Revolution and adopted as a watering cap by the Napoleonic cavalry. A white neck stock and shirt completed the uniform.

Shoes were worn rather than boots. Long stockings woven of woolen thread extended to the thigh. Long gaiters, with supporting garters, covered and protected the leg to the knee. These were strapped under the shoe and prevented its being pulled off the foot in the mud. Each man had one pair of gaiters made of white linen canvass, one water-resistant pair made of linen canvass blackened with tar, and one pair made of black woolen cloth. The gaiters were a new addition to the uniform introduced at the time of Queen Anne's War (1701).

The regulation armament was a sword and a flintlock musket with bayonet. French firearms were generally of superior quality when compared to English military arms of the period. The steel-mounted French weapons were somewhat lighter and more reliable than those of the English. The Tulle Marine Musquet of .69 caliber was carried by all the regulars in French America including the compagnies franches. The *tulle fusille de chase* (hunting musket) was a favorite with militiamen and Indians because it was sturdy and lighter than the standard weapon. A powder horn was slung over the shoulder on a thin leather belt to pro-

This detail from an eighteenth-century manuscript shows part of the military drill used by French infantry. Both the Compagnies Franches de la Marine and the Troupes de Terre in New France would have looked similar to these men. The operation being demonstrated is "Fix Bayonets."

vide priming powder. After 1684 a sword and bayonet were carried in a double frog suspended from the leather waistbelt, which also supported a small cartridge box. These leather boxes seem to have gone through a number of variations, holding from nine to thirty paper-wrapped charges in a wooden block drilled out for the purpose. The flap of the cartridge box carried a medallion engraved with the King's arms and a white anchor representing the Ministry of Marine. The swords had thin straight blades sometimes of triangular cross section with a brass hilt which included a simple knuckle-guard. The wooden grip was wrapped in brass wire.

However, the compagnies franches appeared very different when on campaign in the wilderness. Indian-style moccasins, leather or cloth leggings, and a breechclout were often worn. The large European hat was replaced by the cloth forage cap, and the uniform coat gave way to the blanket capote—a short, hooded, and unlined coat made of blanket-weight wool and tied closed with a woolen or leather belt. In winter, mittens and native American–style snowshoes were issued. In the heat of summer the capote could be used as a blanket at night, and daytime service was performed in a sleeved waistcoat. While the firearms remained unchanged, the cumbersome swords usually gave way to hatchets or tomahawks.[12]

Troupes de Terre. The militia and the compagnies franches were the only military forces available to defend Canada until the middle of the eighteenth century. In 1746 four battalions of regular troops were sent to Canada. These troops were called Troupes de Terre. In 1755, attesting to the military buildup required by the Seven Years' War, four additional battalions arrived with Baron Ludwig August Dieskau, and two more battalions came to America with the Marquis de Montcalm in 1756. Four battalions arrived in 1757 and 1758. The Troupes de Terre were almost always composed of understrength units, and they were reinforced by companies of militia and Indian allies. They included men from a number of European regiments: La Rein, Bourgogne, Languedoc, Guienne, Artois, Royal Roussillon, La Sarre, Bearn, Berry, Cambis, and Volontaires Étrangers. The unit integrity of these regiments was almost always respected during campaigns, so that, for instance, only La Reine and Languedoc were present at the Battle of Lake George in 1755, and only Guienne, Bearn, and La Sarre were at the seige of Fort Oswego in 1756.

The uniforms of the Troupes de Terre was the same grey-white woolen coat found among other royal troops, but their smallclothes and facings were of distinctive colors, including blue, red, and white. The breeches were uniformly grey-white, while the arrangment of buttons, lace, and pocket flaps varied according to regimental standards and traditions.[13]

Small detachments from the Royal Artillery were introduced in 1756 to strengthen the forts and and reinforce the cannoneers of the compagnies franches. The French artillery did good service in the American wars, dragging cannons through the forests and transferring them to and from boats and barges. A Corps of Cavalry was organized in 1759 from among the Canadiens, but this never numbered more than 200 troopers. The mounted forces were led by regular French officers. The Corps of Cavalry served for less than a year, as it was found that horses could not be used as effectively in the deep woods and brush-filled fields of America as they had been on the more open plains of Europe. The uniform worn by these ancillary troops was blue, faced in red. The cavalry may have worn a leather cap trimmed in bearskin.

TO PROVIDE FOR THE COMMON DEFENSE

No formal estabishment of regular army troops was used in America for defense for almost a century and a half after the founding of the first English colony. In part this was due to the character of the colonists, religious dissenters or political outsiders, who distrusted professional military forces. Moreover, the home government itself was in turmoil from 1640 to 1660 during the English Civil Wars and again beginning in

1688 with the Glorious Revolution. Even if the colonists in America had wished a regular army, there was no force available in England to send.

Unlike the French, who were treated to the rule of a single royal family with four monarchs (the Bourbons), the British government or ruling royal houses changed six times and had twelve separate heads of state during the colonial period.[14] These almost continuous political and social upheavals figured prominently in the history of all the English colonies. A major battle was fought between Royalists and Roundheads on Maryland soil, and as many as one-third of all able-bodied male Puritans in Massachusetts returned to England to support the Parliament. Without a concensus about which government in England was lawful during the periods of unrest, the colonies generally reverted to the last form of legitimate governance until such time as the question had been resolved in England. "Confusion in the administration of military, as well as civil, affairs necessarily accompanied these abrupt and bewildering changes." With Royalist planters controlling the southern colonies and Puritans predominating in New England, leaders, both public and military, took sides in these disputes, and many soldiers deserted their posts.[15]

A similar circumstance took place during the Glorious Revolution of 1688. The governor of New York, Sir Edmund Andros, was a "thick-and-thin royalist" who considered the colonists "little better than rebels and traitors." The people, generally believing the king (James II) to be a tyrant, were "disconcerted, angry, and stubborn—by no means the best frame of mind for facing a great public danger."[16] A Dutch rebel named Jacob Leisler, buoyed by the crowning of William of Orange as king of England, raised a group of his countrymen, seized Fort William in lower Manhattan, and attempted to gain control of the colony. However, Albany was still controlled by the Conservative Party under the leadership of Mayor Peter Schuyler. The unrest continued until word came from King William and Queen Mary appointing Leisler governor.[17]

The colonists in Virginia and New England were remarkably dissimilar in their political, economic, social, and religious attitudes. Yet in their beliefs concerning local defense they were very similar, possibly because they both shared the same English military traditions. Without regard to the region of England from which they came, their political party, or their religion, Englishmen came to America armed to the teeth. "The story of the military institutions of the American colonies is an account of efforts to keep as much of the population as possible armed and prepared to fight on short notice." Evidences of lances, crossbows, firelocks, body armor, and helmets reminiscent of the Middle Ages have been found in even remote colonial settlements.[18]

Each English colony designed its own systems of defense, generally fashioned around a militia formed of its male citizens. These organizations were remarkably similar considering the number of individual colonial governments involved in their creation, and any differences are more easily ascribed to regional characteristics rather than any genuine inconsistency. The structure of the militias that were established in the English colonies speaks volumes concerning the daily life of colonials on the frontier.[19]

Neither New York nor Pennsylvania had a large militia establishment beyond local companies. While New Yorkers followed the lead of the original Dutch founders of their colony by relying almost entirely on the good will of the Iroquois for defense, the peace-loving Quakers of Pennsylvannia uniformly resisted raising any local armed forces. Pennsylvania's fortunate geographic position at the center of the English colonies allowed the Quaker majority to pursue their pacifism into the middle of the eighteenth century, with the northern colonies fighting the French on one hand and the southern colonies keeping the Spanish at a distance on the other. Those English who settled in Virginia, Maryland, or the Carolinas came armed and expected to fight off both the native population and any incursions by the Spanish. In fact, as late as 1740 Spanish privateers could be found stalking the Atlantic coast from Florida to the Delaware Bay.

Unlike the other colonies with their mountain barriers to the west, the whole extent of the New England frontier was open to the sudden descent of an enemy by canoe. Rivers flowed to the sea from the interior and through most of the English settlements that made up Massachusetts, Connecticut, and New Hampshire. These were highways into the wilderness, but they were also avenues of danger to be watched.[20] It was almost impossible to efficiently defend this frontier. "To block up the mouths of the rivers with forts, isolated from all support, was equally idle, as was proved by the utter failure of every such attempt. Herein lay the weakness of the English. They were compelled to receive the enemy at their own doors, and that disadvantage they labored under from first to last." The New Englanders initially maintained good relations with the native peoples but joined together in the middle of the seventeenth century to wage a series of wars of annihilation on particular Indian tribes.[21]

Finally, those who settled in the backcountry found that there was simply no adequate passive defense for such isolated habitations. Frontier colonists resorted to the expedient of "forting up" during times of unrest. A chain of log "forts" and garrison houses was established along the colonial frontier. The need to link these outposts led to the development of rangers, who scouted the gaps between forts looking for signs of Indians.[22]

These factors gave the English militia a unique regional flavor even to the type and quality of the soldiers it produced. The Southern colonies preferred to raise more cavalry units than did the colonies of New England. As early as 1672 the Virginia colony claimed to be able to field twenty troops of horse (thirty mounted men each) and an equal number of companies of infantry (thirty musketmen and thirty pikemen). Neither Massachusetts nor Connecticut, with populations equal to or larger than Virginia's, could field such a number or proportion of horsemen at that period.

Bacon's Rebellion

The dangers presented to effective governance by the existence of large bodies of unregulated militia can be seen in Bacon's Rebellion in Virginia in 1676. The causes of the rebellion were complicated and obscure then, and are no less so today. Moreover, much of what was known of it was distorted by the lens of patriotism during the American Revolution.

Nathaniel Bacon was only twenty-six, but he maintained a successful plantation on the James River and had enough wealth and influence to sit on the council of the elderly royal governor, William Berkeley. It is certain that Bacon was neither a hotheaded youth nor a romantic cavalier defending the oppressed. His motives for defying the royal governor at this time are unclear, and his early death prevented him from leaving a detailed written account. Certainly the plantation owners and settlers along the Virginia and Maryland frontier were discontented with the colonial government when Bacon appeared on the scene. "His courage and decisiveness made him at once a popular hero, not only with the small farmers on the frontiers, but with the substantial planters and traders as well."[23]

By 1670 the expansion of plantations into the interior had created increased friction with the natives. The spark that raised the conflict took place in the Potomac River valley in the summer of 1675 when the local militia from Virginia crossed into Maryland and slaughtered almost two dozen Doeg and Susquehannock Indians in a feud over some missing hogs. The Indians retaliated, and the whites demanded further retribution. Back and forth along the frontier, raid and counter-raid followed. In spring 1676 thirty-six persons living on the Rappahannock River were killed during a series of Indian attacks. Virginia settlers, terrified by the renewed hostilities, found themselves clustered for defense in their backwoods settlements. As a consequence the local companies lashed out in unauthorized raids at any Indians they could find.

There was little response from the governor. He rejected the more aggressive course favored by the colonists and ordered an end to any vigilante actions. He also ordered the establishment of a series of weakly garrisoned stronghouses in the border areas secured by a ranging force of 125 cavalrymen. This plan required the establishment of a provincial army of more than 500 men. Although many of the tidewater aristocracy

Some think that Bacon's Rebellion was a spontaneous uprising against a particularly autocratic and stubborn colonial governor. Others view it a precursor to the American Revolution. Neither Nathaniel Bacon nor Governor William Berkeley was without fault in the conflict. Both men seem to have acted in an imprudent and extreme manner.

supported the governor, the frontier planters scoffed at Berkeley's design, as it would raise the level of taxation to a point the planters could not bear. While the governor would do nothing further to stop the frontier massacres, he also absolutely refused to empower the militias to deal with the problem themselves.

Nathaniel Bacon and his followers called for a thousand volunteers to raid the Indian settlements. This action was successful in suppressing the Indian attacks, but Bacon refused to disband his army. Before long, Bacon's followers began to call for sweeping changes in the colonial government. They elected a new House of Burgesses with Bacon as one of its members. This body extended the franchise to all freemen and lowered taxes over the objections of Berkeley and his supporters on the royal council. Even the colony's women played a roll, and they were among the rebellion's most active zealots.[24]

To this point Bacon and his followers had determined their course based on the solid underpinnings of absolute necessity. However, as friction between Berkeley and Bacon increased, Virginia became split between increasingly belligerent factions, and active warfare broke out between the two. Contemporaries considered the ensuing rebellion a spontaneous uprising against the tyranny of an obstinate royal governor. Ultimately the governor fled and abandoned the seat of government at Jamestown to Bacon's followers, who burned the town. Almost immediately thereafter, Bacon contracted a fever and died.

The rebel army simply melted away, and the governor returned with nothing but vengeance on his mind. He captured and summarily hanged all the members of the rebellion whom he could identify. Their property was confiscated and their families were turned out of their homes. Word of Berkeley's program of revenge was reported to King Charles II in London, who was shocked by the governor's lack of restraint and presently recalled and replaced him. Royal troops were sent to the Virginia colony, and thereafter the upheaval slowly died down.

Bacon's forces were "a little reminiscent of European mercenary armies of the sixteenth and seventeenth centuries . . . where the government lost control of the war while trying to wage it more effectively." Bacon's Rebellion was duly noted by the royal authorities at the time, and it may have accelerated and justified the transformation of the Virginia Company's settlements into a royal province. Ultimately Governor Berkeley's forts were built and a few dozen mounted soldiers were hired to range, or patrol, between them—the first rangers in American history.[25]

Southern Militia

A comparision of the organization and function of the militia in New England with that of the southern colonies finds several important differences in their regional character. Most notable was the clustering of settlements and the formation of cohesive towns in New England, while the plantations of Maryland, Virginia, or the Carolinas were virtually isolated outposts separated by many miles. Dense populations served as an advantage to an effective militia system. The early settlements along the James and York Rivers, such as at Jamestown or Williamsburg, offered a small but densely settled pool of potential fighting men who could come together to form a cohesive body, but this was lacking in the later colonial period as farmsteads spread across the frontier.

Once the native Americans of the Chesapeake Bay area were weakened by war and disease, the Virginia militia virtually ceased to exist except as an agency for the control of slaves. White Carolinians were forced to defend themselves from both Spanish aggression directed from Florida and the possiblity of Indian outrages along the frontiers, almost without aid of any kind. Ultimately, the militia of South Carolina became so scattered by the rapid expansion of the frontier settlements as to be incapable of an effective defense. By 1760 the colony's 2,000 militiamen were spread out over 150 miles of frontier. The defensive system became so poor that most of the outlying settlements in Souh Carolina had to be abandoned, with settlers fleeing east to avoid the raids and attacks brought on by the French and Indian War. With the introduction of a regiment of British regulars into the buffer colony of Georgia in 1732, what was left of the South Carolina militia system also evolved from a military force poised to withstand outward agression into a simple slave patrol.[26]

The New England Confederation

An importantly different aspect of the militia in New England from that in the south seems to have been the formation in 1643 of the New England Confederation, which tried to unify the authority and command of the militia of several colonies. The Pequot War of 1637 initially indicated the need for a more organized response to defense needs among the New England colonies. The most important aspect of the formation of the confederation was its central purpose of "joint military and diplomatic action." The New England colonial army, made up of militia volunteers "provided, provisioned, and paid by the colonies in proportion to their fighting male population," functioned well, if not perfectly.[27]

The confederation lasted for forty-two years successfully overcoming various problems posed by the friction between colonial officers and the various colonial commissions. Mobilization of forces was often slow, intercolonial command was awkward, and colonial objectives were sometimes at cross purposes. Although one aspect of the system was its phenomenal inefficiency, it should be noted that the militia in New England "won all the important wars undertaken [by it] in the colonial period." More importantly, the New England militias were able to raise at times upwards of 1,000 men to prosecute and win major wars against the Indian populations—all without revolting against their colonial governments as had the militia in Virginia.[28]

The Pequot War

The Pequot tribe was an Algonquian-speaking people closely related to the Mohegans. They inhabited a narrow strip of coastal New England. At the time of European contact they controlled all of Connecticut east of the Connecticut River to the Pequot River (Thames River) near New London and west to present-day New Haven. There may have been up to 2,500 individuals in the tribe. Initially, they maintained fairly good relations with the Dutch and English in the region.

In 1637 the murder of a local trader caused a breech in these good relations. The New England colonies fielded a large army that surrounded and destroyed the main Pequot stronghold near the Mystic River. Many of the natives were killed outright. Others were burned to death when the village was fired. Between 600 and 700 Indians were

In both the Pequot War and King Philip's War, the colonists of New England reacted to the depredations of their native American neighbors in a drastic and inhumane manner that set a precedent for future generations of colonists in their relationships with Indians.

killed. Of the survivors, a large number were taken captive and sent as slaves to the West Indies. Other survivors scattered to live among other native tribes in the region. One month later, a remnant of the tribe was surrounded in a swamp in the town of Fairfield, Connecticut, by 120 Massachusetts men who had pursued them. All but a few dozen were killed or captured.

The Pequot War was the first major conflict undertaken by the English against an Indian nation. There was no question that so many Europeans with their firearms and light armor would prevail over the Indians with their bows and arrows, tomahawks, and war clubs. This success set the precedent for all other major campaigns against the native Americans undertaken by the English: Attack their villages, burn their crops, enslave those that were not killed. Devastate or totally eradicate the tribe by relentless pursuit.

King Philip's War

Metacomet was a son of Massasoit, the chief of the Wampanoag nation who had greeted the Pilgrims in Massachusetts in 1620. Metacomet, known to the English as King Philip, became the tribal leader after the death of his father and older brother. He led an alliance of coastal New England tribes in a war to end illegal white encroachment on their lands. In June 1675 a series of attacks was made upon the English settlements at Swansea, Rhode Island, and Dartmouth, Taunton, and Middleboro, Massachusetts.

The New England Confederation fielded an army of more than 1,000 men under the command of Josiah Winslow. Captain Benjamin Church, who initially was offered command and would later be regarded as a great "Indian fighter," served as a volunteer. In December this force surrounded the main stronghold of the Narragansett Indians near Kingston, Rhode Island, which was occupied by 3,500 Indian allies of King Philip. The assault lasted three hours, and the English penetrated the defenses of the village. They set some 500 dwellings on fire and retired to stand about the burning stockade shooting any Indians who attempted escape. More than 1,000 natives were killed, but more than 200 colonials were killed or wounded as the survivors broke out into the nearby marshes.

Benjamin Church was wounded twice in the battle, but he was fully recovered when in February 1676 he led the colonial army in a campaign that systematically destroyed the villages and food stores of the Indians of the region. Among the prisoners taken in these raids were the wife and children of King Philip, who were sold as slaves in the West Indies. Finally, in August, Church ambushed Philip in a refuge near Bristol, Rhode Island. King Philip was reportedly killed by the Indian who had betrayed his hiding place to the English. Philip's death effectively ended the war. The methods of warfare employed by the colonials in future wars owed a great deal to the trial-and-error techniques of these earlier encounters.

A WELL-REGULATED MILITIA

A well-regulated and well-trained militia provided a practical solution to the defense needs of most settlements. It had been tested and employed successfully against the Indians in the limited operations that characterized the wars against the Pequots and King Philip. Consequently, militia systems were established throughout the English colonies by the end of the seventeenth century. While less than adequate to substitute as a regular army, such organizations were ultimately able to defend the settlements, drive back the Indians, and hold open the newly abandoned lands for European acquisition.

In lightly populated areas the militia system was an immediate and practical measure for public safety largely necessitated by an ever-shifting string of frontier villages. Yet there remains in America the cherished romantic concept of the milita as "minutemen," a mythical army

The frontiersman often turned out for service in the militia during an emergency with little in the way of military equipment. The author is wearing a broad-brimmed felt hat and linen hunting frock in this photograph. He is carrying an English-style "Brown Bess" musket.

of self-trained and self-armed warriors springing from the colonial soil in times of trouble. While this may seem a natural and sensible means of having, near at hand, contingents of men familiar with the use of weapons, the reality of relying on such a makeshift system for defense could prove a disastrous illusion.

The earliest settlers were seldom effectively organized for warfare when simply formed in hastily assembled and informally constructed groups. It was found that only with training was the colonial soldiery effective. Therefore, periodic training days were instituted, and a cadre of elected or appointed officers was formed. A local stockpile of gunpowder and a few artillery pieces were provided along with armor, pikes, and other items not commonly available to the settlers. These improvements became characteristic of most militia systems.[29]

The Local Company

The structure of the local militia companies in New England has been very well documented.[30] Company strength ranged from 65 to 200 men but often fell below 65, at which time units might be combined from neighboring communities. Local command was invested in a captain, subalterns, and sergeants. These officers were usually elected by the men, but after the middle of the seventeenth century nominations and commissions were being approved by the General Court in New England and colonial governors elsewhere. While military authority generally came from a legislative body or the Crown, the actual management of any war was left to the colonial governors. The overall command structure and the level of authority of individual leaders generally lacked clear definition and varied in form from province to province. Various colonies resorted to the "mode of military organization most proximate to their experience and resources"; others were geographically organized and administered on the town or county level.[31]

As settlement first began, every able-bodied man was a potential soldier and had a legal obligation to serve. For frontier settlers it was impossible to separate defense from the other tasks of daily living such as clearing land, growing food, and building shelters. Men went to church with muskets in hand and set them down nearby in the pew or along the wall. As the character of a village or town became more settled, the nature of the military service changed; but the universal obligation of all able-bodied freemen (including servants) to serve seems to have remained throughout most of the colonial period. Women, magistrates, ministers, slaves, and those who suffered from physical and mental impediments or extreme old age were generally exempt from military duty. In Massachusetts in 1652 it was required that all free Negroes and Indians living in the colony train as part of the militia, but by the end of the century the same persons were legally prohibited from serving. Nonetheless, in times of military emergency, every man, able-bodied or not, became a frontline soldier.[32]

Newly settled villages found it difficult to fulfill their manpower needs, and often several local militias were combined to attain sufficient unit strength to ward off determined attacks. As towns became more settled, militia membership became more social—a mark of full citizenship among the males in the community, but certain minimum property qualifications could exempt those who were wealthy in terms of land and livestock.

Although a lone defense against the attack by even a small enemy force had no practical chance of success, men on the frontier remained reluctant to leave their homes in time of danger to fight in other localities. Small groups of frontiersmen would rather "fort up" in a single defensible position than become part of a larger campaign. This reluctance was somewhat allayed because the laws governing the militia usually prohibited men from serving for long periods far from home or outside their own province or colony.

Provincial Forces

Most of the soldiers who fought for the English colonies prior to the final cataclysm of the French and Indian War were colonials. Only after 1754 were large numbers of regulars sent to the English colonies. However, these colonials were not formed into a simple citizen army but rather were regular provincial troops—formed into regiments and paid by the colony. After the Pequot War of 1637, the Puritans overhauled their militia system to provide for a quick reaction force called a *trained band*, something likened to the concept of a minuteman. They also began to fill their overall manpower needs by imposing quotas on the individual towns.[33]

After the Indian wars of 1675, men were recruited to serve in provincial regiments. These regiments were in some measure bound by kinship ties with fathers, sons, brothers, and cousins all serving in the same unit. The numerous appeals from the colonies for aid during Queen Anne's War and Britain's constant need to maintain a war footing in America during the previous two decades provoked a formal reassessment of colonial policy early in the second decade of the eighteenth century. The Board of Trade began to look at the possibility of putting the individual colonies on a more secure imperial footing and of placing the frontier settlements under the strictures of martial law during times of war. From this point provincial regiments were established to replace the less formal militia units in major operations. In many colonies they became permanent organizations known as the Governor's Foot Guard, or Horse Guard. In later times they became the Royal Americas or the Queen's Rangers.

Fighting Age. Massachusetts and Virginia laws generally agreed that those between the ages of 16 and 60 would be formed into militia units for training. This age range is generally undisputed by historical authorities, but it may leave the student with an incorrect picture of what a provincial army looked like. Exhaustive studies of provincial forces suggest that the average age of men serving in the provincal forces was just under 26, with 80 percent under 35 and less than 2 percent over 55 (many of them officers). Rather than a conglomerate group made up of a spectrum of men of many ages, only a few boys and older men peppered the ranks. Provincial armies were pragmatically composed of adult males in the prime of life. Almost 90 percent of these men were volunteers, and, unlike the soldiers of Europe, most of them were literate—being able to read the Bible and write their names and short letters.[34]

Appearance. In the eighteenth century, militiamen were expected to supply most of their own arms, accouterments, and clothing. Evidence suggests that there was little uniformity of dress, each man wearing what

This historical reenactor is wearing a linen hunting frock, a wide-brimmed hat, a woolen sash, leather leggings, and moccasins. He is carrying a linen haversack on his left hip and a powder horn and ammunition pouch on his right. The handle of his tomahawk can be seen protruding from under the pouch.

he thought best for his own comfort and circumstance. The backcountry militia companies commonly wore the same garments in which they pursued their daily livings on the frontier. This would include a linen shirt in summer and one of deerskin in winter. This was covered with an outer garment known as a hunting shirt, "a kind of loose frock, reaching hafway down the thigh, with large sleeves, open before and so wide as to lap over a foot or more when belted." Each hunting shirt was made of heavy linen and had a shoulder cape of the same material. The garment was usually trimmed in unraveled cloth in the manner of a fringe and was held closed with the same belt that held a knife and hatchet.[35]

An ammunition pouch, powder horn, and a haversack were usually worn on straps which crossed the chest. A wide variety of caps, hats, and kerchiefs were used to cover the head. Most men wore broad-brimmed felt hats and stocking caps. The men wore loose trousers or breeches of wool or linen, moccasins or shoes on their feet, and their lower legs were often covered with Indian leggings or "leather stockings."

The local militia unit from Norwalk, Connecticut, commanded by Thomas Fitch, the governor's son, marching off to join the colonial forces massing in Albany, was dressed in such a variety of common workmen's clothing and civilian dress that it seemed unlike a proper military unit. Fitch's sister, to provide some level of uniformity, gave each man a chicken feather for his hat. When the men arrived at the encampment, a surgeon among the British regulars took the opportunity to write a poem derisive of the colonials. This was later set to a common tavern tune, and became the song "Yankee Doodle." Ironically, the colonials adopted the song as a anthem illustrative of their independent spirit.[36]

Basic Equipment. Although local authorities kept a supply of weapons and gunpowder on hand for emergencies, every colony required that each householder provide himself and his family with specific weapons and equipment. In most colonies each militiaman was required to bring his own musket (or rifle), one pound of lead balls "fitted" to his weapon, powder in proper proportion to the ball, a haversack, a one-quart canteen or water bottle, and a hatchet, tomahawk, or hunting knife. Moreover, few muskets were loaded directly from powder horns. Instead, ammunition was made up ahead of time in paper rolls, kept in a cartridge box or bag, containing both a measure of powder and a leaden ball. The powder horn was generally used only for priming or by riflemen, who might alter their measure of powder depending on range.

There remain many questions about the effectiveness of heavy seventeenth-century equipment (particularly the body armor) in the American wilderness. It seems certain that after King Philip's War (1675), the pike and most of the metal armor all but disappeared. By 1658 the New England Confederation's standing orders to its militia members no

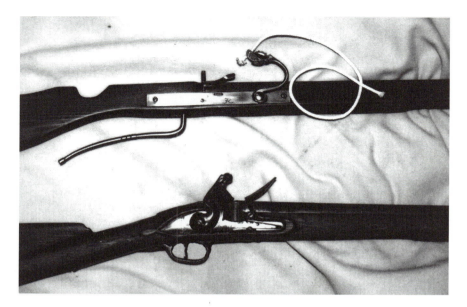

No other technological advance was more important to the direction of native-European interaction than the musket. The earliest muskets brought to the New World had matchlock ignition systems like the example at the top. A glowing rope was dipped into a small pan of gunpowder by the lever. The example at the bottom is a more dependable flintlock from the mid-eighteenth century. The flint, held in the jaws, snapped forward against the upright steel plate sending a shower of hot sparks into the pan. The flashing powder passed through a small hole into the rear of the barrel, igniting the propellant charge behind the lead ball.

longer called for any plate armor other than the gorget—an iron protective collar worn about the neck and shoulders. These changes mirrored similiar developments in Europe.[37]

It has been said that the colonial period bridged the gap between medieval warfare and the onset of the modern warfare of the mid-nineteenth century.[38] Adjustments to military methods, instruments, and tactics came to America somewhat slowly. The mere passage of time eventually marked the evolution of weapons from pole arms, swords, and matchlocks to more convenient tomahawks and knives, and more dependable flintlock muskets and rifles. Moreover, orderly books and journals from the period indicate that militiamen were frequently ignorant of rudimentary drills and were barely able to deal in a military manner with the wide variety of arms available in the colonies.[39]

Firearms. Historians report that matchlock muskets predominated in the Plymouth colony over flintlock (snaphance) muskets before 1645. After that date the colony seems to have been armed completely with the more dependable flintlock weapon. Rapier swords were more numerous than either type of musket during the early colonial period, suggesting that most men were armed with some type of blade.

By the beginning of the eighteenth century almost all of the firearms used by the militia were based upon the same standard smooth-bore flintlock technology used by the armies of Europe. Most firearms, including pistols, fired a generally large lead ball between .63 and .75 caliber, but more than half a dozen different calibers were commonly used during the period. The effective range of the long arms remained under 100 yards, while the visually intimidating pistols were actually wildly inaccurate and useful only at very close quarters. The more accurate rifle did not become a major factor in warfare until the American Revolution.

Rangers

Almost all the colonies used rangers. Only Pennsylvania and New York seem to have neglected the establishment of a formal corps of these paid frontiersmen to watch their outlying borders. Of course New York relied on the ubiquitous Iroquois, but the pacifists in Pennsylvania absolutely refused to take any steps toward creating military units, even defensive ones. Ultimately the non-Quaker settlers of Pennsylvania paid the price of pacifism with their blood on the western frontiers. Virginia, on the other hand, established a system of paid, mounted rangers in the seventeenth century of almost 1,000 men. They patroled the frontiers, held down depredations, and tried to keep abreast of the attitudes of the natives.

Edmond Atkin, a prosperous Charleston merchant familiar with the Indians of the southeastern frontiers, was made an Indian agent by the Board of Trade and asked to submit a plan for the defense during the troubled times of 1755. One of Atkin's proposals was the creation of an extensive line of forts on the frontier to provide not only safe havens, but also trading posts and warehouses for presents and trade goods for the natives. In combination with these he suggested the formation of two troops of rangers from among "men used to the woods" to be paid by the provincial fund. Two rangers were "to be quartered at all times at each fort, in order to carry expresses. And the rest to be employed ranging on the back of the settlements of the several provinces in such manner as shall be found most convenient for their protection. For which purpose they should carry some dogs with them, the more effectually to discover skulking Indians by their scent. Whereby the Indians will be terrified, and the back settlers rendered quiet and safe in their plantations."[40]

The New England colonies established a similar but less extensive system of rangers along their northern borders in the French and Indian War to protect the outlying settlers from the ravages of sudden attack. The best-known group of rangers were those raised by Robert Rogers from among the tough woodsmen of the New Hampshire frontier. Rogers' Rangers could rival any Indian war party in ambush, murder, and scalpings. Like chameleons, they combined Indian moccasins and leggings with uniform coats that were sober green in spring and faded to an almost perfectly camouflaged green-yellow by fall. They were seemingly impervious to weather, bivouacking in the snow, silently flashing past French outposts in winter on ice skates, and penetrating their lines on snowshoes. Rogers' own hairbreadth escape during the Battle on Snowshoes, fought near Lake George in 1758, caused colonial recruits to flock to him. It soon became evident that no British army, provincial or regular, could move safely through the wilderness without a protective screen of rangers.

Although Rogers' Rangers seem to have provided good service to the British regulars, their status as something between regulars and frontiersmen had drawbacks. They were considered chronically unruly, undisciplined, and overpaid by many regular British officers. Ironically, these officers seem to have harbored a special resentment against Rogers, who was personable, charming, and a natural leader, simply because he was a provincial officer. "British army officers who served in North America during the Seven Years' War never tired of reminding one another that the American colonists made the world's worst soldiers."[41]

Rogers' Rangers were important during the colonial period, but they left their mark on American culture as well. The rangers' effective attack on the Abenaki Indian mission at St. Francis in 1759 and their heroic return through the wilderness have become the stuff of novels and of classic cinema and television. The rangers so captured the imagination of Americans that their name was given to the special striking forces of World War II, and Captain Rogers' detailed instructions for his volunteer rangers, written in 1758, still serve as the basis for the irregular tactics used by the Special Forces of the U.S. Army today.

INDIAN WARFARE

The struggle for control of North America was also a contest over which methods and rules of warfare would be used there. For centuries the native Americans had fought among themselves in a conservative if seemingly inhumane manner using knives, clubs, and tomahawks made of wood and stone. The bow and arrow of the eastern woodland Indians of North America was unsophisticated and technologically inferior, not only to those developed by European and Asian cultures, but also to those found in South and Central America. The Indians shifted from traditional weapons to firearms as quickly as they became available, but it has been pointed out that the Indians "never really mastered the white man's weapon."[42] Nonetheless, the native war practices in terms of tactics, prisoners, and personal behavior on the field of battle changed little even with the introduction of firearms.[43]

The tactics employed by native American warriors were simple and effective. They generally struck first without a formal declaration of war, using the basic offensive tactic of surprise. They commonly attacked isolated cabins and remote villages, often at dawn. They often attacked solitary farmers working in their fields after midday, and more than once fell upon farm carts driven by women or children. It was not unusual for an abandoned cart or riderless horse to serve as the first sign of a larger problem. Most attacks, however, took the form of ambushes made in forested regions. These were especially effective against nonmilitary targets such as small parties of settlers or fur traders. The Indians' tactics evolved with time and with contact with Europeans. They abandoned their traditional practice of not fighting through the winter months to launch crucial forays against such targets as Deerfield, Massachusetts, and Schenectady, New York.

Hundreds of miles of ever shifting frontier settlements were not readily defensible against Indian raids, and the only effective strategy was a retaliation so brutal as to deter further incursions. Colonial militias periodically organized punitive expeditions into the frontier regions. Since the Indians rarely chose to stand and fight, colonials learned to threaten and burn the natives' crops and villages. The Indians were thereby forced into an active defense that could be broken by trained soldiers. Recurrent hostilities and the need for repeated colonial forays into the border regions, with all of their political and economic consequences, posed a dilemma for colonial officials that they could never resolve. Nonetheless, a series of overwhelming victories by militia forces in the seventeenth century caused colonials to exaggerate their abilities in this regard.

As a result they tended to look down upon the regular British troops brought to the colonies to fight the French army in the second half of the eighteenth century. However, British colonel Henry Bouquet exhibited an exemplary understanding of Indian offensive tactics during the French and Indian War, which was confirmed by his signal victory at Bushy Run in 1764 during Pontiac's War. He wrote, "[T]here were three basic principles in the Indians' method of fighting: first, fight scattered; second, try to surround; and third, give ground when hard pressed and return when the pressure eased."[44]

Firearms Among the Indians

The effect that weapons technology had on warfare in this period was considerable. By 1676 almost all the tribes of New England Indians had converted to firearms; but they failed develop a technological parody with the colonists. The adoption of firearms, therefore, made the Indian largely dependent on Europeans for powder and ball as well as for repairs. Trade muskets, while widely available, were not as fine as those of the colonists or the regulars.

Even when possessed of firearms the Indians often found themselves with unserviceable weapons for lack of powder or repairs. Those Frenchmen charged with the development and expansion of trade with the native population generally understood this dependence on Europeans for repairs and used it as a means of binding the Indians to them. English traders, on the other hand, understood their role as providers of powder and shot but seem to have avoided dealing in repairs, choosing instead to supply an entirely new weapon to their customers, albeit at an exaggerated cost in terms of furs to the individual Indian.

Tomahawks and Bayonets

Also known as the Indian hachet, the tomahawk was considered an essential piece of equipment on the frontier. So common was its use that it has come to symbolize the very concept of frontier warfare. During the eighteenth century the terms *tomahawk* and *hatchet* were used to convey the very concepts of war and peace, as in "raising the tomahawk" and "burying the hatchet."

Although the Indians sought out firearms and even carried pistols,[45] they continued to rely on the tomahawk and knife for infighting. The origins of the tomahawk have often been misinterpreted to include only the formidable metal hatchet used by native American warriors. In fact, Indians had no iron tomahawks before the period of European contact. They generally used massive wooden warclubs that were quite effective in disabling an opponent. Nonetheless, once they were made available, the native Americans placed a high value on their iron-headed hatchets and war axes.

Very few tomahawks or Indian hatchets have survived the period. Many examples housed in museums may have never belonged to an Indian at all, but were among the prized possessions of some colonial farmer. Indian victories in the seventeenth and eighteenth centuries proved to many frontiersmen the value of the tomahawk as a personal weapon for hand-to-hand combat. In a number of cases swords and bayonets, while available, were disgarded in favor of the tomahawk. The frontiersmen's choice of musket, tomahawk, and knife was largely dic-

These four implements may all have served as weapons. The implement at the top is a typical pipe tomahawk. The bottommost two, each with its point or spike, could serve no purpose other than warfare. The remaining implement is a hatchet, typical of the period, that may have served equally well as a weapon or a camp tool.

tated by the type of warfare practiced by the Indians. The musket could be deadly from ambush or from behind fortifications, and the tomahawk and knife—one in each hand—were equally effective for infighting.

Many tomahawks were simple iron belt axes with a rounded poll that served their purpose in warfare as a weapon, but were mainly used in camp as a tool for cutting firewood, throwing up brushwood barricades, and driving tent pegs. Others were made with lightweight heads fitted with spikes that could serve no general purpose other than warfare. The most highly prized examples were pipe tomahawks. These had an iron head fitted with a steel cutting edge on one side and a hammerlike bowl on the other; a small hole ran from the bowl along a small passage in the handle, terminating in a brass mouthpiece from which tobacco smoke could be drawn. The heads of these pipe tomahawks were often beautifully engraved and ornate. The effectiveness of the pipe tomahawk as a weapon is questionable, however, as the handles were weak. Many of the surviving examples may have been presentation pieces.[46]

Many local militias of the seventeenth century snubbed the bayonet in favor of tomahawks and Indian hachets. This is not surprising. Early

The socket bayonet, at the top, was a technological advance over the "plug"-
style weapon below it. The plug bayonet is often incorrectly identified as a
long-handled hunting knife, a job for which it was, nonetheless, admirably
suited. The socket bayonet had a triangular cross section to its blade and
was used only as a stabbing weapon. The socket bayonet was often used by
soldiers in an unmilitary manner as a candle holder, a convenient skewer for
roasting meat, or a digging tool, all to the dismay of their officers.

bayonets were of the "plug" style, appearing much like long-handled
hunting knives for which they were sometimes mistaken. Fitted into the
muzzle to transform the musket into a long spear, the plug bayonet rendered the weapon useless for firing unless it was first removed.[47]

An improved socket bayonet was developed in 1687 that allowed the
musket to be fired with the bayonet attached. Even with this improvement, however, bayonets did not replace the infantry pike in Europe
until the first decades of the eighteenth century. The bayonet thereafter
became common in European armies, but seemingly played no decisive
part in the forest warfare of North America. British officers often noted
that, but for the lack of a determined bayonet charge, they might have
dispersed a concerted Indian attack. Although great reliance was placed
by these tacticians on the ability of "cold steel" to drive the enemy from
the field, in practice the psychological effect of the bayonet caused one
side or the other to flee. A seasoned soldier noted that "bayonet fighting
occurs mainly in newspaper[s] and other works of fiction." Nonetheless,
both French and British regulars fought with bayonets fixed to their

weapons during battle. Eyewitness reports note the use of bayonet charges at the battles of Lake George, Ticonderoga, and Quebec among others.[48]

British Regulars

It is true that the British officers of the regular army only slowly learned to avoid ambushes in the wilderness by altering their campaigning routines, columns of march, ability to maneuver, and defenses against encirclement. General Edward Braddock's defeat in 1755 and Major James Grant's in 1758 would seem to confirm this statement. Yet the reputation of the British for massive ineptitude under frontier conditions was probably undeserved. Grant mishandled his forces by advancing in separate detachments, which were defeated in detail, and Braddock's men, rather than being poorly led, appear to have panicked and disobeyed their officers.

Without exception, British regular officers seem to have been knowledgeable in the tactics of irregular warfare and the methods of combating them. They were thoroughly acquainted with the concepts of skirmishers, flankers, and advanced parties of scouts, which were included in their technical literature and training manuals. This is not to suggest that European warfare was being "revolutionized," but rather that certain aspects of warfare "were increasingly affected by the activities of irregulars in all theaters of operations" and had been addressed in terms of military training and tactics. The opposite conclusion was somewhat promoted by the actions of inept commanders who ordered a series of unsupported frontal assaults in impossible situations, such as in the British attack on Fort Carillon in 1758 or the attack on the Beauport Lines at Quebec in 1759.[49]

In the provincial armies there was relatively little struggle over the adoption of European-style methods of warfare with their straight lines of soldiers firing at one another across open fields. Colonial regiments paraded, marched, and practiced the evolutions of linear tactics in much the same manner as British regulars, although without their crisp precision. This leaves the student with the unmistakable preception that much of what was said of the inability of the Britsh regulars to wage war in the American wilderness was based in a colonial fondness for griping.[50]

The British record with regard to irregular warfare is exemplary. Parallel with the development of rangers in the colonies was the development of regular light troops by the British. Colonel Thomas Gage is generally given credit for conceiving of the Light Infantry Regiment. Further developed by Lord Augustus Howe and Colonel Henry Bouquet, the Lights were expected to serve as scouts, skirmishers, and flankers as well as to stand in the battalion line. While Howe eliminated many of the useless encumbrances from the light infantry, Bouquet made effective changes in their training. General Braddock's successor, the Earl of Loudoun, was cognizant of the need for his men to fire both kneeling and lying down, to march in a manner suited to forests and mountains, and to take cover when ambushed. General James Wolfe had his men lie down under galling fire from Indians and Canadien militia before the walls of Quebec in 1759, and he used light troops to guard his flanks.

In the field, light troops carried only the basic essential equipment: shot bag and powder horn, cartridge box on a waistbelt, bayonet and hatchet. Many of the muskets carried by light troops were purposely shortened, and some had browned barrels to prevent the reflection of light. The Americans of the back country militia companies were generally looked down upon by regular offices for their disdain of personal discipline, not for their frontier tactics; and they were considered by some regular officers a "portentous variation of [the] light infantry unit." Although the tactics employed by the colonials in combat generally failed to follow any particular pattern, these frontiersmen showed that they knew the arts of scouting, stealth, and ambush as well as any native American.[51]

Many British officers, in particular those regulars with some years in service, had used irregular tactics to repress the risings in Ireland and Scotland in the seventeenth and eighteenth centuries, and special light troops were established who were trained in the prosecution of partisan and irregular warfare. General John Forbes drew on his own European experience and a staff analysis of Braddock's defeat to draw up a highly successful plan of operations against the Indians. Forbes's plan called for the use of Indian allies to reconnoiter the line of march; American frontiersmen to screen the column; disciplined bayonet charges to disperse ambushes; and a well-guarded line of depots and supplies to eliminate long wagon trains. These tactics had been employed by British commanders with whom Forbes had served in 1746 and 1747 in Scotland and in continental Europe.

British prime minister William Pitt fostered the introduction of Scottish Highlander regiments into the army. These kilted warriors with their wailing bagpipes and claymore swords had given the British army a difficult lesson during the last Stuart uprising in Scotland. Rather than live with the apprehension of further violence from that quarter, Pitt had decided to incorporate the Highlanders into the fight against the French. Scottish tactics, more violent and less restrictive than those used by the regulars, proved successful against aboriginal armies in many of the colonial theaters around the world.

NOTES

1. Samuel Adams Drake, *The Border Wars of New England, Commonly Called King William's and Queen Anne's Wars* (Williamstown, MA: Corner House, 1973), 15.

2. Ian K. Steele, *Warpaths: Invasions of North America* (New York: Oxford University Press, 1994), 130.

3. Gary B. Nash, *Red, White, and Black: The Peoples of Early America* (Englewood Cliffs, NJ: Prentice-Hall, 1982), 92–93.

4. David J. Weber, *The Spanish Frontier in North America* (New Haven: Yale University Press, 1992), 23.

5. Nash, 112–113.

6. Maurice Ashley, *Louis XIV and the Greatness of France* (New York: Collier, 1962), 37.

7. Ibid., 37–38.

8. Ibid., 66.

9. Andrew Gallup and Donald F. Shaffer, *La Marine: The French Colonial Soldier in Canada, 1745–1761.* (Bowie, MD: Heritage Books, 1992), 16.

10. Drake, 27.

11. Gallup and Shaffer, 51; Rene' Chartrand, *The French Soldier in Colonial America*, Historic Arms, no. 18. (Alexandria Bay, NY: Museum Restoration Service, 1984), 9–19.

12. For more uniform details, see Rene' Chartrand, *Louis XIV's Army* Men-at-Arms, vol. 203 (Alexandria Bay, NY: Museum Restoration Service, 1988).

13. Ibid., 28–37.

14. The ruling sequence in England/Britain is as follows: Tudor, Stuart, Puritan Republic, Stuart, Orange, Stuart, Hanover. The heads of state: Elizabeth I, James I, Charles I, Oliver Cromwell, Richard Cromwell, Charles II, James II, William III, Anne, George I, George II, George III. The French Boubon dynasty featured an uninterrupted succession: Henry IV, Louis XIII, Louis XIV, Louis XV.

15. Drake, 13.

16. Ibid., 10.

17. Leisler served as interim governor but was later hanged for plotting treason.

18. Daniel J. Boorstin, *The Americans: The Colonial Experience* (New York: Vantage Books, 1958), 353.

19. John W. Shy, "A New Look at Colonial Militia." *William and Mary Quarterly* 35 (1963), 176.

20. At this time Maine was a part of Massachusetts, and Vermont was claimed by New York.

21. Drake, 2.

22. Boorstin, 50–53.

23. Louis B. Wright, *The Atlantic Frontier: Colonial American Civilization, 1607–1763* (New York: Alfred A. Knopf, 1951), 80–81.

24. See Selma R. Williams, *Demeter's Daughters: The Women Who Founded America, 1587–1787* (New York: Atheneum, 1976), 162–163.

25. Shy, 178.

26. Just how widespread the fear of actual slave uprisings was in the early colonial period is debatable, however. Negro slaves were not as numerous or as densely situated as they would be in the nineteenth century.

27. Steele, 95.

28. Jack Radabaugh, "The Militia of Colonial Massachusetts," *Military Affairs* 18 (1954), 15–16.

29. John K. Mahon, "Anglo-American Methods of Indian Warfare, 1676–1794," *The Mississippi Valley Historical Review* 45 (1958), 254.

30. See Fred W. Anderson, *A People's Army: Massachusetts Soldiers and Society in the Seven Years' War* (Chapel Hill: University of North Carolina Press, 1984); Fred W. Anderson, "Why Did Colonial New Englanders Make Bad Soldiers? Contractual Principles and Military Conduct During the Seven Years' War," *William and Mary Quarterly* 3d ser., no. 38 (1981), 395–417; Adam J. Hirsch, "The Collision of Military Cultures in Seventeenth-Century New England," *The Journal of American History* 26 (March 1988), 1187–1212; Mahon, 254–275; Louis Morton, "The Origins of American Military Policy," *Military Affairs* 22 (1958), 75–82; Radabaugh, 1–18; and Shy, 175–185.

·31. Radabaugh, 2.

32. Lorenzo Johnson Greene, *The Negro in Colonial New England, 1620–1776*, (New York: Columbia University Press, 1942), 126–127.

33. Louis Morton, 75, 80.

34. Anderson, *A People's Army*, 231, 44.

35. David Hackett Fischer, *Albion's Seed: Four British Folkways in America* (New York: Oxford University Press, 1989), 732–733.

36. Norwalk, Connecticut, claims the distinction of being the home of Yankee Doodle. A local bridge, part of Interstate 95, is known as the "Yankee Doodle Bridge."

37. Heavy leather coats of this sort are on display at the state museum in Hartford, Connecticut.

38. Philip J. Haythornwaite, *Invincible Generals* (New York: De Capio Press, 1991), 5.

39. Anderson, *A People's Army*, 75.

40. Wilbur R. Jacobs, ed., *The Appalachian Frontier: The Edmond Atkins Report and Plan of 1755* (Lincoln: University of Nebraska Press, 1967), 82.

41. Anderson, "Colonial New Englanders," 395.

42. Mahon, 255.

43. Steele, 222.

44. Mahon, 260.

45. Pierre Pouchot, *Memoir upon the Late War in North America Between the French and English, 1775–1760* vol. 2 (Roxbury, MA: E. Elliot Woodward, 1866), 12.

46. William H. Guthman, "Frontiermen's Tomahawks of the Colonial and Federal Periods," *Antiques* (March 1981), 658–659.

47. Archer Jones, *The Art of War in the Western World* (New York: Oxford University Press, 1987), 267.

48. James H. Croushore, ed., *A Volunteer's Adventure*, by Captain John W. De Forest (New Haven: Yale University Press, 1949), 117–118.

49. Peter E. Russell, "Redcoats in the Wilderness: British Officers and Irregular Warfare in Europe and America, 1740–1760," *William and Mary Quarterly* 3d ser., no. 35 (1978), 635.

50. Steele, 222.

51. Mahon, 274.

11

Flaming Frontiers

Blockhouses and a trembling defensive encourage the meanest scoundrels to attack us.

—British general James Wolfe

Community life on the frontier was by no means secure. Indians were present on the fringes of even the largest settlements along the seacoast. As early as 1607 the English settlers of Jamestown, Virginia, understood the need to create a fortified village for protection against possible attack. With their initial fear of the Indians allayed by the establishment of trade with the local chieftains, the colonists seem to have willingly invited the natives into their compounds and even into their homes, never expecting that the Indians would challenge the advantages provided by European firearms and technology.

The greatest anxiety shared by English colonials was that the Spanish would attack by sailing up the James River from the sea. This fear was not unfounded. The Spanish had destroyed a French Huguenot settlement on the St. John's River in Florida in 1565, showing the heretics no mercy and killing all whom they found. Moreover, in 1570 the Jesuits had established a mission in the Chesapeake Bay area very near the site of Jamestown. Although the mission had failed, the Spanish crown claimed much of what was then Virginia.[1]

The Spanish threat led the Jamestown settlers to construct a stout triangular defensive wall with a palisade of pointed tree trunks and with far reaching cannons mounted upon the parapet—generally facing down the river rather than into the surrounding forest. Within this defensive structure were nestled all the dwellings of the inhabitants, the church, the armory, and other ancillary buildings. Outside the walls were the fields in which staple crops were grown, and then came the almost impenetrable woodlands. As the fear of Spanish attack diminished with time, and as the colonists became more fearful of Indians they did not know, they seem to have taken for granted the loyalty of those most familiar to them.

The English seem to have become somewhat complacent about their personal defenses, spreading out in a short time beyond the reach of aid from the community. The number of settlements along the river increased, as the waterway was the only efficient means of transporting goods and crops. This is a repetitive phenomenon in the development of frontier communities. Initial fear supports community action and substantive defenses. Growing familiarity with the surroundings leads to expansion and personal complacency, which ends in unexpected tragedy, panic, and renewed calls for community action and defense.

For example, in 1622 a concerted effort among the native populations of the Chesapeake Bay area—a well-thought-out conspiracy among several tribes—resulted in the simultaneous destruction of several Virginia settlements and the murder of 375 colonists in a single day. Many of these were killed without warning in their own homes. Only the loyalty of a few Indians, who warned their friends among the English of the coming cataclysm, kept the English settlement at Jamestown from being totally wiped out. One of the more unfortunate English villages to be attacked was Martin's Hundred. So devastating was the attack here that the survivors hastily buried their dead and abandoned the site. There is some reason to believe that the surviving structures were destroyed by the inhabitants.

For more than three centuries the location of Martin's Hundred was lost to memory. Then, in 1969, its location was suddenly rediscovered by archaeologists surveying the grounds of the Carter's Grove Plantation in an attempt to find the location of the nineteenth-century slave quarters known to have been on the property.[2] The archaeolgical evidence and remains found on the site of Martin's Hundred in the 1970s show that there was a fortification at the hub of the village placed to repel attack from the river. Unlike Jamestown, this fort was made of a simple plank stockade slightly taller than a man with a firing step inside so that defenders could fire over the wall. A single residence, rather than group homes, was inside this enclosure. There was also evidence of a gun platform (facing the river) and a watch tower. Within 200 yards of this defensive structure was a series of homes. Each seems to have been fitted with a protective palisade or possibly a stout fence. The surviving post-holes may have supported an enclosure for livestock, but each enclosed area was very small. Moreover, one homesite, nearer to the river and with a better aspect of its length than the others, was also fitted with a gun platform. There was no evidence that any cannons were actually fitted to these positions. The buried remains nearby of almost two dozen murdered settlers—men, women, and children—show that each site was that of a dwelling rather than a military outpost.

The 1622 attack resulted in a retaliatory war between the colonists and the local natives, and it heightened the colonists awareness of the need for a secure and easily accessible retreat in times of trouble. In the next year there was "a massive shipment of muskets and obsolete armor from the Tower of London."[3] Notwithstanding the introduction of improved weaponry, universal service, and mandatory drill, in April 1623 the Virginia militia suffered the loss of thirty men in an ambush by the Indians. It seems that the colonists utterly failed to understand the potential of native warfare and tactics, and they had also failed to make adjustments to their traditional modes of warcraft. Only a number of isolated engagements like this could have taught the colonials something about the motives and methods of Indian warfare, and the disparity between colonial and Indian methods would not come to light until they were directly experienced.[4]

A sudden attack in 1644 similar to the earlier event caused locally available security to become a general policy of the Virginia colony. However, as the colony expanded, the older strongpoints became less appropriate for defense, and new ones were constantly needed in the border areas. In 1675 Governor Berkeley ordered the establishment of a series of weakly garrisioned stronghouses. While they were a visible challenge to the Indians, they were simply unworkable because no single structure with a small garrision could withstand a determined native attack.

THE NEW ENGLAND FRONTIER

In New England the colonists had to learn these lessons for themselves. The outbreak of hostilities in New England at this time quickly showed that forts could not by themselves ensure protection. Only the promise of immediate pursuit of the miscreants by massive details of armed men seemed to deter attacks and raids. Nonetheless, more than 600 colonists lost their lives to Indian attacks during King Philip's War. The frontier settlements of New York and New England were again attacked, this time by Indians from farther afield incited by the French who were prosecuting King William's War (1688–1698) and Queen Anne's War (1702–1713). Many homes were burned, even those in villages with fairly dense populations like Schenectady, New York, which

This photograph was taken during the exercise of the Plymouth colony militia. The historical interpreters and reenactors in the picture are portraying the year 1627. They carry matchlock muskets and are dressed in a wide variety of clothing appropriate to the period.

was burned in 1690. The same grisly story was repeated again and again. Besides the lives lost, fields and livestock were destroyed, placing "a very considerable drain upon the population and prosperity of the Northern New England settlements at the time."[5]

When the wars ended, scores of corpses lay scalped among the ruins of tiny settlements and isolated farmsteads throughout the border regions, and an equal number of despondent and humbled captives had trudged north through the forests to be tormented and sold to the French. Yet few real benefits were derived from the supposed peace agreements. In the brief interlude between open hostilities, the border settlers once again saw the familiar pattern of French-incited raids by the Abenakis and English-inspired counter-raids on the Indians. Consequently, uncounted forest skirmishes took place between small groups of Indians and unfortunate farmers and traders.

The governor of Canada, Philippe de Rigaud, Marquis de Vaudreuil, played a delicate balancing act during the years of peace between England and France. He knew that the English would continue to move further into the forests and that the Indians would come to prefer the cheaper and better English trade goods. Yet Vaudreuil eschewed violence on the New York frontier in the hope of keeping the Iroquois from the warpath, while inciting the Abenaki to raid the New England frontier settlements. "[W]e must do nothing that might cause a rupture between us and the Iroquois; but we must keep things astir in the direction of Boston, or else the Abenakis will declare for the English."[6]

The single event that came to characterize the plight of the frontier settlements was the raid against Deerfield, Massachusetts, on the Connecticut River in 1704. This operation almost mirrored the attack at Schenectady fourteen years earlier. More than one-third of the 300 residents of Deerfield were carried off in a midwinter raid, and between 40 and 50 of the remainder were killed. The news of the Deerfield raid enraged the colonials, and later that same year, Caleb Lymen led a counterstroke on the Abenaki village at Cowass on the upper Connecticut River, driving the Indians to move their villages nearer to Canada. English expeditions like these were used throughout Queen Anne's War. They all shared the common characteristic of having the natives, who were their targets, evaporate into the forests at the approach of the colonial forces. The English saw nothing but deserted wigwams, and the Abenakis became adept at moving from place to place as they were pursued, "leaving only a few cut-throats behind, which kept the country in constant alarm."[7]

The colonists constantly resorted to the same expedient when faced with an Indian war. They raised a large force of inexperienced and only moderately trained men from among their militia, and placed them under the command of untested leaders or provincial officers. They then tried to prosecute a plan of attack requiring precision, secrecy, and flawless execution against targets that were sometimes hundreds of miles away in the geographical vastness of a primeval wilderness. Moreover, most of the colonials were uninterested in how these operations might affect the outcome of a larger American conflict, and only viewed them as a defensive response to their local emergencies. "Disunity among the colonies was a formidable obstacle to military success, as was Britain's habitual lack of interest in the American theater." Not until several decades had passed did the English realize that their frontiers could best be secured by destroying the French presence in Canada.[8]

Forting Up

While the colonial authorities in the coastal cities made plans to take the war to the French by attacking Acadia, Montreal, or Quebec, the initial response of the frontier population to unsettled conditions in the border regions was to "fort up." On the frontier a distinct type of structure evolved to meet the needs of the various communities for protection against human enemies. These local safe-havens became known as garrison houses, stronghouses, blockhouses, and sometimes (euphemisti-

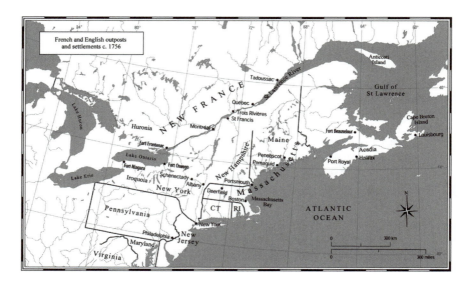

cally) forts. The design and use of these structures was often a balance of unwarranted fear and misplaced optimism, of strategy and counter-strategy, and of isolation and community effort.[9]

The colonists seem to have used many terms interchangeably when speaking or writing about them, but the term *blockhouse* seems to have been saved for a square structure of strongly laid-up logs or timbers with a second floor overhanging the first. The door, if located on the first floor, was heavily barred; if on the second floor, it was accessed by a ladder, hinged at the sill of the door, which could be pulled up like a draw-bridge.[10] Blockhouses were usually surrounded by walls built of timber, with gates securely bolted and barred at night; families whose homes were not considered defensible slept in blockhouses in times of crisis. "In the morning, if all was safe, they went back to their own houses again." Blockhouses were also incorporated into military strong points within or near a fort.[11]

The Garrison House

Another answer that evolved to address the need for a secure local retreat was the garrison house. In each settlement enclave one or two stoutly built houses would be chosen as sites for refuge and local defense. Most of these were private residences given over to the public defense in times of crisis. Examples are DePuey's Fort, a stone building surrounded by a stick-pole stockade located at Shawnee in Pennsylvania, the Old Stone Church in Schoharie, New York, and the group of recon-

This is an eighteenth-century illustration of a timber blockhouse fitted for the use of small cannons on squat wooden "trucks." The items marked "A" are ports from which the cannons might be fired. Those marked "B" are gun slits through which muskets might be fired in relative safety. As most Indian raids lacked artillery, only the use of fire or overwhelming numbers could overcome the defenders.

structed timber garrison houses at Charlestown, New Hampshire, known as Fort No. 4.

Garrison houses were often built of thick wood, either round logs or squared timbers, as this was the most convenient and abundant material available. Buildings laid up in field stone and mortar, or of dressed blocks of limestone, sandstone, or granite, were less frequent but infinitely more defensible against fire. For the same reasons slate roofs were desirable, but wood shingles were more common. In any case, the roof of a garrison house was usually lightly built, but the attic floor was constructed of strong timbers covered with a thick layer of sand or ashes. This ingenious strategy allowed the attic to act as a firestop for the rest of the building if the roof was fired. Garrison houses could be of one or two stories, and it was not uncommon for the second floor to overhang the first. This allowed the defender to shoot down along the wall of the first floor or to pour water on brushfires laid up against the sides of the building.

One necessary characteristic of a good garrison house was a well or large cistern inside the house, or one that was easily accessible by the defenders if outside. The stone trading post built by the French at Fort Niagara had an internal well, even though the entire volume of Lake Ontario was no more than twenty feet from the door. This allowed the defenders access to water for drinking and firefighting without exposing themselves to attack. As the Indians lacked artillery and relied on fire as their primary means of reducing defensive structures, such an arrangement almost certainly allowed the defenders to outwait all but the most determined siege.

Public funds were often appropriated for the fortification of private residences in times of impending crisis. In 1754 Virginia voted funds to build several military posts and to fortify with stockades several garrison houses. At the same time Benjamin Franklin and his supporters were able to press the Quakers in the General Assembly to fund a series of improvements to preexisting garrison houses along the Delaware and Susquehanna Rivers. These forts, actually little more than stockaded homes, were about ten miles apart, allowing settlers to flee in times of unrest. They were useless in a sudden attack.

When planning an attack the enemy usually intended to throw the entire weight of their force on an unsuspecting village and allow terror and confusion to do the rest. The best time for such an attack proved to be at dawn when the inhabitants were first stirring and getting about their chores. A number of circumstances could combine to foil this strategy. The most common of these was that the village had been placed on alert either by a warning from the patrolling rangers or by a chance sighting of the enemy before they were able to ready their attack. The enemy's presence could be given away quite accidentally by the scattering of wildlife, cattle, and hogs from the woods as they were frightened by large groups of men pushing forward toward the village. Additionally, the eagerness of some of the Indian scouts, in particular, to waylay the first inhabitants with whom they came in contact, raising scalping

Picket's Fort in western Pennsylvania is typical of frontier refuge forts built by local communities. Note the blockhouses at the corners (four in all).

halloa (battle cries) and firing upon the terrorized settlers, often served as a first warning to the rest of the village. It was important for survival on the frontier that settlers learn to act upon these implicit warnings immediately. If the attack was truly sudden, or if the unsuspecting settlers were busy in the fields, they might be forced to literally run from their homes for the refuge hoping that they would not be cut off by the marauding band. "The few who did so owed their safety to fleetness of foot."[12]

Undefended houses were easily taken, but the assailants usually met with a rough reception at the garrisons or the blockhouses. However, being in the blockhouse was not a guarantee of safety. In the village of Dover, New Hampshire, the colonists had built five blockhouses, distributed so that the villagers could reach them with little trouble. On the evening of June 27, 1689, all five were considered impregnable, and the inhabitants went peacefully to their beds inside at the usual early hour. Secure in the strength of their barred doors, but mainly because it was raining, they failed to set even one sentinel over the village. However, the town had been under the surveillance of a band of Indians raiding from the Androscoggin and Kennebec Rivers for some days. By morning, all but one blockhouse had been taken either by guile or direct attack during the night. After a stout defense the final blockhouse surrendered rather than watch their fellows, now captives, dispatched before their eyes. Twenty-three persons were killed, twenty-nine more were taken captive, and half a dozen houses and some mills were burned.[13]

According to their diaries and journals, the English seem to have been easily convinced of their inability to withstand a determined attack, and they were often more willing to surrender to groups of assailants led by French officers than to those composed of only native warriors. However, the Frenchmen, often outnumbered by their Indian allies and practically unable to check their vengeance for the losses accumulated in the assault, sometimes allowed the terms of a surrender to be "shamefully violated." Instead of finding the promised protection of the French, the survivors were often "abandoned to the fury of the Indians." At Casco Bay, for instance, the defenders held out for four days before surrendering to the French officers in charge. Following the capitulation, the French simply stood by while the Indians killed more than 100 English of all ages from among the captives.[14]

THE SOUTHERN FRONTIER

The southern colonial frontier was a zone of intercolonial commercial competition. Except during Indian emergencies like the Tuscarora War of 1711 or the Yamasee War in 1715, the usual relations between the separate colonies were characterized by mutual distrust and jealous rivalry. South Carolina had checked Virginia's desire for westward trade expansion by restrictions, discriminatory legislation, and confiscations of trade goods. It had expanded its trade south and west to the many Indian nations of southeastern North America while Virginia sent its traders by a circuitous route through the mountains of North Carolina to the Catawba nation. North Carolina was completely a frontier colony at the time and had little interest in commercial contests. Long before the founding of the colony of Georgia, the chief bases for South Carolina's trade in skins were found along the fall line of the Savannah River. The outpost town of Savannah had been established 140 miles from Charlestown. Traders followed the path along the river opposite Savannah to reach the Cherokee country at Tugaloo, or they went west and south along the widening coastal plain to reach the Creeks. With paths through the southeastern piedmont and trails to the Cherokee, South Carolina was the only English colony to have such an extensive trade network penetrating into the wilderness.

During Queen Anne's War (1702–1713), the colony of South Carolina struck the Apalachee country of northern Florida and the Spanish frontier towns of Pensacola and St. Augustine with such fury and steadfastness of purpose that many tribes abandoned the French and Spanish and sought peace with the English. Although these attacks failed to dislodge the European enemies of the colony, they resulted in renewed loyalty among those tribes friendly to the Carolinas. Consequently, many of the southeastern tribes became an integral part of a Carolinian deerskin trade that stretched from the Atlantic coast to the Mississippi River.

Several tribes moved closer to Charlestown by the end of the seventeenth century to take better advantage of English trade goods. Among these were the Yamasee, whose major villages were so close to the English settlements that the South Carolina colony created a reservation for them near Port Royal to prevent inadvertent settlement by whites on their lands. The Creeks, however, were much more important commercially than the Yamasee, because they served as trading middlemen with the interior tribes. The Creeks were really two closely related peoples who lived inland among the headwaters of the Alabama and Chattahoochee Rivers. The Upper Creeks were further northwest than the Lower Creeks. Together both groups contained over a dozen individual tribes. The combined strength of the two groups was thought to be 2,500 warriors. On the upper branches of the Tombigbee River were also the English-leaning Chickasaws and their enemies the Choctaws, who were probably the strongest tribe in French Louisiana. It was through the middlemen among the Creeks that these western tribes traded with the English.

The Cherokee were an Iroquoian-speaking people described as entirely independent of the other tribes in the region. They may have numbered 3,000 warriors, making them equivalent in strength to the five confederated Iroquois nations in New York, for whom they held great enmity despite being related to them. Aboriginal hatreds had little to do with differences in language, race or customs, and if they were not in response to immediate disputes, they were usually rooted in ancient causes. Nonetheless, every year parties of Iroquois from New York descended the Warrior's Path to the south to attack the Cherokees. These raids caused a great deal of disturbance on the southern frontier, but the colonial governments seem to have been unable to stop them.[15]

The Tuscarora War

The brief uprising known as the Tuscarora War of 1711–1712 was a direct result of such war parties harassing the frontier settlers on the way north. The colony of North Carolina was steadily expanding after 1701 mainly due to the establishment of a large number of widely dispersed farmsteads in the border regions. The settlers quickly occupied lands along the Pamilco, Roanoke, Tar, and Nuese Rivers. These lands were the domain of the Tuscarora Indians, an Iroquoian-speaking people with close ties to the tribes of New York. In 1711 itinerant Indians attacked some isolated farms of mostly Swiss and German settlers near New Bern. The local militias struck out in all directions without design or coordination. The Tuscaroras, once attacked, retaliated, and more than 150 settlers perished in the more remote parts of the colony. Within a year the North Carolina frontier was in ruins with entire regions totally abandoned by terrified whites.

The colonial authorities of North Carolina pleaded for assistance. South Carolina answered with an army of friendly Yamasee warriors led by a few dozen colonials well versed in the complexities of Indian warfare. Virginia sent a few militia units to guard the frontiers, as well as supplies and ammunition. These forces quickly destroyed a Tuscarora fort and several of their villages in the first weeks of a coordinated operation. Within eighteen months more than 1,000 Indians had been killed and many hundreds had been sold into slavery. So extensive was the destruction that the Tuscaroras fled, many to the protection of the Iroquois in New York. In the eighteenth century they became the sixth nation of the Iroquois Confederacy.

The Yamasee War

Although all the native tribes of southeastern North America enjoyed a brisk trade in skins, they complained bitterly to the colonial authorities about the Charlestown traders who visited their villages. It seems certain that many unscrupulous men were trading with the Indians to their disadvantage, abusing rum to facilitate sharp dealing, seducing their wives and daughters, and enslaving their children when the Indians could not pay off their debts. The Yamasee made a formal complaint to this effect in 1711, but the colonial authorities were frustrated and unable to put a stop to these practices.

Embittered by the traders' continued abuses, and incited by the Lower Creeks, who wished to have the traders removed, a group of Yamasee Indians rose and began killing whites in a coordinated attack on April 15, 1715. Up to ninety traders and settlers lost their lives on the first day of the insurrection. "The war came with a terrible suddenness to the dispersed frontier settlers." Those whites who escaped the initial attack spread the news of an Indian uprising all along the frontier settlements. Those colonists in the outlying farmsteads panicked and fled to Charlestown.[16]

Almost all of the surrounding native tribes, with the exception of the Cherokees, eventually allied themselves with the Yamasee against the English. By early summer Yamasees, Creeks, Apalachees, and Savannahs were attacking the colony from both north and south. The Cherokees, traditional enemies of the Creeks, remained loyal to the English. This may have saved South Carolina from utter ruin by giving Governor Charles Craven time to amass an army of colonials. The Cherokee not only refused to join the conspiracy, but they killed several Creek emissaries sent to them to form an alliance and helped the English track down the Lower Creek army in the wilderness.

The South Carolina assembly raised a force of 1,200 men—600 Carolinians, 100 Virginians, and the rest armed Negro slaves and free Indians. Having received arms and support from North Carolina, Virginia, and as far away as New England, Craven counterattacked, successfully vanquishing a large Yamasee force in the southern region of the colony. The immediate response of the Carolina authorities, especially those in Charlestown, had far reaching effects on native American power on the southeastern frontier. Most of the Yamasee women and children fled to the Spanish in St. Augustine, and the Charlestown merchants quickly took the opportunity to sell many native captives to the Caribbean as slaves.

No further major battles were fought, but the surviving Yamasees and Lower Creeks continued their raids from Florida, with the Lower Creeks doing most of the remaining fighting. Until 1717, when a peace was made, these Indian allies continued their scattered raids of the frontier communities. More than twenty plantations in St. Paul's parish were burned and several other parishes were totally deserted by white settlers throughout the two-year emergency. Four hundred whites had been killed. The Yamasees were decimated by the war, but those who remained in the villages near St. Augustine were a constant threat to the colony. The Lower Creeks, chief architects of the conflict, simply moved back to their old territory near the Chattahoochee River.

For the Carolinians, the Yamasee War brought the frightening knowledge of their clear vulnerablity as the southernmost English colony flanking the Atlantic coast. It was from this circumstance that the outlying colony of Georgia would be initiated as a first line of defense. The frontier settlements had been justly terrified, but the failure of the once powerful Yamasee and Creeks to win the war against the English resulted in the total collapse of Indian power in the region. Thereafter, frontier settlers placed no limits on their cruelty and acted with brutal dispatch when dealing with their former Indian enemies—taking their lands and enslaving or killing natives when it suited them.

During the Yamasee War the colony of Virginia openly tried to attract the trade of the Cherokee nation to itself at the expense of the Charlestown merchants. Word of an intercolonial trade rivalry in the midst of an Indian war, however, caused the Board of Trade in London to attempt for the first time "to place Indian affairs in the South upon something like an imperial footing." Thereafter, a more closely coordinated Indian policy was attempted. The board's interest produced a remarkable change in the attitude of Virginia's governor, Alexander Spotswood, who immediately tried to correlate the Indian policy on both the northern and southern frontiers of the English colonies. Virginia joined in the councils with the Iroquois at Albany, and New York's governor, Robert Hunter, tried to engage the warlike Senaca to move against the unfriendly southern tribes.[17]

Georgia

In 1721 the Board of Trade proposed a series of initiatives to strengthen the colonial frontier. These included the building of frontier forts and the transfer of regular British troops to garrison them. The creation of a series of buffer settlements below South Carolina was suggested. Very little came of these plans, although a company of royal infantry was dispatched to build Fort King George at the mouth of the Altamaha River south of Charlestown near present-day Darien, Georgia. The fort failed, however, to stop the Yamasee raids, and in 1728 South Carolina again crossed into Florida to destroy Yamasee villages near St. Augustine.

The founding of the colony of Georgia proceeded directly from these circumstances. James Oglethorpe was a reformer interested in the plight of indebted persons held in civil prisons in England. In a time when English society answered the problem of indebtedness by creating a massive program of imprisonment with all its disadvantages, Oglethorpe came to believe that life on the American frontier was a superior remedy for the problem of what to do with debtors. He wished to combine the philanthropic ideals of personal renewal with the cold, hard needs of the kingdom to found a buffer colony to protect South Carolina.

In 1732 a charter was issued to the colony of Georgia, and the establishment of the colony was prosecuted with the greatest of military expediency. Forts were quickly established at key points, and settlements were planned only for those locations thought to be defensible. Within four years of its founding English and Scottish settlers had pushed the frontiers of the new colony to within twenty miles of St. Augustine, and had established the town of Augusta well inland of Savannah.

The Spanish were outraged at these developments, and by 1738 both sides were preparing for war. London dispatched a regiment of 700 seasoned troops to secure its new colony from Spanish aggression just as King George's War opened in Europe. Incited by the Spanish, the Yamasees attacked the outlying farmsteads. Oglethorpe retaliated by attacking the Spanish outposts on the St. John's River. In 1740, with a combined force of 1,200 troops and colonial militiamen from South Carolina, he attempted a siege of the castillo at St. Augustine. He found himself three weeks later still fruitlessly cannonading that structure when word of a Spanish relieving force from Cuba reached him. Oglethorpe retreated. Two years later the Spanish made a similar foray into Georgia with a force of 1,500 men, which also failed to reach a conclusive result. Thereafter, the war turned to joint colonial-regular army operations in the Caribbean from which South Carolina and Georgia were exempt.[18]

Nonetheless, the depredations of the Indians continued in South Carolina. As late as 1760 an anonymous writer noted the dreadful conditions that continued on the southern frontier throughout the colonial period:

If my capacity would permit to do it, it would be too shocking to paint the melancoly scenes that were presented to us in our little march to the frontiers. Poor families in droves removing, not knowing where to go; several of them wounded and scalped, who were left by the savages for dead, even little infants two and three years old. Strong new houses and well cultivated plantations, the effects of much labor and industry, deserted with plenty of provisions, exposed to the fury and flames of those barbarians.[19]

NOTES

1. David J. Weber, *The Spanish Frontier in North America* (New Haven: Yale University Press, 1992), 6, 60–61.

2. Reinterpretation and analysis of the Martin's Hundred site continues at the present time. See Ivor Noel Hume, *Martin's Hundred* (Charlottesville: University Press of Virginia, 1979).

3. Ian K. Steele, *Warpaths: Invasions of North America* (New York: Oxford University Press, 1994), 43.

4. Adam J. Hirsch. "The Collision of Military Cultures in Seventeenth-Century New England," *The Journal of American History* 26 (March 1988), 1196.

5. Robert G. Miner, ed., *Colonial Architecture in New England* (New York: Arno Press, 1977), 77.

6. Quoted in Robert Leckie, *A Few Acres of Snow: The Saga of the French and Indian Wars* (New York: John Wiley & Sons, 1999), 230.

7. Colin G. Collaway, ed., *Dawnland Encounters: Indians and Europeans in Northern New England* (Hanover: University Press of New England, 1991), 151.

8. John Ferling, *Struggle for a Continent: The Wars of Early America* (Arlington Heights, IL: Harlan Davidson, 1993), 98–99.

9. For a more complete understanding of a fort please, see Chapter 13.

10. Hugh Morrison, *Early American Architecture: From the First Colonial Settlements to the National Period* (New York: Dover, 1987), 76.

11. Samuel Adams Drake, *The Border Wars of New England, Commonly Called King William's and Queen Anne's Wars* (Williamstown, MA: Corner House, 1973), 15.

12. Ibid.,78.

13. Ibid., 20–21.

14. Ibid., 52–53.

15. Francis Jennings, *The Ambiguous Iroquois Empire: The Covent Chain Confederation of Indian Tribes with English Colonies from Its Beginnings to the Lancaster Treaty of 1744* (New York: W. W. Norton, 1984), 206.

16. Verner W. Crane, *The Southern Frontier, 1670–1732* (Durham, NC: Duke University Press, 1928), 167.

17. Ibid., 177–179.
18. See Ferling, 111–118.
19. See Armand Francis Lucier, ed., *French and Indian War Notices Abstracted from Colonial Newspapers, 1759–1760*, vol. 4 (Bowie, MD: Heritage Books, 1999), 121–122.

12

Tedious Days and Frightful Nights

When trouble's near the Lord is kind
He hears the captive's cry.
He can subdue the savage mind
And learn it sympathy.
                    —Susanna Johnson, on her first night of captivity

THE HIDDEN THREAT

The difficulties of living on the colonial frontier were numerous indeed. Carving a homestead from the woodlands required hard and persistent work. Struggling for existence against nature's hostilities demanded determination and commitment. Combating loneliness far from friends and family necessitated strength and faith. The greatest challenge, however, may have been surviving the intense strain created by fear of Indian attack. In a letter printed in the *Pennsylvania Gazette*, the inhabitants of Fort Henry voiced their anxiety after the disappearance of three men: "We are alarmed in the fort almost every night by a terrible barking of dogs; there are certainly some Indians about us."[1]

Susanna Johnson of Charlestown, New Hampshire, painted a stressful picture of her life on the frontier in 1754: "A detail of the miseries of a 'frontier man' must excite the pity of every child of humanity. The gloominess of the rude forest, the distance from friends and competent defense and the daily inroads and nocturnal yells of hostile Indians, awaken the keen apprehensions and anxieties which conception can only picture."[2]

Sending the children to gather berries in the morning, going to the well at dusk, or heeding the call of a sick animal at night was a summons for unbridled trepidation. Susanna Johnson wrote: "The fears of the night were horrible beyond description, and even the light of day was far from dispelling painful anxiety. While looking from the windows of my log-house and seeing my neighbors tread cautiously by each hedge and hillock, lest some secreted savage might start forth to take their scalp, my fears would baffle description."[3]

Word of "outrages on lives and property" kept the settlers in an increasing state of anxiety. When news of the capture of a nearby family reached Charlestown, Susanna Johnson recorded her heightened apprehension: "Imagination now saw and heard a thousand Indians; and I never went around my own house, without first looking with a trembling caution by each corner, to see if a tomahawk was not raised for my destruction."[4]

Writing of the distresses of a frontier farmer, J. Hector St. John de Crevecoeur's description of events in his home, intimately captured the absolute terror that could be unleashed by the simple sound of a snapping twig or the unexpected barking of a dog:

Our sleep is disturbed by the most frightful dreams; sometimes we start awake, as if the great hour of danger was come; at other times the howling of our dogs seems to announce the arrival of our enemy; we leap out of bed and run to arms; my poor wife, with panting bosom and silent tears, takes leave of me, as if we were to see each other no more; she snatches the youngest children from their beds, who, suddenly awakened, increase by their innocent questions the horror of the dreadful moment. She tries to hide them in the cellar, as if our cellar was inaccessible to the fire. I place all the servants at the windows and I myself at the door, where I determine to perish. . . . We remain thus sometimes for whole hours. . . . At last, finding that it was a false alarm, we return once more to our beds.[5]

TAKEN BY SURPRISE

The apprehensions held by the frontier population were not necessarily the fruit of overstimulated imaginations. Individuals were often captured or killed while engaged in their normal daily activities. There are many stories of farmers chased from the fields by small bands of Indians. Moses Willard and his father "were repairing some fence on the rear of the lots, and the Indians, being secreted in the bushes a small distance from them, fired upon them, and shot [his] father dead upon the spot."[6] Moses ran to the fort and, while wounded by a spear, escaped with his

This woodcut engraving from the author's collection clearly represents the effects of Indian raids on the frontier settlements and farmsteads. Note the young captive as he looks back upon the bodies of his slain family and friends.

life. Samuel Burbank "went to the barn to feed the cattle before the rest were up, leaving the door unfastened." The Indians who were hidden nearby in ambush rushed forth and captured him. Steven Farnsworth was captured as he was returning from the sawmill with his team of oxen and a load of boards.[7]

Attacks were not always simply impromptu events brought about by the accidental crossing of settlers' and raiders' paths. At times the raiders entered an area and studied the inhabitants prior to staging their onslaught, or they implemented strategies to draw unsuspecting residents into ambush. William Longley was distressed when he noticed his livestock loose in the cornfields. The Indians had turned the cattle out of the barnyard and then awaited their discovery. As calculated, Longley rushed from the house unarmed in order to drive the cattle back, and the Indians sprang upon and murdered him. They then killed his wife and two of their five children before carrying off the remaining three.

During the course of her captivity Isabella M'Coy discovered that she and her family had been stalked by Indians raiders for some time prior to their attack. She was told that her captors had "looked through cracks around the house, and saw what [we] had for supper" two days prior to the abduction. On the following day, while Isabella was walking, the family dogs ran ahead toward the blockhouse but returned in an agitated state and were growling. She later learned that the Indians had been "concealed there and saw the dogs when they came around." Ultimately the growing uneasiness drove Isabella, her husband, and son to seek the protection of the garrison. Along the way she fell a little in the rear of the others. This allowed the Indians a favorable opportunity of separating her from the others. "They reached from the bushes, and took hold of her, charging her to make no noise, and covering her mouth with their hands."[8]

Premonitions of misfortune were sometimes merely the prelude to real horrors that were much worse than those that the wary might imagine. The burning and pillaging of homes, the murder of women and children, and the abduction of settlers from their families and friends was fated for many if a major attack were under way.

Mary Rowlandson's description of the attack on Lancaster, Massachusetts, included the following report of a man who was shot while running to the garrison for safety: "He begged them for his life, promising them money but they would not hearken to him, but knocked him on the head, stripped him naked, and split open his bowels."[9] She also described the activity in her home during the fighting: "Some in our house were fighting for their lives, others wallowing in blood, the house on fire over our heads, and the bloody heathen ready to knock us on the head if we stirred out."[10]

Pastor John Williams recounted the fate of his two youngest children, two-year-old John Jr. and newborn Jerusha, and the family slave, Parthena, during the raid on Deerfield, Massachusetts: "Some [Indians] were so cruel and barbarous as to take and carry to the door two of my children and murder them, as also a Negro woman." Reports following the Deerfield raid note that death came by gunshot, hatchet, knife, and war-club. Some victims were discovered in the rubble of burned homes. Even those who took refuge in their cellars were not safe. One house's cellar had ten people who had been suffocated from the smoke of the burning home.[11]

Lucy Terry, a sixteen-year-old slave belonging to Ebenezer Wells, described a raid on Deerfield in twenty-eight lines of verse detailing the death of seven men and one woman. The lines that follow serve as examples of her verse:

> Eleazer Hawks was killed outright
> Before he had time to fight . . .
> Simeon Amsden they found dead
> Not many rods distant from his head . . .
> Eunice Allen sees the Indians coming,

And hopes to save herself by running . . .
Young Sammuel Allen, Oh, lack-a-day!
Was taken and carried to Canada.[12]

Mary Rowlandson was among those abducted during the Lancaster raid. The first night of her captivity, Mary reflected upon the "dolefulness" of day: "All was gone, my husband gone [at least separated from me] . . . my children gone, my relations and friends gone, our house and home, and all our comforts within door and without, all was gone [except my life] and I knew not but the next moment that might go too. There remained nothing to me but one poor wounded babe."[13]

THE CAPTIVE JOURNEY

Susanna Johnson was taken from her home in New Hampshire. In her narrative she wrote of the journey to Canada: "My faintness obliged me to sit. This being observed by an Indian, he drew his knife, as I supposed, to put an end to my existence. But he only cut some bands with which my gown was tied, and then pushed me on." She also related an incident where a horse was captured by the Indians and because her "feet and legs were covered with blood" she was given a pair of "moggasons" and "mounted on top" of the bags and blanket that were thrown over the horse. Exchanging a captive's footwear for moccasins was often reported in the narratives of returning abductees. Describing her Indian master, Susanna wrote that he "was as clever an Indian as [I] ever saw; he even evinced, at numerous times, a disposition that showed that he was by no means void of compassion."[14] Johnson concluded the narration of her journey to Canada with this commentary:

"The Indians have been surprisingly patient, and often discovered tokens of humanity. At every meal we all shared equal with them, whether a horse or a duck composed the bill of fare, and more than once they gave me a blanket, to shelter me from a thunder storm."[15]

The scenes portrayed by Susanna Johnson were in harsh contrast to the events recorded by Pastor John Williams following the Deerfield raid. Williams, his wife, Eunice, and five of their seven children were among those taken from the village. On the second day of the trek Williams was permitted to walk and assist Eunice, who was still weak from a recent childbirth. Later that day, after having fallen during a river crossing and nearly having drowned, "the cruel and bloodthirsty savage who took her slew her with his hatchet at one stroke."[16] Pastor Williams also wrote of the slaughter of another woman "who being nigh the time of travail [childbirth], was wearied with her journey." A similar destiny awaited four others who lacked the stamina demanded by such an arduous journey.[17]

An explanation of the considerations shown by one group, compared to the executions of the faint effected by the other, may be made clearer upon review of the circumstances and motivation of the raids. Indians commonly took captives in enemy raids. Like scalps, they were trophies of their conquest. The disposition of captives was the choice of the captor. Susanna Johnson explained: "According to their national practice, he who first laid hands on a prisoner, considered him his property. My master . . . was the one that took my hand when I sat on the bed [as they bust into our home]."[18]

Captives who were weak, who posed a danger to the raiders, or who proved overly troublesome in the least respect were likely to be dispatched, typically with a blow to the head by a tomahawk. Captain of militia Nehemiah How was taken from the Great Meadows fort above Fort Drummer. On the fourth day he recalled that he "became weak and faint; for [he] had not eaten the value of one meal from the time [he] was taken." The next morning his captor said to him, "You must walk quick today or I kill you." Fortunately, they had eaten well the night before and that morning, and How survived to complete the journey.[19]

The Deerfield raid of 1704 yielded 112 captives. Controlling such a large group may have presented difficulties not present with smaller abductions. Verbal taunting was common. A captor might even find it necessary to tomahawk a prisoner as a lesson to control other abductees. Additionally, any person slowing the group represented a liability for the entire party. Overall, 92 of the group survived the trek to Canada. Of the 26 women captured 10 either died or were killed. Three out of four infants, two years of age or less, were killed along the way.

Many northern New Englanders were taken in a series of small raids over a period of forty years. Of the captives taken from Maine and New Hampshire between 1689 and 1730, there have been 270 men, women, and children documented. Of this total, 128 were female and 142 were male. Few escaped. Some died during the arduous journey to Canada. Just over half, were ransomed. If ransom was the goal of abduction, it was in the captor's best interest to see that the captives survived. Susanna Johnson gave birth shortly after her capture. At the onset of labor her captors took her to a brook and made a booth of brush for her. After her daughter was born, they presented her with some clothing that had been plundered during the raid. She was permitted to rest for the remainder of the day, and her captors made a bier upon which the other prisoners carried her when travel resumed. Susanna recalled her captor's response when he learned that he now had two captives: "My master looked into the booth, and clapped his hands with joy, crying two monies for me, two monies for me."[20]

Johnson and her baby survived the journey to Canada. It may seem extraordinary that they could endure the adversity of such a formidable trek through the wilderness, often on limited rations. Remarkably, of the adult women captured in the New England raids, 20 percent were either pregnant or had recently been delivered of a child, and only 3 percent of the women died along the way. Only two of the women lost infants who were born in Indian camps.

Elizabeth Hanson was captured from her New Hampshire home in 1724. She described a difficult journey north with "some very high mountains so steep, that I was forc'd to creep up on my hands and knees." In such instances she deeply appreciated the fact that "my master would mostly carry my babe for me" despite the fact that he had "a very heavy burden of his own." He would "sometimes take my very blanket, so that I had nothing to do, but take my little boy by the hand."[21]

RANSOMING CAPTIVES

The Indians who raided New England tended to take captives for ransom. Captives were frequently ransomed in exchange for valuables, for pledges of peace, or for other prisoners. Some captives were used for prisoner exchange. Susanna Johnson reported, "The Indians brought me here for the purpose of exchanging me for some Micanaw savages, a tribe with whom they were at war; but being disappointed in this, they were exorbitant in their demands, and refused to take less than a thousand livres for me and my child."[22] Following counteroffers and threats, the figure of 700 livres was eventually agreed upon and the transfer concluded.

Phineas Stevens, who was captured by Abenakis as a youth, was appointed emissary to Canada by the governor of Massachusetts and charged with securing the release of New England captives. On one such mission he noted: "John Starkes was brought to Montreal by his Indian master. He was taken hunting this spring. He is given us for an Indian pony in his place, for which we paid 515 livres."[23]

Mary Rowlandson had the opportunity to set her own ransom figure. She described the following negotiations prior to her redemption:

When the letter was come, the Saggamores met to consult about the captives, and called me to them, to enquire how much my husband would give to redeem me. . . . Now knowing that all we had was destroyed by the Indians, I was in a great strait. I thought if I should speak of but a little it would be slighted, and hinder the matter; if of a great sum, I knew not where it would be procured; yet [I] venture[d] [to say] twenty pounds, yet desired them to take less; but they would not hear of that, but sent that message to Boston, that for twenty pounds I should be redeemed.[24]

Funding for redemptions came from both private and public sources, although from time to time New England legislatures tried to forbid the use of public money for such purposes. Obtaining the release of public funding was not always easy. In a 1710 letter, Joseph Dudley, governor of Massachusetts, expressed sympathy for the lot of the captives, but repeated his steadfast resolution "never to buy a prisoner of an Indian, lest we make a market for our poor women and children in the frontiers."[25]

Susanna Johnson's husband, James, was paroled from Montreal in order to return to New England for the purpose of securing the needed funds to effect his redemption and that of his family. His first application was to Governor William Shirley of Massachusetts. Shirley laid the matter before the General Assembly, but they granted Johnson only the sum of ten pounds to defray his expenses. Johnson was then advised to apply to the New Hampshire General Assembly. There the sum of 150 pounds sterling was granted for the purpose of redemption of prisoners. Johnson was also presented with a letter of credit for that amount and advised to "negotiate in the best and most frugal manner."[26]

Captives were commonly sold to the French in Canada. When Elizabeth Hanson was taken to be sold, her captor requested 800 livres for her and her child. The prospective buyer "put him [her master] in a great rage, offering him but 600 livres; he said, in a great passion, if he could not have his demand, he would make a great fire and burn me and babe."[27] Calling the seller's bluff, the purchasing Frenchman made the transaction the following day for the 600 livres.

The purchase of captives from Indians became a regular business endeavor among merchants in Montreal and Quebec. Upon reaching Montreal, Susanna Johnson reported: "Here I had the happiness to find that all my fellow prisoners had been purchased, by persons of respectability. . . . Mr. DuQuesne bought my sister, my eldest daughter was owned by three affluent old maids, by the name of Jaisson, and the other, to wit, Polly, was owned by the mayor of the city."[28]

The French purchasers usually sought reimbursement for the ransom from the families of the captives. Naturally, the purchaser looked forward to enjoying a nice profit in the effort. Phineas Stevens reported the following negotiations in his journal in 1752: "The [N]egro which the Commissary of the fort bought of the Indian taken at Canterbury, we cannot get for the same money we supposed he bought him for. The gentlemen declares he gave 600 livres for him. We have been informed he gave but 400—the captain's lady told us she was offered him for that money."[29] Stevens also indicated that surcharges could be required: "Mrs. Honor Hancock, a prisoner taken from Jebucto was brought to Montreal; which we bought at 300 livres, and 30 livres for the charge of bringing her."[30] Seth Webb, a Maine youth, was captured by Abenakis in 1750. After being purchased in Montreal the following year, he wrote to his father, "I live at Present with Mr. Gamelin at Saint Francois, he has redeemed me from the Indians for 300 livres, I beg you dear father to redeem me as soon as possible you can. I long much to gitt home."[31] By the mid–eighteenth century such negotiations and redemptions had become quite commonplace.

THE TREATMENT OF CAPTIVES IN CANADA

Usually the purchased captives were well treated and enjoyed a fair amount of freedom. Elizabeth Hanson remarked that "the French were civil beyond what I could either desire or expect."[32] Susanna Johnson was able to effect substantial changes in her daughter's situation. Susanna was distressed when she learned that Polly "was not well used; that no proper care was taken of her." She discovered that "the mayor's lady had kept her out at boarding and nursing." It was "fashionable among the higher class of people in Canada to have their own children nursed out till they were about three or four years old." Susanna felt that these boarded children were "not kept so clean a manner by their nurses as the English" and only dressed well when they were presented to their parents during monthly visits. Susanna sought an interview with the mayor's wife, who defended her treatment of Polly. The next morning, however, she sent a servant to Susanna, saying "I could not sleep last night; her observations broke my heart! She may have her child."[33]

Susanna Johnson and her child lived in comfortable circumstances during their time in Montreal, being "treated with great civility; [she] dined frequently in the first families, received cards to attend them on parties of pleasure, and was introduced to a large and respectable acquaintance" until political changes began to unravel their situation. Mr. Johnson had been granted a two-month parole to obtain funding for their ransom, a task in which he had been successful. As Johnson was preparing to return to Canada, however, Governor Shirley wrote to him of intelligence "of the motions of the French in Canada, for further invading his Majesty's territories on the frontiers." The governor refused to let Johnson make his return trip, thus causing him to violate his parole and lose his credit in Canada. This turn of events radically changed Susanna's position. She wrote: "The return of the Indians without Mr. Johnson, boded no good to me. I observed with pain the gradual change in my friends, from coldness to neglect, and from neglect to contempt."[34]

Eventually, Johnson received permission to return to his family in Montreal. Unfortunately, a new governor had been appointed and spirited preparations were being made for war. No considerations were given to the circumstances, which prevented Johnson's return. The Johnsons were attempting to settle their debts with paper money until silver could be obtained, when James was put in jail. James, Susanna, and infant Captive were then shipped to Quebec and imprisoned in a criminal jail. The situation in the jail was odious. Susanna reported: "[W]e were supported by a piece of meat a day, which was served with some rusty crusts of bread, and brought to us in a pail that swine would run from.The straw and lousy blankets were our only lodging, and the rest of our furniture consisted of some wooden blocks for seats."[35] After suffering smallpox and other degradations, the Johnsons were transferred to a civil prison, where Susanna wrote, "We had a decent bed, candles, fuel and all the conveniences belonging to prisoners of war."[36] Complications continued to plague the family, but after three years of imprisonment they finally were permitted to make the journey back home.

The Johnsons were not unique in their imprisonment. After his capture in Autumn of 1745 Nehemiah How was confined in a prison in Quebec. He kept an account of the prisoners who joined the ranks as fellow inmates. From January, 1746, to the following year he recorded the arrival of 215 prisoners. They came as singletons, pairs, and in groups as large as 74. How noted the death of 33 prisoners during the same period.[37] A similar fate also awaited How. He died a prisoner in 1747, a fact that another prison resident recorded as the last entry in How's journal.

INDIAN REVENGE

Revenge was a motive for some abductions. The unfortunates chosen for this purpose—usually men—were subjected to abject humiliation, ritualistic torture, and cruel death. James Smith remained among the Delaware tribe for five years. During his captivity he witnessed a particularly grisly event, which he noted in his journal:

At sundown I beheld a small party coming with about a dozen prisoners, stripped naked, with their hands tied behind their back and their faces and part of their bodies blackened. These prisoners were burned to death on the bank of the Allegheny River opposite the fort. I stood at the fort wall until I beheld them begin to burn one of these men: they had him tied to a stake and kept touching him with fire-brands, red-hot irons, &c., and he screaming in the most doleful manner.[38]

ADOPTION INTO THE TRIBE

Some captives were taken to be absorbed or adopted into the native community. Adoptions were made in order to make up for demographic losses due to war or disease, or to appease those who were in mourning for the loss of a loved one. Warren Johnson, brother to Superintendent of Indian Affairs William Johnson, noted the practice in his journal:

The native American captive in this illustration will probably be
killed. His captor is regaled in typical warrior attire with a scalping
knife held ominously between his teeth. The tattoos on his body indicate that this is an illustration from an early part of the colonial
period. Note the headdress, beads, earrings, and decorated pouch
and loincloth.

"When the Indians lose a man in action, & chance to take an enemy prisoner, he belongs to the family of the deceased, who take great care of him, & look on him in the same light as on the person lost & even leave him the same fortune."[39]

Mary Jemison, a captive who chose to remain among her captors, further explained the process and meaning of adoption:

If they receive a prisoner, it is at their option either to satiate their vengeance by taking his life in the most cruel manner they can conceive of; or to receive and adopt him into the family . . . unless the mourners have but just received the news of their bereavement, and are under the operation of a paroxysm of grief, anger and revenge; or unless the prisoner is very old, sickly or homely, they generally save him.[40]

Those captives who were not ransomed or adopted were generally held as slaves. Being a slave did not mean that the captive could not be ransomed or adopted at a later date; however, the position of a slave came with a heavier workload, harsher treatment, and a good deal of personal humiliation. Mary Fowler, initially held as a slave, complained of "three years hard labor in planting and hoeing corn, chopping and carrying wood, pounding samp, gathering cranberries and other wild fruit." However, these tasks were not far removed from the normal labor of native women.[41]

Writing of her ultimate adoption into a native family, Mary reported, "I was received by two squaws, to supply the place of their brother in the family; and I was ever considered and treated by them as a real sister, the same as though I had been born of their mother."[42] The Indians of Pennsylvania, southern New York, and Ohio did not have the same channels of commerce with Quebec or Montreal that were enjoyed by the Indians in the French missions. Consequently, they kept a larger proportion of their captives for the purposes of adoption or slavery. These Indians commonly stopped at a French fort prior to traveling to their own villages. Older captives were left to be sent to Canada, but younger abductees were kept and adopted into their community.

Adoptees were carefully selected in order to maximize their acculturation into the Indian community. Health, attitude, and age were given important consideration. At the conclusion of hostilities in Pennsylvania in 1764, Colonel Henry Bouquet and his troops encamped on the Muskingum in the Ohio country in order to collect the captives who were to be returned as part of the articles of agreement reached with the Delawares, Shawnees, and Senecas. A total of 81 men and 126 women were returned. Some had been captives for as long as nine years. An additional 88, mainly women and children, remained in Shawnee towns. Eventually, 44 of these were returned to Fort Pitt. All but 4 had been less than sixteen years old, while 37 had been less than eleven when captured.

The adoption process commenced with a ceremony that proved threatening to most captives. Mary Jemison recalled, "During my adoption I sat motionless, nearly terrified to death at the appearance and actions of the company, expecting every moment to feel their vengeance, and suffer death on the spot."[43] The frenzied dancing and "hallooing and yelling in a tremendous manner" proved most intimidating to the abductees.[44] Mary Jemison recalled being engulfed in a circle of squaws who "immediately set up a most dismal howling, crying bitterly, and wringing their hands in all the agonies of grief for a deceased relative."[45] Susanna Johnson recalled: "The figure [of the dance] consisted of [a] circular motion round the fire. Each sang his own music, and the best dancer was the one most violent in motion. The prisoners were taught each a song, mine was, danna witchee natchepung; my son's was nar wiscumpton."[46]

James Smith recalled that his adoption ceremony began with the old chief making a long speech and then presenting him to three squaws, who led him down the riverbank and into the water. "The squaws then made signs for me to plunge myself into the water, but I did not understand them. I thought that the result of the council was that I should be drowned, and that these young ladies were to be the executioners." Eventually one of the women led him to understand that they meant him no harm, and he surrendered himself to be "washed and scrubbed severely." James was then returned to the council house and given new clothes including "a ruffled shirt . . . a pair of leggings done with ribbons and beads, porcupine quills, and red hair; also a tinsel laced cappo." Through an interpreter he was told: "My son, you have now nothing to fear. We are now under the same obligations to love, support and defend you that we are to love and defend one another. Therefore you are to consider yourself as one of our people."[47]

Some captives were surrendered to a gauntlet in which they were hit with axe handles, tomahawks, clubs, and switches by members of the entire village. An ex-captive described the ceremony of running the gauntlet: "There is at the entry of the fort gate a heap of squaws and children who stand ready to receive [the captive] with their sticks, clubs, poles, and fire brands, who lay on with all their force and might till he gets into the wigwam where he is to live."[48] These blows, while real, were not applied in a manner to do mortal harm, however, and in some cases were more symbolic than actual. Young captives were often exempt from this portion of the ritual. Some people believe that the action of Pocahontas throwing her body over John Smith at the moment of his execution was also part of an adoption ritual. Many of these ceremonies have been interpreted to represent the death of a former way of life and rebirth into the Indian community.[49]

Mary Jemison noted: "In the course of that ceremony, from mourning they became serene—joy sparked in their countenances, and they seemed to rejoice over me as over a long lost child. . . . [A]t the close of the ceremony the company retired, and my sisters went about employing every means for my consolation and comfort."[50] Susanna Johnson reported that "the interpreter came to inform me that I was adopted into his family. I was then introduced to the family, and I was told to call them brothers and sisters."[51] The adoptees were often given gifts such as a new pair of moccasins, a shirt, or a dress.

The papers of William Johnson contain the following remarks, which were attributed to the Shawnee who presented the returning captives to Fort Pitt: "We have taken as much care of these prisoners, as if they were [our] own flesh, and blood; they are become unacquainted with your customs, and manners, and therefore, father we request you will use them tender, and kindly, which will be the means of inducing them to live contentedly with you."[52]

Not all captives chose to return to their former communities. Some captives married Indians or other captives, and lived the remainder of their lives among their adopted Indian families. Cadwallader Colden, surveyor-general and member of the king's council of New York addressed this fact in 1747: "No arguments, no entreaties, no tears of their friends and relations, could persuade many of them to leave their new Indian friends and acquaintance[s]; several of them that were by the caressings of their relations persuaded to come home, in a little time grew tired of our manner of living, and run away again to the Indians and ended their days with them."[53]

Benjamin Franklin, serving as a commissioner of the Pennsylvania colony, made a similar observation about the desire of many young captives to remain in their native communities in 1753:

When white persons of either sex have been taken prisoners young by the Indians, and lived a while among them, tho' ransomed by their friends, and treated with all imaginable tenderness to prevail with them to stay among the English, yet in a short time they become disgusted with our manner of life, and the care and pains that are necessary to support it, and take the first opportunity of escaping again into the woods.[54]

Crevecoeur described scenes wherein captive children were presented to their birth parents with surprising and disturbing results. He reported that the youngsters "absolutely refused to follow them and ran to their adoptive parents for protection against the effusions of love their unhappy real parents lavished on them!" He mused, "By what power does it come to pass that children who have been adopted when young among these people can never be prevailed on to readopt European manners?"[55]

The bonds between captor and captive often became very strong on both sides, as Elizabeth Hanson and her husband found when they tried to obtain the release of their daughter: "[T]he affections they have for my daughter, made them refuse all offers and terms of ransom; so that after my poor husband had waited, and made what attempts and endeavors he could, to obtain his child, and all to no purpose, we were forced to make homeward, leaving our daughter to our great grief, behind us, amongst the Indians."[56] John Williams similarly fought long, hard, and unsuccessfully for the release of his daughter, Eunice. Recording the sad news of the Jesuit handling the negotiations, the grieving pastor noted, "The Mohawks would as soon part with their hearts as my child."[57]

Catherine Schyler witnessed a meeting designed to return captive children to their parents in an orchard on her homestead in Albany. She was obviously moved by the scene:

Poor women who traveled one hundred miles from the back settlements of Pennsylvania and New England appeared here with anxious looks and aching hearts, not knowing whether their children were alive or dead or how to identify their children if they should meet them. . . . The joy of the happy mothers was overpowering . . . [as were] the tears of those who after long travel found not what they sought. It was affecting to see the deep silent sorrow of the Indian women and of the children who knew no other mother, and clung fondly to their bosoms from whence they were not torn without bitter shrieks.[58]

Crevecoeur interviewed two men who were captured when they "were grown to the age of men" about their decision to remain among the Indians. After living a number of years among the Indians, these men had been sent a sum of money by friends to ransom themselves from their captors. The young men consulted their masters and were told "they had been long as free as themselves." Among the reasons the men gave Crevecoeur for choosing to remain among their captors were "the most perfect freedom, the ease of living, the absence of those cares and corroding solicitudes which so often prevail with us, and the peculiar goodness of the soil they cultivated."[59]

LIFE AMONG THE INDIANS

Mary Jemison, who lived most of her life among the Iroquois, painted an idyllic picture of the Indian lifestyle: "Their lives were a continual round of pleasures. Their wants were few, and easily satisfied; their cares were only for to-day; the bounds of their calculations for future comfort not extending to the incalculable uncertainties of to-morrow. If peace ever dwelt with men, it was in former times, in the recesses from war, amongst what are now termed barbarians."[60] Crevecoeur speculated: "It cannot be, therefore, so bad as we generally conceive it to be; there must be in their social bond something singularly captivating and far superior to anything to be boasted among us . . . There must be something more congenial to our native dispositions than the fictitious society in which we live."[61]

The labors of an Indian captive were generally light. Mary Jemison described her responsibilities: "I was employed in nursing the children and doing light work about the house. Occasionally I was sent out with the Indian hunters, when they went but a short distance, to help them carry their game. My situation was easy; I had no particular hardships to endure."[62] While Jemison seemed pleased with her duties, Susanna Johnson complained of the dearth of work she had to occupy her time: "It was an unnatural situation to me. I was a novice at making canoes, bunks and trumplines, which was the only occupation of the squaws; of course idleness was among my calamities."[63] Mary Rowlandson used her European skills to her advantage. In her narrative she made numerous references to sewing and knitting for her captors. Rowlandson crafted shirts, caps, and stockings during her captivity. Occasionally she received gifts in recognition of her endeavors. Nine-year-old Stephen Williams was required to do such chores as cutting wood and packing skins and other supplies.

ESCAPES

Not all captives became resigned to their situation. Mary Ingles, her sons (Thomas, aged four, and George, aged two), and her sister-in-law, Bettie Draper, were abducted from the Virginia settlement of Draper's Meadow by a Shawnee raiding party in July 1755. After a month of travel, during which time Mary gave birth to another child, the captives were divided up. Bettie was taken further north. Mary was permitted to keep her baby, but she never saw her young sons again. Mary and a group of other female captives were sent to Big Bone Lick to boil salt. They also spent time gathering wild grapes, walnuts, and hickory nuts. It was during this time that Mary began to plot her escape. She convinced a reluctant captive known only as "the Dutch woman" to accompany her. They each managed to steal a blanket and a tomahawk, and they slipped away one afternoon. Mary left behind her infant, knowing that the cries of the child would surely betray them. She trusted the welfare of her babe to the kindness of some squaw. During her captivity Mary had taken particular care to remember every bend of the river, every landmark. After 100 days and a journey of almost 500 miles, Mary arrived back at Draper's Meadows having lived on nuts, berries, and some corn she found at an abandoned cabin. Never once did she light a fire for warmth. One of Mary's most perilous situations was posed by her companion, who went mad during the journey and attempted to kill her.

Hannah Dunstan, who was immortalized in Cotton Mather's 1702 *Magnalia Christi Americana*, similarly planned and successfully executed an escape. Less than a week after Hannah had given birth, she and her midwife, Mary Neff, were captured at Haverhill, Massachusetts. On their march, Hannah became fearful that they would be "Stript, and Scourg'd, and Run the Gauntlet through the whole Army of Indians." Several days from their destination Hannah, Nurse Neff, and a young English boy named Samuel Leonardson, who had been taken captive about a year and a half earlier, stole some Indian hatchets from their captors as they slept. "[T]hey struck home Blows upon the heads of their Sleeping Oppressors," killing ten, wounding one woman, who escaped, and sparing a youth, who also fled. Whether driven by revenge, greed, or perhaps a desire to confirm their story, the three proceeded to scalp the ten victims and upon their return "received Fifty Pounds from the General Assembly of the Province, as a Recompense of their Action."[64]

CATHOLIC CONVERSION

Accompanying the fear of losing a child to the Indians, was the fear among most New Englanders of losing a child to Catholic conversion. John Williams frequently expressed his extreme concern that his captive children would be exposed to "Latin prayers," the "French tongue," and "popish religion." Speaking with his daughter, he instructed her that "she must be careful she did not forget her catechism and the Scriptures she had learned by heart."[65] His son, Stephen, was purchased by a French merchant in Montreal and sent to a French school, where he came under the tutelage of a priest and succumbed to the influence to embrace Catholicism. Williams recalled, "I mourned when I thought with myself that I had one child with the Mohawks, a second turned to popery, and a little child of six years of age in danger . . . to be instructed in popery."[66] Williams was eventually able to reverse his son's indoctrination.

It was common for Jesuits to pressure captives to forsake their Protestant beliefs and be baptized as Catholics. Captives who were baptized, or who married French men, were released from their bondage. While still among the Indians, Elizabeth Hanson's daughter, Sarah, agreed to marry a Frenchman "in order to obtain her Freedom, by reason that those Captives married by French, are by that Marriage made free among them." Of the 277 captives taken from Maine and New Hampshire between 1689 and 1730, 27 percent of the women and 13 percent of the males chose to remain in Canada and were assimilated among the French.[67]

Jemima Howe had two adolescent daughters who were abducted with her during a raid on Hinsdale, New Hampshire. Unable to find a buyer for her daughter, Submit, they gave her to French governor de Vaudreuil, who placed her in a convent. Her sister, Mary, was designated to be an Abenaki bride. Horrified at this prospect, Jemima was able to persuade the governor to intervene. He then sent Mary to the same convent as her sister, where in Jemima's eyes they were educated "in this school of superstition and bigotry." When the governor returned to France he took the older girl with him and married her to a French gentleman. The younger daughter continued for several years in the convent and was on the verge of being sent to France along with the nuns when Jemima, having been released from captivity, returned to Canada to obtain the release of the young woman. Her daughter refused to go and was released only after Jemima implored the governor to help. Following the threat of soldiers to assist in forcing her to submit to parental authority, the young woman left the convent. Jemima noted that "so extremely bigoted was she to the customs and religions of the place, that after all, she left it with the greatest reluctance, and the most bitter lamentations which she continued as we passed the streets, and wholly refused to be comforted."[68]

Other captives refused to leave Canada as well. Phineas Stevens had negotiated the release of a Dutch girl taken in the war, named Elizabeth Cody, and an English boy named Solomon Metchel, twelve years old. "Upon their refusing to go home the Governor would not give them up."[69] Whether the captors were French or Indian, the most likely abductees to remain transculturated were the young females, between ages seven and fifteen.

INDIANS HELD CAPTIVE

Europeans also understood the value of captives. Abductees could ensure the safety of those in enemy hands, provide bargaining power for political concessions, and assist as instruments of diplomacy as interpreters and intermediaries. Europeans captured Indians and used them in all of these capacities as well as in slavery. Unfortunately, the words and thoughts of these captives were not preserved for us to study. Following the attack upon the Pequot Indians, the settlers enslaved the women and children and, fearing the warriors, sold the surviving men and boys into slavery in the West Indies.

The most famous European captive surely must be the befriender of the Pilgrims, Squanto or Tisquantum. Initially captured with twenty-six other natives by shipmaster John Hunt in 1614, Squanto was sold at the slave market at Malaga, Spain. Eventually, he managed to return home on an English ship only to discover that his village was deserted, having been nearly wiped out by an epidemic. Squanto decided to remain among his captors. He proved to be an able diplomat and assisted in negotiations between the English and the Indians. Squanto helped the settlers to negotiate effectively with the native population for reliable supplies of maize and pelts. He also provided assistance by teaching the settlers how to gather native foods and to cultivate maize. He died among the English in 1622.

Another Indian captive was Pocahontas, daugther of Powhattan, chief of the Indian nation who occupied part of Virginia. She was kidnapped by Jamestown settlers and offered for ransom in return for eight English prisoners and a cache of captured English weapons. While her father, Powhattan, contemplated the exchange, Pocahontas was housed with Anglican minister, Alexander Whitacker, who commenced her religious instruction. After several months Powhattan returned seven captives, each with a broken weapon. The English insisted upon their original demand. Finally, Sir Thomas Dale, then in command of the colony, went to Powhattan with Pocahontas, offering her in return for Powhattan's submission. During the negotiations she is reported to have said that "if her father loved her, he would not value her less than old swords, pieces, or axes: wherefore she should still dwell with the English men, who loved her."[70] Powhattan acceded to her request and asked Dale to care for her as a daughter. Pocahontas married John Rolfe and traveled to London along with their young son, Thomas, in 1616 in an effort to raise funds for the Virginia Company. While in England she contracted a pulmonary infection and died.

Squanto and Pocahontas made the most of their circumstances and were powerful allies to their captors because of their willingness to flourish in their new situations. Many other Indian captives resisted being made instruments of conquest and escaped through suicide. Still others used the knowledge they gained while in captivity against their former captors.

Epenow, a Wampanoag who lived along the northeast coast, was abducted from Martha's Vineyard in 1611. He learned English well and made a favorable impression when shown to potential investors in the Virginia Company. Spinning tales of gold in New England, he managed to inspire an expedition back to the Martha's Vineyard to collect the gold that he said was there. Once home, he escaped and became the leader of Wampanoag resistance against further English expansion and settlement.

A young Algonquian was abducted from the Chesapeake Bay area by the Spanish in 1561. While his traditional name has been lost, he was baptized under the name of Don Luis de Velasco, in honor of the viceroy of New Spain. He traveled to Spain and agreed to lead a party of missionaries to his homeland. Once he returned he moved away from the mission and led an attack on it in which all the priests were killed. Only a native altar boy was spared.

The total number of colonists seized during the colonial period is greatly eclipsed by the number of Indians who were abducted by Europeans to be enslaved or exhibited. What has given the captivity of white colonials such significance is the literary genre that was spawned by the reports of their kidnappings. "These horrid tales required not the aid of fiction, or the persuasive powers of rhetoric, to heighten their colorings, or gain credence to their shocking truths."[71] In a restrained society such as New England, where novels were viewed as corruptive, these narratives provided the excitement of modern escapist literature.

CAPTIVITY NARRATIVES

Perhaps the most famous of what have come to be known as the captivity narratives is Captain John Smith's *General Historie* (1624). One of the earliest accounts, this was written for a European audience. Like similar works it offered its readers firsthand information, if sometimes distorted, about the Indians in the New World. It is probably best read to gain insight into the European mind and perspective of the New World than for insight into the culture of the Native Americans.

More significant in a literary sense, however, were the numerous accounts of captivity, written mainly by or about Puritan and Quaker women that persisted well into the first quarter of the eighteenth century. These writings were as much spiritual autobiographies as descriptions of extraordinary events experienced by ordinary people. They became journeys of salvation through suffering and despair with nothing more than one's saving faith. They epitomized the spiritual trial and redemption theme, which reinforced certain religious beliefs seeking signs of Providence at work in the world, and they were widely read.

Mary Rowlandson's captivity narrative, *The Sovereignty and Goodness of God, Together with the Faithfulness of His Presence Displayed* (1682), was the second of only four works by women authors published in seventeenth-century New England and went through four editions in 1682. Written seven years after the attack on her home in Lancaster, Massachusetts, the work included numerous quotes from scripture that elevate it from being a mere tale of adventure. Prominent clergyman Increase Mather saw the value of attaching a providential meaning to the captivity and redemption experience and included an account of Mary's ordeal in his own *Essay for the Recording of Illustrious Providences* (1684). The renewal of hostilities in the 1690s led Cotton Mather to continue his father's work with colonial warfare and captivity. The younger Mather, however, did more than editorialize. The captivity narratives published by Cotton Mather were heavily edited and generally printed as third-person accounts.

Religious leaders like Cotton Mather warned parents of the loss of their children to heathenism. Settlers who left settlements with established religious communities for more isolated homesteads on the fringe of the frontier were depicted as on the verge of being wild themselves. These people were rebuked for weakening the government by moving beyond its direct control and for tempting the peril of being drawn into heathenish ignorance and barbarism.

Within weeks of his return, John Williams drafted an account of the events from the time of the massacre at Deerfield until his return. He felt a strong need not only to detail his experiences but also to educate the faithful. His narrative was quickly published and in time became a venerable part of the literary canon of Puritanism.[72] It was reissued six times during the eighteenth century and an additional five times in the nineteenth century.

The theme of providential intervention was often heightened by the religious titles of these works. Williams's *The Redeemed Captive Returning to Zion* (1707), like other narratives of this time, seemed almost to be a spiritual allegory of divine favor. Elizabeth Hanson's Quaker narrative, *God's Mercy Surmounting Man's Cruelty, Exemplified in the Captivity and Redemption of Elizabeth Hanson* (1728), continued in the footsteps of Rowlandson and Williams.

By the mid–eighteenth century, captivity narratives had become more secular. The stories became more a recounting of an extraordinary experience. They also, at times, became a vehicle for spreading propaganda against the Indian, the French, or the English, depending on which group was perceived as the enemy at the time.

Naturally, accounts must be read past the possibly jaundiced eye of the writer, whose position was seldom that of ethonographer and who may have easily misinterpreted or misunderstood the actions of his or her captors. Keeping in mind the purpose for which they were written, however, these accounts can provide insight into the customs and way of life of the Eastern Indians. As these native Americans left no written documents, captivity narratives are a major source of study for Indian daily life.

NOTES

1. H.M.M. Richards, "The Indian Forts of the Blue Mountains," in *Report to the Commission to Locate the Site of the Frontier Forts of Pennsylvania*, vol. 1 (Harrisburg: Pennsylvania Historical Commission, 1896), 95.

2. Susanna Johnson, *A Narrative of the Captivity of Mrs. Johnson* (Bowie, MD: Heritage Books, 1990), 18.

3. Ibid., 24–25.

4. Ibid., 25.

5. See J. Hector St. John de Crevecoeur, *Letters from an American Farmer and Sketches of Eighteenth Century America* (New York: Penguin Press, 1981), 202.

6. Johnson, 103.

7. Samuel G. Drake, ed., *Indian Captivities, or Life in the Wigwam* (Auburn: Derby and Miller, 1852), 142.

8. Colin G. Calloway, ed., *North Country Captives* (Hanover, NH: University Press of New England, 1992), 17–18.

9. Mary Rowlandson, *A Narrative of the Captivity and Removes of Mrs. Mary Rowlandson* (Fairfield, WA: Ye Galleon Press, 1974), 4.

10. Ibid., 5–6.

11. John Williams, *The Redeemed Captive Returning to Zion* (Amherst, MA: Edward W. Clark, 1976), 47–48.

12. See Selma R. Williams, *Demeter's Daughters: The Women Who Founded America, 1587–1787* (New York: Atheneum, 1976), 167–168. The individuals so memorialized were killed in the 1746 raid.

13. Rowlandson, 12.

14. Johnson, 29–31.

15. See Ibid., 55.

16. Williams, 48–49.

17. Ibid., 48.

18. Johnson, 31.

19. Calloway, 2–3.

20. Johnson, 36.

21. Kathryn Zabelle Derounian-Stodola, ed., *Women's Indian Narratives* (New York: Penguin Classics, 1998), 68.

22. Johnson, 75–76.

23. Calloway, 38.

24. Rowlandson, 86.

25. John Demos, *The Unredeemed Captive* (New York: Vintage Books, 1994), 92.

26. Johnson, 79–80.

27. Demos, 82.

28. Johnson, 72.

29. Calloway, 38.

30. Ibid., 37.

31. Emma Coleman, *New England Captives*, vol. 2 (Portland, ME: Southworth Press, 1925), 263.

32. Derounian-Stodola, 77.

33. See Johnson, 72–75.

34. Ibid., 84–86

35. Ibid., 93.

36. Ibid., 99.

37. See Drake, 140–143.

38. See Howard H. Peckham, ed., *Narratives of Colonial America, 1703–1765* (Chicago: R. R. Donnelley & Sons, 1971), 87.

39. See "Journal of Warren Johnson," in Dean R. Snow, Charles T. Gehring, and William A. Starna, eds., *In Mohawk Country: Early Narratives About a Native People* (Syracuse, NY: Syracuse University Press, 1996), 257.

40. See James E. Seaver, *A Narrative of the Life of Mary Jemison* (Syracuse, NY: Syracuse University Press, 1990), 22–23.

41. Calloway, 15.

42. Seaver, 23.

43. Ibid., 23.

44. Johnson, 57.

45. Seaver, 20.

46. Johnson, 58.

47. Peckham, 90–91.

48. Demos, 81.

49. See Pauline Turner Strong, *Captive Selves, Captivating Others* (Boulder, CO: Westview Press, 1999), 53–59.

50. Seaver, 22–23.

51. Johnson, 67.

52. James Axtell, *The European and the Indian: Essays in the Ethnohistory of Colonial America* (New York: Oxford University Press, 1981), 175. Quoting Johnson Papers.

53. Cadwallader Colden, *History of the Five Indian Nations of Canada* (New York: A. S. Barnes, 1904), 203–204.

54. See Leonard W. Libra, ed., *The Papers of Benjamin Franklin* (New Haven: Yale University Press, 1959), 481–482.

55. Crevecoeur, 213.

56. Peckham, 95.

57. Williams, 66.

58. Mary G. Humphreys, *Catherine Schyler* (Spartansburg, SC: Reprint Company, 1968), 123.

59. Crevecoeur, 214.

60. Seaver, 48.

61. Crevecoeur, 214.

62. Seaver, 24.

63. Johnson, 68.

64. Derounian-Stodola, 60.

65. Williams, 66.

66. Ibid., 91.

67. Derounian-Stodola, 79.

68. Ibid., 103.

69. Calloway, 38.

70. Strong, 64–65.

71. Seaver, 12.

72. Demos, 51.

13

Frontier Fortifications

A successful battle may leave the victor in control of the countryside for a while, but he still cannot become master of an entire area if he does not take the fortress.
—Marquis de Vauban, seventeenth-century military engineer

FORTS

Forts on the frontiers were constructed of masonry, timber, earthworks, or a combination of these materials. The choice of a particular material was largely a matter of availability, with timber being the most commonly used material for new or temporary structures. When formal construction projects were undertaken, as with Fort Frederick in western Maryland, the initial stages of the work were done in wood and earth, but money was provided by the colonial government for the finished fort to be done in stone. This was also true of Fort Carillon (known as Ticonderoga), begun by the French in 1755 with the initial timber and earthwork structure being replaced after the British captured it with locally quarried stone. While local defense points and stronghouses were often built in a catch-as-catch-can manner, the design of formal fortifications such as Fort Pitt or Fort Augusta in Pennsylvania followed the established dictates of eighteenth-century military engineering.

The systems of military engineering used in the eighteenth century were developed during the preceding hundred years in Europe. Although colonial fortifications built in the forests of North America failed to rival European ones (where whole cities were fortified), they did follow the same predetermined format in most cases. The ostensible purpose of these fortifications was to keep the enemy out. Since the objective of the besiegers was to gain access to the interior of the fortification, or render it untenable, the military engineers of the period devised a series of static defensive structures that would bedevil the attackers. The basic tools of the besiegers were the use of cannons to demolish the walls, the use of miners and sappers to undermine the walls and cause their collapse, or the use of fire to burn out the occupants. Once the walls were breeched and a practicable opening had been established—one large enough to support an attack—a rush of infantry was planned to take the fort.

VAUBAN

Of the many fortification systems developed and used in the seventeenth and eighteenth centuries, one was outstanding. This was the system developed by Sabastien La Prestre, Marquis de Vauban (1633–1707)—a marshal of France and the leading military engineer of his day. As an engineer, Vauban carried the arts of fortification, attack, and defense to a "degree of perfection unknown before his time." He fortified or improved more than 300 citadels in Europe, erected 33 new ones, and conducted at least 53 sieges. His system of approach during sieges, which he first introduced at the siege of Maestricht in 1673, is best known to students of military history as the *System of Parallels*. His abilities as a besieger of fortified positions led him to develop a system of defensive fortifications that would counter his own best efforts.

Vauban's *First System of Fortification* centered on elaborate "star forts" and fortified outstructures. It was scrutinized and imitated by all the European powers of Vauban's day. Baron von Coehorn, the director-general of fortifications in Holland and the inventor of a high-arcing artillery piece known as the Coehorn mortar, used many of Vauban's principles when he published his own system of fortification. It was through the Anglo-Dutch alliance of the late seventeenth century that many British engineers learned to use Vauban's system for British colonial defenses. Ultimately, even the engineering work of Colonel Rufus Putnam, chief military engineer of the American revolutionary army, was influenced by Vauban's precepts.[1]

Vauban improved his own work as a *Second System* and *Third System* within his lifetime, but none of the systems were ever published as separate treatises. Rather, they were incorporated into the *Modern French System* in 1729 by those engineers who had worked closely with Vauban during his career. This document was updated in 1750, but its general

This antique engraving shows a group of military engineers devising a plan
of fortification from a model on the table before them. Military engineers
were well respected professionals who used the best technology of their day
to put their ideas into practice.

precepts were not far removed from those of the *First System* of the previous century. These precepts, with minor modifications, remained the
height of military defense technology until the widespread adoption of
the rifled artillery shell in the mid–nineteenth century overcame most of
their advantages.

The only fortress on the North American continent to have been built
specifically under the precepts of Vauban's system was at Louisbourg
on Cape Breton Island, Canada. Originally designed by the French in
1719, it was further strengthened and modified in 1748. Fortress Louisbourg, unlike most frontier outposts and forts of the colonial period, was
embellished with a large number of outworks and forward structures.
Moreover, the French engineers made extensive use of the natural defensive characteristics of the site. They were also required to defend the
port facilities on an island in the harbor as well as the landward approaches. The surviving structure—the largest fortification attempted on
the North American continent in the eighteenth century—today appears
haphazard and incidental to the untrained eye. Nonetheless, the defenses
were designed to strictly align with Vauban's engineering precepts.

Fort Carillon, built by the French in 1755 at the junction between Lake
George (Lac du St. Sacrement) and Lake Champlain at Ticonderoga in

A view of Fort Carillon at Ticonderoga with its star-shaped outline, outworks, and counterguard taken from an antique postcard in the author's collection. Note that the bastion closest to the viewer is missing. It was blown up with the powder magazine when the French abandoned the fort to the English.

New York, was a true "star fort." Its defenses generally followed Vauban's rules, but its design showed few embellishments. The remains of other eighteenth-century defensive structures that survive in North America, including French, British, and American designs, show a remarkable similarity to the type at Ticonderoga. Unfortunately, no above-ground remains exist for some of the most important forts built in the colonial period, and in many cases their very location is in dispute. Nonetheless, Vauban's *First System* was clearly incorporated into the designs that have been studied, even though almost all of the forts were built well after his death. In each case, deviations from Vauban's system of defense seem to have been simplifications of his precepts rather than innovations.

In order to see how Vauban's theories fit together, it is useful to examine the "drawing board approach" that many military engineers resorted to in designing fortifications. This technique was built upon some of Vauban's most fundamental precepts. First, the limits of the defenses were dictated by the effective range of the artillery available at the time hypothetically loaded with canister (many small leaden balls, as in a shotgun). This was somewhat short of 400 yards. Vauban placed great emphasis on the use of canister against attacking infantry because he believed that a fortress could not fall unless it was physically occupied by attacking troops. Oddly, he had little regard for the effectiveness of musketry for the overall defense of forts primarily because of the wild inaccuracy of the smooth bore musket beyond 100 yards.

Secondly, Vauban relied heavily on simple geometry in his designs, and he used the idea that the trajectory (path) of a bullet or cannonball was always in a straight line. Using these two principles, the plans for a fortification could be made using a drawing compass, a ruled straight edge, and a set of dividers. The actual structure could be taken from a paper layout or model and built at the intended site with simple surveying tools and nothing more than pick-axes and shovels.

DESIGNING A COLONIAL FORT

The first step in designing a fortification was to draw a polygon around the area to be defended. Squares, pentagons, and hexagons were commonly used in Europe, but most forts in North America were based on the square. Ideally these were equilateral figures, but engineers often changed the length of the sides to accommodate the natural defensive features of the ground. They also understood that the area enclosed by the polygon needed to be as small as possible due to the limited number of men available to defend the walls. As an example, historians and archaeologists believe that the interior of Fort Pitt may have been as small as forty-five feet square, requiring the building of an adjacent defensible camp to house the increased number of soldiers in time of war. In 1775 the entire garrison of the fort at Ticonderoga was seventeen men, and they could not have played a game of regulation football on the fort's parade due to its small size.

Most forts built in North America had sides measuring between twenty-five and one-hundred yards. This may reflect the major purpose of the frontier outpost, which was one of resisting small raids and providing a home for the border patrols. It also suggests a greater dependence on the musket rather than the cannon, as a side was rarely made longer than the effective range of a musket shot. The increased reliance on the tactical use of the musket as a defensive weapon on the eighteenth-century frontier was probably brought about by the lack of effective artillery. Most colonial outposts had no more than a few small cannons or swivel guns. By limiting the length of a side, the military engineer could defend adjacent structures without ever being out of range of either musketry or cannon fire.

Once the length of one side of the fundamental polygonal shape had been determined, the "rampart" or the "curtain wall" of the fort was laid out between the points of the star. These points were known as "bastions." Continued planning around the figure formed a defensive work with a bastion at each angle, or corner, of the original polygon. Hexagonal works,

The defensive works at Fort Stanwix National Monument in Rome, New York, as seen by a would-be attacker. This re-creation, by the National Park Service, is one of the most complete ever undertaken. A visitor to the fort would deem it as impregnable as it proved to be. The small sentry box stands atop the bastion at the salient.

therefore, had six bastions; pentagonal ones, five; and squares, four. The resulting figure was known as a "front of fortification."

Notwithstanding minor differences, the bastion remained the basic unit of defense. Its shoulders and flanks, topped by a parapet, commanded an unobstructed field of fire in which there was no cover for attacking infantry. Two adjacent bastions had a geometrically correct field of crossfire everywhere between them. The tip of the bastion was called the "salient angle." A besieger standing directly before the salient was open to fire from either of the adjacent bastions and from the rampart above the curtain wall. In other words, the bastion could not be used as cover by the attacker. The access to the bastion from within the fort was small and elevated above the parade, but every bastion was open to fire from defenders at some other point within the fort, a factor common to all the plans for defensive structures on the frontier.

Bomb-proofs were often built into the base of the bastion for defense against incoming mortar and cannon fire. A water supply, powder room, storeroom, or hospital might be located deep within the bastion with access from within the fort. Behind the curtain walls, or beneath the ramparts, fortified rooms called "casemates" were erected. Barracks, storerooms, offices, and stables could be found herein. The casemates were accessed from the parade and often had firing loops or firing slits that faced outward toward the enemy's position. These often looked out into a great ditch, or dry moat, through which the enemy troops were forced to pass.

The front of fortification was enhanced by an excavation commonly called the "ditch" or "moat." In European castles the original purpose of the ditch (whether dry or wet) was to prevent tunneling or undermining of the walls. A secondary purpose was to raise the relative height of the curtain walls and bastions by lowering the ground around them. This made scaling the wall more difficult. The ditch was usually between fifteen and thirty feet deep. While widths varied, the material dug out of the ditch was often used to raise the bastions and ramparts. The outermost edge of the ditch ran parallel to the shoulders of the bastions, leaving large areas known as "killing grounds" between them. The main entrance to the fort, and one or more "sallie ports," were often directed through the ditch. The entryway to most North American forts in the eighteenth century was either through the ditch or over a narrow bridge that crossed the ditch. This bridge could sometimes be raised. Some forts had wet ditches, or ditches that could be suddenly flooded. Wet ditches better served the purpose of preventing undermining of the walls, but they were particularly unpopular in the colonies because of the health hazard associated with damp air and stagnant water. They also inhibited the defenders' ability to counterattack.

A line of sight taken from the top of the parapet over the ditch to the area surrounding the fort defined the grade of the "glacis." In cross section this smooth sloping area left no cover for approaching troops. The glacis on many North American forts was left undeveloped, and only the trees were cut back, usually to beyond the range of siege cannon. This was often 300 or 400 yards. A military engineer with time, manpower, and money could embed in the glacis diagonal poles or trees with sharpened points that faced the enemy. These "abattis" hampered the enemy's movement toward the fort and made quick rushes impossible.

OUTWORKS AND OUTPOSTS

Vauban and his contemporaries were not satisfied with the limitations of these designs. Military engineers would plan to add a number of embellishments in the form of outworks or outposts around the fort. Some of these were so well integrated into the fundamental front of fortification as to appear part of it. The surviving fort at Ticonderoga has one bastion obscured by two outworks that flank it. To the untrained eye the fort has five points, but it really has only four.

The generally triangular outworks built in the ditch and in front of the curtain wall were called "ravelins." Each served as an island of defense in the ditch and as a platform for mounting additional artillery. Moreover, the body of the ravelin shielded the curtain wall from direct bombardment. The back of the ravelin was open to fire from the parapet atop the curtain wall. If the ravelin fell, the enemy could not maintain the position in safety.

Many forts had independent outposts built on the edge of the glacis. These were called "redoubts." The term *redoubt* was a generic one used to refer to any number of small, defensible positions. In North America they were usually square, though Vauban's redoubts were always triangular. Redoubts, unlike ravelins, could be defended from all sides. Redoubts often served as a strong point or final rallying point in the parade or in the center of a ravelin. The redoubts at Fort Niagara in New York are giant two-story blockhouses made of stone that guard the entrance and flanks of the fort. Other redoubts were made of earth, open to the sky, and had numerous fraises embedded in their sides to prevent scaling. Redoubts often had their own small cannons for defense.

Vauban and his contemporaries envisioned and used a much wider variety of outworks and embellishments than did colonial military engineers. These included counterguards, demi-lunes (half moons), lunettes (small half moons), crownworks, and hornworks. These were not common in North America, but the counterguard appears in many colonial documents and maps. This was a thin line composed of a simple, low parapet placed before the salient angle, the main gate, or the sallie port of the fort. A long, weaving counterguard was constructed at Fort Ticonderoga for the protection of the approach to the main gate.[2]

FRENCH FORTS ON THE FRONTIER

Besides the forts at Louisbourg, Ticonderoga, and Crown Point, the French strongly fortified their posts at Quebec, Montreal, and Niagara. They built less imposing defenses at Detroit, Michmillimacinac, and Sault St. Marie in order to firmly establish control of the Great Lakes–St. Lawrence River trade route. The degree to which an eighteenth-century observer was impressed by these fortifications depended on their experience with forts. The English colonists, whose experience was with garrison houses and blockhouses, might consider anything more elaborate than their own structure a quite formidable fortification. Regular French and British troops who had served in Europe would probably view the same structure as being rather simple. By European standards Louisbourg was fairly small and lightly defended even though it was the largest and most impressive military work attempted in North America during the colonial period.

In 1665 the French military viceroy, Marquis de Tracy, established three forts on the Richelieu River at Sorel, Chambly, and Ste. Therese. He then began a military road between Montreal and Chambly. Finally, he had Isle aux Noix fortified. These served as outposts against attack by the Iroquois, but the French post at Crown Point was meant to be physically and psychologically overwhelming to the English. Placed at the water's edge at a narrows in Lake Champlain in 1749, Fort St. Frederick had limestone walls several feet thick and a bomb-proof tower forty feet tall. There were emplacements for forty cannons. The thick foundations of the walls of this fort still exist, and their outlines testify to the overwhelming control the fort had over the passage of the lake. There was a small stone church outside the fort as well as stone houses for the officers and men of the garrison and a kitchen garden. The immediate area was surrounded by the farmsteads and homes of retired French soldiers.

Geographically, Crown Point controlled the heart of the passage of the Hudson-Richelieu passage from Quebec to Albany. The English Board of Trade was apprehensive about the French presence: "[The] strong fort [built at] Crown Point [will make the French] masters of that part of the country . . . and if they possess themselves of [Ticonderoga] they will intercept all our western fur trade that centers now in Oswego, and will by degrees become entire masters of the whole Six Nations." The French fort at Crown Point was said to be as strong as any in Europe. The nearby French post at Ticonderoga, located below the falls in the LaChute River, which drained Lake George into Lake Champlain, was called Fort Carillon. It was begun in 1755 at the orders of Baron Ludwig Dieskau, and it was strengthened and elaborated by the Marquis de Montcalm. Two great sieges of Fort Carillon were made in the French and Indian War.[3]

By the second half of the eighteenth century the frontier between New France and the English colonies was better defined by these defenses than it had ever before been. The French occupied the portage between Lake Champlain and Lake George at Ticonderoga. Fort Carillon was a square earthwork with four bastions and a redoubt set on a promontory jutting out into Lake Champlain. This was supported by Fort St. Frederick less than two dozen miles to the north along the shore. On the southern shore of Lake George was the English post at Fort William Henry. This was an earthwork faced with logs that was capable of maintaining itself against small arms and sporadic mortar fire, but useless against siege cannons if they could be dragged through the wilderness. It was supported by Fort Edward, which was connected to it by seventeen miles of good wagon road. Logistically, both sets of forts were easily supported by water. The two opposing pairs of fortifications now defined the frontier as Lake George itself, and no European army was going to make speedy progress along the Hudson-Richelieu route without eliminating the presence of one set of forts or the other. As a consequence, this short region of Adirondack wilderness may have been the

Fort Carillon (Ticonderoga) is the small white structure on the peninsula. It controlled the passage from Lake Champlain, on the left, to South Bay, on the right, as well as the passage from Lake George via the LaChute River. This was possibly the most strategic position in all of North America during the colonial period other than Quebec.

most heavily fortified and important strategic position in North American military history.

The French also fortified their presence in the "Ohio" country and the Great Lakes west. The post at Sault St. Marie was established as early as 1641. The location, at the meeting place of three of the Great Lakes (Superior, Huron, and Michigan), intrigued the early French explorers of the region, and attracted many famous French traders and missionaries. As the "sault," or rapids of the St. Marys River, which connected Lake Superior to Lake Huron, fell almost twenty feet in less than a mile, early fur trappers and traders found the rapids to be a barrier to free navigation. Even by canoe or bateau, the long portage of almost forty-nine miles upriver to Lake Superior was quickly deemed impossible with the ever increasing loads of trade goods and furs. In 1662 the French established a permanent settlement on the Lake Huron side of the passage in the hope that the Indians would bring their furs downriver to the trading post. This strategy was generally successful.

Lake Huron was a direct open-water connection with Lake Michigan through the straits of Mackinac near Mackinaw Island. In the colonial period this was known by its native name, Michilimackinac. In 1671 Father Jacques Marquette founded the Jesuit mission of St. Ignace at this

The interior of the commandant's office at Fort Niagara on the shores of Lake Ontario is fitted with period furniture and authentic items such as maps, books, and punched-tin lanterns.

junction. This mission was the focus of French presence in the area. As early as 1676 the French established an outpost, and in 1683 Fort de Baude was built. The fort served primarily as a link in the French fur trade system.

The post at Michilimackinac was closed after the establishment of Detroit but was reestablished in 1715. It quickly became a center of French influence among the native peoples of the region, controlling (better than Detroit) the fur trade route from the west as well as the routes from the Canadian northwest near Lake Winnipeg. The fort provided a post from which French traders could operate and be resupplied with trade goods. The brisk trade in furs somewhat eased the reticence among the Indians to deal with the white traders. Michilimackinac remains one of the most studied and best documented of all the French outposts in the colonial period.[4]

The French also built a series of forts in the middle of the eighteenth century whose establishment set off the final battle of the French and Indian War. Forts Machault, LeBoeuf, and Presque Isle were built in the Ohio drainage area. Fort Niagara was built at the western end of Lake Ontario near the entrance to the portage around the great falls, and it was supported by Fort Frontenac at eastern end of the lake in counteracting the English post at Oswego. The most notable of the western forts built in this period was Fort Duquesne, which sat astride the forks of the Ohio River and was the objective of both Braddock's disastrous campaign and Forbes's more successful one. Ultimately the English built Fort Pitt (Pittsburgh) at almost exactly the same location.

BRITISH ARMY FORTS

Besides the posts already mentioned, the British army maintained a number of strategically important fortifications. Fort William and Fort Bull were built at the Great Carrying Place (Rome, New York) between the Mohawk River and Wood Creek, which led to Lake Onondaga, the Onondaga River, and Lake Ontario at Oswego. Fort Bull was a small, undermanned installation that was overrun in the opening rounds of the French and Indian War. A massacre of thirty of the soldiers who inhabited the post took place, with many of those killed having been burned alive as the wooden fort was fired around them.

Fort Bedford and Fort Ligonier were essential links in the chain of forts and outposts created by General John Forbes in 1758 as he cut a road through Pennsylvania on his campaign against Fort Duquesne. Fort Bedford (Raystown) was allowed to wither, and by 1759 it had a garrison of only seven men. Fort Ligonier (Loyalhanna) had a longer useful life because it was well built and well located in a natural defensive position. The vertical wooden logs and earth-filled cribs were well suited to assault by cannon, and the fort withstood determined Indian attacks in the autumn of 1758 and the summer of 1763.[5]

Forts Loudoun, Lyttleton, and Shirley were further east in Pennsylvania than Bedford, and Fort Frederick, a mighty stone edifice built at great expense, was located near the Potomac River in Maryland. Fort Frederick was used as a fort during the French and Indian War and the American Revolution, and it served as a prisoner-of-war camp in the Civil War. Fort Cumberland at Wills Creek, from which Braddock began his march, made Fort Frederick less important than it otherwise would have been. Fort Augusta, located on the Susquehanna River north of Harrisburg, Pennsylvania, was a 200-square-foot fortification with four bastions and more than six buildings. It had a series of blockhouses outside its walls that controlled the passage of the river. Fort Augusta was designed to house 400 men. Its position was dictated more by the desire to facilitate trade with the Indians than by a need for frontier security.

THE BRITISH PROVINCIAL FORTS

Each of the colonies attempted, with varying results, to build forts and outposts to secure their frontiers. These were built at different times and from many reasons. New York fortified a number of small stone farmsteads along the Mohawk River, including William Johnson's plantation at Fort Johnson and Fort Herkimer, which had a garrison of 200 men. South Carolina established Fort Moore near present-day Augusta, Georgia, early in the eighteenth century. From this post rangers patrolled the frontier against Indian attack and attempted to intimidate French and Spanish traders. However, the colony of Pennsylvania, with a huge frontier left unguarded by decades of neglect fostered by pacifist Quaker control of the legislature, suddenly began a fort-building program after Braddock's defeat. In December 1755 the colony voted to build four major forts in Northampton County. These were Forts Hamilton, Norris, Allen, and Franklin. The last was named for Benjamin Franklin, who was instrumental in moving the appropriations through the legislature.

The intensity of Pennsylvania's fort-building program was best characterized by Franklin's personal direction of the construction of Fort Allen. Repeated attacks on the Moravian missions on the frontier prompted Franklin to travel with 165 colonial soldiers to the proposed site of the fort in the dead of winter. Within just two days a passable stockade was complete. The fort had one bastion centered on each of two opposing walls and two half bastions at the opposite corners to cover the walls. Three blockhouses were erected inside, and the fort contained its own well. This may have been the best built of all the provincial forts, and it was considered by many contemporaries to have been the most strategically important post east of the Susquehanna.[6]

NOTES

1. James M. Volo, "The Fort in America: Military Engineering in the Seventeenth and Eighteenth Centuries," *The Brigade Dispatch,* vol. 20 no. 2 (Autumn 1988), 2–6.

2. The authors suggest the following historic sites: Fortress Louisbourg, Cape Breton Island, Canada; Fort Ticonderoga, Fort William Henry, and Fort Crown Point, Lake George/Lake Champlain region of New York State; Fort Stanwix, Rome, New York; Fort Ligonier, in south central Pennsylvania: Fort Frederick, west of Hagerstown, Maryland; Fort Griswold, New London, Connecticut; Castillo San Marco, St. Augustine, Florida. Many of the embellishments that were placed on colonial forts have been left unreconstructed at historic sites and parks because of the need to provide parking lots.

3. Lt. Governor Clarke, December 6, 1738, to the Board of Trade, found in E. B. O'Callaghan, ed. *Documents Relative to the Colonial History of the State of New York,* vol. 6. (Albany, NY: Weed, Parsons, 1855), 131.

4. The trading post and fort at Michilimackinac is the best-researched archaeological site from the French and Indian War period according to the Fort Michilimackinac Historic Association, the organization that oversees the re-creation.

5. An accurate and impressive reconstruction was undertaken in the 1960s and

completed in 1969. It serves today as a museum, research library, and interpretive facility.

6. See Louis M. Waddell and Bruce D. Bromberger, *The French and Indian War in Pennsylvania, 1753–1763: Fortification and Struggle During the War for Empire,* (Harrisburg: Pennsylvania Historical and Museum Commission, 1996), 32–35.

14

The Opening Rounds of the Conflict

A season of unequaled calamities.

—Susanna Johnson

In fairness to the Europeans who came to North America to settle, the outbreak of hostilities between themselves and the native peoples seems to have been inevitable largely because the native populations were continually warring with each other. In befriending one tribe or another Europeans were almost surely to become targets themselves. Like dominoes in a row, conflicts between one set of native peoples had unforeseeable consequences throughout the native community. It is ironic, however, that the Iroquois, who dispersed so many of their fellow native Americans in the northeastern woodlands, were the last to make a firm and permanent alliance with a European power. Throughout the sixteenth and seventeenth centuries up to the final conflict of the French and Indian War, the Iroquois Confederacy toyed diplomatically with both the English and the French. When the final alliance with the English was made, it was called a "covenant chain," and it was not broken by any of the Iroquois nations until the American Revolution.[1]

THE COLONIAL WARS

The wars that characterized eighteenth-century Europe inevitably spilled over into America. The many conflicts that rocked Europe from

1688 to 1763 can safely be viewed as a single prolonged conflict. It was a period in which trade replaced religion as the fundamental motive for most of the political and social upheavals, and it was during this period that France and Britain fought for control of the North American continent. Both English and French colonists on the frontier were inescapably involved in their own local conflicts during these intermittent wars, and both sides allied themselves with native American tribes. Consequently, European colonists fought not only among themselves, but also with native allies and antagonists.[2]

There were four distinct wars fought during this period, with France and England allied on opposite sides with the other states of Europe: (1) the War of the League of Augsburg, known in America as King William's War (1689–1697); (2) the War of Spanish Succession, or Queen Anne's War (1702–1713); (3) the War of Austrian Succession, or King George's War (in two stages in Europe between 1740 to 1748); and (4) the Seven Years' War, or the French and Indian War (1754–1763 in America; 1756–1763 in Europe). During six decades of Anglo-French conflict over the possession of North America, there were a series of woodland skirmishes, raids, massacres, and major battles that intimately affected the lives of colonists.

None of these conflicts was decisive except the last. Even the catastrophic defeat of General Edward Braddock and his regulars at the hands of the French and their Indian allies on the Monongahela River failed to decide the fate of North America. Only the signal victory by General James Wolfe over the French under the Marquis de Montcalm at Quebec in 1759 fits the characteristics of a decisive battle.

The European context of the conflicts that ripped the frontiers of North America from 1690 to 1763 are largely outside the scope of this book, but the American situations will be discussed here briefly in chronological order. To limit confusion the names used by the colonials for these wars will be used instead of their common European designations.

KING WILLIAM'S WAR, 1689–1697

William of Orange claimed the English throne in 1688 as William III. The Stuart king, James II, was deposed and turned to France for help. William of Orange had been the focus of an anti-French, anti-Papist movement in Europe since his childhood. The alliance of Dutch and English interests in the person of William caused an immediate deterioration of England's relations with France and led to war. In the summer of 1689, Louis de Buade, Comte de Frontenac, was summoned to Versailles and ordered by King Louis XIV to proceed to New France for the second time as governor and to take up the conflict in the American theater. Frontenac carried with him orders that spelled out the king's optimistic plans for the invasion and capture of the English colony of New York. With 1,000 regulars, 600 militia raised from among the habitants, and as many Indian allies as he could attract to the enterprise, Frontenac was to proceed up the Richelieu River, traverse the lengths of Lakes Champlain and St. Sacrement (Lake George), march down the Hudson River, and take Albany by surprise. Thereafter, he was to proceed down the Hudson and take possession of Manhattan Island. The king reminded Frontenac that boldness and speed were of the essence.

Although the king thought the campaign could be concluded within a month of leaving Quebec, Frontenac, of course, was better informed of conditions in the forests of America. He also knew that he was entirely powerless to muster a force capable of carrying out the king's plan. In fact no army in the history of North America ever completely succeeded in carrying out the march from Quebec to New York, although it looked so easy on paper. Nonetheless, Frontenac devised a plan of his own, and he proposed a raid on Schenectady, New York, deep in Mohawk territory, as the first step.

The tiny, palisaded village of Schenectady was founded in 1662 as a trading post above the lower Mohawk falls and rapids. On a bitterly cold night in February, 1690, the gates of the palisade stood open guarded only by a pair of snowmen. The outlying houses and the interior blockhouse were dark. Shortly after midnight, the Frenchmen, supported by their Indian allies, moved out from cover where they had been lying in wait for the village to grow silent. Every house was surrounded and at a signal the doors of every residence were driven in. The garrison in the blockhouse, caught quite by surprise, perished. The town was set ablaze and ransacked of all its valuables. Thirty-eight men and two boys were killed, while only two Frenchmen were reported killed by the defenders. Twenty-two women and children were marched off in the morning through the snow-filled forests toward Montreal, and a few older folk and small babies were left behind. One man, half dead, reached Albany on horseback to report the incident.[3]

To the colonists on the frontier, this seemed like warfare more savage than that practiced in Europe, where nobody fought in winter and where civilians were rarely the primary targets of the enemy. The use of Indians as a striking force added an extra horror to colonial apprehensions. During the next few months the English settlements at Salmon Falls, New Hampshire, and Fort Loyal at Casco Bay in Maine were also burned. The colonial governments were mortified at their inability to effectively protect the frontier settlements. The Iroquois, in particular, were seriously tempted to reassess their English-leaning sentiments, as Schenectady was so near their villages at Canajoharie.

This bloody nighttime raid marked the beginning of seventy years of grim struggle between English and French colonials. Certainly the Indians had attacked farmsteads in the past, but never before had one European power purposely set the Indians against another. Rumors of small bands of Indians stalking around the frontier communities of Northfield and Deerfield in Massachusetts abound before the winter of 1690. It may have been in response to the LaChine raids of the Iroquois that Frontenac sent the Indians to attack Schenectady. He knew that the prestige of the French had been badly damaged by the LaChine raids and hoped to repair it by an aggressive move against the English in the Iroquois' own territory.

The raids of 1690 could not go unanswered by the English. A volunteer army was quickly raised by Governor Simon Bradstreet of Massachusetts to take revenge upon the French. As Quebec was initially considered too far out of reach, Acadia was made the target. Sir William Phips was appointed commander of an expedition of 750 volunteers, who were loaded onto seventeen colonial vessels. Phips won an easy victory at Port Royal, as the overmatched French garrison happily surrendered when given the opportunity. The English destroyed the fort, plundered the town, and burned the church. With no English force left to occupy the place, the French quickly recovered the town.[4]

Meanwhile, the border settlers lived in terror. A joint expedition against Montreal taken up by Connecticut and New York, commanded by Fitz-John Winthrop, son of the Connecticut governor, was so unsuccessful that Jacob Leisler, then the acting governor of New York, arrested Winthrop for cowardice. The failure was hardly Winthrop's fault, however. The combined force of 850 colonials and 2,000 Iroquois failed to materialize largely due to distrust and skepticism among the provincial commissioners who were charged with raising it. Only Connecticut met its quota of recruits, and the expected mass of Iroquois warriors, felled by an epidemic of smallpox, turned out to number only seventy. After three weeks in the field Winthrop had not reached Lake Champlain. With his men sick of dysentery and smallpox, he turned back to Albany.

Encouraged by the ease of his success at Port Royal, Phips assumed the command of an expedition funded by the colony of Massachusetts. This time the target was Quebec itself. Having amassed an army of 2,200 men in Boston, Phips sailed for the mouth of the St. Lawrence with a fleet of thirty-four transports and lightly armed escorts a few days after Winthrop left Albany. The guns of the fleet were to be his siege artillery. When Phips arrived before Quebec in early October, he found an army of 2,000 Frenchmen entrenched along the cliffside of the city. Most of these were poorly trained habitants who had come from Montreal after word of Winthrop's failure. Formed into a militia, but commanded by the wily Frontenac, these men presented a formidable obstacle to Phips's designs.

Phips immediately opened negotiations with Frontenac for the surrender of the city, but the French governor understood that it would be difficult for the English to overcome his defenses in the short time left before the Canadian winter would make military operations impossible. Moreover, any assault on Quebec would require the besiegers to attack either the well-defended promontory or the entrenchments along the St. Charles River where it emptied into the St. Lawrence. Neither strategy appeared promising.

Nonetheless, Phips planned to land 1,200 men under the command of Major John Walley downriver from the city to attempt a frontal assault on the St. Charles lines. Walley's force was put ashore under the protection of the guns of the fleet, and endeavored to cross the river. The French resistance was greater than either he or Phips had imagined, and after four days of fighting in increasingly bad weather the operation was terminated.

The capture of the city of Quebec remained a major objective of the English throughout the colonial wars, but several factors continued to present themselves as formidable obstacles to its accomplishment. The city was built on an all but impregnable cliffside. The approach to the city by way of the Hudson–Lake Champlain–Richelieu River route was so difficult that it took a tremendous toll on an invading force. The approach to the city by ships required a difficult navigation of the St. Lawrence River, and finally the window of opportunity in terms of weather was very narrow. If the invading forces left too early in the season, they tempted foul weather at sea and the last of the melting winter snowfall in the forests. If they left too late they were faced with the possibility of starvation after being frozen in by the early Canadian winter.

With the failure of Phips's campaign, the French subsequently used their Indian allies to mount a series of terror raids on the New England frontier. Never before had French colonial policy so encouraged the Indians to make raids on civilians as part of the prosecution of a general conflict. Since further major campaigns by both the French or the English failed to materialize, the Indian attacks came to characterize the remaining eight years of King William's War. "These forays were of little consequence, except for the grief and anxiety they caused the inhabitants of the backcountry."[5]

TREATY OF RYSWICK

The peace agreement signed in Ryswick, Holland ended the war in Europe in 1697 without settling many of the basic issues that had caused it. Among the provisions were the return of Acadia to the French and the acceptance of the occupation of Nova Scotia by the English. The peace neither ended English settlement in New England nor added a secure frontier to the dominions of New France. In fact the treaty failed utterly to demarcate the frontier boundary between the two. The main point of the agreement was that William III was recognized as the legitimate English king. Nonetheless, the exiled James II and the heirs to the Stuart line continued to create disturbances in Scotland and elsewhere with French help for fifty years.

During King William's War the English colonials perceived an apparent indifference to their needs on the part of the Crown. All of the fighting in North America was left to the colonists or to their Indian allies. The loyalty of the Mohawks was particularly tested as they lost more than one-third of their warriors during the period. Cooperation among the individual colonies proved impossible, and unilateral efforts seemed destined for miserable failure. The armies the colonies fielded were composed of too few men, with too little support, and the commanders were, for the most part, inexperienced in waging war.

QUEEN ANNE'S WAR

King William fell from his horse and died almost at the moment warfare was renewed in Europe, and his sister-in-law followed him on the throne. Unfortunately the Peace of Ryswick (1697), which should have provided Queen Anne with an untroubled reign, proved short-lived. The period of Queen Anne's War is best remembered for the grand battles fought by the Duke of Marlborough and Prince Eugene on the European continent, but there was fighting in America, including some major campaigns in the Carolinas, Acadia, and the Caribbean.

In 1699 the French had taken advantage of the Peace of Ryswick to extend their colonies in America to Louisiana, considered then to encompass a much larger area than the present state. Pierre Le Moyne, Sieur d'Iberville, established a settlement at Biloxi (Mississippi) on the Gulf of Mexico, and in 1702 a seaport town was created at Mobile (Alabama), barely fifty miles from the Spanish outpost at Pensacola (Florida) in the northeast corner of the Gulf of Mexico. Meanwhile, Antoine de la Mothe, Sieur de Cadillac, erected a fort at Detroit, a crucial point for the control of the Great Lakes fur trade. Eventually there would be a chain of forts from Montreal to the Mississippi. These posts were viewed by the French as necessary anchors to the control of the North American interior.

The English colonial authorities in the Carolinas viewed these developments with growing alarm, and panic was said to have briefly gripped the inhabitants of Charlestown when word of a new war reached them in 1702. In addition to the prospects of losing their lucrative deerskin trade with the Indians of the southeastern interior, the Carolinians feared being surrounded by the Franco-Spanish allies and the French-leaning Creek Indians. Governor James Moore of South Carolina hurriedly prepared an expedition against the nearest target available to him, Spanish St. Augustine which lay on the Atlantic coast of the Florida peninsula. The Carolinians were familiar with the Spanish outposts along the border between South Carolina and Florida, and there was little doubt that the French considered St. Augustine the first line of their own defenses for Louisiana.

Moore's force of 500 Carolinians, 300 Indians, and 14 small vessels swept away the Spanish missions north of St. Augustine, and within two days captured the town itself but not the main fort. Moore then laid siege to the Spanish castillo, an entrenched fortification with regular bastions built following the best European designs and capable of supporting 800 troops. Moore was not prepared to overcome such a stronghold with the four cannons he had with him, and during the subsequent eight-week siege he sent for aid. The undisciplined army of colonials quickly became demoralized, and Moore spent much of his time dealing with the increasing discontent evident among his men. Ultimately, two Spanish men-of-war appeared at the bar to the harbor promising relief to the castillo, and Moore had no hope of contending with them successfully. Rightly fearing that his force would be bottled up if he maintained the siege, Moore fired the city and his eight remaining transports, and retreated overland.

Although the St. Augustine expedition failed in its immediate objective, Moore was buoyed by the fact that his casualties had been trifling. He was convinced that for the want of a few warships and a siege train of artillery he would have proved successful, and he immediately set about planning a second strike. "It is a matter of great consequence that we add the conquest of a small Spanish town called Pensacola, and a new French colony [Mobile] . . . both seaport towns. . . . It will make her Majesty absolute and sovereign lady of all the [Gulf coast] as far as the river Mississippi."[6]

In 1703, with an army of 50 Carolinians and 1,000 allied Indians, Moore struck the Apalachee frontier with such fury that the Lower Creek and Alabama tribes abandoned the French and sought peace. This result renewed the loyalty of the tribes friendly to Carolina, but it failed to dislodge the French or the Spanish. In 1706 a joint Franco-Spanish expedition counterattacked at Charlestown itself from the sea. Fortunately for the English this force was poorly led, and the city was well prepared and stoutly defended. The provincial militia was reinforced by 1,500 warriors from among the region's English-leaning tribes and a force of Negroes armed for the purpose. The invaders were repulsed but, thereafter, there were numerous alarms on the Carolina borders. However, the English were effectively mobilizing their Indian allies. Several hundred Talapoosas, led by a few Englishmen, suddenly attacked Pensacola in 1707, burning and pillaging the town and actually entering the fort before being repulsed by a determined counterattack. A subsequent attack was withdrawn when a French relieving force approached from Mobile. Thereafter, Mobile was reinforced and its stockade enlarged to serve as a haven for the tribes friendly to the French, particularly the Choctaw.

On the New England frontier Queen Anne's War was characterized by raids and skirmishes in the border regions, particularly in Maine. Throughout the first five or six years of war the Abenakis and the New England militia sought out each other in the wilderness in a defensive response to the incessant series of raids and counter-raids. Not until several years had passed did the colonists realize that their frontiers could best be secured by destroying the French presence in Canada.

In 1709 the Crown espoused plans for a substantial joint campaign with the colonies against the French in Montreal and Quebec. New York, New Jersey, Pennsylvania, and Connecticut were to furnish a force to be mustered at Albany to strike at Montreal by way of the Lake Champlain route. Meanwhile a force of 3,000 men—mostly regulars and some 1,200 militia from Massachusetts, New Hampshire, and Rhode Island—would be taken aboard a small fleet of warships to Quebec by way of the St. Lawrence River. With the exception of New Jersey and Pennsylvania "the colonies moved with unwonted promptness and vigor to complete their respective assignments." The Montreal expedition under command of Colonel Francis Nicholson of New York moved promptly into the wilderness, built a fort at the Great Carrying Place on the upper Hudson River, and prepared his boats and canoes to traverse the lakes to the north.[7]

The New England troops slated for the Quebec attack gathered at Boston harbor to await the British navy's warships. For weeks and months they scanned the horizon for a sail. Finally, with autumn approaching, word came that the Crown had abruptly canceled the operation and sent the promised fleet to Portugal. When word reached Nicholson, it was found that his force had been stricken by dysentery. Men dropped by the score, and Nicholson had a difficult time retreating the fifty miles to Albany before the winter set in. The colonists were "deeply resentful" of being thus abandoned by the Crown, and the effects of this incident on the future relations of the provinces and the Crown cannot be over-emphasized. British observers would often report a lack of enthusiasm on the part of colonial legislatures in future operations that may be linked to this event in 1709.[8]

Meanwhile in 1710 four loyal Mohawk chiefs arrived in London to be honored by the queen. They were a great hit in London and sat to have their portraits done by the nation's great artists. The Mohawks were accompanied by Peter Schuyler of Albany and by delegates from the New England colonies, who pleaded that British forces be diverted to their own seat of war, particularly against Port Royal in Acadia. A joint

Anglo-American expedition was agreed to by the Crown, but the government would supply only six ships. The colonies of Massachusetts and Connecticut would have to supply the troops. A force of 3,500 men, once again under Nicholson, was raised with great difficulty. Nicholson landed his men, bombarded the fort, and after a few formalities accepted the surrender of the post. The English renamed the place Annapolis Royal in honor of the queen. This expedition was the only real success for the English in America during Queen Anne's War, as it brought into the British empire all of Acadia—renamed Nova Scotia.[9]

The success of the Port Royal expedition led to a second attempt at Quebec that ended in abject failure for the Anglo-American forces. Rear Admiral Sir Hovenden Walker was selected to command the expedition. He had a fleet of 64 ships including 11 men-of-war. A force of 4,300 regulars under General John Hill had been taken from among the Duke of Marlborough's veteran troops in Flanders and reassigned to the venture. A colonial force of more than 3,500 men was recruited from among the New England colonies, New York, and New Jersey to once again attempt the land route by way of the Champlain Valley.

Walker continually delayed his departure from Boston claiming that the colonies had failed to completely supply his needs. Finally, at the end of July he sailed. Twenty days later he proceeded to ascend the St. Lawrence. At night with a fog coming on, he passed the Île aux Oeufs, where the river is some seventy miles wide. Eight of the transports and two of the supply ships ran aground on the rocks of the fog-bound island, and about 900 persons drowned. Walker was now convinced by his pilots that a navigation of the river was impossible, although Phips had negotiated it two decades earlier. While still 160 miles from Quebec, and with one-tenth of his force destroyed, Walker retreated.

Word was once again sent to Nicholson, who had arrived at the foot of Lake George after some days of hard marching. The colonials were very bitter, and their anger increased when the British officials tried to shift the blame for the fiasco onto the provincial legislatures. When Nicholson was told the disgraceful news, he tore off his wig, threw it down, and stamped on it, screaming, "Treachery!" He then burned his forts and marched his men back to Albany once again.[10]

The preparations for the expedition had been filled with colonial fears of regular forces and British recriminations against colonial legislatures, and it ended with the fleet partially destroyed, hundreds of men lost, and the French in Quebec untouched. The citizens of Massachusetts were particularly incensed by these failures, as they had answered every effort to seize either Acadia or Quebec with a laudable immediacy. Public debt in the colony had skyrocketed, and local taxes had almost doubled. In the final years of the war one-third of all the able-bodied males in Massachusetts were in the army, and nearly one in four of the male colonists who had entered the militia or provincial forces between 1690 and 1713 had died in service. Fortunately the war ended before the rhetoric became too extreme.[11]

TREATY OF UTRECHT

The Treaty of Utrecht, signed in 1713, gave the English Hudson Bay, Newfoundland, and Acadia. It recognized the Iroquois as British subjects, a fact that the Crown would use later to claim dominion over all the lands and peoples who were tributaries to the Iroquois Confederacy of the Five Nations. However, the treaty failed to fix the boundary between New France and New England, and it left Cape Breton Island at the mouth of the St. Lawrence in the hands of the French. Here the French would build a base from which to thrust at the New England coast—Fortress Louisbourg.

KING GEORGE'S WAR

For almost a quarter century after the Treaty of Utrecht, Europe was at peace. When the childless Queen Anne died in 1714 the British throne passed to George I of Hanover. Over the next three decades the embers of war smoldered in the American wilderness. From 1739 to 1742, England became involved in a meaningless conflict with Spain known as the War of Jenkins' Ear. This was the first stage of two conflicts known in America as King George's War, named for the throne's present occupant, George II.

In their greed to dispossess the Spanish of some of their most valuable sugar-producing islands in the Caribbean, an expedition was planned in 1740 to attack a fortified Spanish seaport on the coast of South America called Cartegena. The British fitted out a fleet of 124 vessels, 29 of which were ships-of-the-line. Aboard were 12,000 soldiers—among them 3,600 volunteers of Gooch's American Regiment of Foot. The entire enterprise was commanded by Admiral Edward Vernon.

Although Vernon was an admirable seaman, the expedition was an utter failure. The army commander refused to cooperate with the navy, tropical disease laid the troops low, and the colonials insisted on being brought home when their relatively short enlistments expired in the middle of the contest. The refusal to release these Americans immediately created the most meaningful of negative consequences for Anglo-American relations.[12]

Besides the obvious failures of the expedition—fewer than 700 Americans survived to return to the colonies—its most significant result might have been the scarring of American attitudes toward the British regulars. The confinement of so many men for long periods of time during the journey through the Caribbean highlighted the provincial soldiers' unswerving loyalty to their own provincial officers. The regular officers' contempt for the provincial gentlemen was obvious throughout the operation. One British officer wrote that the American officers were "people totally ignorant of military skills." The regular officers constantly refused to consult with their colonial counterparts when planning operations, and often kept the provincial troops out of combat assigning them to ditch-digging and other fatigue duties. Added to the "remarkable ineptitude" with which the campaign proceeded, this attitude created a great deal of resentment, smoldering indignation, and latent hostility between the colonials and the regulars.[13]

Between 1742 and 1744 there was a brief peace, but French opposition to the accession to the Austrian throne of Maria Theresa in 1744 caused the British to become involved in a second round of fighting in Europe. Among the questions that remained in dispute between England and France in 1744 was the ownership of Acadia (Nova Scotia). While the English were firmly established in Annapolis Royal, the Treaty of Utrecht was unclear as to whether the English had gained possession of the entire vast country or only a strip of seacoast. Furthermore both the French and the English continued to claim the Abenakis of Maine as a subject people. When word of a renewed conflict reached the colonies these two problems particularly distressed the governor of Massachusetts, William Shirley, as the loss of Nova Scotia might rekindle the frontier raids of the Indians.

LOUISBOURG

In 1745 several New England colonies agreed to strike a blow at the French by attacking Louisbourg. "To many of the colonists this Catholic stronghold was a den of Satanic iniquity," and their desire to eliminate the French presence there was partly fueled by extreme hatred for the adherents of a rival religion. Not only was Louisbourg a location from which the French could incite Indian raids into the New England frontier, it also directly threatened the ability of the colonial fishing fleets to utilize the cod fisheries of the Grand Banks and dry and salt their catch on the Newfoundland shores.[14]

The colonials assembled a fleet of close to 100 vessels commanded by Captain Edward Tyng of Massachusetts. The land force, composed of more than 4,000 provincial troops was commanded by Colonel William Pepperrell of Maine. More than 80 percent of these troops were from Massachusetts. Connecticut and New Hampshire barely met their quota of men, and no colony south of New England committed any men to the enterprise. This "All New England" expedition was belatedly joined

An antique print of one of the many attacks on the fortress of Louisbourg on Cape Breton Island, probably that of 1759. The fortress was taken by an "all American" force in 1745, but was returned to the French in the Treaty of Aix-la-Chapelle, much to the annoyance of the New England colonies.

by four ships-of-the-line of the Royal Navy, commanded by Commodore Peter Warren. This was the only part of the force provided by the Crown.

The fleet sailed in unseasonably mild weather on April 28, 1745, and arrived at Gabarus Bay about four miles from the fortress without incident. Warren immediately blockaded Louisbourg and silenced the main defensive guns on an island in the harbor. He then covered the amphibious landing of a company of colonial rangers whom Pepperrell had particularly chosen for the task. This landing was carried out in open boats through heavy surf. The rangers secured the beaches with little opposition, and by nightfall 2,000 American soldiers had been ferried ashore. The French commander, Chevalier Duchambon, had 560 regulars, 1,400 militia raised from among the habitants, and a few Micmac Indian allies with whom to defend the place.

Forty-seven days of siege followed, and many of the New England troops grew homesick and tired of army life. Within a month more than 500 men were reporting sick. The sight of wounded and dying comrades eroded their morale, which was further tested when about 20 English stragglers were captured and "scalped and chopped and stabbed and prodigiously mangled" by Micmacs. Nonetheless, Colonel William

Vaughan and a detachment of 400 colonials succeeded in driving the French from their Grand Battery and holding off the French attempt to retake it, largely by their bravado and lusty cheers. Mercifully, the French realized the impossibility of continued resistance before the lack of enthusiasm within the colonial army became too prevalent. American despondency quickly changed to exuberance. New England had scored a great victory at the cost of only 101 lives. The celebrations passed from town to town and from village to village as word of the success spread through the colonies.

Notwithstanding the important part played by Admiral Warren's naval squadron, William Pepperrell was seen as a hero and his success was confirmed by the Crown when he was made a baronet. In the aftermath of the surrender, however, the provincial forces were made to forego their booty while the naval forces snapped up prize money before their eyes as unwary French ships sailed into the harbor. Subsequently, the colonials were forced to garrison the fort into the winter months, whereupon one-third of their number died of exposure and neglect.

France tried unsuccessfully to retake the fortress in 1745 and 1746, and it was clear to Governor Shirley that only a campaign against Quebec would solidify the gains the English had made. With the support of Warren and the Massachusetts legislature, Shirley was able to wrest a commitment from the Crown for an expedition to take Quebec. Eight colonies joined in raising troops for this operation by 1746. Massachusetts alone raised 3,000 men, but the Crown once again demonstrated its lack of regard for the Americans by canceling the operation and leaving the colony of Massachusetts near bankruptcy.

TREATY OF AIX-LA-CHAPELLE

The war ended in 1748 with the Treaty of Aix-la-Chapelle. The war in Europe had proven somewhat of a draw, and the fall of Louisbourg proved to be the one shining accomplishment of British arms. By the terms of the treaty, the British possession of all of Nova Scotia was reaffirmed. They promptly established a major naval base at Halifax. The American colonials were outraged when the government returned Louisbourg to the French in exchange for the city of Madras, which had been lost to French forces in India. The idea that the hard-won fortress would be returned without consulting the provinces rocked many colonists. They began to realize that their interests were not always in accord with those of Great Britain, yet it was obvious that a further final contest was approaching between Britain and France for possession of North America.[15]

NOTES

1. Of the six Iroquois nations (Mohawk, Oneida, Onondaga, Cayuga, Seneca, and Tuscarora), only the Oneida and a few Tuscarora sided with the American colonists in 1776 thus breaking the covenant chain. Of the remainder the Seneca proved to be the staunchest of British allies.

2. Alfred Thayer Mahan, *The Influence of Sea Power upon History, 1660–1783* (New York: Dover 1987), 209.

3. Francis Russell, *The French and Indian Wars* (New York: American Heritage, 1962), 12.

4. John Ferling, *Struggle for a Continent: The Wars of Early America* (Arlington Heights, IL: Harlan Davidson, 1993), 72.

5. Ibid., 74–77.

6. Verner W. Crane, *The Southern Frontier, 1670–1732* (Durham, NC: Duke University Press, 1928), 77.

7. Douglas E. Leach, *Roots of Conflict: British Armed Forces and Colonial Americans, 1677–1775* (Chapel Hill: University of North Carolina Press, 1986), 25–30.

8. Ibid., 25–30.

9. Ferling, 94.

10. Quoted in Robert Leckie, *A Few Acres of Snow: The Saga of the French and Indian Wars* (New York: John Wiley & Sons, 1999), 240.

11. Richard Koebner, *Empire* (New York: Grosset and Dunlap, 1965), 94.

12. See Leach.

13. Ferling, 134; Leach, 57–62.

14. Samuel W. Bryant, *The Sea and the States: A Maritime History of the American People* (New York: T. Y. Cromwell, 1967) 56.

15. See Leach.

15

The Final Struggle for a Continent

I have this minute received the melancholy account of the defeat of our troops, the General killed and numbers of our officers, the whole army taken; in short the account I have received is so bad that, please God, I intend to make a stand here. It's highly necessary to raise the militia everywhere to defend the frontiers.

—General James Innes on Braddock's defeat

THE FRENCH AND INDIAN WAR

The Seven Years' War, called the French and Indian War in America, actually began in 1754 with a skirmish in the wilderness of western Pennsylvania between French colonial troops and Virginia provincial troops commanded by a young officer named George Washington. Governor Robert Dinwiddie of Virginia was very concerned in 1753 when he learned that the French were building forts on the Allegheny River and Lake Erie, and he sent Major George Washington with a strongly worded message of protest to the French commander in the region. The overland journey of more than 500 miles was very difficult. Only the companionship of Jacob van Braam, his interpreter, and the frontier guide, Christopher Gist, had made the journey possible. At Fort le Boeuf Washington presented Dinwiddie's message to the commandant, Captain Jacques Legardeur de Sainte-Pierre. The letter read in part, "by whose authority and instructions [have you] lately marched from Canada with an armed force, and invaded the King of Great Britain's territories." Sainte-Pierre had carefully penned an answer promising to "transmit [the] letter to the Marquis Duquesne, Governor of New France, for his orders."[1]

This brief exchange was followed by the arduous return of Washington to Williamsburg. Without the help of Gist, Washington might have perished in the wilderness. Not far above the junction of the Monongahela and the Allegheny Washington fell into the freezing water, and Gist was forced to rescue him. Had they not been close to the trading post of John Fraser, both might have died of exposure. The story of Washington's journey made him an overnight sensation.

It was not surprising, therefore, that Dinwiddie placed Washington in charge of expelling the French from the "Ohio country" in 1754. Dinwiddie raised a regiment of 400 Virginians and two independent companies of regular troops. Captain Joshua Fry of the Virginia regiment was made second in command. Washington was promoted to lieutenant colonel.[2]

As Washington's troops advanced toward Wills Creek Station, about 140 miles from the forks of the Ohio River, he sent ahead a detachment of troops under Captain William Trent, who was to build a fort to house and protect the command when it arrived. Meanwhile the French governor sent his own aide, Captain Pierre de Contrecouer, with a force of 1,100 men to reinforce the western forts and to build a new post at present-day Pittsburgh.

About 100 miles south of the point chosen by the French for their new post, the English detachment under Captain Trent were already building a fort. It was by no means complete. When Contrecouer arrived at the English works with a force of 500 men, he found Ensign Edward Ward in temporary command of about 40 soldiers, Trent having gone to retrieve supplies. Contrecouer politely demanded Ward's surrender, and it was given. The English were permitted to retire from the region as the French demolished their works. The French commander then returned to the forks of the Ohio to complete his own post, Fort Duquesne.

Contrecouer had been advised by friendly Indians that most of Washington's force was camped in the Great Meadows east of the Monongahela. Colonel Fry was still at Wills Creek. The French commander chose Ensign Coulon de Jumonville de Villiers to lead a small group of soldiers to meet the English en route and require them to leave the dominions of France. If they refused, Contrecouer promised to bring his entire force down upon them. That these two young men, de Jumonville and Washington, would meet in the wilderness of North America was fated to set almost all the kingdoms of Europe at odds.

MURDER IN THE WILDERNESS

The night of May 27, 1754, was a rainy one, and de Jumonville and his small detachment had taken the opportunity offered by an overhanging cliff to spend the night out of the rain. Meanwhile, Washington with a small group of soldiers and friendly Seneca Indians, under the chief Monakaduto, had gone forward from the Great Meadows to attempt an observation of Contrecouer's camp at the forks and accidentally found de Jumonville's camp. Washington placed his men around the campsite in a semicircle, and caught the French party totally unaware. A brief fight ensued during which the French party suffered eight dead and twenty-one captured. Two Frenchman escaped in the dark.

At this point Monakaduto grabbed de Jumonville and murdered him with a single blow of his hatchet to his skull. The English soldiers quietly watched as the Seneca scalped the dead. The death of de Jumonville was to cause an immediate diplomatic embarrassment for the British government because the French claimed that Washington had assassinated a diplomat.

FORT NECESSITY

After this engagement Washington retreated to the Great Meadows and immediately began fortifying the camp. In the center of a large field he had his men dig a poor earthwork entrenchment. This was well within musket shot of the surrounding forests, leaving some question as to the tactical thinking of Washington and his officers. A rough stockade was erected to house the sick and wounded, and the resulting structure was named Fort Necessity by Washington.

Contrecouer, having learned of the murder of de Jumonville, immediately sent word to the young man's brother, Captain Coulon de Villiers, to assemble a force of 1,400 French troops and Indian allies to attack Washington's poorly constructed fort. Washington had perhaps 150 men, but he expected any day to be joined by Captain Fry's detachment of more than 300. These arrived on June 3 under Captain Mackay of the regulars, who reported that Fry had died in a fall from his horse. Mackay was less than pleased with the situation, declaring it insanity to attempt a defense of the place.

On July 4 the French attacked. The English were forced to keep under cover as the French and Indians peppered their positions with musket shot from two hills. The light swivel guns of the English were the only effective defense for the approaches to the fort. A heavy downpour filled the entrenchments with water and caused the muskets to refuse to fire. By nightfall, twelve of Washington's volunteers were dead as well as eighteen of Mackay's regulars. Seventy men were wounded. With the situation becoming worse by the moment, Washington chose to accept an offer to surrender.

The terms were very generous. Washington could retire with drums beating and flags flying, but he was required to sign a statement to the effect that he had "killed" de Jumonville. Jacob van Braam, Washington's interpreter, translated the articles of surrender that were in French, for Washington. The section assigning responsibility for the death of de Jumonville actually read as an "assassination" or "murder"—*l'assassinat du Sieur de Jumonville*. This was clearly untrue, and there is no evidence that Washington had personally killed anyone.

Washington had brought Great Britain to the brink of a world war and pushed. The series of misadventures and military escapades he had experienced ultimately brought him a good deal of personal recognition in the colonies. However, the French had swept the Ohio country practically clean, and it seemed the end of the English west of the Allegheny.

It was at this time that an illustration, which first appeared in Benjamin Franklin's Philadelphia Gazette, began to be seen in many other colonial newspapers. A writhing snake was broken into eight segments representing South Carolina, North Carolina, Virginia, Maryland, Pennsylvania, New Jersey, New York, and New England. Beneath the broken snake were the words "Join, or Die."

A WORLD AT WAR

The war begun in the remote forests of North America escalated into a worldwide conflict by 1756. Battles on sea and land were fought in North America, the West Indies, Europe, India, the East Indies, and the Pacific between vast alliances on both sides, making it a true world war. England understood that it could not fight the French on the land in Europe, India, and North America and simultaneously maintain a fleet strong enough to beat them at sea. While the British would concentrate on fighting the French in North America and the Caribbean, their allies would carry the fight in Europe.

The French used the time between the surrender of Washington and the declaration of war to fill Quebec with reinforcements and rebuild and strengthen Louisbourg. Six full battalions of 1,000 men each were brought from France. The French forts in the Ohio country and Fort Duquesne were completed and garrisoned. Finally a new and highly experienced officer was given command of all the French forces in America. This was the Baron Ludwig August Dieskau, a professional soldier of German birth who had learned his trade in the wars on the continent of Europe.

The conflict in North America would require the cooperation of the provincials and the Crown to a degree never before experienced, but the regulars viewed the colonial volunteers as undisciplined, untrained, or worse. A British officer wrote, "If [the American levees] are as bad as I apprehend, it is a most horrid imposition." Two regiments of British regulars from Ireland, the 44th and 48th of Foot under Colonel Sir Peter Halkett and Colonel Thomas Dunbar were transferred to Virginia. They would ensure discipline and order. Colonel Sir John St. Clair was made quartermaster-general to prevent colonial incompetency in securing supplies. Finally, Major-General Edward Braddock of the Coldstream Guards was made commander of all military affairs in North America so that the colonials might come to learn how a war should be fought.[3]

Governor William Shirley, who retained his rank of colonel from King George's War, was made second in command of all English forces. Decentralized authority and a myriad of incoherent policy positions, residing in the many colonial governments, made a concerted English response to the French difficult to accomplish. Although Shirley immediately began the recruitment of forces, virtually no one in British North America was prepared for the war. New France, with its centralized authority, well-trained and well-organized army, and a small but undivided peasantry, had gained the allegiance of the majority of the Indian tribes. Moreover, Canada's military needs were supplied by money and material from France, which might easily neutralize the English advantage in population.[4]

As one of his first official acts, Shirley made a proclamation offering bounties of from twenty to fifty pounds for the capture or the scalps of the Indians allied to the French: "I do hereby require His Majesty's subjects . . . to embrace all opportunities of pursuing, capturing, killing, and destroying all and any of the aforesaid Indians."[5]

THE ALEXANDRIA CONFERENCE

Braddock arrived in February 1755. By April he had called upon the colonial governors to meet at Alexandria, Virginia, to develop a strategy for the forthcoming campaign. The governors of North Carolina, Pennsylvania, Maryland, New York, Virginia, and Massachusetts met with Braddock and Commodore Augustus Keppel of the Royal Navy at Charleton House. Also in attendance was William Johnson, a fur trader and frontier diplomat from the Mohawk River valley of New York who had been given complete control of British Indian policy as superintendent of Indian affairs by King George II.

The Alexandria meeting was historic. Having no centralized army to place into the field, the colonies had been forced to improvise a new army from among their scattered parts at the beginning of each campaigning season. "Each of them watch its neighbors, or, jealous lest it should do more than its just share, waited for them to begin." The plans for several campaigns were undertaken by the men at the Alexandria meeting. For the first time the Crown was taking an active leadership role in America.[6]

Unfortunately the Crown officials should have been met by the colonials with an atmosphere of self-sacrifice and gratitude. Instead when the colonial legislatures resisted their propositions for prosecuting the war, most of the British viewed them as shortsighted, selfish, and even maliciously unpatriotic. A British officer wrote of his disillusion with the colonies, "I reckon the day I bought my commission the most unhappy in my life, excepting that in which I landed in this country." It would be necessary for the colonials and the British to overcome this mutual distrust and suspicion if they wished to prosecute a successful war against the French.[7]

The first proposal of the Alexandria meeting was for an expedition to secure the forks of the Ohio River and destroy Fort Duquesne. This operation was to be under the command of General Braddock. The second plan was for a complete removal of all the French inhabitants left in Nova Scotia and the reduction of the French post at Fort Beausejour. This was the responsibility of the British royal governor of Nova Scotia, Charles Lawrence, who would be aided by 2,000 Massachusetts volunteers. Shirley would lead an expedition to reinforce Fort Oswego before undertaking the reduction of the French post at Niagara. Finally, a colonial force raised in New York, New Jersey, and New England was placed under the command of William Johnson. His objective was the French post at Crown Point, and he was given the rank of major-general of provincial forces.

At the end of the conference General Braddock wrote to the representatives of the Crown in London; "Mr. Shirley with the other northern governors met me at this place last week [and] we settled a plan for operations . . . [but] I have been greatly disappointed by the neglect and supineness of the assemblies of those provinces, with which I am concerned. They promised great matters and have done nothing whereby, instead of forwarding, they have obstructed the service."[8]

Braddock immediately faced a torrent of supply problems for his army of several thousand men. "[One hundred fifty] waggons, with 4 horses to each waggon, and 1500 saddle or pack-horses are wanted for the service of His Majesty's forces." Appraised of this problem, Benjamin Franklin noted: "[T]he General . . . had sent thro' the back parts of Maryland and Virginia to collect wagons . . . [which] only amounted to twenty-five, and not all of those were in serviceable condition. The General . . . exclaimed against the ministers for ignorantly landing him in a country destitute of the means of conveying their stores, baggage, etc." Through tact and ingenuity Franklin was able to furnish the wagons and horses that Braddock needed from the farmsteads of Pennsylvania, "as in that country almost every farmer had his wagon."[9]

Braddock set off into the wilderness from Fort Cumberland at Wills Creek, building a road for his army ahead of him. The physical achievement of clearing this road exceeded any other road-building project undertaken in North America to that time. Braddock's route ran from the

Potomac River in Maryland along Nemacolin's Path, a route blazed by Christopher Gist and Thomas Cresap and authorized by the Ohio Company of Virginia in 1752. These frontiersmen had been assisted by a Delaware guide for whom the path was named. Governor Dinwiddie was one of the investors in the Ohio Company of Virginia, which sought land rights and trade opportunities west of the Appalachians, and he has been incorrectly charged with a conflict of interest in suggesting this route instead of others that were supposed to be less demanding. The western end of the alternate route was found to be impassable less than a decade later.

"Moving an army as large as Braddock's involved far more than simply traversing the wilderness the way groups of individual traders and surveyors had often done." The great weight of Braddock's cannons and supply wagons made them especially cumbersome on the trail even after it had been cleared and leveled by the troops. In anticipation of these difficulties a detachment of sailors was added to the expedition who were considered expert in moving heavy objects with blocks and tackle. Finally, Braddock's route gradually wound past Christopher Gist's plantation and toward the Great Meadows, where Washington, now an aide to Braddock, had built Fort Necessity.[10]

The main strength of Braddock's command of 2,500 was the corps of regulars of the 44th and 48th of Foot commanded by Peter Halkett and Thomas Dunbar, respectively. These were filled out with companies of Virginia recruits. The rest of the force was made up of three companies of Virginia and Maryland rangers, two New York companies, a South Carolina unit, and teamsters and wagoneers for the baggage train. There were eighty-six officers, and a mounted troop of thirty Virginia dragoons.

Braddock dismissed all but ten of the Indian scouts provided by Dinwiddie. His contempt for wilderness warfare can be seen in his attitude toward the Indians: "These savages may, indeed, be a formidable enemy to your raw American militia but upon the King's regular and disciplined troops, sir, it is impossible they should make any impression."[11] Although he was relying on their ability to protect his column from surprise attack, he was almost as contemptuous of his ranger companies as he was of the Indians.[12]

DEATH ON THE MONONGAHELA

Braddock's defeat at the Monongahela River was the most significant event in British colonial history to that time. The historical accounts of this battle are extensive and well supported by primary sources. In its aftermath, the British regulars blamed the colonies for withholding essential support and even for alienating the allied Indians scouts from

them, but the colonials claimed the regulars were simply inept and ineffective in the wilderness. One explanation of the defeat was based in
the fact that sixty-three of the eighty-six officers involved in the action
were casualties. Another explanation rests on the poor performance of
the British regulars, who were said to have panicked and become hope-
lessly entangled with their fellows in the woods. Finally the question of
whether the standard British field tactics used in European warfare were
impractical in the American woodlands is still being debated by military
historians. That these problems reappeared with nearly every subsequent
campaign of the French and Indian War makes their status as genuine
causes for the defeat all the more feasible.[13]

Nonetheless, the "arrogant, aggressive, and unyielding personality" of
General Braddock seems to have been the main cause of the tragedy by
any test of history. It seems certain that the party of 200 to 300 French
and Indians led by Captain Hyacinth de Beaujeu, who was killed early
in the engagement, was bent on combat despite its numerical inferiority.
"All the Indian nations were called together and invited to join and assist
the French to repulse the English who came to drive them out of the
land they were then in possession of."[14]

ANATOMY OF DEFEAT

Besides food and ammunition, the British baggage train that accompanied Braddock carried hospital supplies, horseshoes, felling axes,
whipsaws, and three sets of miner's tools. It soon became obvious that
the wagons were slowing Braddock's advance, and at the suggestion of
Washington, Braddock moved forward with 1,500 of his best men as he
approached within eight or ten miles of Fort Duquesne. "The soldiers
[were] to leave their shoulder belts, waist belts and hangers (swords)
behind and only to take with them to the field one spare shirt, one spare
pair of stockings, one spare pair of shoes and one pair of brown gaiters."[15]

Although he knew that he outnumbered the French garrison, Braddock advanced in an alert and careful manner with flankers out and
rangers "afoot and mounted" in the forefront of his column. The exact
spot on which the battle was fought is now considered part of Pennsylvania, but at the time it was also claimed by Virginia. Captain Robert
Orme, Braddock's aide, on July 9, 1755, reported; "The General ordered
a halt, and the whole formed in their proper line of march. . . . No sooner
were the pickets upon their respective flanks . . . but we heard an exces-
sive quick and heavy firing in the front. The general, imagining the advanced parties were very warmly attacked . . . ordered Lieutenant
Colonel Burton to reinforce them with the vanguard [of] eight hundred
men."[16]

Duncan Cameron, a private in the 44th of Foot, noted: "[W]e crossed the Monongahela in two places, and soon after the second crossing, when our advanced guard had got about one mile from the river, a firing began in the front. The enemy were advantageously posted on two hills, one each side of our way, which hills joined in our front."[17]

Washington wrote: "In the early part of the action some of the irregulars (as they were called) without directions advanced to the right in loose order [spread out] to attack, but this unhappily [was] mistaken for cowardice ... and the confusion became general."[18] William Dunbar a British Regular officer continued: "[W]e were alarmed by the Indian hollow [war cry] and in an instant found ourselves attacked on all sides. ... [M]ost of our advanced party were laid sprawling on the ground. Our men unaccustomed to that way of fighting, were quite confounded and ... were seized with the same panic and went into much disorder, some part of them being 20 deep."[19]

A French observer reported: "Soon [after the death of Beaujeu], the English abandoned two pieces of artillery, and fell back toward the rear of their columns, which still pressed towards the front, to attack, but they lost their cannon one by one, and were thinned out by musketry during the space of five hours. The Indians ... rushed upon them with their tomahawks, as did the French also when they disbanded, and a great massacre followed."[20] A British officer noted: "The men from what stories they had heard of the Indians in regard to their scalping ... were so panic struck that their officers had little or no command over them."[21]

Another British officer noted: "The main body was with Col. D. or the whole army would have been destroyed. ... The military chest with £25,000 to pay the army, and all the General's papers is lost [including the plans for the Crown Point expedition]. Capt. Waggoner, with 170 Virginians, went up to where the enemy was hid and routed them: but O unhappy! Our infatuateds seeing a smoke, fired and killed him with several of his men. Capt. Polson, another brave Virginian, with his company, attacked the enemy a little before retreat was beat, which they [the enemy] hearing surrounded these brave fellows, and cut the Captain and most of them to pieces."[22]

Washington was busy during the battle and noted, "many attempts were made to dislodge the enemy from an eminence on the right but they all proved ineffectual and fatal to the officers who by great exertions and good examples endeavored to accomplish it. In one of these the General received the wound of which he died. ... No person knowing ... who the surviving senior officer was and the troops by degrees going off in confusion; without a ray of hope left of further opposition from those that remained; G.W. placed the General in a small cart ... and in the best order he could ... brought him over the first ford of the Monongahela."[23]

Ensign Godefroy of the French army noted; "The enemy [English] . . . [w]hen they left the field, they did so in such good order it did not seem a retreat, that instead by half-ranks they wheeled right and left, and regrouped to charge from the rear."[24] Another French officer reported: "[S]ieur [Jean-Daniel] Dumas . . . fell on the English with such vigor that [he] forced them to fall back in their turn. The latter continued to fight boldly for some time, but finally after four hours of fierce firing they collapsed, and the rout was general."[25]

Washington continued: "At an encampment near the Great Meadows the brave, but unfortunate General Braddock breathed his last. He was interred with the honors of war, and as it was left to G.W. to see this performed, and to mark out the spot for the reception of his remains, to guard against a savage triumph, if the place should be discovered, they were deposited in the road over which the army, wagons, etc. passed to hide every trace by which the entombment could be discovered. Thus died a man whose good and bad qualities were intimately blended."[26]

A French Canadien soldier wrote from Fort Duquesne: "Messrs. de Montigny and Corbrere returned from the field of battle and brought in their canoes the body of Monsr. de Beaujeu in a coffin sent on purpose. He was buried with all the marks of honor due his bravery . . . There is all the appearance that the [English] army will not rally again as the principal officers are left on the field of battle. That army marched not to attack a wooden fort, but the strongest fortified in Canada. Without saying too much of it, one can not say enough."[27]

The defeat of General Braddock shocked the British public. "Our danger is also further increased by the melancholy defeat of General Braddock . . . a whole army . . . routed and several hundred cut off by inhuman brutes perhaps scare a tenth of their number," wrote one editor. Another newspaper printed; "In consequence of this shameful defeat the frontiers of several southwestern provinces lay exposed to the enemy and how much innocent blood may be inhumanly sacrificed to the cowardice of the British soldiers in that action. . . . [W]e have the highest reason to fear the worst."[28]

The year 1755 was a bad one for the colonies. Besides Braddock's staggering defeat, William Shirley had delayed his advance on the French fort at Niagara. His own son had been killed on the Monongahela, and his men had become disheartened by the news of Braddock's disaster. The first signs of bad weather caused Shirley to cancel the operation against Fort Niagara. Shirley was now the commander of all British forces in the colonies, but his failure to attempt the reduction of Fort Niagara damaged his otherwise good reputation.[29]

Meanwhile, the provincials under Governor Charles Lawrence of Nova Scotia had captured Fort Beausejour and were well forward in securing the region. The 6,000 French inhabitants of Nova Scotia were rounded up and shipped away throughout the colonies in scattered groups. They managed to retain some of their heritage and were the object of Henry Wadsworth Longfellow's poem "Evangeline." The British defeat at the Monongahela, coupled with provincial success in Nova Scotia, left the regulars with an extreme sense of frustration. One last operation of the four planned in Alexandria had yet to play out, and it would provide a significant counterpoint to Braddock's defeat.

THE CROWN POINT EXPEDITION

William Johnson opened a trading post in the Mohawk River valley in 1738 after emigrating from Ireland to manage the lands of his uncle. He was one of the most important men on the continent in 1755 because he was beloved by the Iroquois. The Iroquois trusted him and called him Warraghiyagey—He Who Does-Much. He had treated the natives fairly, learned their language, joined their war parties, and taken one of their women as a wife. Johnson built a great stone house near present-day Johnstown, which he called Johnson Hall. Here he entertained hundreds of Indians at a time, mostly at his own expense. No single person in North America had as much influence with the Iroquois.

At the Alexandria conference, William Johnson had been assigned the campaign against Crown Point. The English received information that Crown Point was defended by only 800 Frenchmen and whatever Indians they could muster. The same spies brought word that the fort was in very good repair and defended by cannon. However, the French had word of Johnson's coming through the papers captured at the Monongahela, and would confront Johnson with 3,000 troops under the Baron Dieskau.

In August 1755 Johnson disembarked his troops at the Great Carrying Place near the falls of the Hudson River. His entire force numbered about 2,900 men, but reinforcements were expected to follow. With him, Johnson had Captain William Eyre of the regular British artillery, and ten field pieces: two 32-pounders, two 18-pounders, two 10-pounders, and four 6-pounders, with powder and shot for more than one hundred rounds per gun as well as the personnel to man them. Braddock had insisted that Eyre be attached to Johnson's command as he "did not choose to send an officer [Johnson] who had not seen service" alone into the wilderness in charge of an army.[30]

Leaving a skeleton force at the Carrying Place to build Fort Edward, Johnson moved to the southern shore of Lake St. Sacrement. He immediately renamed that body of water Lake George, for the English king. Of the Lake George site, Johnson wrote:

I found it a near wilderness, not one foot cleared. I have made a good wagon road to it from Albany, distance about 70 miles; never was house or fort erected

These are the remains of the soldiers' barracks of the fort built by the British at Crown Point during the 1760s. This fort was the largest earthwork fortification of its kind built on the North American continent. Lake Champlain can be seen clearly in the background. The fort is near the modern bridge across the lake from Crown Point, New York, into Vermont. It was near this site that Champlain intervened in an intertribal native battle in 1609.

here before. We have cleared land enough to encamp 5000 men. The troops now under my command and the reinforcements on the way will amount near that number.[31]

A temporary camp was created on the lakeshore from brushwood and logs stacked among the stumps of the new-cut forest. The artillery pieces were emplaced to defend the breastwork and one field piece was very well situated on a small eminence on the flank. Johnson designated his partially completed post Fort William Henry after one of the king's grandsons.

Dieskau knew of Johnson's occupation of the Lake George shoreline and of the lightly held camp at Fort Edward. After ordering the construction of a fort at Ticonderoga, he quietly moved the French army up Lake George to within striking distance of Johnson's camp. The capture of a courier to Fort Edward suggested that Johnson was unaware of the French presence in the region.

Finally learning of the French approach on the morning of September 8, 1755, Johnson sent a large party back along the wagon road toward

Fort Edward as a precaution. This detachment became known as the "Early Morning Scout." Johnson's own account of the battle of Lake George in the form of a dispatch was reported in the colonial newspapers less than a week later:

[I]n order to catch the enemy in their retreat from their camp . . . 1,000 men were detached under the command of Col. [Ephraim] Williams, of one of the Boston Regiments, with upwards of 200 Indians. They marched between 8 and 9 o'clock. In about an hour and a half afterwards we heard a heavy firing, and . . . we beat to arms, and got our men all in readiness. The fire approached nearer, upon which I judged our people were retreating, and I detached Lt. Cole with about 300 men to cover their retreat. . . .

About half an hour after 11 the enemy appeared in sight, and marched along the road in a very regular order directly upon our center. They made a small halt about 150 yards from our breastwork, when the regular troops (whom we judged to be such by their bright and fixed bayonets) made the grand and center attack. The Canadiens and the Indians squatted and dispensed on our flank. The enemy's fire we received first from the regulars in platoons, but it did no great execution, being at too great a distance, and our men defended by the breastwork. Our artillery then began to play upon them . . . [and] the engagement now became general on both sides.

The French regulars kept their ground and order for some time with great resolution, but the warm and constant fire from our artillery and troops put them into disorder. . . . This was about 4 o'clock, when our men and Indians jumped over the breastwork, pursued the enemy, slaughtered numbers and took several prisoners, amongst whom was Baron de Dieskau . . . badly wounded in the leg and through both hips, and the surgeon fears for his life. [He died in a few days.][32]

In the morning engagement the colonials had suffered their greatest losses of the battle. These included Colonel Williams, seven officers, and the Iroquois sachem Tiyanoga, known as King Hendrick. During the battle Johnson received a wound in the thigh that was "very painful; the ball lodged and can not be got out." Nonetheless, one week later he was still planning to move against Crown Point. However, the expedition was fated to stall on the shores of Lake George.[33]

Several factors caused the objective to be abandoned. Johnson's own wound was one. The death of many Indians, especially King Hendrick, caused those friendly to the English to return home to mourn their dead, as was their custom. Although Johnson had rangers with him under Captain Robert Rogers, he lost his most effective Indian scouts. Moreover, documents found among the French dead showed that they had fortified Ticonderoga and were expecting 6,000 troops and Indians to mass there. Ticonderoga was closer to Johnson than Crown Point. It would have to be reduced first. Finally, the colonial governments seemed satisfied to end the campaign with a victory in hand rather than risk another engagement.

Governor Hardy of New York wrote to Johnson as the campaigning season faded, "As early as possible dismiss the militia if it should appear that the enemy are not advancing, but remain quiet in their post at Ticonderoga."[34] The provincial commissioners "unanimously agreed that the army under command of Major General Johnson destined against Crown Point . . . be discharged [they being] detained no longer than their respective enlistments." They also made provision for the ten tons of supplies needed by the garrisons at Fort William Henry and Fort Edward. These could be carried to Fort Edward in about a dozen bateaux from Albany in six days, and to Fort William Henry in one more day by wagon.[35]

Governor Hardy wrote to the Board of Trade in January, 1756, emphasizing the importance of Johnson's victory and the new British forts on the New York frontier:

The advantages resulting from these forts are very considerable. Fort Edward stands at the Great Carrying Place on Hudson's River near 50 miles above Albany, and is the common passage from Canada to Albany, whether they come by Lake George, the South Bay [of Lake Champlain], or Wood Creek. Fort William Henry secures the pass[age] by Lake George to Hudson's River, Schenectady, and the Mohawk's country. . . . By Fort William Henry . . . we shall be masters of the waters that lead to Crown Point and may facilitate any enterprise on that place or further up Lake Champlain should such be thought advisable.[36]

MOHAWK BARONET

William Johnson's stature had never been higher. A Bostonian wrote, "This is the first time Mr. Johnson or any of his men ever fought an enemy . . . so that the . . . militia of New England have all the glory of the most obstinate and long engagement."[37] A Boston newspaper reported that the respect shown to Johnson "was equal to what might have been paid to a Marlborough on his return with victory from Flanders." His Royal Majesty, George II, made Johnson a baronet for life. He was thereafter Sir William Johnson.[38]

The *New York Gazette* reported of Sir William's arrival from Albany on January 5, 1756:

Last Tuesday . . . [a]bout six miles out of town, he was met by a considerable number of gentlemen on horseback, who conducted him to the King's Arms Tavern, where most of the principle inhabitants were assembled to congratulate him on his safe arrival. The ships in the harbor saluted him as he passed the streets, amidst the acclamation of the people. At night the city was beautifully illuminated.[39]

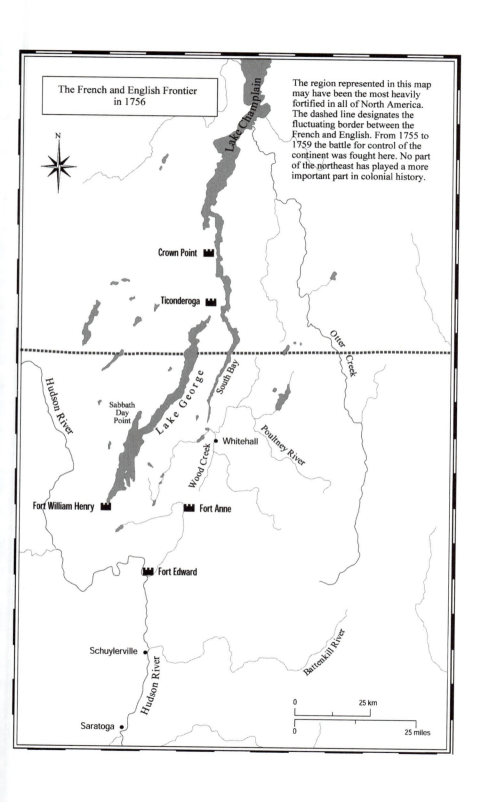

The French and English Frontier
in 1756

N

The region represented in this map
may have been the most heavily
fortified in all of North America.
The dashed line designates the
fluctuating border between the
French and English. From 1755 to
1759 the battle for control of the
continent was fought here. No part
of the northeast has played a more
important part in colonial history.

Lake Champlain

Crown Point

Ticonderoga

Otter Creek

Hudson River

Sabbath
Day
Point

Lake George

South Bay

Poultney River

Wood Creek

Whitehall

Fort William Henry

Fort Anne

Fort Edward

Schuylerville

Hudson River

Battenkill River

Saratoga

0   25 km

0   25 miles

Meanwhile an unaccustomed quiet settled over the frontier. Both the English and the French had lost their military leaders leaving their military organizations under the direction of seconds in command. More importantly for the frontier communities, the Indian nations began to vacillate in their traditional loyalties. The initial reaction to Braddock's defeat was to attract many of the Indian nations who had formerly been neutral, to the French, but Dieskau's defeat had made even the tribes closely allied to the French apprehensive.

The Mohawks seem to have been encouraged by the faith they had placed in their brother, Warraghiyagey. They chose to remain staunchly bound to the English. However, a delegation from the other Iroquois nations went to Quebec during 1756 to reaffirm their friendship with the French. For most of the Iroquois this was just good politics, but for the Senecas it was more. The fortified trading post built by the French at Niagara had attracted their trade, and even Johnson became unsure of their loyalty.[40] Sir Charles Hardy considered the reduction of Fort Niagara of the utmost consequence, claiming that the loss of Niagara would "soon oblige the French to abandon their encroachments [in the Ohio country] as it will be scarce possible for them to support those forts with garrisons or supply them with provisions."[41]

There was now speculation in the English colonies that had the initial objectives of Shirley and Johnson been reversed both men would have been better off. Shirley from Massachusetts would have commanded mostly New England troops, and Johnson would have marched through the Mohawk River valley supported by fellow New Yorkers and the Mohawks. There were numerous calls for Johnson to supplant Shirley as commander in chief of colonial forces. Moreover, Shirley and Johnson embarked upon a personal confrontation through the fall and winter of 1755–1756 over Sir William's authority as Indian agent. Johnson noted "the imperious style he [Shirley] writes to me since General Braddock's death . . . his threatening intimidations and his temper."[42]

Johnson immediately requested that the Board of Trade clearly delineate his position. "Governor Shirley's interfering in the authorative and ill judged manner he has done, was injurious to the true system of Indian affairs, a violation of my commission and an arbitrary insult upon my character."[43] Johnson received the support of the Board of Trade, which issued him a new royal warrant and a commission as colonel, agent, and sole superintendent of the affairs of the Six Nations. These events seem to have ended the influence formerly enjoyed by Shirley with the Board.[44]

OSWEGO

Shirley's reputation was further damaged when word came in 1757 that the French and Indians had burned Fort Oswego. The post, which was actually two positions under the command of Colonel Hugh Mercer, was on Lake Ontario at the mouth of the Oswego River. The total garrison of 1,600 men was composed largely of regular troops but about a third were colonials. Oswego was important because it largely neutralized the French presence on the lake at both Fort Niagara and Fort Frontenac. The French victory at Oswego "wrought marvels among the Indians, inspired the faithful, confirmed the wavering, and daunted the ill-disposed. The whole west was astir, ready to pour itself again in blood and fire against the English border."[45]

When Lord John Campbell, Earl of Loudoun arrived in America in the summer of 1756 to replace Braddock as military commander, he blamed the loss of Oswego on Shirley's inaction, and suggested the governor's recall to England. Thereafter, he dismissed all of Shirley's former plans and replaced them with his own scheme, which was directed once again at Louisbourg. Along with Loudoun came an influx of British officers into the colonies. Among these were several officers who would figure prominently in the final stages of the war: General Daniel Webb, Major-General James Abercromby, Lieutenant Colonel George Munro, General Jeffrey Amherst, Brigadier-General Lord Augustus Howe, and Major-General James Wolfe.

FORT WILLIAM HENRY AND THE MASSACRE

The initial steps of Loudoun's campaign of 1757 resulted in a botched attempt to retake the fortress on Cape Breton Island by Admiral Francis Holbourn. The English fleet sailed up to the harbor, saw sixteen large French warships ranged about the fortress, and retreated precipitously without engaging. This failure was particularly noted by the Anglo-Americans, who were still smarting over the return of the fortress at the end of the last war.

Meanwhile, Montcalm, who had taken over the military defense of New France after Dieskau's death, gathered an army of 6,000 regulars and Canadiens and 2,000 Indians, and a large train of artillery at Ticonderoga in July 1757. His objective was Fort William Henry, which stood on the Lake George battlefield. The fort's commander was Lieutenant Colonel George Munro, a hard-bitten Scottish veteran of the European wars. The garrison had recently been enlarged to 1,500 with the arrival of provincial troops from New York, New Jersey, and New Hampshire, as well as a large number of women and children. These were frontier families who had come in for the security of the fort or dependents of the soldiers who regularly traveled with the army. But the fort could house no more than 500. Consequently, a fortified camp was hastily established to accommodate most of the garrison and to control the high ground that would otherwise have been freely occupied by the French.

"The cannon of Fort William Henry, with the heaviest guns positioned to cover the lake, were to be the first and last line of defense." No attempt was made to provide obstacles to an enemy landing on the shores.[46]

General Daniel Webb was at Fort Edward within easy support of Munro. During the first three weeks of July, Munro sent out no fewer than six separate scouting parties, but the inability of the English to penetrate the screen of French allied Indians at the northern end of Lake George proved frustrating. Finally, Colonel John Parker was ordered to undertake a reconnaissance in force. With five companies of New Jersey Blues and a few New York militiamen (about 350 men in total), Parker left the south shore of the lake in some two dozen whaleboats heading for the sawmill at the falls of the LaChute River near Ticonderoga.

Montcalm's Indians spied Parker's whaleboats traveling north just before nightfall, and arranged an ambush at Sabbath Day Point on Sunday, July 24, 1757. Parker's troops allowed the intervals between their craft to become irregular and sometimes very large. Three of the leading boats, much separated from the others, stumbled into the French ambush, and brought the other English vessels to their aid just north of the point. Here the Indians, firing from the shore and launching their canoes into the lake, fell upon the detachment. All but four of the whaleboats were captured or overturned. In the initial attack about 100 of Parker's men were shot, drowned, or hunted down in the forests to which they fled after reaching shore. About 100, including Parker, retreated to Fort William Henry either by boat or on foot through the woods. The rest were taken prisoner.[47]

The Indians were overjoyed with their success. Montcalm almost immediately sent out Brigadier de Levis with 3,000 men to march down the western shore of Lake George and prepare a fortified camp near present-day Bolton's Landing. Montcalm brought the rest of the army and the all-important artillery down the lake by boat. Once combined, the two forces moved to within three miles of Fort William Henry and nestled in a cove well suited to the army's protection and security. Montcalm then initiated a formal siege with entrenchments and parallels.

Six days of bombardment convinced Lieutenant Colonel Munro that further resistance was unless. Munro was brave enough, but the fort had not been built to withstand a classic artillery bombardment. Moreover, a letter from General Webb to Munro, intercepted by the French, declared that no reinforcements from Fort Edward would be coming. Having been assured that help was impossible, Munro acceded to Montcalm's offer of an honorable surrender. It was agreed that the British would march out with the honors of war, and be escorted to Fort Edward by a detachment of French troops.[48]

The English passed a troubled night in Fort William Henry as the Indians pillaged the fortified camp. When they marched out on the morning of August 10, they were terrified that the French could not control the Indians. When the column of English at last began to move "the Indians crowded upon them, impeded their march, snatched caps, coats, and weapons from men and officers, tomahawked those that resisted, and, seizing upon shrieking women and children, dragged them off or murdered them on the spot. . . . A frightful tumult ensued, when Montcalm, Levis . . . and many other French officers, threw themselves among the Indians, and by promises and threats tried to allay their frenzy."[49]

Montcalm was said to have pleaded for the Indians to kill him and spare the English, who seem to have been so stunned as to make little or no defense. The broken column straggled forward in disorder seeking the protection of the French advance guard, who seem to have acted with unseemly detachment. Others retraced their steps to take refuge in the fort. The massacre ended in fits and starts with as many as fifty English dead. To his credit, Montcalm succeeded in ransoming about 400 English in the course of the day, but the Indians decamped in a body toward Montreal with about 200 captives.

Word came to Montcalm that a large reinforcement of Fort Edward was expected shortly from Albany. This made an investment of that English post impossible. More importantly, since it was felt that successful war in the wilderness required the services of the Indians—and they had left—no advance toward Fort Edward was possible. Montcalm, therefore, burned Fort William Henry and retired.

A WINNING STRATEGY

William Pitt became the prime minister of England in June 1757. His administration almost completely revitalized the British government, and he proposed a strategic plan for winning the war in North America. His objectives were the three gatekeepers to Quebec—Fortress Louisbourg, Fort Carillon at Ticonderoga, and Fort Duquesne at the forks of the Ohio River. Two of these had been the targets of colonial campaigns in the past, but the new fort at Ticonderoga had never before been tried.

In 1758 a new fleet was assembled at Halifax to attack Louisbourg once again. Numerous warships were committed to the task under the command of the capable Admiral Edward Boscawen. A land force of 12,000 British regulars was placed under Generals Jeffery Amherst and James Wolfe. After Boscawen blockaded the Louisbourg harbor, Amherst and Wolfe successfully landed their troops very close to the spot where the colonials had landed in 1745. With the fortress besieged and with no hope of a relieving force breaking the blockade, the outnumbered French garrison surrendered within a few weeks.

General Wolfe had been the life of the siege, and although Amherst

The entrance to Fort Ticonderoga is through the surrounding counterguard. Note the curtain wall to the left and the bastion to the right. The large pair of weapons near the gateway are Coehorn mortars.

was called away with six regiments to support a planned operation against Ticonderoga, Wolfe wanted to press forward to Quebec immediately with the remainder of the army. He wrote to Amherst, with whom he was on good terms: "An offensive, daring kind of war will awe the Indians and ruin the French. . . . If you will attempt to cut up New France by the roots, I will come with pleasure to assist." However, Wolfe's health, always questionable, failed him within the next month, and he returned to England to rest after having secured Cape Breton Island to the English.[50]

Meanwhile, the attack on Ticonderoga in 1758 was entrusted to Major-General James Abercromby, who was considered inept and infirmed at age fifty-one. Pitt had meant the command to go to Lord Augustus Howe, brigadier-general and second in command of the forces under Abercromby, but the old general had precedence.[51] Augustus Howe was a model soldier, young and highly regarded by the colonials. Howe placed himself in the hands of Robert Rogers and learned, firsthand, his methods of woodland warfare and ranger tactics. He insisted that the British army be sent to the frontier to learn to live and fight as rangers did. Regulars as well as provincials were made to cut down the tails of their regimental coats to ease their travel through the wilderness. He limited their equipment to weapons, canteen, a haversack, and a single blanket and bearskin. Even officers were required to follow these instructions, and it was remarkable to see his Lordship and his staff eating around the campfire like private soldiers. Colonel Thomas Ellison of the New York militia noted: "Both officers and men packed their bundles on their backs, and the colonel [himself] though an old man and afflicted with rheumatism marched on foot with his musket on his shoulder at the head of his men and waded through rivers crotch deep. . . . Some of the men complained that their officers marched too hard for them."[52]

Had Howe's influence continued throughout the campaign it might have proved successful. Unfortunately, Howe, brave to the point of being oblivious to personal danger, went forward with a small party under provincial Major Israel Putnam to reconnoiter a possibly line of attack from the rear of Fort Carillon. Near the rapids of the LaChute River they encountered a detachment of French and Indians numbering about 350 whom Montcalm had sent to harass the British. A sharp fight ensued and in the first moments Howe was killed by a shot to the chest.[53]

In that instant the French had effectively overcome the English. Major Thomas Mante wrote: "In Lord Howe the soul of General Abercromby's army seemed to expire." More importantly, in Howe the British lost the only person of high rank and prestige in the British army to have recognized the potential effectiveness of colonial fighting men and American-style tactics. Had he lived to effect a change in British military attitudes toward colonials, the War of American Independence might have taken a different course or might never have happened at all.

The British efforts under Abercromby to take the entrenchments around Fort Carillon by unremitting and seemingly senseless frontal assaults ended in a series of bloody repulses even though the Highland troops among the British regulars and the Rhode Island regiment of the colonials fought stubbornly. Abercromby lost almost 2,000 men while Montcalm lost less than 400. Thereafter, the English army seems to have panicked somewhat in its retreat up Lake George, leaving hundreds of barrels of provisions scattered along the shore, and it did not stop until it reoccupied the ground that held the burned ruins of Fort William Henry.[54]

Here they were greeted with glorious news. A colonial army of 3,000 men under the command of Lieutenant Colonel John Bradstreet had attacked and destroyed Fort Frontenac on the north shore of Lake Ontario. The colonials had moved up to the site of Fort Oswego, taken to whaleboats and bateaux in the night, and by the morning had made a lodgment within 200 yards of the lightly garrisoned French post. The French commander, outnumbered by almost thirty to one, quickly surrendered. Bradstreet burned the fort and the outbuildings and captured the entire French lake fleet of nine armed vessels and scores of canoes. He then retired up the Oswego River to present-day Rome, New York, where

1,000 men were detached to build a new English post named Fort Stanwix.

The advantages to the English wrought by this "All-American" victory were many. The French lost command of Lake Ontario, and the supply line from Montreal to their western forts was threatened. Meanwhile, the French-leaning Indians, initially buoyed in their alliances by series of victories wrought by Montcalm, now wavered. Henceforth, except for small parties of Shawnees on the western frontiers, they remained neutral and took no further part in the war.

In late autumn 1758 Brigadier-General John Forbes, with a force of 5,000 provincials and 1,500 Scots Highlanders, moved across Pennsylvania toward Fort Duquesne cutting a new road through the forests of the colony and leaving a series of fortified posts behind him. A detachment of 800 Highlanders, Royal Americans, and provincials under the command of Major James Grant advanced toward Fort Duquesne and were caught in an ambush almost as fatal as that of Braddock years earlier. The entire affair was mismanaged by Grant, who advanced his forces in separate detachments who were defeated in detail. The English lost almost 300 men before retiring. Two months later when Forbes advanced toward Fort Duquesne with his main body, the French blew up their magazines and burned their own works. Forbes, who was all but bedridden and near death, ordered a new fort built at the forks of the Ohio. This was named Fort Pitt in honor of the prime minister.

THE CAMPAIGN OF 1759

The French began the year of 1759 discouraged by the loss of many of their posts in the preceding year. Yet they still held Fort Niagara at the western end of Lake Ontario, Fort Carillon at Ticonderoga, Crown Point, and the massive citadel of Quebec. The English campaign to reduce these important posts formed the core of English strategy in 1759. Brigadier-General John Prideaux and Sir William Johnson would lead the attack on Fort Niagara. Jeffery Amherst, replacing Abercromby as commander in chief, would lead a renewed attack at Ticonderoga and Crown Point, and James Wolfe would attack Quebec.

The first two of these operations moved forward rapidly. By July Amherst invested Fort Carillon with 11,000 men—half regulars and half colonials—and he began a bombardment. Under orders from the governor of New France, the French left a force of only 400 at Carillon and withdrew the remaining forces to Montreal. The fort's commandant abandoned Fort Carillon in the night and meant to destroy the magazines. A great explosion ripped the night, but only a single bastion was destroyed. Amherst followed the retreating French to Crown Point, which was also abandoned and destroyed. Amherst was an active and capable officer

This photograph was taken from the battlements of Old Fort Niagara. The tall square building in the rear is a stone and mortar redoubt. A drawbridge passing under this structure allows entrance to the fort. The open area at the top of the redoubt houses a platform for cannons.

who, with his primary objectives achieved, planned to move on Montreal thereby providing a diversion for Wolfe's attack on Quebec. By August, Amherst was on the Richelieu River.

Meanwhile, General Prideaux and Sir William Johnson had reached Niagara with their army in June. This force was made up of two regiments of regulars, a battalion of Royal Americans, and 3,000 provincials. Johnson had also attracted 900 Iroquois to the English for this offensive. This large turnout of Indians serves as a barometer of the war and shows how important the small English victories of the previous year really were.

While Fort Niagara had been renovated and well supplied in anticipation of an attack, it had only 600 men to defend it. These were ably led by Captain Pierre Pouchot. The siege was begun with classical form, but an error in laying out the approaches was made by the British engineers, which cost a number of unnecessary casualties. Early in the operation General Prideaux was accidentally killed when a British mortar shell burst unexpectedly upon being fired. Johnson assumed command of the operation and within three weeks he had the French post in dire straits.

At this point a French column from the forts to the west approached to give Fort Niagara succor. This force was attacked by Johnson and was convincingly put to rout. The survivors retreated all the way to Detroit burning many of their western posts and forts. Lacking the promise of reinforcement, Pouchot had no choice but to surrender. The capture of Niagara on July 25 was a masterstroke for British arms because it cut off the entire French colony to the west from the rest of colonial Canada.

THE SIEGE OF QUEBEC

Bolstered by the successes at Louisbourg, Frontenac, Niagara, and Duquesne, General James Wolfe returned to Canada in 1759 to attack Quebec with a massive body of regular troops supported by 49 men-of-war, almost 200 transports, and sailors and marines numbering 14,000 men. His army was composed almost completely of British regulars. In all this great number, there were only two battalions of Royal Americans, one of Scots Highlanders, and six companies of American rangers. Although the rangers were considered by Wolfe to be the worst sort of soldiers, he instituted many of the sensible reforms in uniform and equipment that had been suggested by Lord Howe.

Temporarily delayed by late-season ice, Wolfe's force was brought safely up the St. Lawrence in June by Admiral Charles Saunders. The navigation of the St. Lawrence without the loss of a ship from among so many was an amazing feat of seamanship. The fleet anchored in the St. Lawrence River off the Ile de Orleans about four miles below Quebec, and a detachment under General Robert Monckton was sent at once to occupy Point Levis on the south shore opposite the citadel.

The French were stunned. It was bad enough that Montcalm and Governor de Vaudreuil were at loggerheads even though the general had been given precedence in deciding military matters, but no more than 16,000 fighting men could be mustered in all of Canada, among them only 3,000 Troups de Terre. Nonetheless, the French position atop the cliffs overlooking the river appeared impregnable, and the passage of ships up the river to the west seemed impossible. In preparing for a defense, Montcalm had carefully laid out a line of strong entrenchments, called the Beauport lines, from the eastern edge of the city at the mouth of the St. Charles River to the great falls of the Montmorenci River. The French would have to hold out just long enough to allow the Canadien winter to drive the English away. Meanwhile, Montcalm initiated a series of ineffective attacks by fireship and burning rafts on the anchored British fleet.

With great difficulty Wolfe was able to erect batteries of artillery on Point Levis opposite the city. From here a brisk, if ineffective, fire was directed upon the city proper. Coureurs de Bois and French Indians constantly raided these positions, killing sentries and leaving behind mutilated bodies. The American rangers seemed incapable of preventing these incursions. This caused a great deal of concern among the English troops, and the number of desertions consequently increased.

In mid-July a small number of British ships with part of Wolfe's army slipped past the Quebec garrison and took position upstream of the city. These floated back and forth with the six-knot tide in tedious regularity unable to land any troops at the foot of the nearly vertical cliffs that lined the river. Nonetheless, Montcalm was required to detach a strong force of 1,500 men to guard the clifftops west of the city to prevent just such a landing. These Frenchmen, under the direction of Montcalm's aide, Colonel Louis Antoine de Bougainville, were required to guard between fifteen and twenty miles of shoreline. Moreover, word of the fall of Ticonderoga and Amherst's advance toward Montreal had caused Montcalm to send General Levis with 1,800 men to protect that town.

At the end of July an ill-advised attempt was made upon the French entrenchments near the Montmorenci falls. The British regulars, having landed from boats, became disordered as they tried desperately to cross the mud flats that lined the shore, and they could not bring a concerted effort to bear on the French positions. More than 400 men lost their lives, including 33 officers, before the attackers could be brought off. Wolfe was deeply moved by the disaster, and the French were equally buoyed by it, believing that the British campaign was winding to an end.

As late August approached, Wolfe's health again began to fail, but he nonetheless sent his light troops, rangers, and highlanders into the surrounding farmsteads to burn and generally terrorize the habitants in an effort to draw out Montcalm. Vaudreuil denounced these tactics as barbaric atrocities, but Montcalm let the parishes burn, refusing to "imperil all Canada to save a few hundred farmhouses."[55]

As September loomed, Wolfe found that the passage of the river at Quebec could be made with little damage given a brisk wind and a favorable tide. He, therefore, changed his strategy from an attack below the city to one from above it. Here the Plains of Abraham (named for Abraham Martin, a farmer) made a generally flat expanse before the walls of the city upon which regular lines of attack could be established. A reconnaissance of the 175-foot-high cliffs was begun from the south bank of the river. A number of flatboats were ferried upstream and 1,200 additional men were marched overland to embark on them in anticipation of finding some means to scale the cliffside. Wolfe chose a small cove at the base of the cliffs called the Anse de Foulon as a landing place. Here the vertical walls seemed to be scaleable by a small party.

On the night of September 12–13 Wolfe loaded his men aboard thirty flatboats and drifted down the river on the ebb tide toward the chosen landing place. Almost 2,000 additional men would follow if the cliffs could be scaled. Bougainville's men had been broken into detachments

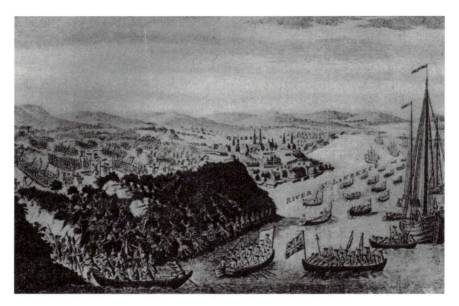

This print from the authors' collection represents the final attack on the French stronghold of Quebec by the British under the command of General James Wolfe. The cliffs that the British scaled are actually much steeper and forbidding than they appear in this illustration. The troops are arrayed on the Plains of Abraham, and the Old City with its many church spires can be seen in the background.

in order to effectively patrol the cliffs. The sentries had become somewhat complacent watching the British ships drifting back and forth twice a day. In the dark the little flotilla made quiet progress. When challenged, French-speaking men among the English bluffed their way past the guards by claiming to be a provisions convoy from Montreal. Almost miraculously, they were believed. Having arrived at the landing, the British light infantry scrambled up the woody precipice and overran a French guard post at the top. With very little loss, and a great deal of discipline and organization, Wolfe had his entire force lined up on the Plains of Abraham by sunrise.

When the news was brought to Montcalm he was only somewhat alarmed, thinking that a small force of the enemy had achieved a limited lodgment. But what he saw as he rode onto the Plains of Abraham at dawn on September 13 stunned him. An entire British army of 4,800 regular troops and two artillery pieces was drawn up in the best linear order facing the walls of the city with the Light infantry on the flanks and the Royal American held in reserve. Montcalm was reported to have said, "I see the enemy where they have no business to be. This is a serious affair!"[56]

Montcalm could have stayed behind the walls of the city, but Wolfe had set the stage for the type of battle that both he and Montcalm understood best: a standup European encounter between long lines of regulars on a fairly even and level piece of ground. Montcalm immediately ordered the veteran regiments of Bearn, LaSarre, Languedoc, and Royal Rousillion to form a line outside the wall, where the Regiment Guienne had already taken their post. Imperative messages were sent to Bougainville to fall back on Quebec in the hope of catching Wolfe between two fires. Coureurs de bois and Indians were called from the Beauport lines to beat back a wide turning movement by the British light infantry on the flanks. Montcalm set the Compagnies Franches de la Marine and the Canadien militias to the left and right of his regulars, and called up three pieces of artillery.

The French took three hours to order their forces. Meanwhile, the English awaited the result with feigned composure as they were peppered by musket fire from the French Indians and plied with canister from the French artillery. British skirmishers were set out to deal with these, and the infantry were told to lie down in the grass to avoid the artillery shells.

Brigadier General George Townsend made the following observations of the battle: "[I]t is most certain that the enemy formed in good order and that their attack was very brisk and animated. . . . Our troops reserved their fire till within forty yards, which was so well continued that the enemy every where gave way."[57] Sir John Fortescue was less appreciative of the order demonstrated by the French, claiming that they came on the run, which at once broke their lines, and that they fired too soon. Of the British regulars he noted that the line fired like a single shot, repeated the feat, and followed with a charge of bayonets and claymores (Scottish swords) when the French fled the field.[58]

Wolfe had been active along the lines and had received a wound in the wrist. Just as the enemy broke he was struck in the chest and groin by musket fire. He staggered and sat on the ground. Those around him came to his aid and sent for a surgeon, but Wolfe knew he was finished. Having been informed that the French were in rout, he gave a few barely coherent orders and murmured, "Now, God be praised, I will die in peace!"[59]

Montcalm tried to bring order to the retreat, but he was borne along on horseback within the stream of panic-stricken soldiers. As he neared the walls of the city, a stray shot passed through his body. He kept his seat until he had ridden through the St. Louis Gate and then was placed in the house of the army surgeon. Montcalm was dying, heavy of heart and lost in the reflections of a defeated general. The Bishop of Quebec,

Pontbriand, attended his deathbed and administered the last rites of the Catholic Church. He died at 4 A.M. on the day after the battle, and was buried in a shell-hole in the chapel of the Ursuline convent.

Governor Vaudreuil did not arrived from the Beauport lines until after the French regulars began their retreat, and he blamed the defeat on Montcalm's decision to open the battle without him. Nonetheless, the brave Canadiens whom Vaudreuil commanded made a fight of it, throwing themselves into the bushes and ravines on the British left and pouring a brisk, if distant and ineffective, fire upon them. These marksmen were ultimately driven off, and they crossed the St. Charles River to the Beauport lines by way of a bridge well covered by French artillery. However, before midnight the British fortified themselves on the battlefield, brought up additional cannons, and occupied the general hospital of the city. The British lost about 660 killed, wounded, and missing in the battle, and the French most likely lost about the same number—the official reports by each side differ widely.[60]

The city was still in French hands, and the majority of the French army was safely ensconced behind the St. Charles lines. The British, exhausted by a night of cliff-climbing and a day of fighting, were spent and in no condition to continue offensive operations. Vaudreuil called a council of war among his officers, and there was much sentiment among them to fight on. However, the governor decided upon an immediate retreat, and Quebec was left to its fate. The cannons were left in the lines of Beauport, the tents in the encampments, and provisions enough in the storehouses to supply the army for a week.

One of only a dozen undisputedly decisive battles in world history was finally over. The great citadel at Quebec had fallen to the ill-fated Wolfe. Montcalm, possibly the best French general officer to serve in the colonial period, was dead, and the governor of New France had humiliated himself by his precipitous withdrawal in the face of the enemy. But the threat of having the fleet frozen in during the coming Canadien winter caused Admiral Saunders to withdraw his ships, leaving a small land force to hold the city until relieved in the spring. The importance of the prompt arrival of the Royal Navy at Quebec of 1760 cannot be underestimated. It confirmed the victories of 1759 and led directly to the fall of Montreal and all of French Canada with it.

The struggle for North America was over. In the Peace of Paris (1763), France lost almost all its possessions in North America except a few islands in the Caribbean. By the provisions of the treaty, Havana and Manila, taken by the British Royal Navy were restored to Spain, which had belatedly entered the war as a French ally. In exchange Britain received Florida and all the Spanish territory east of the Mississippi River. Britain kept Minorca in the Mediterranean and the Grenadas, Dominica,

Tobago, and St. Vincent in the Caribbean. France gave the Spanish all of Louisiana as compensation for their losses.

The British won a great worldwide empire in the Seven Years' War, but their grip on North America was a tenuous one. The accumulated effects of almost a century of colonial neglect, widespread prejudice against provincials, and a growing hatred of British regulars would cause the Anglo-American colonists to attempt to sever their ties with Britain in 1775.[61]

NOTES

1. See Allen W. Eckert, *Wilderness Empire* (New York: Bantam Books, 1980), 253–254.

2. Washington wanted an appointment to the regulars, which was denied him largely because he was a colonial. This circumstance reinforces the idea that militia officers were held in contempt by the regulars and aids in understanding Washington's motivations for seeking high rank during the American Revolution.

3. The first quote is from a letter by St. Clair to Braddock on April 10, 1775. The second is from an unidentified British officer to his friends in London on April 8, 1755. Both can be found in Andrew J. Wahll, ed., *The Braddock Road Chronicles, 1755* (Bowie, MD: Heritage Books, 1999), 124.

4. Reported in Armand Francis Lucier, ed., *French and Indian War Notices Abstracted from Colonial Newspapers*, vol. 1, (Bowie, MD: Heritage Books, 1999), 282. See Francis Parkman, *Montcalm and Wolfe* (New York: Atheneum, 1984), 244.

5. Reported in Lucier, 196–197.

6. Parkman, 244.

7. John Ferling, *Struggle for a Continent: The Wars of Early America* (Arlington Heights, IL: Harlan Davidson, 1993), 197. Also see Timothy J. Todish, *America's First World War: The French and Indian War, 1754–1763* (Ogden, UT: Eagle's View, 1987).

8. A letter to Sir Robert Napier from Braddock, April 19, 1755, found in Wahll, 354.

9. A journal entry found in ibid., 151, 154.

10. Louis M. Waddell and Bruce D. Bromberger, *The French and Indian War in Pennsylvania, 1753–1763: Fortification and Struggle During the War for Empire* (Harrisburg: Pennsylvania Historical and Museum Commission, 1996), 10–11.

11. Quoted in Francis Russell, *The French and Indian Wars* (New York: American Heritage 1962), 94.

12. Braddock's general orders of April 8, 1755, found in Wahll, 115.

13. See Waddell and Bromberger, 14–15.

14. The French have a few eyewitnesses. Monsieur Roucher was a French Canadien soldier at Fort Duquesne. Pierre Pouchot likewise left a memoir. Pierre de Contrecour and Jean-Daniel Dumas both commanded troops during the battle. See Wahll 344.

15. Ibid., 115.

16. Captain Robert Orme, quoted in ibid., 345.

17. Captain Robert Orme to Sir John St. Clair April 16, 1755, and a journal entry found in ibid., 137, 354.

18. Journal entries from Washington, found in ibid., 348.

19. Journal entries from William Dunbar, found in ibid., 349.

20. Quoting Monsieur Roucher and Ensign Godefroy, in ibid., 367, 368.

21. Journal entries from an anonymous British officer, found in ibid., 349.

22. Journal entries from an anonymous British officer, found in ibid., 353.

23. Journal entries from Washington, found in ibid., 348.

24. Quoting Monsieur Roucher and Ensign Godefroy, in ibid., 367, 368.

25. Quoting a French Officer, in ibid., 370.

26. Journal entries from Washington, found in ibid., 377.

27. Quoting Monsieur Roucher, in ibid., 379.

28. Reported in Lucier, 264–265.

29. John A. Schutz, *William Shirley* (Chapel Hill: University of North Carolina Press, 1961), 198.

30. Major-General Edward Braddock, May 17, 1755, to Major-General Johnson, found in Almon W. Lauber, ed., *The Papers of Sir William Johnson*, vol. 9 (Albany: State University of New York, 1939), 171.

31. Major-General Johnson, September 3, 1755, to the Board of Trade, found in E. B. O'Callaghan, ed. *Documents Relative to the Colonial History of the State of New York*, vol. 6 (Albany, NY: Weed, Parsons, 1855), 997.

32. A Boston newspaper account of Johnson's dispatch after the battle, reported in Lucier 305–308.

33. Ibid., 309.

34. Governor Charles Hardy, November 14, 1755, to Major-General Johnson, found in Lauber, vol. 13, 69.

35. Minutes of the meeting of the provincial commissioner, November 20, 1755, found in ibid., 71–72.

36. Sir Charles Hardy, January 16, 1756, to the Board of Trade, found in O'Callaghan, vol. 7, 4.

37. Reported in Lucier, vol. 2, 29–30.

38. Reported in ibid., 3.

39. Reported in ibid., 7.

40. Lauber, vol. 9, 785.

41. Governor Charles Hardy, January 6, 1756, to the Lords of Trade, found in O'Callaghan, vol. 6, 6.

42. Major-General Johnson, September 3, 1755, to Governor George Clinton, found in ibid, 996.

43. Major-General Johnson, September 3, 1755, to the Board of Trade, found in ibid., 991–996.

44. Secretary of the Board Pownall, December 2, 1755, to Major-General William Johnson, found in ibid., 1022.

45. Parkman, 271.

46. Ian K. Steele, *Betrayal: Fort William Henry and the "Massacre"* (New York: Oxford University Press, 1990), 97.

47. See Steele, 87–89; and Parkman, 281–282.

48. Several historians claim that Daniel Webb, then holding the rank of general, refused to support Munro when requested, an infamous circumstance set

in history over the intervening years and made a part of American folklore by James Fennimore Cooper and numerous Hollywood film directors. The text of this letter was reported by Parkman, who claimed to have seen a complete copy in Colonel Joseph Frye's journal. The bloodstained original is reproduced in Steele, 103.

49. Parkman, 296–297.

50. Quoted in ibid., 350.

51. Howe was the older brother of two men—William and Richard—who would appear in American history as the respective army and navy commanders of British forces during the American Revolution.

52. Letter of Thomas Ellison, November 1, 1757, to Mr. Gain, found in *Magazine of American History* 24 (August 1890), 84.

53. Putnam was to become an important general in the Continental Army in the American Revolution, as was General John Stark, who served as second in command of Roger's Rangers.

54. Robert Leckie, *A Few Acres of Snow: The Saga of the French and Indian Wars* (New York: John Wiley & Sons, 1999), 309–311.

55. Parkman, 459.

56. F. Van Wyck Mason, *The Battle for Quebec* (Boston: Houghton Mifflin, 1965), 158.

57. Brigadier-General Townsend to Mr. Secretary Pitt, September 20, 1759, found in Lucier, vol. 4, 109–111.

58. Robin May, *Wolfe's Army* (London: Osprey, 1989), 37.

59. Parkman, 478.

60. Ibid., 481–483.

61. See Dorothy Denneen Volo and James M. Volo, *Daily Life in the Age of Sail* (Westport, CT: Greenwood Press, 2002).

Selected Bibliography

Alexander, William. *The History of Women from the Earliest Antiquary to Present Time: Giving an Account of Almost Every Interesting Particular Concerning That Sex Among All Nations, Ancient and Modern.* Philadelphia: J. H. Dobelbower, 1796.

Anderson, Fred W. *A People's Army: Massachusetts Soldiers and Society in the Seven Years' War.* Chapel Hill: University of North Carolina Press, 1984.

———. "Why Did Colonial New Englanders Make Bad Soldiers? Contractual Principles and Military Conduct During the Seven Years' War." *William and Mary Quarterly* 38 (1981), 395–417.

Armstrong, Edward, ed. *Good Order Established in Pennsylvania and New Jersey in America by Thomas Budd.* New York: Williams Gowans, 1865.

Ashley, Maurice. *Louis XIV and the Greatness of France.* New York: Collier, 1962.

Axtell, James. *The European and the Indian: Essays in the Ethnohistory of Colonial America.* New York: Oxford University Press, 1981.

Bacon, Richard M. *The Forgotten Art of Growing, Gardening and Cooking with Herbs.* Dublin, NH: Yankee, 1972.

Bennett, Ralph, ed. *Settlements in the Americas: Cross-Cultural Perspectives.* Newark: University of Delaware Press, 1993.

Berkin, Carol. *First Generations: Women in Colonial America.* New York: Hill and Wang, 1996.

Biggar, H. P., ed. *The Works of Samuel de Champlain.* Vol. 6. Toronto: Champlain Society, 1933.

Boorstin, Daniel J. *The Americans: The Colonial Experience.* New York: Vintage Books, 1958.

Bryant, Samuel W. *The Sea and the States: A Maritime History of the American People.* New York: T. Y. Cromwell, 1967.

Calder, Isabel M. *Colonial Captives, March, and Journeys*. Port Washington, NY: Kennikat Press, 1935.

Calloway, Colin G., ed. *Dawnland Encounters: Indians and Europeans in Northern New England*. Hanover, NH: University Press of New England, 1991.

———. *New Worlds for All: Indians, Europeans, and the Remaking of Early America*. Baltimore: Johns Hopkins University Press, 1997.

———. *North Country Captives*. Hanover, NH: University Press of New England, 1992.

———. *The Western Abenakis of Vermont, 1600–1800: War, Migration, and the Survival of an Indian People*. Norman: University of Oklahoma Press, 1990.

Carver, Jonathan. *Travels Through the Interior Parts of North America in the Years 1766, 1767, and 1768*. Minneapolis: Ross & Hanes, 1956.

Chartrand, René. *The French Soldier in Colonial America*. Historic Arms. Alexandria Bay, NY: Museum Restoration Service, 1984.

———. *Louis XIV's Army*. Men-at-Arms. Alexandria Bay, NY: Museum Restoration Service, 1988.

Clement, W. H. P. *The History of the Dominion of Canada*. Toronto: William Briggs, 1897.

Colden, Cadwallader. *History of the Five Indian Nations of Canada*. New York: A. S. Barnes, 1904.

Coleman, Emma. *New England Captives*. Portland, ME: Southworth Press, 1925.

Connecticut Historical Society. *Children at Work*. Hartford: Connecticut Historical Society, 1993.

Coolridge, Guy Omeron. *The French Occupation of the Champlain Valley from 1609 to 1759*. Fleischmanns, NY: Purple Mountain Press, 1999.

Crane, Elaine Forman, ed. *The Diary of Elizabeth Drinker*. Boston: Northeastern University Press, 1994.

Crane, Verner W. *The Southern Frontier, 1670–1732*. Durham, NC: Duke University Press, 1928.

Cresswell, Nicholas. *The Journal of Nicholas Cresswell, 1774–1777*. New York: Dial Press, 1928.

Cronon, William. *Changes in the Land, Indians, Colonists, and the Ecology of New England*. New York: Hill and Wang, 1983.

Cummins, George W. *History of Warren County*. New York: Lewis Historical, 1922.

de Bougainville, Louis Antoine. *Adventures in the Wilderness. The American Journals of Louis Antoine de Bougainville*. Norman: University of Oklahoma Press, 1964.

de Crevecoeur, J. Hector St. John. *Letters from an American Farmer and Sketches of Eighteenth Century America*. New York: Penguin, 1981.

Demos, John. *The Unredeemed Captive*. New York: Vintage Books, 1994.

Derounian-Stodola, Kathryn Zabelle, ed. *Women's Indian Narratives*. New York: Penguin Classics, 1998.

Dow, George Francis, ed. *The Holyoke Diaries*. Salem, MA: Essex Institute, 1911.

Doyle, Marian I. "A Plentiful Good Table." *Early American Life* (December 2001), 47–50.

Drake, Samuel Adams. *The Border Wars of New England, Commonly Called King William's and Queen Anne's Wars*. Williamstown, MA: Corner House, 1973.

Drake, Samuel G., ed. *Indian Captivities, or Life in the Wigwam.* Auburn: Derby and Miller, 1852.

Duncan, David Ewing. *Calendar: Humanity's Epic Struggle to Determine a True and Accurate Year.* New York: Avon Books, 1998.

Dunn, Shirley W. *The Mohicans and Their Land, 1609–1730.* Fleischmanns, NY: Purple Mountain Press, 1994.

Earle, Alice Morse. *Child Life in Colonial Days.* New York: Macmillan, 1940.

———. *Customs and Fashions in Old New England.* Williamson, MA: Corner House, 1969.

———. *Home Life in Colonial Days.* Stockbridge, MA: Berkshire House, 1993.

Eckert, Allan W. *Wilderness Empire.* Toronto: Bantam Books, 1980.

Edmonds, Walter D. *The Musket and the Cross: The Struggle of France and England for North America.* Boston: Little, Brown, 1968.

Ferling, John. *Struggle for a Continent: The Wars of Early America.* Arlington Heights, IL: Harlan Davidson, 1993.

Fischer, David Hackett. *Albion's Seed: Four British Folkways in America.* New York: Oxford University Press, 1989.

Ford, Worthington Chauncey, ed. *Diary of Cotton Mather.* New York: Frederick Ungar, 1911.

Gallup, Andrew, ed. *Memoir of a French and Indian War Soldier: Jolicoeur Charles Bonin.* Bowie, MD: Heritage Books, 1993.

Gallup, Andrew, and Donald F. Shaffer. *La Marine: The French Colonial Soldier in Canada, 1745–1761.* Bowie, MD: Heritage Books, 1992.

Grant, Anne. *Memoirs of an American Lady: With Sketches of Manners and Scenery in America as They Existed Previous to the Revolution.* New York: Samuel Campbell, 1805.

Greene, Lorenzo Johnson. *The Negro in Colonial New England, 1620–1776.* New York: Columbia University Press, 1942.

Guthman, William H. "Frontiermen's Tomahawks of the Colonial and Federal Periods." *Antiques* (March 1981), 658–665.

Hawke, David Freeman. *Everyday Life in Early America.* New York: Harper & Row, 1988.

Haythornwaite, Philip J. *Invincible Generals.* New York: De Capo Press, 1991.

Herrick, Cheesman A. *White Servitude in Pennsylvania: Indentured and Redemption Labor in Colony and Commonwealth.* Philadelphia: John Joseph McVey, 1926.

Hirsch, Adam J. "The Collision of Military Cultures in Seventeenth-Century New England." *The Journal of American History* 26 (March 1988), 1187–1212.

Holliday, Carl. *Woman's Life in Colonial Days.* Boston: Cornhill, 1922.

Hume, Ivor Noel. *Martin's Hundred.* Charlottesville: University Press of Virginia, 1979.

Humphreys, Mary G. *Catherine Schyler.* Spartansburg, SC: Reprint Company, 1968.

Hunt, George T. *The Wars of the Iroquois: A Study in Intertribal Trade Relations.* Madison: University of Wisconsin Press, 1972.

Jacobs, Wilbur R., ed. *The Appalachian Frontier: The Edmond Atkins Report and Plan of 1755.* Lincoln: University of Nebraska Press, 1967.

Jennings, Francis. *The Ambiguous Iroquois Empire: The Covent Chain Confederation of Indian Tribes with English Colonies from Its Beginnings to the Lancaster Treaty of 1744*. New York: W. W. Norton, 1984.

Johnson, Michael G. *American Woodland Indians*. Men-at-Arms, vol. 228. London: Osprey, 2000.

Johnson, Susanna. *A Narrative of the Captivity of Mrs. Johnson*. Bowie, MD: Heritage Books, 1990.

Jones, Archer. *The Art of War in the Western World*. New York: Oxford University Press, 1987.

Kalm, Peter. *Peter Kalm's Travels in North America*. New York: Dover, 1964.

Keegan, John. *Fields of Battle: The Wars for North America*. New York: Alfred A. Knopf, 1996.

Knight, Sarah Kemble. *The Journal of Madame Knight: A Woman's Treacherous Journey by Horseback from Boston to New York in the Year 1704*. Boston: Small, Maynard, 1920.

Koebner, Richard. *Empire*. New York: Grosset and Dunlap, 1965.

Lauber, Almon W., ed. *The Papers of Sir William Johnson*. Albany: State University of New York, 1939.

Leach, Douglas E. *Roots of Conflict: British Armed Forces and Colonial Americans, 1677–1775*. Chapel Hill: University of North Carolina Press, 1986.

Leckie, Robert. *A Few Acres of Snow: The Saga of the French and Indian Wars*. New York: John Wiley & Sons, 1999.

Libra, Leonard W., ed. *The Papers of Benjamin Franklin*. New Haven: Yale University Press, 1959.

Loudon, Archibald. *A Selection of Some of the Most Interesting Narratives of Outrages Committed by the Indians in Their Wars with the White People*. London: S. Hooper and A. Morley, 1808.

Lucier, Armand Francis, ed. *French and Indian War Notices Abstracted from Colonial Newspapers*. Vols. 1–4. Bowie, MD: Heritage Books, 1999.

Mahan, Alfred Thayer. *The Influence of Sea Power upon History, 1660–1783*. New York: Dover, 1987.

Mahon, John K. "Anglo-American Methods of Indian Warfare, 1676–1794." *The Mississippi Valley Historical Review* 45 (1958), 254–275.

Marcus, G. J. *The Formative Centuries: A Naval History of England*. Boston: Little, Brown, 1961.

Mason, F. Van Wyck. *The Battle for Quebec*. Boston: Houghton Mifflin, 1965.

May, Robin. *Wolfe's Army*. London: Osprey, 1989.

McCallum, John H., ed. *Francis Parkman, The Seven Years War: A Narrative taken from Montcalm and Wolfe, The Conspiracy of Pontiac, and A Half-Century of Conflict*. New York: Harper Torchbooks, 1968.

McElrath, Joseph R., Jr. and Allan P. Robb, eds. *The Complete Works of Anne Bradstreet*. Boston: Twayne, 1981.

Metz, Elizabeth. *Sainte Marie Among the Iroquois*. Syracuse, NY: Midgley, 1995.

Miner, Robert G., ed. *Colonial Architecture in New England*. New York: Arno Press, 1977.

Morrison, Hugh. *Early American Architecture: From the First Colonial Settlements to the National Period*. New York: Dover, 1987.

Morton, Louis. "The Origins of American Military Policy." *Military Affairs* 22 (1958), 75–82.

Nash, Gary B. *Red, White, and Black: The Peoples of Early America.* Englewood Cliffs, NJ: Prentice-Hall, 1982.

Nash, Roderick. *Wilderness and the American Mind.* New Haven: Yale University Press, 1971.

O'Callaghan, E. B., ed. *Documents Relative to the Colonial History of the State of New York.* Albany: Weed, Parsons, 1855.

O'Neil, James F., ed. *Their Bearing Is Noble and Proud: A Collection of Narratives Regarding the Appearance of Native Americans from 1740–1815.* Dayton, OH: J.T.G.S., 1995.

Parkman, Francis. *La Salle and the Discovery of the Great West.* New York: Modern Library, 1999.

———. *Montcalm and Wolfe.* New York: Atheneum, 1984.

Peckham, Howard H., ed. *Narratives of Colonial America, 1703–1765.* Chicago: R. R. Donnelley & Sons, 1971.

Pennsylvania Historical Commission. *Report to the Commission to Locate the Site of the Frontier Forts of Pennsylvania.* Vols. 1–2. Harrisburg· Pennsylvania Historical Commission, 1896.

Phipps, Frances. *Colonial Kitchens, Their Furnishings, and Their Gardens.* New York: Hawthorn Books, 1972.

Pouchot, Pierre. *Memoir upon the Late War in North America between the French and English, 1775–1760.* Roxbury, MA: E. Elliot Woodward, 1866.

Radabaugh, Jack. "The Militia of Colonial Massachusetts." *Military Affairs* 18 (1954) 1–18.

Romans, Bernard. *A Concise Natural History of East and West Florida.* Gainesville: University of Florida Press, 1962.

Rouse, Parke, Jr. *The Great Wagon Road from Philadelphia to the South.* New York: McGraw-Hill, 1973.

Rowlandson, Mary. *A Narrative of the Captivity and Removes of Mrs. Mary Rowlandson.* Fairfield, WA: Ye Galleon Press, 1974.

Russell, Francis. *The French and Indian Wars.* New York: American Heritage, 1962.

Russell, Peter E. "Redcoats in the Wilderness: British Officers and Irregular Warfare in Europe and America, 1740–1760." *William and Mary Quarterly* 3d ser., no. 35 (1978), 629–652.

Schutz, John A. *William Shirley.* Chapel Hill: University of North Carolina Press, 1961.

Seaver, James E. *A Narrative of the Life of Mrs. Mary Jemison.* Syracuse, NY: Syracuse University Press, 1990.

Shipton, Clifford K. *Sibley's Harvard Graduates.* Boston: Historical Society, 1975.

Shurtleff, Nathaniel, and David Pulsifer. *Records of the Colony of New Plymouth in New England.* New York: AMS Press, 1968.

Shy, John W. "A New Look at Colonial Militia." *William and Mary Quarterly* 35 (1963), 175–185.

Smith, Richard. *A Tour of Four Great Rivers: The Hudson, Mohawk, Susquehanna, and Delaware in 1769.* New York: Charles Scribner's Sons, 1906.

Snow, Dean R., Charles T. Gehring, and William A. Starna, eds. *In Mohawk Country: Early Narratives About a Native People.* Syracuse, NY: Syracuse University Press, 1996.

Spenser, Emanuel. "Glimpses of Log-cabin Life in Early Ohio." *Magazine of American History* 24 (August 1890), 101–111.

Steele, Ian K. *Betrayal: Fort William Henry and the Masaacre*. New York: Oxford University Press, 1990.

———. *Warpaths: Invasions of North America*. New York: Oxford University Press, 1994.

Stone, Albert E., ed. *Letters from an American Farmer and Sketches of Eighteenth-Century America by J. Hector St. John de Crevecoeur*. New York: Penguin Classics, 1986.

Strong, Pauline Turner. *Captive Selves, Captivating Others*. Boulder, CO: Westview Press, 1999.

Swan, Susan Burrows. *Plain and Fancy: American Women and Their Needlework, 1650–1850*. Austin, TX: Curious Works Press, 1995.

Thomas, M. Halsey, ed. *The Diary of Samuel Sewall, 1674–1729*. New York: Farrar, Straus and Giroux, 1973.

Timberlake, Henry. *Lieutenant Henry Timberlakes's Memoirs*. Marietta, GA: Continental, 1948.

Todish, Timothy J. *America's First First World War: The French and Indian War, 1754–1763*. Ogden, UT: Eagle's View, 1987.

Todorov, Tzvetan. *The Conquest of America*. New York: Harper Perennial, 1987.

Turner, Frederick Jackson. *The Significance of the Frontier in American History*. New York: Henry Holt, 1920.

Ulrich, Laurel Thatcher. *Good Wives: Image and Reality in the Lives of Women in Northern New England, 1550–1750*. New York: Vintage Books, 1991.

U.S. Department of Agriculture. *Early American Soil Conservationists*. Washington, DC: Soil Conservation Service, 1990.

Volo, Dorothy Denneen, and James M. Volo. *Daily Life in Civil War America*. Westport: Greenwood Press, 1998.

Volo, James M. "The Fort in America, Military Engineering in the 17th and 18th Centuries." *The Brigade Dispatch* (Autumn 1988), 2–6.

Volo, James M., and Dorothy Denneen Volo. *Encyclopedia of the Antebellum South*. Westport: Greenwood Press, 2000.

———. *Daily Life in the Age of Sail*. Westport: Greenwood Press, 2001.

Wacker, Peter O. *The Musconetcong Valley of New Jersey: A Historical Geography*. New Brunswick, NJ: Rutgers University Press, 1968.

Waddell, Louis M., and Bruce D. Bromberger. *The French and Indian War in Pennsylvania, 1753–1763: Fortification and Struggle During the War for Empire*. Harrisburg: Pennsylvania Historical and Museum Commission, 1996.

Wahll, Andrew J., ed. *The Braddock Road Chronicles, 1755*. Bowie, MD: Heritage Books, 1999.

Wallace, Paul A. W. *Conrad Weiser: Friend of Colonist and Mohawk, 1696–1760*. Lewisburg, PA: Wennawoods, 1996.

Weber, David J. *The Spanish Frontier in North America*. New Haven: Yale University Press, 1992.

Weiser, Reuben. *Regina, the German Captive*. Baltimore: T. N. Kurtz, 1860.

Wilbur, C. Keith. *The Woodland Indians: An Illustrated Account of the Lifestyles of America's First Inhabitants*. Guilford, CT: Globe Pequot Press, 1995.

Williams, John. *The Redeemed Captive Returning to Zion.* Amherst, MA: Edward W. Clark, 1976.

Williams, Selma R. *Demeter's Daughters: The Women Who Founded America, 1587–1787.* New York: Atheneum, 1976.

Wilson, Lisa. *Ye Heart of a Man: The Domestic Life of Men in Colonial New England.* New Haven: Yale University Press, 1999.

Wright, Louis B. *The Atlantic Frontier: Colonial American Civilization: 1607–1763.* New York: Alfred A. Knopf, 1951.

Index

Page references to illustrations are in boldface type.

330   Index

effectiveness of, 279, 286, 292, 295, 296, 302, 303; equipment, 201–202, 290, 301; weapons, 202–203
Putnam, Major Israel (ranger), 118, 303
Putnam, Colonel Rufus (mentioned), 256
Pychon, John (English fur trader), 179

Quebec (city) (*See also* trading posts, battles and crucial operations), viii, ix, xi, xv, 22, 56–61, **57**, 79, 174, 184, 219, 238, 272, 276, 277, 281, 297, 301, 304, 305–310, **308**

Radisson, Pierre-Espirit, (fur trader), xi, 86, 175–176
Raleigh, Sir Walter (English), 98
Rangers, xv, xvi, 203–204, 223, 289, 295, 301, 306
Ransom (of captives), 237–239, 244, 245
Rappahannock River and Valley, 191
Rasiers, Isaac de (Dutch trader), 74–75
Rasles, Father Sabastian, 64
Regular military forces; considered incompetent, 287, 290, 291, 292, 302; English, xv; 188–189, 193, 205, 209–210, 228, 277, 289, 298, 301, 304, 305, 307; equipment, 290, 301, 305, 309; French, xv, 169, 183–188, 295, 300, 305, 306, 307–308; organization of, 169, 184, 301, 304, 305, 306, 307–308; Scotch Highlanders, 285, 303; Spanish, xvii, 182–183, 186, 229; tactics and methods of warfare used by, 209–210, 256, 259, 263, 290, 302, 303, 306, 308, 309
Religion (as an influence on the frontier), **31**, 35, 51- 71, 95–97; bigotry, xx, 52–54, 64, 96, 106; church buildings, 58, 66, **67**, 263; established religions, 53, 96, 104; sects, 104, 106
Religious groups in America; Anglicans (including Church of England and Episcopal), 53, 103, 104–105; Baptists (including Dunkers), 52, 104, 110, 111; Catholics (see Roman

Catholicism); Congregationalists, 52; Dutch Reform (Calvinist), 52, 106; Huguenots (French Calvinist), viii, 100, 106, 215; Jews, vii, 53, 107; Lutherans, 52, 110; Methodists, 112; pietists (including Moravians and Mennonites), 55, 68–69, 70, 110, 111–112 Presbyterians, 105; Puritans, 51, 52, 98, 99, 103–104, 189; Quakers, xii, 68–69, 98, 108–110, 223; Wallons (Flemish Calvinists), 106
Religious orders or clergy, 159, 160; Franciscans, vii, 52, 183; Jesuits, vii, x, xi, xii, xiii, 22, 56–68, 69, 89, 107, 160, 247; Recollets, ix, xi, 60, 159; Sulpicians, x, 159; Ursulines, 159, 168, 310
Rhode Island colony, x, 51, 96, 104, 276
Richelieu, Cardinal, 160
Richelieu River, xi, 8, 10, 263, 271, 304
Roads, 12–14, 15, 109–110, 294
Rogers, Major Robert (provincial commander), xv, 63, 204, 295, 302
Roman Catholicism (papists), vii, ix, xi, xii, xix, 51–52, 96, 98, 103, 247–248, 309; conversions to among Protestants, 247–248; Counter Reformation, viii, xx, 215; Indian Missions (*See also* separate heading), xxii, 61–67, **67**, 86, 160, 242
Rowlandson, Mary (captive), 234, 235, 237, 246, 250
Royal American Regiment, 303, 304, 305, 307, 308
Royal houses (families) of the period in England and France, 211
Royalists, 98, 99, 189

Sabbath Day Point, 300
Saguenay River, 174
Sainte-Pierre, Captain Jacques Legardeur de (French officer), 283–284
Salmon Bay (Falls), New Hampshire (raid), xii, 166, 271
Salt, 152
Saunders, Admiral Charles (Royal Navy), 306, 310

About the Authors

JAMES M. VOLO is a teacher, historian, and living history enthusiast. He has been an active historic reenactor for more than two decades, participating in a wide range of living history events, including television and screen performances. With Dorothy Denneen Volo, he is co-author of *Daily Life in the Age of Sail* (Greenwood, 2001).

DOROTHY DENNEEN VOLO is a teacher and historian. She has been an active living history reenactor for 20 years and has been involved in numerous community historical education projects. With James M. Volo, she is co-author of *Daily Life in the Age of Sail* (Greenwood, 2001).